THE CLASS ACTIONS CONTROVERSY

PATRONS OF THE SOCIETY

Constance Backhouse

Blake, Cassels & Graydon, LLP

Chernos, Flaherty, Svorkin, LLP

The Law Foundation of Ontario

McCarthy Tétrault LLP

Osler, Hoskin & Harcourt LLP

Paliare Roland Rosenberg Rothstein LLP

Torys LLP

WeirFoulds LLP

The Osgoode Society is supported by a grant from
The Law Foundation of Ontario

THE LAW
FOUNDATION
OF ONTARIO

The Society also thanks The Law Society of Ontario
for its continued support.

THE CLASS ACTIONS CONTROVERSY

The Origins and Development of the Ontario *Class Proceedings Act*

SUZANNE CHIODO

IRWIN LAW

The Class Actions Controversy: The Origins and Development of the Ontario *Class Proceedings Act*

Published in 2018 by
Irwin Law Inc
Suite 206, 14 Duncan Street
Toronto, ON M5H 3G8
www.irwinlaw.com

ISBN: 978-1-55221-476-3 e-book ISBN: 978-1-55221-477-0

The law is stated as at 16 October 2017 (except for some later developments that occurred during the manuscript editing process and to which brief reference has been possible).

Library and Archives Canada Cataloguing in Publication

Chiodo, Suzanne, 1978–, author
The class actions controversy : the origins and development of the Ontario Class Proceedings Act / Suzanne Chiodo.

Includes bibliographical references and index.
Issued in print and electronic formats.
ISBN 978-1-55221-476-3 (softcover).—ISBN 978-1-55221-477-0 (PDF)

1. Class actions (Civil procedure)—Ontario—History. 2. Ontario. Class Proceedings Act, 1992. I. Title.

KEO1129.C45 2018 347.713'053 C2018-904658-9
KF8896.C45 2018 C2018-904659-7

Canada

Ontario
Ontario Media Development Corporation
Société de développement de l'industrie des médias de l'Ontario

Printed and bound by CPI Group (UK) Ltd, Croydon, CR0 4YY
1 2 3 4 5 22 21 20 19 18

SUMMARY TABLE OF CONTENTS

DETAILED TABLE OF CONTENTS

FOREWORD

The publication of this book could not be more timely. The Ontario *Class Proceedings Act, 1992* (*CPA*) not only changed the face of civil litigation in this province, but was the legislative model for the other common law provinces. After the United States and Quebec, the Ontario *CPA* was one of the first class action statutes in the world.

However, twenty-five years after its enactment, the *CPA* continues to generate discussion and is decidedly ready for significant review and reform. The overarching objective—greater access to justice—is probably being achieved, but the actual design and content of the underlying legislation needs adjustment and refinement. It is time to address the questions that have materialized over the last quarter century. Are the certification requirements working as intended? What is the ideal costs rule? What about third party funding? Contingency fee awards? National class actions? Are measures needed to help police conflicts of interest on the part of class counsel and minimize the potential for self-dealing? And what should be the ongoing role of the class actions judge?

The answers to these questions very much depend on one's view of where we are and how we got here. The former is arguably well understood; the latter not so much.

As a class actions judge, I have an abiding interest in the ongoing evolution of the class action vehicle. But I have long been troubled by the realization that we know very little about the *CPA*'s historical roots. Unlike other law reform initiatives that involved extensive study and significant legislative debate, the *CPA* materialized almost overnight. The genesis of the class proceeding in Ontario can be traced most directly to the *Report of the Attorney General's Advisory Committee* in 1990. The ten members of the Advisory Committee, each representing a key stakeholder or special interest group, understood that Attorney General Ian Scott was expecting a consensus report. Scott, brilliant, determined, and by all accounts, a master tactician, understood that a meaningful class proceedings law would not be enacted if the matter was left to lobbying and legislative debate. His plan: Get the key stakeholders in a room and force them to generate a consensus report that would then allow him to tell the legislature that no further discussion was needed.

Scott succeeded. His Advisory Committee managed to produce a unanimous report after just ten meetings, and in due course the *CPA* was enacted with little to no legislative debate. I know this because I was a member of this Advisory Committee, representing the Consumers' Association of Canada. However, I have long forgotten the details about how and why we did what we did; what compromises had to be made; and how, to our collective surprise, we managed to achieve unanimity.

In this groundbreaking publication, Suzanne Chiodo provides the first in-depth analysis of the history of the *Class Proceedings Act, 1992* and the political and social influences that shaped it. The book details, for the first time, the work of the Advisory Committee—the meetings, the issues, and the deals that had to be made.

Ms Chiodo begins the book by providing an engaging review of the equitable origins of the class proceeding and the subsequent development of class actions in the United States, Australia, and Canada, debunking several myths in the process. Her focus on Canadian developments includes both the common law provinces and Quebec. She then delves into the impact of the Ontario Law Reform Commission's 1982 report and provides a detailed understanding of the *Report of the Attorney General's Advisory Committee*. In her concluding chapter, Ms Chiodo dissects the current topics: certification, costs, third party funding, overlapping and national class actions, carriage motions, and the ethical pitfalls confronting modern class action litigation. As an experienced class actions lawyer, Ms Chiodo provides important and practical insights that will better inform our understanding of the current law and the reforms that are required.

Ian Scott noted in his autobiography that, "[i]n the long run the legislation allowing class actions may be the most important legacy of my time as Attorney General." He was right. In an era of crippling legal costs, the class action remains the only viable vehicle for meaningful access to justice. We just have to get it right. This book will help us get there. It is a must-read for class actions lawyers and judges, and, indeed, anyone interested in public policy and civil litigation.

I congratulate Suzanne Chiodo on this seminal publication.

Justice Edward P Belobaba
Superior Court of Justice—Ontario
30 September 2017

FOREWORD

FROM THE OSGOODE SOCIETY FOR CANADIAN LEGAL HISTORY

The *Class Proceedings Act* of Ontario, passed in 1993, represented a major innovation in civil procedure, making it possible to join together thousands of plaintiffs in a single action. Suzanne Chiodo's new book is the first to analyze comprehensively the history of the origins of this highly significant legislation. It looks in turn at the origins of representative proceedings in equity, the rise of modern-day class actions around the world (particularly in the United States and Quebec), and at the debates about, and the passage of, the Ontario legislation. The book presents an in-depth analysis of the political and social influences that shaped this momentous legal change. It explains the importance of the Ontario Law Reform Commission's 1982 *Report on Class Actions*, and how the Attorney General's Advisory Committee Report in 1990 pulled together so many divergent interests where previous attempts had failed. With the twenty-fifth anniversary of the Act upon us, and the Law Commission of Ontario currently reviewing it, this is a most timely contribution to a current debate as well as an instructive historical analysis.

The purpose of the Osgoode Society for Canadian Legal History is to encourage research and writing in the history of Canadian law. The Society, which was incorporated in 1979 and is registered as a charity, was founded at the initiative of the Honourable R Roy McMurtry, and officials of the Law Society of Upper Canada. The Society seeks to stimulate the study of legal history in Canada by supporting researchers, collecting oral histories, and publishing volumes that contribute to legal-historical scholarship in Canada. This year's books bring the total published to 103 since 1981, in all fields of legal history—the courts, the judiciary, and the legal profession, as well as on the history of crime and punishment, women and law, law and economy, the legal treatment of ethnic minorities, and famous cases and significant trials in all areas of the law.

Current directors of the Osgoode Society for Canadian Legal History are Dr Susan Binnie, Bevin Brooksbank, Shantona Chaudhury, David Chernos, Linda Silver Dranoff, Michael Fenrick, Timothy Hill, Ian Hull, Trisha Jackson, Mahmud Jamal, Virginia MacLean, Waleed Malick, Rachel McMillan, The Hon R Roy McMurtry, Yasir Naqvi, Dana Peebles, The Hon Paul Reinhardt, William Ross, Paul Schabas, The Hon Robert Sharpe, Jon Silver, Alex Smith, Lorne Sossin, Mary Stokes, and The Hon Michael Tulloch.

ACKNOWLEDGEMENTS

This book arises from the thesis I wrote for my master of laws degree at Osgoode Hall Law School, and thanks must go to those who helped me complete it. I owe this book most of all to my husband Joe, who supplied a constant flow of tea and support (which, to an English woman, are pretty much the same thing). My family was also an enormous help, particularly my sister, brother, and aunt, who hosted me in England while I wrote and took bets on where I would write the most pages.

My thesis supervisor Philip Girard helped me transform my idea into a full-length book, which I would not have thought possible three years ago. I am also grateful to Justice Paul Perell, who was the second reader for my thesis and provided helpful comments, and to Janet Walker and Jamie Benidickson, who formed my examining committee, and gave useful feedback. This book was also improved by the input of the members of the Osgoode Society Legal History Workshop, especially Jim Phillips.

Justice Edward Belobaba has written the foreword to this book, and I thank him for his endorsement and support. I am also grateful to my former colleagues at Rochon Genova LLP, with whom I gained my practical experience of class actions and who continue to encourage me in my academic career.

The support I have received throughout this process, along with the positive feedback from so many quarters, has encouraged me to pursue my research in the field of class actions. Thanks to everyone who has helped me, whether or not I have mentioned you by name (and if I haven't, I owe you a beer).

Suzanne E Chiodo
Oriel College, Oxford
October 2017

Chapter 1

OVERVIEW

A. INTRODUCTION

On 24 June 1982, Attorney General Roy McMurtry announced to the Ontario legislature[1] that the Ontario Law Reform Commission had completed its *Report on Class Actions*.[2] The result of six years of deliberation and running to nearly 900 pages, the OLRC Report was widely hailed as one of the most comprehensive treatments of the subject, covering almost every aspect of class actions in exhaustive detail. It was accompanied by draft legislation and had been especially commissioned by the attorney general, with McMurtry stating the following year that he regarded class action reform as "a high priority. I would expect to be discussing these issues . . . with my cabinet colleagues in the early autumn, with a view to possibly bringing first reading legislation before the House by the end of the year."[3]

1 Ontario, Legislative Assembly, *Official Report of Debates (Hansard)*, 32nd Parl, 2nd Sess (24 June 1982) (Roy McMurtry), online: http://hansardindex.ontla.on.ca/hansardeissue/32-2/l087.htm.

2 Ontario Law Reform Commission, *Report on Class Actions* (Toronto: Ministry of the Attorney General, 1982) [OLRC Report].

3 Ontario, Legislative Assembly, *Official Report of Debates (Hansard)*, 32nd Parl, 3rd Sess (17 June 1983) (Standing Committee on Administration of Justice, Estimates, Ministry of the Attorney General), J-173, Ontario Law Reform Commission files, Nov 1976–Dec 1982, Project name: class actions, RG 4-66, BA77, Box No B380537, North York, Archives of Ontario.

The draft Act was never passed. The OLRC Report gathered dust on the shelves of the Ministry of the Attorney General for more than five years, while the Conservative government was voted out of power and a minority Liberal government took its place, continuing the reformist agenda initiated by the 1985 Liberal–NDP accord once it won a majority in 1987. While certain interest groups made submissions to the ministry on the OLRC Report and class actions, virtually no steps were taken towards reform. Then, in 1988, and with the strong backing of a Liberal government, Attorney General Ian Scott turned his activist eye towards class actions. Focused on the subject of access to justice, Scott saw class actions as a way of securing justice for consumers, environmental groups, and others, on a mass scale, while levelling the playing field between plaintiffs and powerful defendants.

Ready to help him was Michael Cochrane, an ambitious young lawyer who had joined the Policy Development Division (PDD) of the Ministry of the Attorney General just weeks before Scott was appointed. The OLRC Report was just one of a number of projects that had been idling at the PDD, and Cochrane volunteered to dust it off and move it forward.[4] Together, the two men were to create a unique consultation process whereby key stakeholders from business, the legal profession, consumer groups, and environmental organizations engaged in a mediation-style process. This process involved a political commitment to undertake reform; a commitment by the group to reach a consensus (or there would be no legislation at all); a public and up-front commitment by the participants to several written terms of reference, which were non-negotiable and around which the legislation would be designed; and a willingness to discuss interests and goals, rather than lock into particular positions.[5] Trained as a mediator, Michael Cochrane chaired the Attorney General's Advisory Committee on Class Action Reform and successfully negotiated

4 Interview of Michael Cochrane (28 June 2016).

5 Michael G Cochrane, "The Process of Principled Negotiation of Public Policy: An Overview" (unpublished, on file with the author) at 5–8. This approach borrows from the principled negotiation approach developed by Roger Fisher et al in *Getting to Yes: Negotiating Agreement Without Giving In*, 2d ed (New York: Penguin Books, 1991). There is some overlap between Cochrane's paper and the principles outlined in *Getting to Yes*, including focusing on interests, not positions; and insisting on objective criteria for negotiation. These principles were based on the work of the Harvard Negotiation Project, and taught as part of the project's Program of Instruction for Lawyers (see notes in *Getting to Yes*). Cochrane was almost certainly exposed to these principles when he took part in negotiation training at Harvard in 1989.

a compromise between the vastly differing viewpoints at the table.[6] The resulting consensus on such a controversial topic was a surprise to everyone, including Premier David Peterson.[7]

However, it was not without compromise. The OLRC Report had called for various mechanisms to level the playing field for plaintiffs and remove procedural and substantive barriers to class actions. In particular, it recommended that traditional costs rules ("two-way" costs, where the losing party paid the successful party's legal costs) should not apply to class actions. Instead, each party should pay its own costs, no matter which party was successful (the "no-way costs" rule).[8] Cochrane and Scott had originally proposed the same costs mechanism, and it was one of the Cabinet-approved terms of reference for the work of the Advisory Committee. However, it quietly fell to the wayside, as the business groups asserted their position that class actions should depart as little as possible from the traditional rules of litigation: for them, it was either traditional costs rules or no class actions at all. The no-way costs rule was one of the casualties of the compromise struck by the Advisory Committee, and the decision not to include it has been questioned by class actions lawyers to this day.[9]

In addition, the consultation process led to compromises not only in the shape of reform itself, but also in the process by which the legislation was created. Some on the Advisory Committee—and also those who had not been invited to participate—questioned a process that invited only certain parties to the table, leaving other major stakeholders, such as women's groups, out in the cold. The members of the Advisory Committee worked long and hard to agree to a compromise, and were justifiably

6 Ontario, Ministry of the Attorney General (MAG), Policy Development Division, *Report of the Attorney General's Advisory Committee on Class Action Reform* (Toronto: Ministry of the Attorney General, 1990) [Advisory Committee Report].

7 Interview of Michael Cochrane (21 April 2016) [Cochrane interview 1].

8 Another costs mechanism put forward by various commentators, such as Neil Williams who prepared draft legislation for the Consumers' Association of Canada in 1974, was that of "one-way" costs. Under this scheme, successful plaintiffs would be awarded costs by the court, but successful defendants would have to pay their own costs. Neil J Williams, "Consumer Class Actions in Canada—Some Proposals for Reform" (1975) 13 *Osgoode Hall Law Journal* 1 at 51–52 [Williams, "Some Proposals"]; Neil J Williams, *Consumer Class Actions in Canada: A Report for the Consumers' Association of Canada* (Ottawa: Consumers' Association of Canada, 1974).

9 Law Commission of Ontario, *Review of Class Actions in Ontario: Issues to Be Considered* (Toronto: The Commission, 2013) at 9–11, online: www.lco-cdo.org/wp-content/uploads/2014/01/class-actions-issues-to-be-considered.pdf [LCO 2013].

proud of the consensus that resulted. Unfortunately, that pride took a proprietary turn in that they were unwilling to allow legislative counsel a free hand in drafting the statute. The usual process would dictate that legislative counsel draft the legislation (using the Advisory Committee's report as guidance only), which would then be debated by the legislature and any necessary amendments made. This was not the process followed for the *Class Proceedings Act, 1992*.[10] In that case, legislative counsel drafted the statute clause by clause, in regular consultation with the members of the Advisory Committee, who signed off on the finished draft to ensure that it reflected their consensus. Before the bill was tabled in the legislature, Scott made a commitment to the Advisory Committee that he would get the bill through the readings and committee stages with no substantive changes.[11] That is what happened, and the *CPA* received royal assent on 25 June 1992—with virtually no input from the democratically elected representatives of the Ontario legislature.

The process by which class action reform came about in Ontario, therefore, reflects an uncomfortable tension between an innovative mediation-style process that brought many of the major stakeholders to the table to negotiate a compromise, and the democratic process with its avenues of consultation and statute-creation. The departure from the usual process meant that certain compromises were never reviewed or approved by a wider audience—including crucial decisions on the issue of costs. Although several Advisory Committee members argue that reform might never have come about otherwise,[12] those compromises continue to affect class proceedings to the present day, often to the detriment of the philosophy of access to justice that underlies the *CPA*.

B. WHY A HISTORICAL STUDY OF THE *CPA*?

A quarter of a century has passed since class action reform came about in Ontario. Since then, the *CPA* has become one of the most frequently debated procedural mechanisms of its kind. Plaintiff lawyers proclaim the *CPA* as the bastion of access to justice, while defence lawyers emphasize its safeguards against frivolous use and the requirements that must be met before class actions can proceed.

10 SO 1992, c 6 [*CPA*]. The companion statute to the *CPA* is the *Law Society Amendment Act (Class Proceedings Funding), 1992*, SO 1992, c 7 [*LSAA*].

11 Cochrane interview 1, above note 7.

12 *Ibid*; interview of Advisory Committee member (13 April 2016).

At the same time, the Law Commission of Ontario (LCO)[13] has begun a wide-ranging review of the Act, acknowledging that "[i]t is unclear whether the *CPA* is working as intended and many unforeseen challenges associated with it have become fodder for discussion in conferences, academic papers, professional associations, social media and other commentary."[14]

In light of the LCO's review, a study of the genesis of the *CPA* is timely. By examining the origins of the Act, the controversies to which it gave rise, and the views that were present at the time of its passage, clarity can be brought to issues that are currently under the LCO's spotlight, as well as the manner in which the *CPA* is used and interpreted by stakeholders today. For example, one subject of the LCO's review is the issue of costs. Numerous commentators have questioned why the Attorney General's Advisory Committee did not follow the OLRC's recommendations on no-way costs. In the case of *Bayens v Kinross Gold Corporation*,[15] Perell J stated that the loser-pays regime creates a strong economic disincentive for plaintiffs to bring claims. He concluded that "[i]t may be wise for the Legislature to revisit whether any of this is what it intended when it rejected the Law Reform Commission's recommendation that class actions not be governed by the loser pays principle."[16] Justice Strathy came to a similar conclusion in the 2011 case of *Dugal v Manulife Financial Corp*:[17]

> One of the important goals of class proceedings is to provide access to justice to large groups of people who have claims that cannot be economically pursued individually. In Ontario, the costs rules applicable to ordinary actions apply to class proceedings—the loser pays. The costs of losing can be astronomical—well beyond the reach of all but the powerful and very wealthy—not exactly the group the legislature had in mind when the *CPA* was enacted.[18]

---

13 The LCO is the successor to the Ontario Law Reform Commission.

14 LCO 2013, above note 9 at 2. After stalling for some time, this project was relaunched in 2017 and renamed "Class Actions: Objectives, Experience and Reforms," announcement online: www.lco-cdo.org/wp-content/uploads/2013/04/CA-Press-Release-FINAL-Sept-22-2017.pdf [LCO 2017]. See also Law Commission of Ontario, *Class Actions: Objectives, Experiences and Reforms: Consultation Paper* (Toronto: Law Commission of Ontario, 2018), online: www.lco-cdo.org/wp-content/uploads/2018/04/Class-Action-Consultation-Paper.pdf.

15 2013 ONSC 4974 [*Bayens*].

16 *Ibid* at para 35.

17 2011 ONSC 1785 [*Dugal*]. Both *Dugal* and *Bayens*, above note 15, are cited in LCO 2013, above note 9.

18 *Dugal*, above note 14 at para 27.

This discussion on the subject of costs can be informed by the history of the *CPA*, and especially the deliberations of the Attorney General's Advisory Committee and the subsequent passage of the legislation. These deliberations provide vital insight as to why the Advisory Committee rejected the OLRC's recommendations on costs. A review of these reasons will inform any reassessment of the *CPA* today.

A review of the history of the statute also reveals the political influences that shaped it. Economic theory has shed light on the politicization of law reform by positing two grounds for legal change: public interest grounds (both economic—for example, correcting a market failure—and non-economic, such as fair distribution of resources or protection of vulnerable groups) and private interest grounds (for example, pressures from various interest groups).[19] The literature on the history of class proceedings has focused almost exclusively on public interest grounds. For example, both Shaun Finn and Bill Bogart state that class proceedings legislation came about as a response to market failure (in that small claims were not being litigated because they were not individually economically viable) and, to a certain extent, fair distribution of resources and paternalism (for example, to modify the behaviour of corporate and other actors who hold power and privilege, and to protect consumers and other relatively vulnerable groups).[20] However, a review of the historical record reveals that private interests were also at play in the creation of class proceedings legislation.[21]

19 See, for example, Anthony Ogus, *Regulation: Legal Form and Economic Theory* (Oxford: Clarendon Press, 1994); Richard A Posner, *Theories of Economic Regulation* (New York: National Bureau of Economic Research, 1974), online: www.nber.org/papers/w0041.pdf.

20 Shaun Finn, "In a Class All Its Own: The Advent of the Modern Class Action and Its Changing Legal and Social Mission" (2005) 2:2 *Canadian Class Action Review* 333 [Finn, "In a Class"]; Shaun Finn, *Étude d'un recours évolutif: redéfinir la procédure sui generis du recours collectif Québécois* (LLM Thesis, Faculté de Droit, Université Laval, 2011) [unpublished] [Finn, *Étude*]; WA Bogart, Jasminka Kalajdzic, & Ian Matthews, "Class Actions in Canada: A National Procedure in a Multi-jurisdictional Society?" (Report for the Globalization of Class Actions Conference, Oxford University, December 2007) [Bogart, Kalajdzic, & Matthews].

21 While there is extensive work on the role of private interests in the conduct of class proceedings, virtually no scholarship exists on the role of these interests in the creation of the legislation itself. Examples of the former include Deborah R Hensler et al, *Class Action Dilemmas: Pursuing Public Goals for Private Gain* (Santa Monica: RAND Institute for Civil Justice, 1999); Alberto Cassone & Giovanni B Ramello, "Private, Club and Public Goods: The Economic Boundaries of Class Action Litigation" in Jürgen G Backhaus et al, eds, *The Law and Economics of Class Actions in Europe: Lessons from America* (Cheltenham, UK: Edward Elgar Publishing, 2012) 101; John

While public interest grounds acted as the pull towards reform, private interests, such as business groups, acted as the pull away from it. Business groups opposed reform for as long as they could and, when reform seemed inevitable, sought to influence the creation of the legislation (most notably through the groups' influence on the Attorney General's Advisory Committee) to ensure that it was as conservative as possible. Business groups were able to do this because of the unique nature of the consultation process instituted by Ian Scott, as detailed above.

This book also presents a more nuanced picture of the class proceedings debate than has been presented to date. For example, the widely accepted narrative is that, after more than two decades of controversy, an activist attorney general (Ian Scott) commissioned the 1990 Attorney General's Advisory Committee Report and thereby "broke the logjam" that had prevented the advent of class actions.[22] That narrative, however, does not explain how the report suddenly pulled together so many divergent interests and why those interests had not been reconciled before. This book compares and contrasts the OLRC and Advisory Committee reports and also examines the surrounding debate and the changes in the wider legal culture, to answer precisely those questions.

In light of the Law Commission of Ontario's current review of the Act, the results of this research will be of assistance not only to the LCO but also to lawyers, other stakeholders, legal academics, and policy makers. This detailed historical study, looking at class actions from an interdisciplinary perspective, builds upon and contributes to the existing literature on the history of class proceedings and access to justice.

C. EXISTING SCHOLARSHIP ON THE HISTORY OF CLASS ACTIONS

For the most part, historical analyses of class action reform in Ontario have been limited to brief overviews involving the seminal Supreme

Beisner et al, "Class Action 'Cops': Public Servants or Private Entrepreneurs?" (2005) 57 *Stanford Law Review* 1441.

22 Bogart, Kalajdzic, & Matthews, above note 20 at 3; Michael G Cochrane, "Conditions for Instituting Class Actions" in A Prujiner & J Roy, eds, *Class Actions in Ontario and Quebec: Proceedings of the First Yves Pratte Conference* (Montreal: Éditions Wilson & Lafleur Ltée, 1992) at 3 [*Yves Pratte Conference*]. Even Cochrane, chair of the Attorney General's Advisory Committee, writes (without explanation) that the committee's delivery of a unanimous report occurred "much to everyone's surprise."

Court of Canada decision in *GM (Canada) v Naken*,[23] in which the Court severely narrowed the scope of class actions at common law; the OLRC Report; and the Advisory Committee Report.[24] Slightly more detailed analyses have included the increased activity of the Ministry of the Attorney General leading up to the formation of the Advisory Committee, including Ian Scott's Conference on Access to Civil Justice in Toronto in June 1988,[25] and the recommendations on class actions of the Uniform Law Conference of Canada in August of that year.[26] Such narratives can be found in the work of Michael Cochrane, chair of the Attorney General's Advisory Committee, in the years following the enactment of the *CPA*.[27] Cochrane's narrative has, for the most part, been picked up uncritically by other commentators.[28]

Very little academic scholarship has looked further than that. The relatively short articles that have touched on the history in Ontario generally cover the entire history of class actions, from their beginnings in the Court of Chancery to the present day. They treat each period in a fairly cursory manner—including the crucial period during which the device was actually being debated in Ontario.[29] The more in-depth treatments stick largely to the caselaw on class actions. For example, John Kazanjian looks at the roots of class actions in equity, and then conducts a useful review of the caselaw in England and in Ontario and other provinces.[30] However, this is where his historical analysis ends, and the structure of the article clearly indicates that he is conducting such an analysis simply to answer present-day questions. This is largely true for other articles that look at the equitable beginnings of class actions and

23 [1983] 1 SCR 72 [*Naken*].

24 See, for example, Paul Perell, "Class Action Devils and Angels" (2013) 30:3 *Thomas M Cooley Law Review* 285, although Perell J also discusses the roots of the class action in equity.

25 Ministry of the Attorney General, *Conference on Access to Civil Justice: June 20–22, 1988* (Toronto: Ministry of the Attorney General, 1988).

26 Uniform Law Conference of Canada (ULCC), "Proceedings of the Seventieth Annual Meeting" (Toronto, August 1988), online: www.ulcc.ca/images/stories/Past_Proceedings_PDF/1988ULCC0070.pdf.

27 Michael G Cochrane, *Class Actions: A Guide to the Class Proceedings Act, 1992* (Aurora, ON: Canada Law Book Inc, 1993) at 1–4; "Conditions for Instituting Class Actions," in *Yves Pratte Conference*, above note 22 at 3.

28 See, for example, Michael A Eizenga & Emrys Davis, "A History of Class Actions: Modern Lessons from Deep Roots" (2011) 7 *Canadian Class Action Review* 3.

29 *Ibid*; Perell, above note 24.

30 John A Kazanjian, "Class Actions in Canada" (1973) 11 *Osgoode Hall Law Journal* 397.

review the caselaw.[31] Although these provide a useful overview of how the Ontario courts handled class actions prior to the enactment of the *CPA*, they reflect a narrow view that legal history consists purely of prior court decisions. Such articles do not look at the wider context of the *CPA*, and the political and social influences that shaped it.

There have been fairly detailed historical treatments of the class action device in other jurisdictions. With regard to Quebec, the most in-depth work is that of Shaun Finn.[32] Finn discusses the genesis of Quebec class proceedings legislation, with reference to the debates in the legislature and the reports from the Standing Committee on Justice. He provides a useful analysis of the cultural and political context of the movement for reform, but he does so without reference to wider "non-legal" sources, such as newspaper articles and correspondence of key players. Catherine Piché has also looked at the history of the class action in Quebec,[33] relating her review to an overarching analysis of the cultural impact of class actions, and the way in which class actions are also informed by culture. Again, however, Piché does not look at other historical sources. Both scholars rely almost exclusively on caselaw, academic commentary, and (in their discussion of other provinces) the reports of the provincial law commissions on class actions.[34]

The most notable historian of class actions is Stephen Yeazell, who looks in depth at the roots of class actions in equity and English history.[35] Yeazell focuses on group litigation in the sixteenth, seventeenth, and eighteenth centuries, and finds that such litigation was the result of the two relationships that governed the lives of many English people: the manor–copyholder (or landlord–tenant) relationship, and the parishioner–priest

31 Williams, "Some Proposals," above note 8; Colin Gillespie, "The Scope of the Class Action in Canada" (1981) 11 *Manitoba Law Journal* 215; Lucy Nissen, "Class Actions in Canada: An Environmental Perspective" (1984) 48 *Saskatchewan Law Review* 29; Jennifer K Bankier, "Class Actions for Monetary Relief in Canada: Formalism or Function?" (1984) 4 *Windsor Yearbook of Access to Justice* 229.

32 Finn, "In a Class," and Finn, *Étude*, above note 20.

33 Catherine Piché, "The Cultural Analysis of Class Action Law" (2009) 2 *Journal of Civil Law Studies* 101 at 120 and 123.

34 For an overview of class actions in each Canadian province, see Mathew Good, "Access to Justice, Judicial Economy and Behaviour Modification: Exploring the Goals of Canadian Class Actions" (2009) 47 *Alberta Law Review* 185.

35 Stephen Yeazell, "Group Litigation and Social Context: Toward a History of the Class Action" (1977) 77:6 *Columbia Law Review* 866 [Yeazell, "Group Litigation"]; Stephen Yeazell, *From Medieval Group Litigation to the Modern Class Action* (New Haven: Yale University Press, 1987).

relationship. Both involved various rights and duties, including the payment of rent (to the manor) and tithes (to the parish priest). As these groups struggled to work out the customary laws that governed their relationships, they turned to the Court of Chancery to declare what those customary laws were. In that sense, early modern litigation was not really litigation by classes, but requests by pre-existing groups to declare what the law was. Yeazell argues that such "group litigation" was fundamentally different from the modern class action, because (1) the groups existed as social entities independent of the lawsuit (whereas aggregation in modern class actions increases the power of individuals by grouping them together), and (2) the issues at stake involved status and declaratory remedies (whereas modern class actions involve individual claims of right which are generally remedied by monetary damages).[36]

In doing so, Yeazell undermines the assumptions of many other scholars of class actions, who state that class actions have an unbroken history that stretches back to the Court of Chancery. Indeed, even the proponents of reform in Ontario pointed back to this history in order to legitimize what appeared to be a procedural novelty. Attorney General Ian Scott did this when he addressed the Canadian Manufacturers' Association in September 1989:

> [Class actions] have been a part of our legal system for a great many years and in fact can be traced to the early part of the eighteenth century. Until the fusion of law and equity in 1873 in England, and in 1881 Ontario, this procedural device was employed only in Courts of Chancery.[37]

Yeazell argues persuasively that such arguments are incorrect. This would explain why courts, such as the Supreme Court of Canada in *Naken*, were so reticent to adopt class actions in the absence of legislative authority: there was little historical precedent for doing so. It also explains why there was a dearth of group claims for monetary damages in the twentieth century after the fusion of the courts, a phenomenon commented on by Kazanjian:[38] class actions were overwhelmingly an equitable and declaratory device. The modern class action is therefore fundamentally

36 Yeazell, "Group Litigation," above note 35 at 876–77.

37 "Notes for Remarks by the Honourable Ian Scott, Attorney General" (Delivered at the Luncheon Meeting of the Canadian Manufacturers' Association, 19 September 1989) at 2, speeches and notes for remarks by Ian Scott, F 4339-1, Box No B222612, North York, Archives of Ontario.

38 Kazanjian, above note 30 at 433–36.

different from its forebears.[39] This fact was conveniently overlooked by many of the proponents of class action reform in Ontario and elsewhere, but it explains why the device provoked such bitter opposition from business interests and other more conservative groups. H Patrick Glenn, in his scholarly commentary on and opposition to class actions, noted that group litigation throughout history was highly exceptional in character, a "serious judicial usurpation of the functions of the legislature," and "an instrument of royal political and social policy rather than ... a strictly 'adjudicative'" procedure.[40]

Yeazell was not the first to write of the equitable origins of class actions,[41] but his work is so authoritative that it has guided most of the subsequent scholarship on the subject.[42] However, his work on US class actions in the twentieth century has since been built upon, most notably by David Marcus, who has conducted significant original historical research on the genesis of Rule 23[43] and its political, social, cultural, and economic context.[44] Through the lens of the philosophical tension within

39 Curiously, the modern defendant class action (involving a class of defendants) bears much more similarity to group litigation in equity: Suzanne Chiodo, "Defendant Class Actions: Awkward Twin or Distant Cousin?" (2015) 10:3 *Class Action Journal* 649.

40 H Patrick Glenn, "Class Actions in Ontario and Quebec" (1984) 62:3 *Canadian Bar Review* 247 at 271–72. Glenn took the position that judicial activism in the context of class actions was inappropriate even if it were authorized by legislation, because it would involve a distortion of the traditional judicial function. He did not specifically discuss how the *Canadian Charter of Rights and Freedoms* (Part I of the *Constitution Act, 1982*, being Schedule B to the *Canada Act 1982* (UK), 1982, c 11) factored into this analysis. The effect of the *Charter* on the class actions debate in Ontario will be addressed in Chapter 3.

41 See Zechariah Chafee, "Bills of Peace with Multiple Parties" (1932) 45 *Harvard Law Review* 1297; Joseph Story, *Commentaries on Equity Pleadings*, 8th ed (Boston: Little, Brown, and Company, 1870), online: Hathi Trust Digital Library http://babel.hathitrust.org/cgi/pt?id=njp.32101068559671;view=1up;seq=7; Frederic Calvert, *A Treatise upon the Law Respecting Parties to Suits in Equity* (New York: Gale Academic, 2010).

42 See, for example, Geoffrey C Hazard Jr et al, "Historical Analysis of the Binding Effect of Class Suits" (1998) 146:6 *University of Pennsylvania Law Review* 1849; and Francisco Valdes, "Procedure, Policy and Power: Class Actions and Social Justice in Historical and Comparative Perspective" (2008) 24 *Georgia State University Law Review* 627.

43 Rule 23 of the *Federal Rules of Civil Procedure* governs class actions in the United States district courts: *Federal Rules of Civil Procedure*, Title IV: Parties, Rule 23: Class Actions, 383 US 1029 (1966), online: Legal Information Institute www.law.cornell.edu/rules/frcp/rule_23 [Rule 23].

44 David Marcus, "The History of the Modern Class Action, Part I: *Sturm und Drang*, 1953–1980" (2013) 90 *Washington University Law Review* 587 [Marcus]; David Marcus,

class actions (do they confer substantive rights, or are they merely procedural?), Marcus looks beyond the caselaw and academic commentary relied on by most other scholars of class actions history. He refers to primary "non-legal" sources such as newspaper articles, records of institutional proceedings, reports and submissions from interest groups, and writings and speeches of key players. He not only looks at the official reports of the committee that drafted the various revisions to Rule 23, but also their working papers, notes, and correspondence. In addition, Marcus refers to events occurring in the wider society that affected the development of Rule 23. His contrast between the "regulatory conception" of class actions (whereby proponents of Rule 23 saw it as a mechanism for regulation of big business, environmental polluters, and others) and the "adjectival conception" (whereby more conservative interests held that Rule 23 should not depart from the traditional rules of court and was merely procedural in nature)[45] is compelling and is reflected in the history of class actions in Ontario.

Marcus's work on US class actions therefore provides a model for a detailed look, in the broader legal historical sense, of the genesis of class proceedings legislation. Few scholars have undertaken a similar legal historical analysis of the genesis of the *CPA*. There are some exceptions. For example, Bill Bogart has written numerous articles on the influence of the *Canadian Charter of Rights and Freedoms* and its role in changing the legal and cultural landscape that preceded class action reform.[46] Bogart argues persuasively that the *Charter* changed perceptions of the judicial function, as well as of individual and collective rights, and thereby helped prepare the ground for the *CPA*.[47] He also links the evolution of class actions with wider societal developments, such as the rise of mass consumerism and government bureaucracy, and the increased use of the class action mechanism in the United States.[48] Catherine Piché also discusses the influence of the *Charter*[49] and links class actions with the wider culture. However,

"The History of the Modern Class Action, Part II: Litigation and Legitimacy, 1981–1994" (2017) Arizona Legal Studies Discussion Paper No 17-17, online: SSRN https://ssrn.com/abstract=3015581.

45 Marcus, above note 44 at 4–11.

46 WA Bogart, "*Naken*, the Supreme Court and What Are Our Courts For?" (1984) 9 *Canadian Business Law Journal* 280 [Bogart, "*Naken*"]; WA Bogart, "Questioning Litigation's Role—Courts and Class Actions in Canada" (1987) 62:3 *Indiana Law Journal* 665. *Charter*, above note 40.

47 WA Bogart, "Ambiguity" in *Yves Pratte Conference*, above note 22 at 3.

48 Bogart, "*Naken*," above note 46.

49 Piché, above note 33 at 120 and 123.

Piché's work focuses largely on Quebec, and neither author discusses the genesis of the Ontario *CPA* with regard to the historical record.

This book follows Marcus's example by using a wide array of historical sources to study the development of class actions law in Ontario in relation to its social, economic, political, and legal background. It looks at the legal institutions and players and their work in society, as well as the dynamics of lawmaking in general. In studying legal history in this way, scholars such as Brian Simpson have found that the sources reveal an underlying story that often explains why cases were decided a certain way or legislation passed in a certain form.[50] Presently, there is no such analysis of class action reform in Ontario. That forms the subject of this book, in which the underlying story of the *CPA* is revealed.

D. SCOPE AND STRUCTURE

The focus of this book is Ontario, the first common law jurisdiction in Canada to enact class proceedings legislation. Apart from a handful of cases,[51] there appears to have been very little interest in class actions in the province until the reform to Rule 23 of the US *Federal Rules of Civil Procedure* in 1966 and the subsequent debate in Quebec. The debate in Ontario in fact did not begin until the early 1970s, and my investigation therefore begins at that point. It ends upon the coming into force of the *CPA* on 1 January 1993.[52] Although I conduct a thorough study of primary historical sources within the scope of my research, I rely almost exclusively on secondary sources when referring to other jurisdictions and time periods.

The debate on class action reform in Ontario was preceded by the origins of class actions and group proceedings in the Court of Chancery, the limited jurisprudence in the United Kingdom and subsequently Ontario, and the rise of class actions in the United States and elsewhere.

50 For a discussion of "external" legal history, see AWB Simpson, "The Rise and Fall of the Legal Treatise: Legal Principles and the Forms of Legal Literature" (1981) 48:3 *University of Chicago Law Review* 632; AWB Simpson, *Cannibalism and the Common Law* (Chicago: University of Chicago Press, 1984); and W Wesley Pue & Barry Wright, *Canadian Perspectives on Law & Society: Issues in Legal History* (Ottawa: Carleton University Press, 1988).

51 Examples are cited in the OLRC Report, above note 2 at 18–32.

52 The legislative history of the *CPA* essentially ends with its coming into force on 1 January 1993. The *CPA* has remained in its original form since then, except for a minor amendment in 2006 to reflect the fact that the Ontario Court (General Division) was renamed the Superior Court of Justice.

That forms the second chapter of this book. Chapter 3 covers the period from the early 1970s, when class actions began to be discussed in Ontario in the context of federal competition legislation and provincial consumer protection laws, to 1985, encompassing the release of the OLRC Report and the Supreme Court of Canada's decision in *Naken*. Chapter 4 looks at the reform debate under the tenure of Ian Scott as attorney general, the lead-up to and release of the Advisory Committee Report, and the subsequent passage of the *CPA*. Chapter 5 provides an analysis of why the Advisory Committee Report succeeded in forming the basis of a class action statute in Ontario, and why the OLRC Report did not. Finally, Chapter 6 assesses the use of the *CPA* since its enactment, issues with class actions that the drafters of the *CPA* did not foresee, and how the Act's history affects the practice of class actions lawyers today.[53]

Of the period leading up to the enactment of the *CPA*, Shaun Finn writes eloquently:

> Common law Canada was becoming increasingly sensitized to the class action. Beneath the surface, the seed planted by the provincial [OLRC] report was slowly taking root, stretching out, and sending tentative, unseen shoots towards the sunlight.[54]

This book investigates, for the first time, the history of class action reform in Ontario in depth, revealing those shoots as well as the factors that aided or hindered their growth.

53 I will assume that the reader has a basic knowledge of civil procedure in Ontario. However, terms of art pertaining specifically to class actions—particularly those that tend to be the object of controversy in the policy-making context—are listed in the appendix to this book.

54 Finn, "In a Class," above note 20 at 364.

Chapter 2

CLASS ACTIONS IN ENGLAND, NORTH AMERICA, AND AUSTRALIA

A. REPRESENTATIVE PROCEEDINGS IN EQUITY AND ENGLISH LAW

Class actions have their forebears in equity. Representative proceedings first emerged in medieval England in about the year 1200,[1] and involved pre-existing groups suing for a declaration of rights: for example, villagers suing for a declaration against the manorial lord that they had a right to graze common land. Representative actions reached their ascendancy in England in the seventeenth century, and since that time, as Stephen Yeazell has written, they have been put to three chronologically separate and distinct uses.[2] In the first phase, such proceedings were used to modernize and adjust the customary law governing manorial (landlord–tenant) and parochial (priest–parishioner) relationships on the eve of the agricultural revolution. In the second phase, in the late eighteenth and nineteenth centuries, the proceedings were instead used in disputes between new sets of groups, such as business persons and trade unions. For Yeazell, the third phase involves the emergence of the modern class

1 Stephen Yeazell, *From Medieval Group Litigation to the Modern Class Action* (New Haven: Yale University Press, 1987) at 38 [Yeazell, *Medieval*]. See also Raymond B Marcin, "Searching for the Origin of the Class Action" (1974) 23 *Catholic University Law Review* 515, which outlines the history of the class action in the British Isles from the fourteenth century onwards.

2 Stephen Yeazell, "Group Litigation and Social Context: Toward a History of the Class Action" (1977) 77:6 *Columbia Law Review* 866 at 867 [Yeazell, "Group Litigation"].

action in the United States. The first two phases will be examined below, while the third phase will be reviewed later in this chapter.

Prior to 1873, judicial authority was vested in two systems: the common law courts, which dealt with strictly "legal" matters, and the Court of Chancery, which dealt with "equitable" rights. Common law courts saw disputes as purely a two-party affair; they took a narrow view of the joinder rule and allowed permissive joinder only if the judgment would affect the direct and immediate interests of the people to be added. The court of equity, however, existed to adjudicate not only the immediate dispute but also the rights that would be affected by it. This court called for compulsory joinder of all persons whose interests would be affected by the suit, so that the eventual judgment would bind everyone and no further related suits would be brought.[3]

There were occasions, however, where all interested parties could not be located or it would be impractical to join them, so the court of equity began to make use of the representative action. Under this device, one person could bring a suit on behalf of all interested persons, and any judgment would bind all those people. In this way, the compulsory joinder rule would not prevent the parties from "com[ing] at justice,"[4] and the court could still avoid an inefficient multiplicity of suits.[5] This relaxation of the rule was essential for groups such as tenants who had disputes with their manorial lord,[6] or parishioners who wished to assert their rights against their parish priest.[7] As society industrialized and commerce became more complex, business people also combined and collectivized, but these collectives lacked separate legal personality (this was prior to the birth of the modern corporation). They therefore exercised their group claims through the court of equity.[8]

---

3 John A Kazanjian, "Class Actions in Canada" (1973) 11 *Osgoode Hall Law Journal* 397 at 399–400; Neil J Williams, "Consumer Class Actions in Canada—Some Proposals for Reform" (1975) 13 *Osgoode Hall Law Journal* 1 at 8–9 [Williams, "Some Proposals"].

4 *Duke of Bedford v Ellis*, [1901] AC 1 at 8 (HL) [*Ellis*], cited in William E McNally & Barbara E Cotton, "Guiding Principles Regarding the Constitution of a Representative Defendant and a Defendant Class in a Class Action Proceeding" (2003) 27 *Advocates' Quarterly* 110 at 115–16.

5 Kazanjian, above note 3 at 401.

6 See *How v The Tenants of Bromsgrove* (1681), 23 ER 277, and *Brown v Howard* (1701), 21 ER 960, both cited in Kazanjian, *ibid* at 402.

7 See *Brown v Vermuden* (1676), 1 Chan Ca 271, and *Brown v Booth* (1690), 121 ER 960, both cited in Kazanjian, *ibid* at 402.

8 Kazanjian, *ibid* at 401. See also *City of London v Richmond* (1701), 23 ER 870, and *Chancey v May* (1722), 24 ER 265, both cited in Kazanjian, *ibid* at 402.

It was considered acceptable to bind people even if they did not know about the judgment, because equitable suits did not involve claims for damages and therefore did not directly affect people's financial interests. Relief was generally declaratory or injunctive, and the declaration or injunction usually involved the rights of a pre-existing group.[9] Stephen Yeazell is one of the few scholars to have noted this distinction between representative actions at equity and modern-day common law class actions (generally involving damages and class members with no pre-existing bond):

> Once one realizes that the relief sought was a declaration of custom, the problem [of absent class members] seems far less urgent. Having one's day in court loses some of its significance if what the court does at the end of that day is simply to declare what shall be the law tomorrow, without retrospectively applying that law to a specific dispute.[10]

The declaration of the rights of one member of the group was a declaration of the rights of all. The subject matter of the dispute simply had to be a general proprietary right in which all parties had a common interest, and the parties had to be so numerous that actual joinder would be impracticable.[11]

From about the mid-1800s, the popularity of group litigation at equity began to decline. The birth of the corporation meant that businesses had standing to sue and be sued in their own right.[12] In addition, Parliament enacted several statutes that dealt with the issues regularly faced by corporations, which reduced business peoples' tendency and desire to resort to group litigation to clarify those issues.[13] Equity litigation in general began to fall out of favour, with the publication of Dickens's *Bleak House*

9 See, for example, *Lloyd v Loaring* (1802), 31 ER 1302 (lodge of Freemasons seeking injunction against dissident member), and *Adair v New River Company* (1805), 32 ER 1153 (shareholders seeking an account of moneys owing against the corporation), both cited in Kazanjian, *ibid* at 405.

10 Yeazell, "Group Litigation," above note 2 at 891.

11 Two other criteria (privity between the group and the adversary, and privity between members of the group) were abandoned by the Lord Chancellor in *Mayor of York v Pilkington* (1737), 26 ER 180. The Lord Chancellor reasoned that equity courts entertained Bills of Peace even though they did not necessarily involve such privity, and that representative actions should be no different. The requirement that the right in question be proprietary also disappeared in 1901, in the *Ellis* (above note 4) and *Taff Vale* (below note 19) decisions. See Kazanjian, above note 3 at 403 and 419.

12 Yeazell, *Medieval*, above note 1 at 124–25.

13 *Ibid* at 210–12.

between 1852 and 1853 illustrating the torturous delays and overly complex nature of that system. A campaign for court reform led to the fusion of the courts of law and equity with the passage of the *Supreme Court of Judicature Act, 1873*.[14] From this point onwards, representative actions could be brought in the courts of common law in England (under Rule 9) and Ontario (under Rule 10). Both rules were very similar to Ontario's later Rule 75 and read as follows:

> Where there are numerous parties having the same interest in one action, one or more of such parties may sue or be sued or may be authorized by the Court to defend in such action on behalf of or for the benefit of all parties so interested.[15]

However, because of their equitable roots, representative actions were not well received by the courts when those actions involved monetary damages. This is because, as noted above, binding absent class members was much more troublesome when financial interests were involved. Damages were also generally different for each class member, as opposed to declaratory relief that was the same for everyone. Equitable representative actions were simply a different beast than common law class actions for damages, and the courts treated them differently.

Many commentators, including the authors of the OLRC Report, have noted that class actions began promisingly after the fusion of the courts, but express confusion at the courts' restrictive interpretation of them from the beginning of the twentieth century.[16] When one looks at the difference between equitable and common law group actions, however, the reason for this restrictive interpretation is clear: the major representative actions brought in England after 1873 were received favourably by the courts because they involved equitable relief only. The restrictive interpretation began in 1910, with the bringing of a class action that involved claims for damages. To understand this explanation, however, is to acknowledge that there is a profound difference between representative actions in equity and class actions at common law, and this is to acknowledge that the modern-day class action is a substantial departure from precedent. Such

---

14 (UK) 36 & 37 Vict, c 66. The fusion took effect in Ontario in 1881 by way of *The Ontario Judicature Act, 1881*, 44 Vict, c 5.

15 Rules of Court, Order XII, Rule 10, enacted as a schedule to the *Ontario Judicature Act*, *ibid*.

16 Ontario Law Reform Commission, *Report on Class Actions* (Toronto: Ministry of the Attorney General, 1982) at 10–13 [OLRC Report].

an acknowledgement did not fit in with the twentieth-century reformers' efforts to play down the innovative nature of class proceedings and thereby reassure business and other groups supporting the status quo.[17]

The two major representative actions for equitable relief after 1873 were *Duke of Bedford v Ellis*[18] and *Taff Vale Railway Co v Amalgamated Society of Railway Servants*.[19] *Ellis* involved a group of fruit and vegetable growers who claimed to be entitled to certain statutory rights regarding the use of Covent Garden Market. They sought equitable relief in the form of a declaration and an injunction. A majority of the House of Lords found that a class action could be brought, because three criteria had been satisfied: there was a common interest, there was a common grievance, and the relief sought was beneficial to all whom the plaintiff proposed to represent.[20] The second case, *Taff Vale*, involved a registered trade union and whether it could be sued for an injunction in its registered name. The law lords found in *obiter* that a defendant class action was a viable procedural alternative. Given that both these cases involved claims for equitable relief, they did not pose the procedural difficulties that were presented by claims for damages.

These difficulties arose in a 1910 case, *Markt & Co Ltd v Knight Steamship Co Ltd*,[21] which was a representative action for damages. The plaintiffs' goods had been damaged when a Russian warship destroyed the defendant's vessel, on the suspicion that it was carrying contraband. The plaintiffs sued on behalf of forty-four other shippers and sought "damages for breach of contract and duty in and about the carriage of goods by sea."[22] The English Court of Appeal found that the plaintiffs could not bring a representative action, because there was no common interest. First, the shippers all had separate contracts with the defendants (no common interest); second, their damages were all different; and third, the defendants might be able to raise different defences against different shippers.[23] The relief sought (monetary damages) was necessarily personal to each shipper, and this relief could not therefore be beneficial to all whom the

17 Yeazell, "Group Litigation," above note 2 at 866–67.

18 Above note 4.

19 [1901] AC 426 (HL) [*Taff Vale*], cited in OLRC Report, above note 16 at 11.

20 *Ellis*, above note 4 at 8.

21 [1910] 2 KB 1021 (CA) [*Markt*], cited in OLRC Report, above note 16 at 11–12.

22 *Markt*, above note 21 at 1022. See also Mark Stiggelbout, "The Recognition in England and Wales of United States Judgments in Class Actions" (2011) 52:2 *Harvard International Law Journal* 433 at 446.

23 *Markt*, above note 21 at 1029–30, 1035, and 1040; Stiggelbout, *ibid* at 447.

plaintiffs proposed to represent. The case therefore failed the test articulated in *Ellis*, and could not proceed as a representative action.[24]

The subsequent jurisprudence followed the ruling in *Markt*. Very few representative actions could satisfy the three-part test articulated in *Ellis*: common interest; common grievance; and relief beneficial to all. The exceptions were largely cases that sought equitable relief or damages from a common fund (such as a trust—trusts also being part of the law of equity), or involved groups that pre-existed the litigation, such as unions, who were not simply bound together by individual contracts against the same defendant.[25] There were also some cases in which the courts allowed representative actions for a declaration of liability; in those cases, class members would then have to follow up with their own individual suit for damages.[26] However, the seeking of monetary relief, or the presence of individual contracts, was a major impediment to representative actions in England.[27]

The situation was similar in Ontario, where the caselaw generally followed the precedent set by *Markt*. Representative actions in which the claims of class members were based on separate contracts were found not to satisfy the "common interest" requirement,[28] as were actions that sought monetary relief.[29] Courts in Ontario continued to be largely unreceptive to class actions until the 1970s, when group litigation began to increase in popularity following class action reform south of the border.

B. CLASS ACTIONS IN THE UNITED STATES

Class actions in the United States have a long and complex history. This history is further complicated by the fact that class actions are available at

---

24 *Markt*, above note 21 at 1035 and 1040–41.

25 *EMI Records Ltd v Riley*, [1981] 2 All ER 838 (Ch) (suit brought on behalf of all members of a music industry trade association), cited in OLRC Report, above note 16 at 16.

26 *Prudential Assurance Co Ltd v Newman Industries Ltd*, [1979] 3 All ER 507 (Ch), cited in OLRC Report, *ibid* at 13–14.

27 *Electrical, Electronic, Telecommunication and Plumbing Union v Times Newspapers Ltd*, [1980] 1 All ER 1097 (QB); *Smith v Cardiff Corporation*, [1954] 1 QB 210, both cited in OLRC Report, *ibid* at 16 and 20.

28 *Preston v Hilton* (1920), 48 OLR 172 (HC); *Shields v Mayor*, [1953] OWN 5 (CA); *Agnew v Sault Ste Marie Board of Education* (1976), 2 CPC 273 (Ont HCJ), all cited in OLRC Report, *ibid* at 22.

29 *Turtle v City of Toronto* (1924), 56 OLR 252 (SCAD), cited in OLRC Report, *ibid* at 25–26. See also Williams, "Some Proposals," above note 3 at 30.

two levels of courts in the United States—the state level and the federal (national) level. The discussions on reform in Ontario, as well as the various reports on class actions in that province, were influenced far more by the federal rules than those at the state level. The focus of this section will therefore be on federal class actions in the United States.[30] Because the United States was the first jurisdiction in the world to explicitly allow class actions for damages when the federal rules were reformed in 1966, other jurisdictions have looked to the United States as both an example and a warning in structuring their own class actions regimes. Ontario is one of these jurisdictions.

The concept of representative litigation entered the United States in the early nineteenth century, when Supreme Court Justice Joseph Story discussed the mechanism in his treatise on equity.[31] Story also looked at the representative action in the case of *West v Randall*,[32] a decision he wrote as a judge of the United States Court of Appeals for the First Circuit. The case arose from a dispute over the estate of West involving numerous individuals, and the issue before Story was which of those individuals should be made parties to the lawsuit. The action originated in equity (as it involved a trust), and Story held that the same rule that applied in equity in England should apply in the United States: namely, that all persons materially interested in the subject matter of the suit should be joined as parties.[33] The rule applied for the same reason as it did in England—to ensure a complete adjudication of all the issues between the parties, to prevent a multiplicity of suits, and to protect the rights of everyone involved.[34] Where it was not possible to bring all the parties before the court, "a few may sue for the benefit of the whole."[35] In other words, representative litigation could be resorted to in the context of

30 A good overview of US class actions at the state level can be found in the OLRC Report, above note 16 at 64–70. Until the 1980s at the earliest, class action litigation in the US federal courts was far more significant than litigation at the state level: David Marcus, "The History of the Modern Class Action, Part I: *Sturm und Drang*, 1953–1980" (2013) 90 *Washington University Law Review* 587 at 591.

31 Joseph Story, *Commentaries on Equity Pleadings*, 8th ed (Boston: Little, Brown, and Company, 1870), online: Hathi Trust Digital Library http://babel.hathitrust.org/cgi/pt?id=njp.32101068559671;view=1up;seq=7. The history of US class actions generally is discussed in Yeazell, *Medieval*, above note 1.

32 29 F Cas 718 (RI 1820), online: https://law.resource.org/pub/us/case/reporter/F.Cas/0029.f.cas/0029.f.cas.0718.pdf.

33 *Ibid* at 1 of online version.

34 *Ibid* at 8.

35 *Ibid* at 10.

equity, if it was required for justice to be done. However, this was not a blanket rule: "A bill cannot be sustained in equity, which is multifarious and embraces distinct matters, affecting distinct parties, who have no common interest in the distinct matters."[36]

In 1833, Story's ruling was codified in Equity Rule 48. Although this rule allowed for representative litigation where it was impractical to join all interested parties, such litigation could not bind absent parties. For practical purposes, therefore, the rule was ineffective.[37] The Supreme Court got around this problem by interpreting the rule so that absent parties could be bound.[38] However, uncertainty as to the binding nature of such judgments persisted, even after a revision of the Equity Rules in 1912.[39] In the early part of the twentieth century, Equity Rule 48 became Rule 38 as part of a major restructuring of the rules. When the courts of law and equity were fused in the United States at the federal level in 1938, Equity Rule 38 became *Federal Rules of Civil Procedure*, Rule 23,[40] and representative actions became available for both legal and equitable relief.

The original Rule 23 attempted to provide some guidance to the courts as to the types of actions that would be amenable to class treatment. The rule described three different types of class actions: true, hybrid, and spurious.[41] True actions involved rights that were enjoyed jointly; hybrid actions involved rights to specific property, where the rights were several; and spurious actions involved several rights, with only common questions of law or fact affecting them.[42] The true actions were closest to their equitable forebears, because they involved a pre-existing group (property owners) with a common interest (property).[43] Hybrid actions still involved a pre-existing group (owners of specific property), even though their property rights were not held in common. It was the spurious actions, however, that gave the courts the most trouble. Most courts

36 *Ibid* at 1.

37 Yeazell, *Medieval*, above note 1 at 221.

38 *Ibid* at 221–22.

39 OLRC Report, above note 16 at 8.

40 308 US 653 (1938) [original Rule 23].

41 These terms are not used in the original Rule 23, *ibid*, but over time they came to be used to describe the categories laid out in that rule: OLRC Report, above note 16 at 8.

42 William J Landers & B Wayne Vance, "Comments: Federal and State Class Actions: Developments and Opportunities" (1975) 46:1 *Mississippi Law Journal* 39 at 75.

43 This conclusion was supported by Landers & Vance, *ibid*, who stated that the purpose of this categorization was "to give meaning to the terminology of 'common or general interest' as used in the Field Code version of the class action rule" (at 74–75).

allowed binding judgments as to absent class members only in the first two categories, so the spurious category soon became completely worthless.[44] In other words, it was essentially only the actions that were closest to their equitable forebears (those with a pre-existing group and/or a common interest) that survived as class actions under the new regime. The US federal experience, in this sense, was similar to the English and early Ontarian experiences.

The categorizations under the old Rule 23 proved overly conceptual and extremely difficult for courts to follow. In addition, there were significant problems with notice, and this affected the due process rights of absent class members.[45] These problems, and the virtually useless nature of the "spurious" category, led to calls to reform the rule. These were answered in 1966.[46] Under the 1966 rule, all class actions bound absent class members[47] and contained specific safeguards for their rights, including requirements for notice. In addition, actions had to be certified by the court before they could proceed as a class action, and the certification requirements included the following:

1) the class is so numerous that joinder of all members is impracticable;
2) there are questions of law or fact common to the class;
3) the claims or defenses of the representative parties are typical of the claims or defenses of the class; and
4) the representative parties will fairly and adequately protect the interests of the class.[48]

Most importantly, the 1966 rule did away with the old categories, constructing in their place a new tripartite structure:

- Rule 23(b)(1) class actions were designed to avoid the risk of individual judgments that would impose incompatible standards of conduct on defendants, or be dispositive of or impair the interests of other members of a group;
- Rule 23(b)(2) class actions involved class injunctive and declaratory relief;

44 *Ibid* at 75.

45 *Ibid.*

46 *Federal Rules of Civil Procedure*, Title IV: Parties, Rule 23: Class Actions, 383 US 1029 (1966), online: Legal Information Institute www.law.cornell.edu/rules/frcp/rule_23 [Rule 23].

47 *Ibid.*

48 *Ibid*, Rule 23(a).

- Rule 23(b)(3) class actions could be maintained where questions of law or fact common to class members predominated over individual issues, and where a class action was superior to other methods for adjudicating the controversy.[49]

It was Rule 23(b)(3) that was the most revolutionary part of the new rule. The other two kinds of class actions were fairly close to their equitable predecessors: Rule 23(b)(1) actions largely encompassed pre-existing rights or members of a pre-existing group, and thus were closer to the "true" actions under the old rule;[50] and Rule 23(b)(2) actions were only for equitable relief. Rule 23(b)(3) actions, however, encompassed class members who might be tied together only by the conduct of the defendant.[51] The first two parts of the new tripartite structure had arguably always been available, albeit without the new protections and requirements applicable to all class actions. The third part, however, was a drastic departure from precedent and constituted the birth of the modern class action as we know it today.

One of the reasons Rule 23(b)(3) was so revolutionary is that it allowed the aggregation of claims that were not economically viable on an individual level, without any pre-existing ties between class members. The departure from equitable claims also meant that class actions for damages were suddenly available,[52] opening up the horizons for class litigation in a massive way. Combined with contingent fees and no-way costs, the incentives for entrepreneurial class counsel were plentiful.[53] However, the due process protections specific to Rule 23(b)(3), including the requirement to provide individual notice of each class member's right to opt out, could also cripple a class action, leading to procedural delays and rendering the action economically unviable.[54] Notice also had to be provided where any certified class action was dismissed or settled, and such dismissal or settlement could not occur without court approval.[55]

49 Linda Silberman, "The Vicissitudes of the American Class Action—With a Comparative Eye" (1999) 7 *Tulane Journal of International and Comparative Law* 201 at 204.

50 *Ibid.*

51 *Ibid.*

52 OLRC Report, above note 16 at 54–55.

53 Silberman, above note 49 at 205.

54 This is essentially what happened in *Eisen v Carlisle & Jacquelin*, 417 US 156 (1974) [*Eisen*], cited in Silberman, *ibid* at 206.

55 Rule 23, above note 46, r 23(e).

The provisions of Rule 23 were used prolifically from 1966 to the early 1970s in a range of proceedings, from civil rights lawsuits to consumer actions, in order to "dispens[e] justice to socially or economically disadvantaged groups as well as to small claimants generally."[56] Class actions were also used to supplement government securities and anti-trust regulations,[57] with many plaintiff class actions lawyers styling themselves as "private attorneys general."[58] As enthusiasm for the new class actions device ran high, courts were initially liberal in their willingness to certify.[59]

However, this tendency slowed from the early 1970s.[60] Several landmark decisions at that time stymied class actions for damages at the federal level.[61] In *Snyder v Harris*[62] and *Zahn v International Paper Co*,[63] the US Supreme Court held that the $10,000 minimum requirement for the federal courts to take jurisdiction applied per class member. In other words, it was not sufficient for the claims of the class to total more than $10,000; each class member's claim had to total more than that amount. This removed almost every consumer class action, and many others as well, from the federal courts' jurisdiction.[64] In *Eisen v Carlisle & Jacquelin* the Supreme Court held that, as far as possible, individual class members must receive notice in a Rule 23(b)(3) suit, and the costs of that notice must be paid by the representative plaintiff. This had the effect of removing many damages actions from the federal courts, as they would be cost prohibitive. *Eisen* also removed district courts' ability to conduct preliminary hearings on the merits of a case, which had generally been favourable

56 Arthur Miller, "Of Frankenstein Monsters and Shining Knights: Myth, Reality, and the 'Class Action Problem'" (1979) 92 *Harvard Law Review* 664 at 678.

57 This concept was first suggested by Harry Kalven Jr and Maurice Rosenfield in their 1941 article, "The Contemporary Function of the Class Suit" (1941) 8 *University of Chicago Law Review* 684.

58 Adolf Homburger, "Private Suits in the Public Interest in the United States of America" (1974) 23 *Buffalo Law Review* 343 at 345; Mauro Cappelletti, "Vindicating the Public Interest Through the Courts: A Comparativist's Contribution" (1976) 25 *Buffalo Law Review* 643 at 660; John C Coffee Jr, "Rescuing the Private Attorney General: Why the Model of the Lawyer as Bounty Hunter Is Not Working" (1983) 42:2 *Maryland Law Review* 215. The plaintiff in *Eisen*, above note 54, was one such "private attorney general."

59 Silberman, above note 49 at 205.

60 Miller, above note 56 at 679.

61 A summary of these cases can be found in the OLRC Report, above note 16 at 58–62.

62 394 US 332 (1969).

63 414 US 291 (1973).

64 Silberman, above note 49 at 205–6.

to plaintiffs. Finally, courts were far more reluctant to award lawyers' fees. Although the United States had no-way costs, courts could make an exception for the "private attorney general," lawyers whose successful prosecution of the case had furthered the public interest. However, the Supreme Court effectively wiped out this exception in *Alyeska Pipeline Service Co v Wilderness Society*,[65] stating that lawyers' fees were not recoverable absent express statutory authorization.

From the mid to late 1970s, the class actions pendulum swung back towards the middle, in "a period characterized by increasing sophistication, restraint, and stabilization in class action practice."[66] Plaintiffs' lawyers defined the scope of their claims and classes much more carefully and realistically, and defence lawyers, in turn, became less resistant to the prospect of class actions.[67] Judges also began to exercise their managerial functions in a much more nuanced way, redefining classes, granting partial certification, and bifurcating cases where necessary.[68] The US Supreme Court had softened its stance so that, by 1982, the OLRC Report could conclude that "the attitude of that Court to class actions ... in recent years, may be characterized as one of cautious acceptance."[69] This was something of a boon to the reformers in Ontario, as they could refer to the US experience to show how the class action was, for the most part, a balanced remedy that treated the rights of plaintiffs and defendants with equal concern.

C. ONTARIO IN THE 1970S: THE PRECURSOR TO REFORM

As noted earlier in this chapter, Ontario was largely unreceptive to class proceedings until the 1970s, when the effects of the United States' new Rule 23 began to make themselves felt. Representative proceedings in Ontario were governed by Rule 75, which was similar to the previous Rule 10 and stated that, "[w]here there are numerous persons having the same interest, one or more may sue or be sued or may be authorized by the court to defend on behalf of, or for the benefit of, all."[70] An increasing

65 421 US 240 (1975).

66 Miller, above note 56 at 680.

67 *Ibid.*

68 *Ibid* at 680–81.

69 OLRC Report, above note 16 at 62.

70 Rule 75 of the Rules of Practice of the Supreme Court of Ontario.

number of actions in Ontario, including those involving separate contracts and those for monetary relief, were found to satisfy the "same interest" requirement. As John Kazanjian has noted, the phrase defies clear and specific meaning, which was ideal for the flexible approach of the court of equity, but invited arbitrary treatment once it was codified as a rule of civil procedure.[71] Where earlier in the twentieth century the "same interest" requirement had been interpreted inflexibly, then, the Ontario courts began interpreting it more generously from 1970 onwards,[72] to mean "the same interest in winning the action."

In adopting this interpretation, the Ontario courts took the lead from several decisions in British Columbia. The two most notable were *Shaw v Real Estate Board of Greater Vancouver*[73] and *Chastain v British Columbia Hydro and Power Authority*.[74] In *Shaw*, a group of real estate salespersons brought a representative action for an accounting in order to recover portions of commissions that they claimed had been wrongfully withheld by the defendant. The court held that it was immaterial that the group members had been wronged in their individual capacity, "provided, of course, that their claims were not for personal damages."[75] Because the group had brought their action for equitable relief—that is, for an accounting and not for damages at common law—it did not matter to the court that calculating the entitlement of each class member would involve "long, detailed and difficult accountings."[76] What was important was that the class had the "same interest" in that they had a common interest in the success of the action:

> A class action is appropriate where if the plaintiff wins the other persons he purports to represent win too, and if he, because of that success, becomes entitled to relief whether or not in a fund or property, the others also become likewise entitled to that relief . . . .[77]

71 Kazanjian states that the phrases "same interest" and "common interest" were used interchangeably in equity: Kazanjian, above note 3 at 416–18.

72 As the OLRC Report has noted, courts did not have difficulty with the "numerous persons" requirement, unless there were so few class members that they could just as easily have been joined in an ordinary action: OLRC Report, above note 16 at 18–19, citing *Goodfellow v Knight* (1977), 2 CPC 209 (Alta SCTD).

73 (1973), 36 DLR (3d) 250 (BCCA) [*Shaw*], cited in OLRC Report, above note 16 at 26.

74 (1973), 32 DLR (3d) 443 (BCSC) [*Chastain*], cited in OLRC Report, *ibid* at 26.

75 *Shaw*, above note 73 at 253–54.

76 *Ibid* at 255.

77 *Ibid* at 254.

This "common success" criterion was also followed in *Chastain*.[78] In that case, the plaintiff brought a representative action on behalf of hydro customers who had been required to pay a security deposit (the practice was discriminatory because only customers with poor credit histories were required to pay the deposit). The action sought equitable relief, in the form of a declaration that the defendant had no authority to require deposits, as well as an injunction preventing the defendant from keeping current deposits. The injunction was effectively a claim for monetary relief (which would involve returning different amounts to each customer), but the court nevertheless allowed it to proceed. Justice McIntyre concluded that the plaintiffs and those whom they represented "form a group having the same interest in the cause."[79] In other words, all class members had the same interest in the success of the action.

The caselaw in Ontario in the 1970s reflects the dual strands of *Shaw* and *Chastain*: first, the adoption of the "common success" test, and second, the creative use of equitable remedies to bypass the restrictions of *Markt* and claim monetary relief on behalf of the class. *Farnham v Fingold*[80] was a representative action brought on behalf of non-controlling shareholders, who claimed they had been unjustly deprived of a premium that had been paid to the controlling shareholders upon the sale of the company. They sought several forms of relief, including a declaration, an accounting, and damages. Despite the plaintiffs' creative efforts to seek relief by equitable means, the Court of Appeal in fact chose to treat the action as one for damages. Justice Jessup treated the holding in *Markt* as *obiter*, and instead preferred the holding in *Taff Vale*, which would permit a more flexible approach to representative actions.[81] It helped that the plaintiffs in *Farnham* sought a *pro rata* share of damages, so that individual assessments would not be required. Justice Jessup expressed circumspection about class actions for damages where such assessments would be required. Not only would such an action deprive the defendant of the ability to conduct discoveries to establish individual entitlement, but, in the event of success, the defendant would only have recourse for costs against the plaintiff, even though their costs had been increased

78 This case is discussed in Williams, "Some Proposals," above note 3 at 12–13.

79 *Chastain*, above note 74 at 443.

80 [1972] 3 OR 688 (HCJ), rev'd [1973] 2 OR 132 (CA), cited in OLRC Report, above note 16 at 26.

81 Above note 80 at 135 (CA).

by multiple separate claims.[82] The Ontario courts therefore continued to view class actions for separately assessed damages as problematic.[83]

The case of *Cobbold v Time Canada Ltd*[84] built on the success of *Farnham* and adopted the "common success" test from the BC jurisprudence. The plaintiff in *Cobbold* brought an action for breach of contract, on behalf of himself and other subscribers with unexpired subscription contracts, when the defendant suspended publication of its magazine in Canada. The defendant had since been supplying the US version of *Time* and, because that version was more expensive, it had curtailed the length of the class members' contracts. The plaintiff sought relief in the form of specific performance (delivery of *Time* for the full length of the original contracts) or a declaration that the class members were entitled to damages. This case is another example of the creative use of equitable relief in order to bypass the restrictions of *Markt*. Nevertheless, the defendant objected that the action was essentially one for damages, and also pointed out that each class member had a separate contract with the defendant. The court allowed the action to proceed anyway pursuant to the "common success" test in *Shaw*. Citing that case, Stark J stated that "a class action is appropriate if it can be shown that success for the plaintiff means success for the other members of the class, especially where the same measure of success applies equally to all."[85] Again, as in *Farnham*, the class members were not claiming damages that had to be individually assessed, but were instead seeking damages that could be assessed in the aggregate.[86]

This same approach was successful at the Court of Appeal for Ontario in *General Motors of Canada Ltd v Naken*.[87] The representative plaintiff was suing on behalf of persons who purchased new models of the Firenza,

82 *Ibid* at 136.

83 Kazanjian, above note 3 at 435–36; Williams, "Some Proposals," above note 3 at 32–33. The issue of individually assessed damages was one of the factors that later prevented *Naken* from proceeding as a class action: *General Motors of Canada Ltd v Naken*, [1983] 1 SCR 72 [*Naken*].

84 (1976), 13 OR (2d) 567 (HCJ) [*Cobbold*], cited in OLRC Report, above note 16 at 23.

85 *Cobbold*, above note 84 at 569.

86 The action was, however, dismissed at trial on the grounds that the class members who had been sent the US version of *Time* instead had not suffered any damages. The class members who instead received a refund from *Time* were found to have settled with the defendant, and were therefore excluded from the class. Costs were awarded against the plaintiff in an unspecified amount: *Cobbold v Time Canada Ltd*, 1980 CanLII 1879 (Ont HCJ).

87 1979 CanLII 1983 (OCA) [*Naken* (CA)].

manufactured by General Motors, in 1971 and 1972. The Firenza was a notoriously unreliable vehicle, finding its place in automotive history next to the flaming Pinto.[88] As a Canadian newspaper reported more than a decade later:

> The Firenza made mechanics rich. Owners picketed car lots all over Ottawa, Montreal, Oshawa and Toronto, protesting its low resale value. They sued dealerships. They formed an association and drove a motorcade to Parliament Hill to protest—along the route one Firenza broke down, barfing smoke at the sky.[89]

The plaintiffs in *Naken* (CA), not surprisingly, alleged that the vehicles were in breach of the manufacturer's collateral warranty. They sought *pro rata* damages in the same creative way as in *Farnham*, alleging that each class member had suffered $1,000 in damages based on the reduced resale value of each car caused by the breach of warranty.

At the first instance, the defendant's motion to strike was dismissed.[90] However, the Divisional Court saw through the plaintiffs' creative presentation of their damages claim and allowed the defendant's appeal.[91] It held that individual assessments for damages would be required, and that the class members' damages could not be disguised as aggregate damages simply by capping the claims at $1,000 each.[92] In addition, the court held that the claims involved individual contracts.[93] The class members did not have the "same interest," and could not claim that their case involved a "common fund" out of which all class members would be paid if the

---

88 The Pinto was a vehicle manufactured by Ford that became infamous in the 1970s for bursting into flames if its gas tank was ruptured in a collision. It is now the subject of one of the main exhibits at the American Museum of Tort Law.

89 Brad Evenson, "The Lemon Car Legacy" *Ottawa Citizen* (26 July 1992) A4 ["Lemon Car Legacy"], in Ministry of the Attorney General, Policy Development Division (PDD) Counsel correspondence files, Class Proceedings—Media, RG 4-40, Box No B703283, North York, Archives of Ontario [PDD Media].

90 *Naken v General Motors of Canada Ltd*, 1975 CanLll 498 (Ont HCJ).

91 *Naken v General Motors of Canada Ltd*, 1977 CanLll 1317 (Ont Div Ct).

92 *Ibid.*

93 The plaintiffs acknowledged that the main contracts were formed between class members and various automobile dealers, not the manufacturer; however, they claimed that GM had established a preliminary or collateral contract with class members by inducing them to purchase their vehicles through advertising and other means. The court held that this question of reliance was inescapably individual, and that a common cause of action was therefore missing (*ibid*).

case succeeded. The suit could not therefore proceed as a class action under Rule 75.[94]

At the Court of Appeal, Arnup JA allowed the plaintiffs' appeal and permitted the pleading to stand.[95] Although the contracts between the class members and various automobile dealers were not common, there was a collateral contract between GM and some of the class members, whereby GM's advertisements and other representations had induced those class members to buy the vehicles. The only members of that class, however, were those that had relied upon the advertisements. The pleading therefore had to be amended to narrow the class to those people, so that there would be a "common interest" among the class.[96] In that way, the plaintiffs' damages would be sought on behalf of the class as a class, and could therefore be assessed in the aggregate without the need for individual damages assessments. Although individual proceedings would be necessary in order for each class member to demonstrate that they had relied upon the manufacturer's warranty, Arnup JA held that such proceedings could be held after the common questions were answered, and that this should not be a bar to a class action.[97]

This was a promising development towards the increased use of class actions in Ontario.[98] It was not an unqualified win, however. Two subsequent decisions from the Court of Appeal for Ontario clarified the jurisprudence on damages class actions, making it clear that a class action could not proceed where individual assessments for damages were required. In *Seafarers International Union of Canada v Lawrence*,[99] the plaintiffs sought damages for defamation. The court concluded that the damages for each class member would be different, and that it would not be possible to establish the exact amount of damages and pro-rate that amount among

---

94 *Ibid.*

95 *Naken* (CA), above note 87. See also "Judge Rules Firenza Action Is Proper, if Change Made" *Globe and Mail* (13 October 1978) 5, in Ontario Law Reform Commission files, Nov 1976–Dec 1982, Project name: class actions, RG 4-66, BA77, Box No B380543, North York, Archives of Ontario [Box No B380543].

96 *Naken* (CA), above note 87.

97 *Ibid.*

98 Unfortunately, the development was cut short when the Supreme Court of Canada overturned the Court of Appeal's decision and said the case could not proceed as a class action: *Naken*, above note 83. The Supreme Court's decision will be reviewed in detail in the next chapter.

99 (1979), 24 OR (2d) 257 (CA) [*Seafarers International*], cited in OLRC Report, above note 16 at 31.

the class.[100] In *Stephenson v Air Canada*, the Court of Appeal for Ontario[101] affirmed the earlier judgment of Southey J.[102] This judgment held that a group of people who had bought Air Canada flights in August 1978, only to find the flights were subsequently cancelled due to a strike, could not proceed with a class action for damages. Again, there was no common fund available in this case, and no way in which damages could be assessed in the aggregate. Individual enquiries as to damages would have to be conducted, and this meant that a class action would not be fair to the defendants.[103]

Nevertheless, it was clear that Ontario courts were becoming accustomed to the idea of class actions in general, even if they would still not permit Rule 75 proceedings involving individual damages or individual contracts. This development was reflected in other jurisdictions in Canada and internationally, where class actions were being researched, debated, and even legislated.

D. DEVELOPMENTS IN OTHER JURISDICTIONS

1) New Brunswick

The vanguard of the movement for class actions was led by consumer protection and environmental rights advocates. Post-war Canada, like many other countries in the West, saw a dramatic rise in mass production and the availability of consumer products. However, this development took place without many of the institutions that were required to protect consumers and ensure that transactions were fair. This led to a nationwide movement advocating for consumer rights and the means for enforcing them.[104]

100 *Seafarers International*, *ibid*, at 263–64.

101 The Court of Appeal for Ontario gave its decision on 10 February 1981 without reasons. Its decision is cited in the OLRC Report, above note 16 at 24.

102 (1979), 26 OR (2d) 369 (HCJ).

103 *Ibid* at 369–70. See also "Class Action Suit Against Air Canada Ruled Out" *Toronto Star* (12 February 1981), in Box No B380543, above note 95.

104 One of the organizations that sprang out of this movement was the Consumers' Association of Canada, which was instrumental in bringing about class action reform in Ontario and elsewhere: Anna Sadovnikova et al, "Consumer Protection in Postwar Canada: Role and Contributions of the Consumers' Association of Canada to the Public Policy Process" (2014) 48:2 *Journal of Consumer Affairs* 380.

In New Brunswick, this movement led to the creation of the Consumer Protection Project in the Law Reform Division of the New Brunswick Department of Justice. This project looked into various consumer protection mechanisms over a number of years, one of which was class actions. The project's third report, released in 1976, recommended that legislation permitting class actions be enacted.[105] However, like many initial proposals for statutory change, the New Brunswick report adopted the new Rule 23 of the US *Federal Rules of Civil Procedure* with very little change. Such proposals were troublesome in that they imported the weaknesses of Rule 23, such as the requirement for individual notice in damages class actions that, as noted above, could cripple class actions and even prevent them.

Nevertheless, the report of the Consumer Protection Project was an important first salvo in the fight for reform. While New Brunswick would not end up introducing class action legislation until 2006,[106] its officials informed other jurisdictions' research into class actions, as well as that of the Uniform Law Conference of Canada.[107]

2) British Columbia

British Columbia also undertook early research into the possibility of class action reform. In August 1977, J Douglas Lambert, the BC delegate to the Uniform Law Conference of Canada (ULCC) and member of the BC Law Reform Commission, presented the ULCC annual meeting with a memorandum on class actions.[108] The memorandum was only a preliminary outline of the issues to be discussed, with more in-depth research to follow once the ULCC had given guidance. Lambert suggested that the ULCC adopt the model for class actions that had been proposed as part of

105 Karl J Dore & Richard W Kerr, *Third Report of the Consumer Protection Project*, vol 1 (Fredericton: New Brunswick Department of Justice, Law Reform Division, 1976).

106 *Class Proceedings Act*, SNB 2006, c C-5.15, since repealed and replaced by RSNB 2011, c 125.

107 The correspondence between Basil Stapleton, director of the New Brunswick Law Reform Branch, and Michael Cochrane is detailed in Chapter 4. Stapleton encouraged Cochrane to have Ontario class actions placed on the Uniform Law Conference of Canada (ULCC) agenda.

108 Uniform Law Conference of Canada, "Proceedings of the Fifty-Ninth Annual Meeting" (St Andrews, New Brunswick, August 1977) 208–13, online: www.ulcc.ca/images/stories/Past_Proceedings_PDF/1977ULCC0059.pdf [ULCC 1977].

the further amendments to the federal *Combines Investigation Act* (CIA).[109] Although the ULCC established a committee to monitor developments in the field and possibly prepare model uniform provisions for consideration the following year,[110] these discussions had little immediate effect for two reasons. First, the CIA proposal had been tailored to fit the federal criminal law power that was then the sole basis for competition law prosecutions, and it became apparent that it could not easily be modified for the purposes of provincial civil litigation.[111] Second, as discussed further below, the model for class actions under the CIA itself died on the order paper not long after Lambert submitted his memorandum. By the time of the 1978 meeting, the committee was able to report[112] that legislation had been introduced and passed in Quebec,[113] which was to prove a major influence on the movement for class proceedings reform in Ontario. Further discussions on the subject of class actions for the common law provinces would, however, have to wait until well into the next decade.

109 *Ibid* at 208–10. The federal *Combines Investigation Act*, as well as the work of the OLRC on class actions (also referred to in Lambert's memorandum), are discussed in Chapter 3. The proposal suggested by Lambert was contained in Neil J Williams & Jennifer Whybrow, *A Proposal for Class Actions Under Competition Policy Legislation* (Ottawa: Department of Consumer and Corporate Affairs, 1976).

110 ULCC 1977, above note 108 at 29. The committee consisted of J Douglas Lambert (BC) as chair, Professors Hubert Reid and Daniel Jacoby (Quebec), and Derek Mendes da Costa and Simon Chester (Ontario). Mendes da Costa was the chair of the OLRC at the time. Chester was executive counsel to the deputy attorney general from July 1977 to February 1982 (having formerly worked as a legal research officer with the OLRC from December 1974 to July 1977, including work on the class actions project). He was later counsel at the Policy Development Division at the MAG (from February 1982 to mid-1985), and thereafter joined the law firm of McMillan Binch. Because of McMillan Binch's lobbying work against class actions (discussed below), Chester ceased all discussion on class actions after joining the firm: correspondence with Simon Chester (now counsel at Gowling WLG (Canada) LLP) (4 December 2017) [Chester email].

111 Chester email, *ibid*.

112 Uniform Law Conference of Canada, "Proceedings of the Sixtieth Annual Meeting" (St John's, Newfoundland, August 1978) at 111–12, online: www.ulcc.ca/images/stories/Past_Proceedings_PDF/1978ULCC0060.pdf [ULCC 1978]. Marie José Longtin, assistant director of legislation at the Department of Justice of Quebec, who had replaced Daniel Jacoby, reported on the passage of the Quebec legislation (at 111).

113 *An Act Respecting Class Actions*, CQLR c R-2.1 [Quebec *CPA*]. The passage of the Quebec legislation will be detailed later in this chapter.

In 1979, British Columbia introduced a form of class action as part of the *Trade Practice Act*[114] that empowered the director of trade practices, or any other person, to bring an action for a declaration or an injunction on behalf of aggrieved consumers.[115] The action could be brought on behalf of consumers generally, or on behalf of a specific group of consumers. This was not a class action statute of general application (such legislation would not be passed in British Columbia until 1996),[116] and it allowed only equitable relief. However, several commentators at the time noted that section 18(3) allowed courts, in an action for a permanent injunction, to restore to consumers any property or money of which they had been deprived by an unconscionable act.[117] Effectively, then, a consumer class action for damages could be brought under this statute. As such, it was very widely applicable and reflected the wider movement for consumer protection and class action reform.

3) Saskatchewan

Similarly, in 1978, Saskatchewan passed *The Department of Consumer Affairs Act*,[118] pursuant to which the provincial attorney general could maintain an action on behalf of any person or class of persons who alleged that they had suffered loss as a result of illegal conduct affecting consumers.[119] This statute was of narrower application than the BC *TPA*, because only the attorney general could bring a consumer class action; however, unlike the BC *TPA*, class actions for damages could be brought with a view to compensating consumers.[120] The provisions of the *DCAA* were partly the result of a study by the Saskatchewan Law Reform

114 RSBC 1979, c 406 [BC *TPA*], cited in the OLRC Report, above note 16 at 284, and Edward Belobaba, "Unfair Trade Practices Legislation: Symbolism and Substance in Consumer Protection" (1977) 15 *Osgoode Hall Law Journal* 327 at 329.

115 BC *TPA*, above note 114, s 18(1).

116 *Class Proceedings Act*, RSBC 1996, c 50. British Columbia was reportedly waiting for the outcome of the debate in Ontario before enacting legislation: J Robert S Prichard, "Class Action Reform: Some General Comments" (1984) 9 *Canadian Business Law Journal* 309 at 313.

117 Belobaba, above note 114 at 365.

118 RSS 1978, c D-9 [*DCAA*], cited in the OLRC Report, above note 16 at 284.

119 *DCAA*, above note 118, s 10.

120 The statute is not very clear on this point; however, see OLRC Report, above note 16 at 293, particularly note 75 and accompanying text.

Commission as part of its Consumer Credit Law Project,[121] commenced in 1975, which looked at the potential for class actions as a means of protecting consumer credit rights.

Although Saskatchewan made some headway towards reforming its consumer protection laws, there appears to have been little other movement towards class action reform until after Ontario passed the *CPA*. In the end, a class action statute of general application was not passed in Saskatchewan until 2001.[122]

4) Australia

In 1977, in its *Thirty-Sixth Report Relating to Class Actions*,[123] the Law Reform Committee of South Australia[124] recommended legislation enacting a class actions procedure. The proposals included a draft statute that was modelled on the new Rule 23 of the US *Federal Rules of Civil Procedure*. This draft statute was never passed. However, legislative amendments allowing for representative proceedings were enacted in 1987.[125] Under these provisions, a quasi-class action may be commenced "where numerous persons have common questions of fact or law requiring adjudication."[126] The plaintiffs must bring a motion for certification and for directions, but certification will not be refused simply because the action involves individual damages or separate contracts.[127] In September 2006,

121 Law Reform Commission of Saskatchewan, *Fourth Annual Report* (Saskatoon: Law Reform Commission of Saskatchewan, 1977).

122 *The Class Actions Act*, SS 2001, c C-12.01.

123 Law Reform Committee of South Australia, *Thirty-Sixth Report Relating to Class Actions* (Adelaide: Government of South Australia, 1977).

124 Australia is a federation of six states, with two federal territories. South Australia and Victoria are two of the states discussed in this section.

125 An overview of the South Australian class action regime can be found in Vince Morabito, "Taxpayers and Class Actions" (1997) 20:2 *University of New South Wales Law Journal* 372 at 377 [Morabito, "Taxpayers"]. See also Vince Morabito, "Group Litigation in Australia—'Desperately Seeking' Effective Class Action Regimes" (National report for Australia prepared for the Globalisation of Class Actions Conference, Oxford University, December 2007), online: http://globalclassactions.stanford.edu/sites/default/files/documents/Australia_National_Report.pdf [Morabito, "Litigation"].

126 *Supreme Court Rules 1987* (SA), r 34.01.

127 *Ibid*, rr 34.02 & 34.03, cited in Morabito, "Taxpayers," above note 125 at 377. According to Rule 81 enacted in 2006, a judicial order authorizing a class proceeding must (1) define the group on whose behalf the action is brought; (2) define the nature of the claims made on behalf of the members of the group and specify the remedy

rules 80 and 81 of the new *Supreme Court Civil Rules 2006* (SA) came into operation. The major difference under the new rules is the "opt-in" mechanism: a class can only consist of members who have provided the class representative with written authorization to represent them.[128]

Another state that has undertaken its own reform initiative is Victoria.[129] In 1986, the Victorian Parliament introduced class actions by way of amendment to the *Supreme Court Act*.[130] The procedure allowed for representative proceedings where three or more people had the right to the same (or substantially the same) relief against the same person, or where there were common questions of law or fact.[131] However, the procedure was extremely limited.[132] It was opt-in and all represented persons had to consent to the procedure in writing[133] and be named in the originating process.[134] The statutory provisions did not provide any other guidance to the courts, but merely empowered them to give directions concerning the administration of a class action.[135] As a result, the new procedure came under heavy fire from both the courts and the federal Australian Law Reform Commission. The latter was particularly critical of the limits posed by the opt-in procedure. The courts were frustrated by the vague nature of the provisions, combined with their restrictive nature that stopped the courts from using their discretion to overcome the deficiencies.[136] No class actions ever reached trial under these provisions.[137]

---

sought; (3) define the common questions of law or fact that are to be determined in the action; and (4) give directions about the determination of other issues raised in the action that are not common to all members of the group: Morabito, "Litigation," above note 125 at 2.

128 Morabito, "Litigation," *ibid.*

129 An overview of the Victorian class action regime can be found in Morabito, "Taxpayers," above note 125 at 375–76.

130 1986 (Vict), ss 34(a) and 35(2)(a) [*Supreme Court Act*], cited in S Stuart Clark & Christina Harris, "Multi-plaintiff Litigation in Australia: A Comparative Perspective" (2001) 11 *Duke Journal of Comparative & International Law* 289 at 294 [Clark & Harris, "Multi-plaintiff"].

131 *Supreme Court Act*, above note 130, s 34(a).

132 Clark & Harris, "Multi-plaintiff," above note 130 at 294–95.

133 The consent had to occur either before the proceeding was commenced, or afterwards with leave of the Court: *Supreme Court Act*, above note 130, ss 35(2)(a) and 35(4).

134 *Ibid*, s 35(3).

135 *Ibid*, s 35(5).

136 Clark & Harris, "Multi-plaintiff," above note 130 at 294–95.

137 *Ibid* at 295.

In 1997, the Victorian Attorney General's Law Reform Advisory Council recommended to the Victorian government that comprehensive class actions legislation, similar to Part IVA of the *Federal Court of Australia Act*, be introduced. The Victorian government did not respond, so the Supreme Court of Victoria took the initiative and established a class action regime that was virtually identical to Part IVA by way of a new Order 18A to the *Supreme Court (General Civil Procedure) Rules 1996*. A constitutional challenge to the validity of the new regime came about shortly thereafter, on the basis that Order 18A exceeded the Court's power to draft rules of court.[138] The challenge was rejected by the Court of Appeal for Victoria, but the fear that the High Court of Australia might declare Order 18A invalid led the Victorian Parliament to intervene and introduce legislation.[139]

At the federal level, the commonwealth attorney general first referred the question of class action reform to the Australian Law Reform Commission (ALRC) in 1977.[140] In 1979, the ALRC published a discussion paper calling for reform.[141] The report discussed the arguments for and against class actions, before concluding that reform was necessary in order to keep up with the technological and marketplace developments of the twentieth century.[142] The proposals in this discussion paper were closely modelled on US Rule 23. Various consultations were conducted on these proposals, with draft legislation being released for public comment in June 1988,[143] and the ALRC's final report tabled in the legislature in December of that year.[144] However, the legislation did not come into force until March 1992,[145] just months before the Ontario *CPA* came into force.

138 *Schutt Flying Academy (Australia) Pty Ltd v Mobil Oil Australia Ltd* (2000), 1 VR 545 (CA).

139 *Courts and Tribunals Legislation (Miscellaneous Amendments) Act 2000* (Vict), s 14. The background to this legislation is explained in Morabito, "Litigation," above note 125.

140 S Stuart Clark & Christina Harris, "The Push to Reform Class Action Procedure in Australia: Evolution or Revolution?" (2008) 32 *Melbourne University Law Review* 775 at 780 [Clark & Harris, "Push"].

141 Law Reform Commission of Australia, *Access to the Courts II: Class Actions* (Sydney: Law Reform Commission, 1979).

142 *Ibid* at 34.

143 This development is discussed in detail in Chapter 4.

144 Australian Law Reform Commission Report No 46, *Grouped Proceedings in the Federal Court* (Canberra: Government of Australia Publishing Service, 1988), online: www.alrc.gov.au/sites/default/files/pdfs/publications/alrc46_Summary.pdf [ALRC Report], cited in Clark & Harris, "Push," above note 140 at 776 and 780.

145 *Federal Court of Australia Act 1976* (Cth); Part IVA was inserted into this Act to allow for class actions, by way of the *Federal Court of Australia Amendment Act 1991* (Cth), s 3: see Clark & Harris, "Push," *ibid* at 780 and accompanying notes.

The federal legislation followed the ALRC Report and discussion paper, except for the fact that it did not include a class actions fund (publicly financed or otherwise).[146] Like the ALRC Report and discussion paper, the legislation was based largely on US Rule 23, but differed from those provisions in several important respects.[147] First, it contained no certification requirement. Second, it did not require that common issues predominate over individual issues. Third, it expressly provided for the determination of individual issues such as causation, so that even personal injury claims could proceed as part of a class action.[148] In this sense, the federal Australian legislation was more plaintiff-friendly than US Rule 23.

In more recent years, the parliaments of both New South Wales and Queensland have passed legislation allowing for class actions. New South Wales enacted part 10 of the *Civil Procedure Act 2005* in March 2011, allowing for a comprehensive class actions regime that is based on the federal legislation.[149] The Queensland regime, enacted in November 2016, largely adopts the framework already existing in Victoria, in New South Wales, and at the federal level.[150] Similar legislative change is also expected in Western Australia.[151]

5) Quebec

Class proceedings, a development of the equitable and common law traditions of English-speaking countries, would not appear to fit comfortably with a francophone civil law jurisdiction. Nevertheless, Quebec was the

146 Clark & Harris, "Push," *ibid* and accompanying notes. However, changes introduced around the same time sanctioned contingency fee arrangements, albeit with a ban on agreements that calculated the fee by reference to a percentage of the amount recovered: Clark & Harris, "Multi-plaintiff," above note 130 at 295 and accompanying notes.

147 Clark & Harris, "Multi-plaintiff," *ibid* at 296–98.

148 In the United States, personal injury claims are not permitted to proceed as a class action. Instead, if hundreds or thousands of personal injury claims that share common issues of fact are filed, the Judicial Panel on Multidistrict Litigation will group them together for the purposes of efficiency in a "multidistrict litigation" (MDL) and transfer them to one district.

149 Vince Morabito, "Replacing Inadequate Class Representatives in Federal Class Actions: Quo Vadis?" (2015) 38:1 *University of New South Wales Law Journal* 146 at 146.

150 Damian Grave & James Page, "State Based Class Action Regimes—25 Years On" (19 December 2016), online: Herbert Smith Freehills LLP www.herbertsmithfreehills.com/latest-thinking/state-based-class-action-regimes-%E2%80%93-25-years-on.

151 *Ibid.*

first province in Canada to enact class action legislation, and it spearheaded reform for the rest of the country. This was part of an increasing trend towards law reform in the province following the Quiet Revolution.[152] Quebec had enacted other ground breaking legislation such as *An Act Respecting Matrimonial Regimes*[153] that, like class actions, was studied by the OLRC.[154]

The class actions device does not seem to have been subject to a longstanding debate in Quebec.[155] The Parti Québécois government was voted into power on 15 November 1976 on a platform of promoting access to justice and implementing social and remedial legislation.[156] Bill 39 respecting class actions was introduced in the legislature just a few months later in 1977,[157] as part of a wider reformist agenda that included labour reform and the enactment of a consumer protection statute.[158] The Bill itself had a strong consumer protection purpose. During the legislative debates, one member declared that it was "destined to re-establish a balance between the isolated citizen and companies."[159] The Quebec Council of Employers took issue with this characterization in its report on class actions,[160] objecting to the

> rhetoric[,] according to which[,] all large companies are exploitative, profit is immoral, and (when profits have indeed been earned) they were

152 Claire L'Heureux-Dubé, "The Quebec Experience: Codification of Family Law and a Proposal for the Creation of a Family Court System" (1984) 44:6 *Louisiana Law Review* 1575 at 1578.

153 SQ 1969, c 77, cited in Ontario Law Reform Commission, *Report on Family Law, Part IV: Family Property Law* (Toronto: Ministry of the Attorney General, 1974) at xii.

154 *Ibid.*

155 A brief history of class actions in Quebec is provided in Shaun Finn, "In a Class All Its Own: The Advent of the Modern Class Action and Its Changing Legal and Social Mission" (2005) 2:2 *Canadian Class Action Review* 333 at 352–61 [Finn, "In a Class"]. This account is reproduced in French in Shaun Finn, *Étude d'un recours évolutif: Redéfinir la procédure sui generis du recours collectif Québécois* (LLM Thesis, Faculté de Droit, Université Laval, 2011) [unpublished] at 31–43 [Finn, *Étude*].

156 Catherine Piché, "The Cultural Analysis of Class Action Law" (2009) 2 *Journal of Civil Law Studies* 101 at 118.

157 Finn, "In a Class," above note 155 at 352.

158 *Ibid*, citing Projet de Loi 39, *Loi sur le recours collectif*, 3rd Sess, 31st Leg, Quebec, 1978.

159 *Journal des débats*, Troisième session—31ième Législature: audition des mémoires sur le projet de loi no 39 (le 7 mars 1978) B-262 (Member of the National Assembly (MNA) Fernand Lalonde), cited in Finn, "In a Class," above note 155 at 353.

160 Conseil du patronat du Québec, *Mémoire à la Commission parlementaire de la justice sur le projet de loi 39: Loi sur le recours collectif* (Montreal: Le Conseil, 1978).

> acquired illegally and on the back of someone else ... Is it necessary, when seeking to protect the vulnerable, to automatically assume that the adverse party is a thief?[161]

Nevertheless, despite the concerns of employers and other business groups, there was wide public support for reform. This support extended to the legal profession, with the Barreau du Quebec submitting its *Mémoire* in January 1978.[162] The Barreau welcomed the introduction of class actions, having been studying the procedure since 1974,[163] although it pointed out that class actions should not create new substantive rights, and must be compensatory rather than punitive.[164]

On 8 June 1978, *An Act Respecting the Class Action*[165] was adopted in the legislature, adding an entire book to the *Code of Civil Procedure*.[166] The Act was based heavily on US Rule 23, as well as the Civil Practice Law and Rules of the State of New York.[167] As the Quebec delegation to the ULCC reported at its annual meeting in 1978,[168] the salient points of the new legislation included the following:

1) Only "natural persons" could bring a class proceeding (in other words, the remedy was foreclosed to corporations and other purely legal persons);[169]
2) Leave of the court had to be sought for the bringing of a class action, in the form of a "motion for authorization," which would not involve an assessment of the merits of the action;[170]

---

161 *Ibid* at 33–34, cited in Finn, "In a Class," above note 155 at 353.

162 Barreau du Québec, *Mémoire à la Commission parlementaire de la justice sur le projet de loi 39: Loi sur le recours collectif* (Québec: Barreau du Québec, 1978).

163 *Ibid* at 1.

164 *Ibid* at 3.

165 Quebec *CPA*, above note 113.

166 Book IX of the *Code of Civil Procedure*, which came into force on 19 January 1979, cited in Finn, "In a Class," above note 155 at 354.

167 Finn, "In a Class," *ibid* at 352.

168 ULCC 1978, above note 112 at 113–20.

169 *Ibid* at 114. This requirement was lifted in December 2015, such that class membership is now available to anyone: Vincent de l'Étoile, "Quebec's Own Class Action Authorization Regime" *Canadian Lawyer* (25 April 2016), online: www.canadianlawyermag.com/6005/Quebecs-own-class-action-authorization-regime.html.

170 ULCC 1978, above note 112 at 115. "It is not the wish of the legislator to allow an examination on the merits of the action at the motion stage [but] it will be possible to examine the person alleging the facts as to [their] veracity."

3) On the motion for authorization, the court would consider the allegations and whether "they seem to justify the conclusions sought," the existence of a group, the existence of common questions of law or fact, whether other group proceedings would be difficult or impractical, and whether the plaintiff would adequately represent the group;[171]
4) Notice at the certification stage was compulsory;[172]
5) Class members were included in the class unless they opted out, and they had a right to do so;[173]
6) Collective recovery (aggregate damages) was permitted, with discretion given to the Court as to the distribution of any residue;[174]
7) With regard to costs, traditional costs rules continued to apply—however, legal fees could be taken out of any settlement or judgment before distribution to the class;[175] in addition, a Class Action Assistance Fund (*Fonds d'aide aux recours collectifs* or the "Fonds") paid the plaintiff lawyer's fees, the costs of notification and general disbursements.[176]

There were some aspects of the Act that had not been borrowed from the United States. These included the "natural persons" requirement; the requirement that the allegations "seem to justify the conclusions sought" (basically, a requirement that the facts as pleaded support one or more causes of action); and, most importantly, the Class Action Assistance Fund. The idea of a government-supported fund to reimburse fees and disbursements did not exist in the United States and was completely new to Quebec. It was to form an important precedent for Ontario and was significant in facilitating class proceedings legislation there.

The Quebec legislation had rather an uninspiring start. In the first five years following its enactment, an average of only twenty class actions per year were commenced (compared to an average of 55,000 cases brought annually in Quebec Superior Court).[177] The Fonds was also vastly underutilized, with only $15,500 of the $100,000 available to claimants

171 *Ibid* at 115.
172 *Ibid* at 115–16.
173 *Ibid* at 116.
174 *Ibid* at 117–18.
175 *Ibid* at 118–19.
176 *Ibid* at 119.
177 H Patrick Glenn, "Class Actions in Ontario and Québec" (1984) 62:3 *Canadian Bar Review* 247 at 255.

being used in 1979.[178] As a result, amendments were introduced in 1982 upon the advice of consumer groups and the Fonds.[179] Co-operatives were added to the organizations entitled to act as class representatives, without requiring that someone in the class had to have been a member of that organization when the action arose. Immediate appeals as of right from certification orders were repealed for defendants.[180] Most importantly, the powers of the Fonds to finance class actions were extended, and a controversial supplementary counsel fee was repealed. These changes retained the traditional two-way costs rules, but provided greater protection from costs risks for representative plaintiffs.

Unfortunately, however, the Quebec courts showed reluctance to give the legislation full effect. This persisted even into the 1980s, with two major decisions from that decade showing the courts' cautious approach. In both *Nault v Canadian Consumer Co*[181] (a consumer class action) and *Comité de citoyens et d'action municipale de St-Césaire c Ville de St-Césaire*[182] (an action by residents against a municipality for passing a series of bylaws), the courts stated that a class action was not the appropriate vehicle for resolution of the class members' claims.[183] In the same conservative manner as the Ontario courts prior to the early 1970s, the Quebec courts emphasized the differences between class members (different contracts in *Nault*, and different interests in the outcome in *St-Césaire*) rather than the common issues that bound them together.

This approach changed in 1990, at the same time as Ontario was debating the *CPA* in the legislature. *Tremaine c AH Robins Canada Inc*[184] involved the notorious Dalkon Shield, a contraceptive device that the

178 Canadian Press, "Class Action Fund Plan Needs Better Publicity, Quebec Officials Say" *Canadian Press* (31 January 1981) P3, in Box No B380543, above note 95.

179 Glenn, above note 177 at 257–59. See also WA Bogart, "Questioning Litigation's Role—Courts and Class Actions in Canada" (1987) 62:3 *Indiana Law Journal* 665 at 687.

180 This provision was re-enacted in December 2015, providing defendants with a right of appeal with leave of a judgment authorizing a class action: de l'Étoile, above note 169.

181 [1981] 1 SCR 553 at 354–55, cited in Finn, "In a Class," above note 155.

182 [1986] RJQ 1061 (CA), cited in Finn, "In a Class," above note 155 at 355–56. This proceeding was commenced under the class action provisions of the *Code of Civil Procedure*, although there were alternative avenues of redress for the petitioners (plaintiffs) under the *Code* (for example, by way of joinder under art 59 or 67). The court pointed to these alternative avenues when denying the petitioners' motion for authorization.

183 Canadian Press, "Court Denies Class Action" *Globe and Mail* (12 May 1981) 11, in Box No B380543, above note 95.

184 [1990] RDJ 500 [*Tremaine*], cited in Finn, "In a Class," above note 155 at 357.

plaintiffs alleged was faulty and that had led to pregnancies and pregnancy-related complications among class members. The Court of Appeal held that differences between class members should not prevent the authorization of a class action, and stated that the plaintiffs' case rose and fell on the question of whether the design of the Dalkon Shield was faulty. It disagreed with the court of first instance when it called the class action "an extraordinary procedure," holding instead that a class proceeding was purely a procedural vehicle like any other contained in the *Code of Civil Procedure*.[185] This reasoning was followed in numerous subsequent cases,[186] showing that the class action provisions of the *Code* were receiving a more liberal interpretation consistent with consumer rights and corporate responsibility.

The Quebec class action began to be truly effective when the *CPA* came into force in Ontario. While Quebec's reform had blazed a trail for the rest of Canada, its courts' tardiness in recognizing and giving effect to the innovative nature of the device meant that Ontario was able to quickly catch up.

E. CONCLUSION

The rise of class actions in North America and Australia was accompanied by a rising sympathy towards the device in the Ontario courts. The liberal interpretation of the "common success" test meant that class actions could proceed under Rule 75 even where class members did not all have the same contract (as long as their contracts were substantially identical) and even if damages were claimed (as long as those damages could be assessed in the aggregate).

However, despite these developments, it became increasingly clear to all observers that Rule 75 was inadequate to deal with complex litigation such as the modern class action. Academic commentators noted that courts were procedurally ill-equipped to deal with issues such as damages

185 *Tremaine*, above note 184 at 507.

186 See, for example, *Comité d'environnement de La Baie inc c Société d'electrolyse et de chimie Alcan Ltée*, [1990] RJQ 655 (CA) (class action allowed to proceed on behalf of 2,400 residents who claimed loss of enjoyment of their properties due to the defendant's pollution); and *Québec (Curateur public) c Syndicat national des employés de l'Hôpital St-Ferdinand (CSN)*, [1994] RJQ 2761 (CA), aff'd [1996] 3 SCR 211 (class action allowed to proceed on behalf of hospital patients who suffered as a result of the defendant union's thirty-three-day illegal strike). Both cases are cited in Finn, "In a Class," above note 155 at 358–61.

assessments and distribution,[187] notification of absent class members, and disposition of unclaimed awards.[188] Although it allowed that class action to proceed, even the Court of Appeal in *Naken* (CA) asked for legislative intervention:

> [T]he plaintiffs face many procedural and evidentiary difficulties if this action is allowed to proceed. If we are to have consumer class actions in Ontario it would be highly desirable that there be enacted legislation or rules of practice or both, pursuant to which such actions could be conducted.[189]

Such a plea was highly prescient, and would be echoed by the Supreme Court of Canada in the same case. The Supreme Court's decision in *Naken* was one of the many catalysts to reform that would occur in the years leading up to the Attorney General's Advisory Committee Report and the passage of the *CPA*.

187 Williams, "Some Proposals," above note 3 at 53–54.

188 Kazanjian, above note 3 at 436.

189 *Naken* (CA), above note 87.

Chapter 3

THE EARLY CAMPAIGN FOR REFORM AND THE OLRC REPORT

The latter part of the twentieth century, particularly from the late 1960s onwards, saw an expansion of bureaucracy in public administration, while mass production became ever more pervasive in private industry.[1] As the size of institutions and businesses grew, they became increasingly distant from the citizens that used them.[2] A wider swath of citizens was being affected by the actions of those institutions and businesses at the same time as it was becoming increasingly difficult to obtain recourse against them. This era saw activists such as Ralph Nader rise to prominence—individuals who campaigned for consumer, environmental, and other rights, as well as for recourse for breach of those rights. The cost of litigation meant that very few individuals would be willing to sue the government or a multinational corporation for a wrong done to them; however, class actions rose in popularity as people began to see that there was strength in numbers. As Neil Williams has observed:

> No matter how just the claim, it is the exceptional person who will embark on litigation against an intransigent business corporation or

1 Jamie Benidickson, "From Empire Ontario to California North: Law and Legal Institutions in Twentieth-Century Ontario" in DeLloyd J Guth & WW Pue, eds, *Canada's Legal Inheritances* (Winnipeg: Canadian Legal History Project, Faculty of Law, University of Manitoba, 2001) at 620 and 644–47.

2 James O'Grady, "Consumer Remedies" (1982) 60:4 *Canadian Bar Review* 549 at 550–51. See also Anna Sadovnikova et al, "Consumer Protection in Postwar Canada: Role and Contributions of the Consumers' Association of Canada to the Public Policy Process" (2014) 48:2 *The Journal of Consumer Affairs* 380.

> government agency, particularly if the individual stake is only small. However, a vindication of rights becomes a realizable prospect when the citizen sues not just for himself but also for hundreds and possibly thousands of others in an identical position.[3]

This enthusiasm occurred not only in the United States with the enactment of the new Rule 23 that allowed for class actions for damages; as noted in the previous chapter, it arose in numerous jurisdictions, including Canada. Following the developments occurring in their neighbour to the south, the passage of the new Rule 23 was viewed with interest by Canadian advocates of consumer, environmental, and civil rights. With the increasingly liberal attitude of the courts towards class actions, these advocates were encouraged to press for a similar remedy in Canada. Their efforts were boosted by a number of developments that helped prepare the ground for class proceedings legislation, familiarizing politicians and lawyers with the device, and turning public opinion in its favour.

A. THE FIGHT FOR CONSUMER RIGHTS

Consumer rights were on the rise in the late 1960s and 1970s in North America, with the enactment of public regulation, such as the Ontario *Consumer Protection Act*,[4] and the establishment of consumer protection agencies, such as the federal Department of Consumer and Corporate Affairs.[5] These measures were taken to redress the imbalance of power between consumer and producer, and to protect consumers against economic losses.[6] As consumer rights proponents occupied the vanguard for the campaign for class actions in Canada,[7] the issue was increasingly debated in the press. Consumer advocates argued that expanding rights was pointless without a machinery to enforce those rights. Because consumers would not bother bringing a small individual claim arising

---

3 Neil J Williams, "Consumer Class Actions in Canada—Some Proposals for Reform" (1975) 13 *Osgoode Hall Law Journal* 1 at 3 [Williams, "Some Proposals"].

4 RSO 1970, c 82.

5 Public Interest Advocacy Centre, *Consumer Protection in Canada and the European Union: A Comparison* (2009) at 23–25, online: www.piac.ca/wp-content/uploads/2014/11/piac_report_consumer_protection_in_canada_and_the_europeon_union_a_comparision.pdf.

6 Iain Ramsay, *Consumer Law and Policy: Text and Materials on Regulating Consumer Markets*, 3d ed (Oxford: Hart, 2012) at 4–5.

7 Williams, "Some Proposals," above note 3 at 2.

from shoddy goods because of the expense, delays, and inconvenience, an effective machinery had to include class actions.[8] Class actions under Rule 75 were brought against corporations such as GM[9] and Ford.[10] The lawyers in those cases rose to prominence as consumer rights advocates, with Jeff Lyons (counsel for the plaintiffs in the Ford action and the *Naken* case against GM) being dubbed "Canada's Ralph Nader."[11]

On the other side, business interests argued that allowing class actions would harm legitimate businesses; place an enormous burden on the courts; and prove expensive, slow, cumbersome, and ineffective for consumers.[12] The case for consumer class actions was also made in several working papers commissioned by the Canadian Consumer Council

8 Michael Trebilcock, "Our 'Legal Machine Can't Enforce Rights'" *Globe and Mail* (11 September 1972) 6 [Trebilcock, "Legal Machine"], in Ontario Law Reform Commission files, Nov 1976–Dec 1982, Project name: class actions, RG 4-66, BA77, Box No B380537, North York, Archives of Ontario [Box No B380537]. Trebilcock, a University of Toronto law professor, made similar arguments in his article, "Private Law Remedies for Misleading Advertising" (1972) 22 *University of Toronto Law Journal* 1. He later worked on the OLRC Report on class actions.

9 *General Motors of Canada Ltd v Naken* [*Naken*], further discussed in Section J, below in this chapter. The *Naken* action was commenced in July 1973, and the defendant brought a motion to strike two years later (on the grounds that the pleading disclosed no reasonable cause of action). *Naken*'s journey through the courts is detailed in Chapter 2.

10 As a result of the publicity surrounding *Naken*, the plaintiffs' lawyer in that case, Jeffery Lyons, also represented owners of Ford vehicles that were prone to rusting: Rusty Ford Owners' Association, "Civil Litigation Against Manufacturers of Defective Automobiles" (1976), Jeffery Lyons Fonds, MIKAN No 4583565, Container 1, Item 17, Ottawa, Library and Archives Canada. However, Lyons learned from his experience with GM and advised his Ford clients to fight in the court of public opinion instead. This tactic succeeded, with a settlement forthcoming later that year: Estelle Dorais, "Ford to Pay $300 Rust Compensation," and Clayton Sinclair, "Rust Settlements Will Polish Ford's Image" *Montreal Gazette* (25 September 1976) B1, both available online: Google Newspaper Archives http://bit.ly/2hsooeC.

11 John Lorinc, "Jeffery Lyons Paved the Way for Consumer Lawsuits" *Globe and Mail* (7 August 2015), online: www.theglobeandmail.com/news/jeffery-lyons-paved-the-way-for-consumer-lawsuits/article25891542/?. For contemporaneous news coverage of Lyons's role in the *Naken* case, see P Dalby, "Father and Son Geared for Battle with Auto Giant" *Toronto Star* (15 September 1981); W Darroch, "GM Pulls Out Big-Gun Lawyers" *Toronto Star* (17 September 1981); both articles can be found in Ontario Law Reform Commission files, Nov 1976–Dec 1982, Project name: class actions, RG 4-66, BA77, Box No B380543, North York, Archives of Ontario [Box No B380543].

12 Anthony Abbott, ". . . But Proposal 'May Do More Harm Than Good'" *Globe and Mail* (11 September 1972) 7 [Abbott, "Proposal"], in Box No B380537, above note 8. Abbott was then president of the Retail Council of Canada.

in the early 1970s. Two of those papers looked at the subject of consumer advocacy, and both recommended the facilitation of class actions for the purpose of enforcing consumer rights.[13]

As the debate continued and complaints about the condition of manufactured goods (particularly vehicles) increased, the Ontario government asked the Ontario Law Reform Commission (OLRC) to study the subject.[14] The OLRC's *Report on Consumer Warranties and Guarantees in the Sale of Goods*[15] was tabled in the Ontario legislature in June 1972. The OLRC Consumer Report made various recommendations in order to increase the availability of consumer remedies in Ontario, including giving the Consumer Protection Bureau the power to mediate all warranty disputes, and also to bring test cases to determine important questions of law.[16] However, although the OLRC considered whether to recommend amending the Ontario law to allow for the bringing of consumer class actions, it ultimately decided that class actions needed to be investigated separately as they raised broader questions of a substantive and procedural nature.[17]

The question of class actions in the consumer context was raised again in July 1974 in a study commissioned by the Consumers' Association of Canada (CAC) that focused directly on the subject.[18] The CAC study recommended class action reform in order to facilitate consumer claims. Specifically, the study stated that class action provisions should include a certification test; that class members should receive notice following certification and be permitted to opt out; that discontinuance, dismissal, or settlement only occur with court approval; and that class actions should

13 Michael Trebilcock, *The Case for a Consumer Advocate* (Ottawa: Canadian Consumer Council, 1972); Edward Belobaba et al, *On the Question of Consumer Advocacy: A Working Paper* (Ottawa: Canadian Consumer Council, 1972). See also Edward Belobaba, "Unfair Trade Practices Legislation: Symbolism and Substance in Consumer Protection" (1977) 15 *Osgoode Hall Law Journal* 327 at 363–65. Both authors would go on to participate in the two major reports that led to class action reform in Ontario—Trebilcock in the Ontario Law Reform Commission Report, and Belobaba in the Attorney General's Advisory Committee Report.

14 Jacob Ziegel, "Review: *Report of the Ontario Law Reform Commission on Consumer Warranties and Guarantees in the Sale of Goods*" (1973) 22:2 *International and Comparative Law Quarterly* 363 at 364.

15 (Toronto: Ministry of the Attorney General, 1972) [OLRC Consumer Report].

16 *Ibid* at 108–9.

17 *Ibid.*

18 Neil J Williams, *Consumer Class Actions in Canada: A Report for the Consumers' Association of Canada* (Ottawa: Consumers' Association of Canada, 1974).

not be barred simply because they make a claim for individual damages.[19] With regard to costs, the CAC study was particularly controversial in that it recommended a "one-way" costs rule whereby costs could be awarded to a successful plaintiff, but the plaintiff would not have to pay costs to a successful defendant.[20]

These numerous reports gradually built up the case for consumer class actions throughout the 1970s. However, consumers were not the only group advocating for reform. As consciousness of consumer rights grew, so did consciousness of the environment and the damage that was being done to it.

B. ENVIRONMENTAL RIGHTS AND STANDING

The late 1960s and early 1970s also saw the rise of environmental awareness in Canada. The formation in the United States of groups such as Friends of the Earth, as well as the publication of books such as *Silent Spring* (on the damage caused by the spraying of pesticides),[21] led to a parallel movement in Canada, with the foundation of Greenpeace and Pollution Probe, and the establishment of government agencies such as Environment and Climate Change Canada. Similarly, disasters such as the nuclear meltdown at Three Mile Island in the United States[22] and stories of widespread pollution in Canada[23] led to greater awareness of the harm that increasing industrialization could cause to both humans and their environment.[24]

For those wishing to sue corporations for widespread environmental harm, however, there was virtually no recourse.[25] Three barriers stood

19 Williams's recommendations are also summarized in Williams, "Some Proposals," above note 3.

20 *Ibid* at 51–52.

21 Rachel Carson, *Silent Spring* (Boston: Houghton Mifflin, 1962).

22 A class action was filed with regard to this disaster, resulting in a $25-million settlement in 1981: B Franklin, "Concerns Agree to Pay $25 Million for Losses Caused by 3 Mile Island" *New York Times* (22 February 1981) 1, in Box No B380543, above note 11.

23 See, for example: R Platiel, "Fluoride Threat Started 20 Years Ago" *Globe and Mail* (18 June 1979) 10, in Box No B380543, *ibid*.

24 Benidickson, above note 1 at 644–45; John McLaren, "The Common Law Nuisance Actions and the Environmental Battle—Well Tempered Swords or Broken Reeds" (1972) 10 *Osgoode Hall Law Journal* 505 at 505–6.

25 An environmental rights bill, introduced as a private member's bill by the Liberals in 1979, was voted down by the legislature: unknown author, "Environmentalists

in the way of these environmental actions.[26] The first was the "common interest" requirement that prevented many such actions in the 1970s.[27] Class actions for private nuisance involved numerous individual issues and therefore did not satisfy this requirement;[28] class actions for public nuisance were problematic for different reasons, as described below.

The second barrier was financing, as the application of traditional costs rules would have prevented many litigants from undertaking the risk of an environmental action.[29] The 1970s saw the advent of a publicly funded legal aid program in Ontario, as well as the establishment of clinics (partly funded by the government) such as the Canadian Environmental Law Association.[30] The financing of public participation in environmental actions was a subject dear to Ian Scott (then in private practice).[31] When he later became attorney general, he oversaw the introduction of the *Intervenor Funding Project Act*[32] that provided qualified intervenors with advanced funding.[33]

The third and major obstacle was that of standing. Environmental suits at common law were generally brought by way of an action for public

---

Worried as PCs Set to Kill Private Bill" *Globe and Mail* (5 December 1979) 4, in Box No B380543, above note 11.

26 Very few environmental class actions were brought in the United States, largely because individual issues (such as defences) were generally held to predominate over common issues: Simon Chester, "Class Actions to Protect the Environment: A Real Weapon or Another Lawyer's Word Game?" in John Swaigen, ed, *Environmental Rights in Canada* (Toronto: Butterworths, 1981) 60 at 78.

27 Lucy Nissen, "Class Actions in Canada: An Environmental Perspective" (1984) 48 *Saskatchewan Law Review* 29 at 47; Ontario Law Reform Commission, *Report on Class Actions* (Toronto: Ministry of the Attorney General, 1982) at 275 [OLRC Report].

28 OLRC Report, *ibid* at 274–75.

29 Ian Scott & Raj Anand, "Financing Public Participation in Environmental Decision Making" (1982) 60 *Canadian Bar Review* 81 at 114–19 [Scott & Anand]. Scott intervened in several environmental court actions after becoming attorney general, and had also been counsel to the Berger Inquiry on the Mackenzie Valley Pipeline: Benidickson, above note 1 at 652; Ian Scott with Neil McCormick, *To Make a Difference: A Memoir* (Toronto: Stoddart, 2001) at 57 [Scott].

30 Benidickson, above note 1 at 642–43.

31 Scott & Anand, above note 29.

32 SO 1988, c 71.

33 Benidickson, above note 1 at 652. Scott's support for intervenor funding can also be seen in his impromptu promise to the Women's Legal Education and Action Fund (LEAF) to give them $1 million to fund their intervention in constitutional challenges: Scott, above note 29 at 134–35. Scott was also a firm supporter of legal clinic funding (at 175).

nuisance, because they involved interference with a public right (such as the right to fish or the right to clean air).[34] However, the infringement of public rights was a matter for the attorney general, who was guardian of public rights and therefore the only one who could sue to remedy their breach.[35] The only way anyone else could have standing to sue is if they suffered particular direct damage over and above that suffered by the public generally.[36] This was a major impediment to environmental class actions, as many interest groups readily acknowledged.[37]

This rule was relaxed throughout the 1970s, in a series of cases beginning with *Thorson v Canada (Attorney General)*.[38] *Thorson* was an action brought by a taxpayer who was suing on the basis that the *Official Languages Act* was unconstitutional, as was the *Appropriation Act* that provided money to implement the *OLA*. Although the lower courts decided that Thorson did not have standing, a majority of the Supreme Court of Canada held that he did. They reasoned that the question sought to be adjudicated would otherwise be immune from judicial review because there was no one particularly aggrieved, the government was unwilling to direct a reference, and the attorney general was unwilling to institute proceedings on behalf of the public. Two subsequent decisions, *Nova Scotia (Board of Censors) v McNeil*[39] and *Canada (Minister of Justice) v Borowski*,[40] were decided on a similar basis. According to the three cases, the requirements for public interest standing would be met where there

---

34 Wilfred Estey, "Public Nuisance and Standing to Sue" (1972) 10 *Osgoode Hall Law Journal* 563 at 565.

35 *Ibid* at 566.

36 *Ibid* at 568. See also *Cowan v Canadian Broadcasting Corporation*, 1966 CanLII 225 (Ont CA). For a list of environmental representative actions that were not permitted to proceed because the plaintiff was held not to have standing, see Nissen, above note 27 at 46–49.

37 Letter from Marc Denhez, lawyer for Heritage Canada, to the Civil Procedure Revision Committee (Williston Committee) (7 June 1978) in Box No B380537, above note 8; letters from John Swaigen, general counsel of the Canadian Environmental Law Association, to Roy McMurtry (9 November 1978) and Derek Mendes da Costa, OLRC chairman (13 November 1978), asking that the OLRC projects on standing and class actions be made a priority: both letters can be found in Box No B380543, above note 11.

38 [1975] 1 SCR 138.

39 [1976] 2 SCR 265 (Nova Scotia resident challenging the constitutionality of the censorship provisions under the *Theatres and Amusements Act*, RSNS 1967, c 304).

40 [1981] 2 SCR 575 (Saskatchewan resident challenging the constitutionality of the provisions of the *Criminal Code* permitting procurement of miscarriage).

was a serious issue as to the validity of the Act in question; where the applicant was directly affected by the Act or had a genuine interest in its validity; and where there was no other reasonable and effective way of bringing the issue before the Court.[41]

In making these decisions, the Supreme Court of Canada loosened the reins on the requirement that the ability to sue must be based on a traditional legal interest and the one-to-one adversarial model.[42] This would have important ramifications for class actions. Indeed, many of the actors involved in the later work on class actions by the Ministry of the Attorney General (MAG) were involved in the efforts to change the law on standing—including Ian Scott.[43] In addition, the rapidly evolving law of standing led the Ontario Law Reform Commission to commence a study of the subject, although the report was not completed until long after the OLRC Report on class actions.[44]

In the midst of this rise in consumer and environmental activism, and combined with developments in the United States and changes in the common law to accommodate the cases that were increasingly being brought before the courts in Ontario, Attorney General Roy McMurtry decided that the time had come for the OLRC to study class actions as well. In his letter to the commission,[45] McMurtry acknowledged that

---

41 *Ibid* at 575–76.

42 WA Bogart, "Questioning Litigation's Role—Courts and Class Actions in Canada" (1987) 62:3 *Indiana Law Journal* 665 at 667–68 [Bogart, "Questioning Litigation's Role].

43 R Furness, "Inquiry Must Hear Waste Site Opponents" *Globe and Mail* (3 November 1977), in Ontario Law Reform Commission files, Nov 1976–Dec 1982, Project name: class actions, RG 4-66, BA77, Box No B380538, North York, Archives of Ontario [Box No B380538]. The article reports on the efforts of north Toronto residents to have standing to appear before the Royal Commission on Waste Management to challenge the approval of a landfill permit. The Divisional Court granted them standing. Ian Scott appeared as counsel on that case, along with John Swaigen of the Canadian Environmental Law Association (CELA). CELA was later to participate in the Attorney General's Advisory Committee on Class Action Reform.

44 Ontario Law Reform Commission, *Report on the Law of Standing* (Toronto: Ministry of the Attorney General, 1989). Curiously, there is no evidence that the OLRC Report on standing influenced the deliberations of the Attorney General's Advisory Committee on Class Action Reform, whose report was released in 1990: Ministry of the Attorney General (MAG), Policy Development Division, *Report of the Attorney General's Advisory Committee on Class Action Reform* (Toronto: Ministry of the Attorney General, 1990).

45 Letter from Attorney General Roy McMurtry to Allan Leal, chairman of the OLRC (17 November 1976) [AG Reference], in Box No B380537, above note 8. According to Simon Chester, who at that time was a legal research officer at the OLRC, the

court decisions in Ontario would continue to change the law on class actions, and also that the commission was studying the related law on standing. He also referred to the OLRC Consumer Report and its position that class actions was a complex area of the law that merited separate study,[46] before concluding, "I think that the time has come for a comprehensive look at the nature of the class action and the advisability or inadvisability of its development, in one form or another, in Ontario."[47] It was to be another six years, however, before the commission released its recommendations. In the meantime, there would be further significant developments in the debate on class actions.

C. CLASS ACTIONS AND THE *COMBINES INVESTIGATION ACT*

In 1975, the federal government amended the *Combines Investigation Act*[48] to permit civil actions for violations of the Act. Persons who had suffered loss or damages as a result of a failure to comply with either the Act, a court order, or an order of the Restrictive Trade Practices Commission, could sue the person who had failed to comply. Offences included conspiracy, bid-rigging, discriminatory pricing, and misleading or false advertising. Consumers and corporations alike could use these provisions.[49]

Two years later, in March 1977, the government proposed further amendments to the *CIA*, including provisions specifically for class actions. The provisions not only allowed people to sue as a class for damages sustained as a result of competition-related offences, but also provided a detailed guide as to the procedural and substantive rules governing such

AG Reference was prompted by a letter from Andrew Roman of the Public Interest Advocacy Centre to Roy McMurtry, suggesting a reference to the OLRC: correspondence with Simon Chester (now counsel at Gowling WLG (Canada) LLP) (4 December 2017).

46 H Allan Leal, then chairman of the OLRC, had reviewed the class actions section of the OLRC Consumer Report just one week before McMurtry wrote the AG Reference, above note 45: Letter from H Allan Leal to Simon Chester, OLRC legal research officer (10 November 1976) in Box No B380537, above note 8.

47 AG Reference, above note 45 at 1.

48 RSC 1970, c C-23 [*CIA*].

49 Government of Canada, "Class Actions: Recent Developments in Canada" (1978) 4 *Commonwealth Law Bulletin* 128 at 144 ["Recent Developments"].

class actions.[50] This was the first time any comprehensive class action legislation had been introduced in Canada.[51] Consumer and Corporate Affairs Canada minister, Anthony C Abbott,[52] announced that the Act's framework for class actions would include the following:

- Requirement for certification, including whether the proceedings were brought in good faith and appeared to have merit;
- Plaintiffs who were unsuccessful on certification, on an interlocutory motion or at an individual issues trial would have costs awarded against them; however, no-way costs rules would apply at a common issues trial;
- Counsel fees would be paid out of individual damage awards on a pro-rata basis;
- Where a court refused to certify an action, the Competition Policy Advocate could bring a substitute action on behalf of class members, and damages would be paid to the Federal Treasury to prevent the unjust enrichment of the defendant; and
- Jurisdiction would initially vest with the Federal Court, but the Superior Courts of the provinces could be empowered to hear such cases once agreement had been reached with the provincial Attorneys General.[53]

Certification would not be denied based solely on the fact that an action involved individual damages or separate contracts; class members would be included in the class unless they opted out; and notice at any stage of the action would be optional and within the court's discretion.[54] In addition, leave of the court would be required for discontinuance, abandonment, or settlement.[55] The Act would be renamed the *Competition Act*.

50 *Ibid* at 128.

51 *Ibid* at 146.

52 This is the same Anthony Abbott who had opposed class actions in a *Globe and Mail* editorial just five years earlier, in September 1972 (Abbott, "Proposal," above note 12).

53 Consumer and Corporate Affairs Canada, News Release (16 March 1977), with accompanying Backgrounder [CCAC backgrounder], in Ontario Law Reform Commission files, Nov 1976–Dec 1982, Project name: class actions, RG 4-66, BA77, Box No B319672, North York, Archives of Ontario [Box No B319672]. See also Department of Consumer and Corporate Affairs, *Proposals for a New Competition Policy for Canada, Second Stage* (Ottawa: Supply and Services Canada, 1977) at 73–77 [DCCA *Proposals*].

54 "Recent Developments," above note 49 at 145.

55 DCCA *Proposals*, above note 53 at 74.

The class actions proposals for the new *Competition Act* were based substantially on a report written for Consumer and Corporate Affairs Canada.[56] The recommendations on costs for the new *Competition Act* were particularly interesting. The proposals and the report assumed that giving plaintiffs immunity for costs at the common issues trial would remove the financial deterrent to bringing class actions.[57] However, they failed to consider that the certification stage, especially where (as in this case) there was a *prima facie* assessment of the merits, could be just as cost prohibitive for plaintiffs. This was a sign of Canada's inexperience with class actions at this point. The new Rule 23 in the United States (where parties bore their own costs) had been in existence for just over a decade, and class action legislation had not yet been enacted in Quebec. There was very little indication that certification would one day become the main battleground in class actions. Canada still had a lot to learn.

The reaction to the class actions proposals for the new *Competition Act* was indicative of the later debate that was to rage over the *Class Proceedings Act*. The press was mostly positive about the concept of class action reform, but lukewarm towards the actual provisions of the *Competition Act*. Criticisms were directed towards the restrictions on class actions (for example, limitation periods and the inability to sue for breach of implied warranty and defective products)[58] and other provisions of the Act, such as the wide and arbitrary powers given to the Competition Board.[59] *Canadian Consumer* magazine encouraged its readership to lobby their provincial governments for class action reform instead.[60] Jeff Lyons, class counsel in *Naken*, stated that the certification requirements were too restrictive and that the legislation as a whole made "too many

56 CCAC backgrounder, above note 53 at 2; DCCA *Proposals*, above note 53 at 73. See also Neil J Williams & Jennifer Whybrow, *A Proposal for Class Actions Under Competition Policy Legislation* (Ottawa: Department of Consumer and Corporate Affairs, 1976) [Williams & Whybrow].

57 Williams & Whybrow, *ibid*; DCCA *Proposals*, above note 53 at 77; Williams, "Some Proposals," above note 3 at 52, 63, and 86–87.

58 Canadian Press, "Ottawa Bill Clears Way for Class Action Suits" *Toronto Star* (17 March 1977) ["Ottawa Bill"], in Box No B380543, above note 11; unknown author, "Class Actions" *Canadian Consumer* (August 1977) 36 at 38 and 41 [*Canadian Consumer*], in Policy Development Division Counsel correspondence files, Class Actions—Miscellaneous Material, 1977–1981, RG 4-40, CA226, Box No B248633, North York, Archives of Ontario [Box No B248633—Miscellaneous Material].

59 "Competition Act Can Be Improved," Editorial, *Toronto Star* (18 March 1977) B4, in Box No B380543, above note 11.

60 *Canadian Consumer*, above note 58 at 41.

concessions to big business."[61] Consumer advocates and the press mostly agreed.[62]

For its part, "big business" strongly opposed the proposals. The Canadian Chamber of Commerce called for the complete deletion of the provisions on class and substitute actions.[63] It disagreed with the principle implicit in the Williams and Whybrow Report and the legislation that there was a pressing need or public demand for widespread civil enforcement of the Act's provisions.[64] It took particular issue with the costs proposals,[65] stating that making defendants pay their own costs whatever the outcome was "iniquitous," and as a result, "a powerful weapon has been added to the 'legal blackmail' arsenal"; instead of discouraging frivolous suits, the costs provisions would make class actions "a vehicle for harassment."[66] The Chamber submitted that, if class and substitute actions were to be permitted, then the actions should be on an opt-in basis and traditional costs rules should apply.[67] The Independent Petroleum Association objected to "[t]he prejudice against business underlying the Act," and stated that "class actions in the United States of America have proved to be highly beneficial to lawyers and of little use to anyone else."[68] Like the Chamber, it took issue with the costs provisions of the Act,[69] stating they were consistent with

61 "Ottawa Bill," above note 58. See also Jeffery Lyons, "Ottawa's New Class Action Legislation Still Lacks Teeth" *Toronto Star* (25 March 1977) B4, cited in *Canadian Consumer*, above note 58 at 41.

62 *Canadian Consumer*, *ibid* at 40. See also "Consumer Action Bill 'Not Tough Enough,'" Editorial, *Montreal Star* (17 March 1977) A1 & A2; "Give Consumers Better Class Actions Law," Editorial, *Toronto Star* (28 March 1977), both cited in *Canadian Consumer*, above note 58 at 41.

63 The Canadian Chamber of Commerce, Submission on Bill C-42, the *Competition Act*, to the House of Commons Standing Committee on Finance, Trade and Economic Affairs (2 June 1977) at 2 and 5 [CCC Submission], in Box No B380538, above note 43.

64 CCC Submission, above note 63 at 3.

65 When the proposal for one-way costs was presented at a Competition Policy Conference held 12–13 May 1977, there were "gasps of astonishment [from the] audience," which consisted mainly of corporate representatives: Memorandum from Simon Chester, legal research officer at the OLRC, to other members of the OLRC (16 May 1977), in Ontario Law Reform Commission files, Class Actions—General 1976–1980, in RG 4-66, Box No B319671, North York, Archives of Ontario [Box No B319671].

66 CCC Submission, above note 63 at 4.

67 *Ibid* at 5.

68 Independent Petroleum Association of Canada, Submission on Bill C-42, the *Competition Act*, to the House of Commons Standing Committee on Finance, Trade and Economic Affairs (8 June 1977) at 1 [IPAC Submission], in Box No B380538, above note 43.

69 IPAC Submission, above note 68 at 2.

"the philosophy that business, being per se undersirable [sic], should be penalized more heavily than others."[70] It too recommended total deletion of the sections on class and substitute actions.[71]

Other business interests, however, were a little less categorical in their opposition. While the Canadian Manufacturers' Association (CMA) stated that substitute actions should not be allowed, it would permit class actions if they were limited to prevent abuse.[72] It particularly objected to the possibility of aggregate damages assessments,[73] although, surprisingly, it made no submissions on the issue of costs. The Retail Council of Canada similarly called for the scrapping of the substitute actions provisions, and stated that class actions "involving large classes who have individually suffered small losses [are] anomalous, unfair to defendants and should not be permitted."[74] However, it acknowledged that class actions had limited value in certain circumstances,[75] provided that certain protections were built in. These included a requirement to opt in, to individually prove damages, and the application of traditional costs rules,[76] as well as a stringent and mandatory requirement for notice.[77]

The legal profession also objected to the class actions section of the *Competition Act*, because class actions would involve procedural and substantive changes to the law, and a wider review of the subject (as well as consultations with the provinces) was required.[78] The Canadian Bar Association (CBA) also voiced a concern that was held by many in the bar and the wider population,[79] and which posed a cultural and philosophical

70 *Ibid.*

71 *Ibid* at 3.

72 Canadian Manufacturers' Association, Submission on Bill C-42, the *Competition Act*, to the House of Commons Standing Committee on Finance, Trade and Economic Affairs (2 June 1977) at 1–2 [CMA Submission], in Box No B380538, above note 43.

73 CMA Submission, above note 72 at 2–3.

74 Retail Council of Canada, Submission on Bill C-42, the *Competition Act*, to the House of Commons Standing Committee on Finance, Trade and Economic Affairs (7 June 1977) at 3 and 6–7 [RCC Submission], in Box No B380538, above note 43.

75 RCC Submission, above note 73 at 3 and 13.

76 *Ibid* at 3 and 8–11.

77 *Ibid* at 8.

78 Canadian Bar Association, Submission on Bill C-42, the *Competition Act*, to the House of Commons Standing Committee on Finance, Trade and Economic Affairs (7 June 1977) at 2 [CBA Competition Submission], in Box No B380538, above note 43.

79 See, for example, the following opinion editorial on the introduction of an environmental rights bill: "Smith's Idea Fatally Flawed" *Toronto Star* (6 December 1979) ["Fatally Flawed"], in Box No B380543, above note 11. The opposition to judicial

barrier to the institution of class actions in general—that the *Competition Act* would lead to an undermining of the power of the democratically elected legislature:

> To the extent that class action damage suits might in time become the predominant method of enforcement of the [*Competition Act*], the direction of public policy in this area of the law may be taken to a substantial degree out of the hands of law enforcement officers and Ministers of the Crown and placed in the hands of aggressive and innovative plaintiffs' counsel and the courts, which appears to have been the experience in the United States.[80]

The concerns of the bar and the business community were made even clearer in the oral submissions to the Standing Committee on Finance, Trade and Economic Affairs. The vice-president for Canadian Pacific submitted that the provisions on class and substitute actions were "certainly over-kill. More than that, we certainly do not know of any real basis that would indicate that that kind of provision is necessary at this time . . . [it] should be completely deleted."[81] As in its written submission, the Canadian Chamber of Commerce stated that the benefits of class actions had not been proven and that, on the contrary, the US experience showed it to be "a circus."[82] These business groups were not reassured when Robert Bertrand, the assistant deputy minister of Competition Policy, made it clear that they did not have to fear frivolous suits because protection would be provided by the certification test in the Act.[83] The business groups responded by stating that the main deterrent to frivolous suits was traditional costs rules, and they expressed their concern that the Act was departing from these rules in the context of class actions.[84] They also reiterated their desire that the mechanism, if enacted, be on a strictly opt-in

activism will be covered in more detail in the section on the *Charter* later in this chapter.

80 CBA Competition Submission, above note 78 at 6–7.

81 Bill C-42, the *Competition Act*, Minutes of Proceedings and Evidence of the House of Commons Standing Committee on Finance, Trade and Economic Affairs (2 and 9 June 1977) (Mr Maxwell, vice-president and general counsel, Canadian Pacific) [*Competition Act* oral hearings], in Box No B380538, above note 43.

82 *Competition Act* oral hearings, above note 81 (RF Booth, chairman, Executive Council, Canadian Chamber of Commerce).

83 *Ibid* (Robert Bertrand of the Department of Competition Policy, and Mr Gray of the Standing Committee on Finance, Trade and Economic Affairs).

84 *Ibid* (Robert Law, general counsel, Canadian Tire Corporation Ltd).

basis,[85] otherwise class actions could be used as a "club against corporate defendants" and would "end up clogging the courts."[86] The Standing Committee recommended amendments to the class action provisions, including a requirement that the plaintiff demonstrate that a certain proportion of the class supported their claim, as well as restrictions on damages.[87]

It was the Proceedings of the Standing Senate Committee on Banking, Trade and Commerce,[88] however, which sounded the death knell of the *Competition Act*'s class action provisions. While the advocates for class actions had been active in the preparation of the legislation and in the media, it was the business interests that predominated at the Senate Committee hearings. Representatives of Imperial Oil and Dominion Foundries and Steel (Dofasco) made submissions regarding the "legalized blackmail" and "undesirable temptation to have litigation" posed by class actions.[89] They asserted that representative plaintiffs would not be truly representative of the class, which would not even be well informed enough to make a claim, and even the committee chair agreed that to think otherwise would be "a pious hope."[90] The business groups strongly submitted that traditional costs rules should apply to class actions, and if the government thought plaintiffs should be subsidized, it should provide a public fund for that purpose.[91]

The business groups referred frequently to the US experience with class actions, and, from the senators' response, this appears to have been the most persuasive part of their submissions. Dofasco obtained an opinion letter from a Buffalo-based law firm that had worked in this area.[92] The firm supported the submissions made by the business interests,

85 *Ibid.*

86 *Ibid* (Alasdair McKichan).

87 Bruce Wildsmith, "An American Enforcement Model of Civil Process in a Canadian Landscape" (1980) 6 *Dalhousie Law Journal* 71 at 91.

88 Bill C-42, the *Competition Act*, Minutes of Proceedings and Evidence of the Standing Senate Committee on Banking, Trade and Commerce [Senate Committee hearings], in Box No B319672, above note 53.

89 Senate Committee hearings, above note 88 (15 June 1977) (HG Batt, QC, associate general counsel, Imperial Oil Limited); (29 June 1977) (HG Wilson, secretary, Dofasco).

90 *Ibid*, 15 June 1977 (Senator Hayden, chair of the Senate Committee); (29 June 1977) (Wayne McCracken, legal counsel, Dofasco).

91 *Ibid* (15 June 1977) (HG Batt, QC, associate general counsel, Imperial Oil Limited). This is one of the first times a public fund is mentioned in the historical record; such a fund would be incorporated into the Quebec class action legislation the following year.

92 *Ibid* (29 June 1977) (Letter to Senate Committee from Joechle, Fleischmann & Mugel (JFM), reproduced in Senate Committee minutes in full).

describing its experience with US federal class action procedures as "horrible."[93] It provided statistics demonstrating the substantial increase in the courts' caseload following the enactment of the new Rule 23,[94] and stated that the rule had been plagued by the fact that there was no meaningful standard for certification, so that broad classes would be certified and would drive defendants to settle even unmeritorious actions.[95] In light of this dire warning from the United States, the senators asked the business groups why they accepted class actions at all—to which they responded that "we accept the inevitable."[96]

The business community's serious reservations persuaded the Senate Committee to recommend that the class actions section of the *Competition Act* be deleted.[97] In the alternative, if the section were to be retained, then the Senate Committee recommended that traditional costs rules should apply and that representative plaintiffs should put up security for costs. The committee cynically reasoned that these costs rules would not form an insuperable barrier to class actions, because plaintiffs would probably be bankrolled by a consumer organization or a class actions lawyer.[98]

Unfortunately for advocates of class actions, the Senate Committee's recommendations carried the day.[99] On 18 November 1977, a watered-down version of the *Competition Act* was introduced in the legislature[100] in order "to head off an angry confrontation with Canada's business

93 *Ibid.*

94 *Ibid.* For example, between 1967 and 1971, the number of class actions filed in the Federal District Court for the Southern District of New York increased four-fold, and more than half the actions commenced in 1966 were still pending in 1971.

95 *Ibid.*

96 *Ibid* (29 June 1977) (John G Sheppard, executive vice president—financial, Dofasco).

97 Interim Report of the Standing Senate Committee on Banking, Trade and Commerce, Section 18: Class Actions (6 July 1977), in Box No B319672, above note 53.

98 *Ibid.*

99 These advocates included Simon Chester, then executive counsel to the deputy attorney general. Chester wrote to Patricia Burton at the Information Secretariat for the *Combines Investigation Act*, enclosing the minutes of the Senate Committee hearings pertaining to class actions (above note 88), stating that they were "for our 'Know your Enemies—Who Killed C-42' file" (Letter from Chester (27 September 1977) in Box No B319672, above note 53).

100 Wildsmith, above note 87 at 91–92. This new version of the Bill required that the representative plaintiff provide proof that a certain portion of the class supported the action, and that the claims of the class were likely to be large enough to justify the cost in administering them. It also removed the substitute action provisions. See also Jacob Ziegel, "Consumer Has Little Muscle in Court" *Toronto Star* (1 November 1978), in Box No B380543, above note 11.

community."[101] However, even that version of the Act drew heavy fire from business.[102] The entire statute eventually died on the order paper prior to the general election in 1979, and the next Progressive Conservative government did nothing to revive it.[103] Class action reform would not be debated again in the legislature until well into the next decade.

D. THE REPORT OF THE WILLISTON COMMITTEE

Nevertheless, the device was being discussed in many other contexts in the intervening period. In 1980, the Civil Procedure Revision Committee released its report on the revision of the rules of court.[104] Chaired by Walter Williston, a Bay Street QC,[105] the committee had begun its work in December 1975[106] and was directed by Attorney General McMurtry to simplify the procedure and reduce the number of rules in order to decrease costs and delay.[107] McMurtry had mentioned the Williston Committee's work in his reference to the OLRC in 1976, but had decided that a subject as complex as class actions merited separate study.[108] For the same reason, after the OLRC commenced its study, McMurtry asked the committee to stop its work on a class actions rule.[109]

---

101 John Honderich, "Trust-Buster's Powers Limited Under New Bill" *Toronto Star* (18 November 1977) B7, in Box No B380543, *ibid.*

102 Report of the Standing Senate Committee on Banking, Trade and Commerce on the Subject Matter of Bill C-13, *Debates of the Senate*, Vol 125, No 91 (29 June 1978) at 1004–20, cited in WT Stanbury, "Half a Loaf: Bill C-29, Proposed Amendments to the *Combines Investigation Act*" (1985) 10:1 *Canadian Business Law Journal* 1 at 6.

103 Stanbury, *ibid* at 6.

104 Walter B Williston, *Report of the Civil Procedure Revision Committee* (Toronto: Ministry of the Attorney General, 1980).

105 Williston was an early proponent of contingency fees in Ontario: see Williston, "Contingency Fee," below note 119 at 201, where he likened contingency fees to sex: "At an early age one is taught to abhor it. The first direct encounter with it may come somewhat as a shock. Maturity and experience develop a keen appreciation for its merits."

106 Walter B Williston, "Revising the Ontario Rules of Practice—The Work of the Civil Procedure Revision Committee" (1977) 1 *Advocates' Quarterly* 18 at 18.

107 *Ibid* at 21–22.

108 AG Reference, above note 45.

109 Letter from Williston to Derek Mendes da Costa, OLRC chair (26 April 1979), enclosing draft class actions rule, in Box No B380537, above note 8. A new section on class actions had recently been added to the *Ontario Rules of Civil Procedure* to reflect recent judicial interpretations of Rule 75: Garry D Watson & Neil J Williams, *Canadian Civil*

Although the final Williston Report contained no reform of the existing Rule 75 on representative actions, the committee's draft of the class actions rule is revealing. The Williston Committee recommended, among other things, a certification test (but not on the merits),[110] notice within the discretion of the court,[111] and the ability to award aggregate damages.[112] However, it contained no provisions for opting-out (or in),[113] or for costs, in which case traditional costs rules would have continued to apply. The rule is skeletal and reflected the preliminary nature of the committee's work on the subject. The committee knew enough, however, to conclude in its final report that, "we are convinced that the present procedure respecting class actions is in a very serious state of disrepair."[114] This phrase would be picked up time and again by advocates seeking to reform the law on class actions.[115]

E. PRIVATE MEMBERS' BILLS ON CLASS ACTIONS

Two of these advocates attempted to bring about reform by way of three private members' bills (PMBs), all of which were worded in exactly the same way. NDP MPP Patrick Lawlor introduced the first two bills in 1977[116] and 1980,[117] and Mel Swart (also NDP) introduced the third in 1982.[118] None of them progressed past first reading.

Procedure Cases and Materials, 2d ed (Toronto: Butterworths, 1977) at 5-82 to 5-110, reviewed by George R Stewart, "Book Reviews" (1978) 56 *Canadian Bar Review* 545.

110 Draft class actions rule, above note 109 at 1.

111 *Ibid* at 2.

112 *Ibid* at 4.

113 However, a judgment could not be enforced against a class member without leave of the court: *ibid* at 5.

114 Williston, above note 104 at 16.

115 See, for example, the numerous policy and Cabinet submissions drafted by Michael Cochrane, cited in Chapter 4.

116 Bill 12, *An Act to Provide for Class Actions*, 4th Sess, 30th Leg, 1977 (Private Member's Bill, Mr Lawlor), in Box No B380543, above note 11.

117 Bill 30, *An Act to Provide for Class Actions*, 4th Sess, 31st Leg, 1980 (Private Member's Bill, Mr Lawlor), in Box No B380543, *ibid*. Patrick Lawlor was later commissioned by the attorney general to undertake a study on group defamation, which included a section on recourse in the courts by way of a class action: Patrick Lawlor, *Group Defamation: Submissions to the Attorney General* (Toronto: Ministry of the Attorney General, 1984) [Lawlor, *Defamation*].

118 Bill 122, *An Act to Provide for Class Actions*, 2d Sess, 32nd Leg, Ontario, 1982 (Private Member's Bill, Mr Swart), in Box No B380543, above note 11.

The bills contained a certification requirement, including a requirement that it is *prima facie* in the interests of the class that the action be brought as a class proceeding. They also stated that individual damages or separate contracts were not to be an impediment to certification. Notice would be within the discretion of the court, and class members would have a right to opt out. Cases could not be settled or discontinued without court permission. Other than these provisions, however, the bills were very bare indeed. They said nothing about rights of discovery or how damages were to be determined, and they were silent on costs (meaning that traditional costs rules would apply). Given these deficiencies, it is likely that these bills would have done little to encourage class actions or clear up the confusion in the caselaw, even if any of them had been passed.

F. CLASS ACTION LEGISLATION IN QUEBEC

As noted in the previous chapter, in 1978 Quebec became the first province in Canada to enact class action legislation. This was a major boost to the movement for reform in Ontario, as class actions advocates could now point to an example other than the United States (a jurisdiction that Canada had been historically reluctant to emulate on this matter). The authors of the OLRC Report relied heavily upon the Quebec experience as an example of how class actions could work, as did the Attorney General's Advisory Committee. Although the Quebec courts were initially restrictive in their interpretation of class actions, they eventually began to interpret the device more liberally, and this helped prepare the ground for reform in Ontario.

However, although the Quebec experience demonstrated how class actions could work outside the United States, there were still several barriers to class action reform in Ontario, and breaking down those barriers would require a change in the legal culture. One of them was contingency fees, another US device to which the Ontario bar was historically averse.

G. THE DEBATE ON CONTINGENCY FEES

Contingency fees were regarded with hostility and suspicion by many of the business groups and others involved in the class actions debate, to the extent that they were seen as "legal leprosy."[119] An agreement to charge

119 Walter B Williston, "The Contingent Fee in Canada" (1968) 6 *Alberta Law Review* 184 at 184 [Williston, "Contingent Fee"].

fees on the contingency that the lawyer won or settled the case was traditionally seen as champerty (where a plaintiff pursues a lawsuit in their own name in return for sharing any eventual award with their lawyer) and maintenance (where, for improper motives, a person assists someone else with a lawsuit in which the person has no interest).[120] They were also forbidden by statute in Ontario, pursuant to the *Solicitors Act*[121] and *An Act Respecting Champerty*.[122] However, there was some evidence in the later part of the twentieth century that lawyers were pursuing cases on a de facto contingency basis, collecting their fees from the client only once a case had been resolved successfully.[123]

To fully understand the debate, however, the term "contingency fee" must be clarified, as there are several ways in which such fees can be calculated:

1) Fee as a percentage of the client's net recovery;
2) Fee based on hourly billing; or
3) Fee based on hourly billing, multiplied by a certain number agreed upon in advance (a "multiplier") in order to reflect the risk assumed by the lawyer.

It is apparent that the de facto contingency basis which was largely accepted in Ontario in the later twentieth century was a simple fee based on hourly billing (lawyers then collected their fee once the litigation was successfully resolved).[124] During the course of the contingency fee debate that began in the late 1960s in Ontario, some commentators expressed support for a "controlled" contingency fee, that is, the third option above, with the added requirement of court approval.[125] Because of the perceived excesses of their US counterparts, very few in the legal profession were in

120 Philip Girard, "The Making of the Canadian Legal Profession: A Hybrid Heritage" (2014) 21:2 *International Journal of the Legal Profession* 145 at 160; Williston, "Contingent Fee," *ibid* at 184–87.

121 RSO 1960, c 378, s 59. They were also prohibited by the Rules of Professional Conduct: Williston, "Contingent Fee," *ibid* at 190.

122 RSO 1897, c 327. See also Girard, above note 120 at 161.

123 Girard, *ibid* at 163.

124 This type of arrangement was also known as a "speculative action": Williston, "Contingent Fee," above note 119 at 197–98: "It is clear that there is nothing wrong in a proper case with a solicitor undertaking litigation when he knows that he will not get paid unless the action is successful."

125 See, for example, Donald Dewees, J Robert S Prichard, & Michael Trebilcock, *Class Actions as a Regulatory Instrument* (Toronto: Ontario Economic Council, 1980). This was also the option put forward by the OLRC Report, above note 27.

favour of the first option—a fee as a percentage of the client's net recovery—at least until the 1980s.[126] When commentators referred to classic US-style contingency fees, it was invariably the first option to which they were referring.[127]

The prevalence of contingency fees in the United States was a major reason why they were regarded with such repugnance in Ontario.[128] Courts decried the "'American Ambulance-Chaser' [that] has become a visible factor in so called professional life."[129] Law reform advocates assured their opponents that Ontario was not a "California North,"[130] full of "bounty-hunter lawyers looking ... [for] a fat contingent fee"[131] because such fees were not permitted there. Even newspapers sympathetic towards class actions bore headlines stating, "Don't give lawyers a cut" and opposing US-style contingency fees.[132] The Ontario branch of the CBA stated that "contingent fee systems are typically American and sprang from a legal system which did not have court costs or Legal Aid."[133]

The CBA also took the position, as many other opponents did, that contingency fees would compromise the integrity of the legal profession because "a lawyer becomes a litigant rather than an officer of the court"[134]

126 Williston, "Contingent Fee," above note 119 at 184. The LSUC's approval of contingency fees in 1988 is detailed in Chapter 4.

127 Williston, "Contingent Fee," *ibid* at 188 and 198–99. See also Canadian Bar Association (Ontario) and The Public Interest Research Centre, *Report on Class Actions*, Submission to the Hon R McMurtry, QC, attorney general of Ontario (November 1983) at 38 [CBA/PIAC Report], in Policy Development Division Counsel correspondence files, Class Actions—Canadian Bar Association—brief—File #1, 1982–1991, RG 4-40, CA226, Box No B248633, North York, Archives of Ontario [Box No B248633-CBA].

128 Although it does not explain why Ontario was the last Canadian province to allow them: Girard, above note 120 at 161.

129 *Re Solicitor* (1907), 14 OLR 464 (HCJ), cited in Williston, "Contingent Fee," above note 119 at 190.

130 David W Slater, *Final Report of the Ontario Task Force on Insurance*, vol 1 (Toronto: The Task Force, 1986) at 53, cited in Benidickson, above note 1 at 651. However, Slater pointed out that there was every indication that Ontario could become a "California North" in the foreseeable future, due to the continuing expansion and extension of liability.

131 Trebilcock, "Legal Machine," above note 8 at 2.

132 "Don't Give Lawyers a Cut," Editorial, *Toronto Star* (24 March 1980), in Box No B380543, above note 11.

133 Report of the Professional Organizations Committee of the CBA, Submission to the Ministry of the Attorney General Professional Organizations Committee (30 April 1979), in Box No B380537, above note 8.

134 *Ibid* at 84.

and the lawyer would be put in a position of conflict with his or her client.[135] The overall position of the CBA was that the drawbacks of contingent fees outweighed their advantages.[136] The attorney general himself was opposed to any change in the law,[137] and as a result the Law Society of Upper Canada decided not to conduct an in-depth study of the issue,[138] having received "considerable" correspondence, almost all of which was opposed to contingency fees.[139] Finally, in April 1980, the MAG Professional Organizations Committee recommended that "[t]here should be no relaxation of the current prohibition of contingent fees as a payment mechanism for legal services in Ontario."[140]

Even into the 1980s, therefore, there was staunch and widespread opposition to the introduction of contingency fees in Ontario. The issue was to prove a major point of contention in the continuing debate on class actions, as well as in the eventual deliberations of the Attorney General's Advisory Committee.[141]

H. THE *CHARTER* AND ITS IMPACT ON LEGAL CULTURE

Not all opposition to class actions was purely pragmatic or self interested —some of the opposition was also on the basis of principle. A significant concern of business interests and other opponents was the discretion and case management power that the device gave to judges. Commentators observed that class action legislation would take power out of the hands of the democratically elected legislature and place it in the hands of the judiciary. They stated that the class action was not "merely a new

135 *Ibid* at 86.

136 *Ibid* at 84.

137 LSUC Minutes of Convocation (23 April 1976) 175 at 178 (Report of the Special Committee on Contingent Fees), in Box No B380537, above note 8.

138 *Ibid*.

139 *Ibid* at 176.

140 Larry Fox, "Ban on Contingency Fees Remains in Ontario" *Ontario Lawyers Weekly* (12 August 1983) 5, in Policy Development Division Counsel correspondence files, Class Actions, 1988–1990, RG 4-40, Box No B502275, North York, Archives of Ontario. Larry Fox was a legal research officer who worked on the OLRC Consumer Report, above note 15 (especially regarding costs) and was later instrumental in setting up the Class Proceedings Fund. His article was cautiously in favour of contingency fees.

141 The adoption of contingency fees in the context of the *CPA*, however, was to open the way for their adoption generally: Girard, above note 120 at 161.

adjudicative procedure. It is highly exceptional in character . . . and it is quite possible to see in it . . . a 'serious judicial usurpation of the functions of the legislature.'"[142]

This was a concern that was not limited to class actions. It also related to other statutes that gave judges a high level of discretion, such as an environmental rights bill introduced by the Liberals in 1979. The power this bill would have given to the courts was even remarked upon with concern by a traditionally more left-leaning newspaper—the *Toronto Star*:

> Judges would be given legislative powers . . . This clashes with a primary principle of democracy: That laws can only be made by popularly elected legislators, and that they are implemented by government ministers who are directly accountable to those legislators. The function of the courts and their judges is to arbitrate disputes over what the law is and to determine fact. It is not to make the law.[143]

Of course, the main focus of fears about judicial activism in the late 1970s and early 1980s was the *Canadian Charter of Rights and Freedoms*.[144] Historically, Canadian courts had not been nearly as activist as their American cousins; while the American courts played a unique role created by their constitutionally entrenched *Bill of Rights*, prior to 1982 the Canadian courts had had no such role (and in fact the highest court in Canada had, until 1949, been in England).[145]

However, with the advent of the *Charter* in 1982, the courts began to have a role not simply in interpreting law but in articulating fundamental values, and the legal culture of Canada took one step closer to that of the United States.[146] Indeed, after a few years, legal academe, the bar, and the public in general came not only to acknowledge that the judiciary was taking on a legislative function, but also to accept and perhaps even

142 H Patrick Glenn, "Class Actions in Ontario and Québec" (1984) 62:3 *Canadian Bar Review* 247 at 271. See also Submission of the Canadian Manufacturers' Association to Ministry of the Attorney General, December 1982, at 2–3 [CMA 1982], in Policy Development Division Counsel correspondence files, Class Actions—General—File #1, 1985–1987, RG 4-40, Box No B248633, North York, Archives of Ontario [Box No B248633—General File #1].

143 "Fatally Flawed," above note 79.

144 *Canadian Charter of Rights and Freedoms*, Part I of the *Constitution Act, 1982*, being Schedule B to the *Canada Act 1982* (UK), 1982, c 11 [*Charter*].

145 Wildsmith, above note 87 at 118–20.

146 WA Bogart, "*Naken*, the Supreme Court and What Are Our Courts For?" (1984) 9 *Canadian Business Law Journal* 280 at 287.

welcome it.[147] The class action simply fit conveniently into this contemporary judicial role,[148] as a more activist judiciary (together with changes to the classic two-party adversarial model of litigation that *Charter* litigation began to entail)[149] was an essential ingredient of the class action device.[150] The *Charter*, therefore, caused many of the more philosophical arguments against class actions to fall by the wayside.

This marked change in legal culture began in 1982, the same year the OLRC Report was released. With the *Charter* still in its infancy, however, the ground was not yet sufficiently prepared for the OLRC Report to take root. It was released into a world that still clung to traditional modes of litigation and a conservative role for the judiciary, and therefore, to a significant extent, was ignored.

I. THE OLRC REPORT

Six long years after the attorney general's reference on the subject of class actions, the OLRC released its report. The only public consultations that took place during this time consisted of a series of advertisements placed in the Ontario Reports, various legal publications, and public newspapers, inviting submissions on the subject of class actions.[151] The OLRC received several responses, although the vast majority of the more detailed submissions were from business interests.

These groups made the same objections as they had to the earlier amendments to the *Combines Investigation Act*, and indeed some of them sent in the same submissions they had made to the House of Commons and Senate Standing Committees on that occasion.[152] They opposed

147 Glenn, above note 142 at 272; WA Bogart, Jasminka Kalajdzic, & Ian Matthews, "Class Actions in Canada: A National Procedure in a Multi-jurisdictional Society?" (Report for the Globalization of Class Actions Conference, Oxford University, December 2007) at 34; Ian Scott, "The Role of the Attorney General and the *Charter of Rights*" (1987) 29 *Criminal Law Quarterly* 187.

148 Glenn, above note 142.

149 For example, many of the cases on public interest standing, detailed in Section B, above in this chapter, involved either the *Bill of Rights* or the *Charter*. See also WA Bogart, "Questioning Litigation's Role," above note 42 at 669.

150 Bogart, Kalajdzic, & Matthews, above note 147 at 2–3.

151 Class Actions Project—Advertising for Briefs (19 January 1977) [the advertisement appeared in various newspapers], in Box No B380543, above note 11.

152 Submissions to Ontario Law Reform Commission by Dofasco (27 May 1977) and Imperial Oil (4 July 1977), both in Submissions to OLRC on Class Actions 1977, in Box No B319671, above note 65.

contingency fees as well as any changes to the traditional costs rules,[153] and also objected to the concept of aggregate damages.[154] Where they conceded that class actions could be permitted in some limited fashion, they advocated for an opt-in regime and a merits-based certification test, and stated that other safeguards should be employed to reduce the possibility that class actions could be used to blackmail defendants into a settlement.[155]

Those in favour of class actions made much less detailed submissions, with some of these organizations stating that they did not have the resources to produce anything more substantial.[156] Environmental organizations expressed concerns regarding the law of standing,[157] and other groups advocated for contingency fees[158] and noted the deterrent effect of the "loser pays" costs rules.[159]

153 Submissions to Ontario Law Reform Commission by the Institute of Chartered Accountants of Ontario (10 June 1977); Ontario Chamber of Commerce (June 1977) [OCC Submission]; Insurance Bureau of Canada (17 June 1977) [IBC Submission]; Canadian Bankers' Association (31 May 1977) [Bankers' Association Submission]; Ontario Risk & Insurance Management Society (12 May 1977) [ORIMS Submission]; Legislative Committee of the Ontario Urban Development Institute (27 April 1977) [UDI Submission]; all in Submissions to OLRC on Class Actions 1977, in Box No B319671, *ibid.*

154 Bankers' Association Submission, above note 153.

155 OCC Submission, IBC Submission, ORIMS Submission, UDI Submission, Bankers' Association Submission, all above note 153; Submission to Ontario Law Reform Commission by Retail Council of Canada (5 May 1977), in Submissions to OLRC on Class Actions 1977, in Box No B319671, above note 65.

156 Submissions to Ontario Law Reform Commission by Great Lakes Tomorrow (24 January 1977); Thorncliffe Park Community Organization (2 March 1977); all in Submissions to OLRC on Class Actions 1977, in Box No B319671, *ibid.*

157 Submission to Ontario Law Reform Commission by National and Provincial Parks Association of Canada (26 January 1977), in Submissions to OLRC on Class Actions 1977, in Box No B319671, *ibid.*

158 Submission to Ontario Law Reform Commission by Melvyn L Solmon, partner at the law firm of Outerbridge, Manning & Mueller (9 May 1977) [Solmon Submission], in Submissions to OLRC on Class Actions 1977, in Box B319671, *ibid.* Solmon also enclosed an unpublished paper on class actions for damages; however, this paper does not appear to be in the archival record.

159 Solmon Submission, *ibid*; Submissions to Ontario Law Reform Commission by David W Mossop, counsel to the Vancouver Community Legal Assistance Society and counsel for the plaintiff in *Chastain v British Columbia Hydro and Power Authority* (1973), 32 DLR (3d) 443 (BCSC) [*Chastain*] (1 February 1977) (although Mossop took the more general position that no change was needed to facilitate class actions); Ian G Waddell, legal director of the Western Canada Institute of Legal Research & Reform and counsel for the plaintiff in *Chastain* (15 March 1977); Board of Directors of the Community & Legal Aid Services Programme (CLASP) at Osgoode Hall Law

The OLRC only provided a short letter of acknowledgement in response to these submissions.[160] In the years between the call for submissions and the release of the OLRC Report, there were very few announcements or public statements regarding the project. No public hearings were held despite the OLRC's express intention of doing so.[161] As far as the outside world was concerned, nothing was heard until June 1982 when the attorney general tabled the OLRC Report in the Ontario legislature.[162] Any momentum that the movement for class action reform had had when the report was commissioned had been lost by the time it was released. There is very little explanation as to why the report took so long,[163] and why, when it was finally released, it was 880 pages of unnecessarily long and repetitive "dense legal prose"[164] that likely discouraged many less well-resourced groups from commenting on it.[165]

School (5 September 1978); in Submissions to OLRC on Class Actions 1977, in Box No B319671, *ibid.*

160 Letters from the OLRC (January to July 1977) in Class Actions—General 1976–1980, in Box No B319671, *ibid*; letters from the OLRC (25 June 1982) [the day after the OLRC Report was tabled in the legislature] in Class Actions Correspondence 1981–1984, in Box No B319671, *ibid.*

161 Letter from WP Richardson, OLRC counsel, to JA Whybrow, Research Branch of Corporate and Consumer Affairs Canada (14 February 1977) in Class Actions—Correspondence 1976–1980, in Box No B319671, *ibid.*

162 Ontario, Legislative Assembly, *Official Report of Debates (Hansard)*, 32nd Parl, 2nd Sess (24 June 1982) (Roy McMurtry), online: http://hansardindex.ontla.on.ca/hansardeissue/32-2/l087.htm [Hansard, 24 June 1982].

163 The OLRC did not even meet on the subject of class actions until 5 June 1978, nearly two years after it received the AG Reference: Memorandum from Patricia Richardson, OLRC counsel, to OLRC members re: Class Actions (29 June 1978), in Box No B380538, above note 43. However, it is also clear from this memorandum that a fair amount of material had been written and researched by that time. Simon Chester, legal research officer at the OLRC, wrote his initial memo on the subject less than a month after the OLRC received the AG Reference: Simon Chester to OLRC (6 December 1976) in Class Actions—Initial Memorandum, in Box No B319671, above note 65.

164 E Roseman, "Class Actions Are Needed, Commission Report Says" *Globe and Mail* (7 July 1982) 9 [Roseman]; "Facilitate Class Actions," Editorial, *Toronto Star* (28 June 1982) A12 ["Facilitate"]. Both articles can be found in Box No B380537, above note 8.

165 Letter from WL Hetherington, chairman, Ontario Division, of the Canadian Manufacturers' Association, to the Honourable R Roy McMurtry, QC (15 September 1983) at 1 [CMA Letter 1983], in Policy Development Division Counsel correspondence files, Class Actions—Correspondence, RG 4-40, CA226, Box No B248633, North York, Archives of Ontario; Memorandum to File from Peter Bernhardt, student-at-law, re: Meeting 8 February 1983 with representatives of the Canadian Manufacturers' Association (11 February 1983) at 1 [Bernhardt Memo February 11], Policy Development Division Counsel correspondence files, Class Actions—Consultations,

Despite the warm reception the report received, therefore, it is very unlikely that most of the people praising it had read it in its entirety. Attorney General McMurtry praised it as "the culmination of [a] massive project of research and scholarship [that] has reviewed every aspect of the law relating to class actions" and as a major contribution to the class actions debate.[166] Academics stated that it "deserves to become a basic reference work on the subject"[167] and that it "demands the attention of all procedural reformers."[168] Consumer advocates and the wider public welcomed the report's call for class action reform in Ontario.[169] However, Andrew Roman, head of the Public Interest Advocacy Centre (PIAC) who was later to sit on the Attorney General's Advisory Committee, stated "the OLRC's proposals for reform were not as persuasive as its research."[170]

Not only was the OLRC Report so long that it was virtually unreadable for most people,[171] but its template for class action reform departed substantially from the traditional model of litigation, so much so that the business community and the legal profession strongly opposed many of its recommendations. The report's draft legislation adopted a procedure similar to that of Rule 23 in the United States,[172] but in addition it made several quite controversial recommendations, including the following:

- The Attorney General was to be given notice of every class action brought in the province, with a right to intervene in any case that raised a matter of public interest, and a discretion given to the court

1983–1988, CA226, RG 4-40, Box No B502275, North York, Archives of Ontario [Box No B502275—Consultations].

166 Hansard, 24 June 1982, above note 162.

167 Benjamin S DuVal, Jr, "Book Review: Ontario Law Reform Commission *Report on Class Actions*" (1983) 8:3 *Law & Social Inquiry* 783 at 783.

168 Thomas A Cromwell, "An Examination of the Ontario Law Reform Commission Report on Class Actions" (1983) 15 *Ottawa Law Review* 587 at 587 [Cromwell].

169 Roseman, above note 164; "Facilitate," above note 164.

170 Andrew J Roman, "Class Actions in Canada: The Path to Reform?" (1988) *Advocates' Society Journal* 28 at 28 [Roman, "Class Actions"]. See also Cromwell, above note 168 at 9–12.

171 The final product was nevertheless a significant improvement on the draft, which was more than 2,000 pages long: Draft OLRC Report (March 1982 Minister's Copy), Table of Contents, in Ontario Law Reform Commission files, Nov 1976–Dec 1982, Project name: class actions, RG 4-66, BA77, Box No B380546, North York, Archives of Ontario [Box No B380546].

172 OLRC Report, above note 27 at 307.

to allow the Attorney General to act as the representative plaintiff in certain circumstances.[173]

- A certification requirement included a preliminary merits test, which would certify only those actions "brought in good faith with a reasonable possibility that material questions of fact and law common to the class will be resolved at trial in favour of the class."[174]
- The certification test would also allow the court to determine whether the representative plaintiff had competent legal representation that was adequate to protect the interests of the class.[175]
- Part of the onerous certification test would involve a "cost-benefit" analysis, which would be different from the "superiority" test (also a requirement); this would allow the court to embark on a wide-ranging enquiry into whether the impact of the litigation on the administration of justice would be outweighed by the compensatory or deterrent value of the suit (the draft legislation gave very little other guidance to the courts in this regard).[176]
- Class members would not be allowed to opt out without leave of the court.[177]
- Traditional costs rules would not apply to class actions—no costs would be awarded to any party (unless it would be unjust to deprive the successful party of costs; in the event of vexatious, frivolous, or abusive conduct; and in the case of interlocutory proceedings); traditional costs rules would apply to individual proceedings.[178]
- A modified contingency fee arrangement would be allowed, to be approved by the court; a lawyer's fee would come out of any recovery to the class.[179]
- Aggregate damages could be awarded, and any unclaimed residue of a damages award could be distributed in a way that would benefit uncompensated class members, or could even be forfeited to the Crown.[180]

173 *Ibid* at 307–8.
174 *Ibid* at 309–24.
175 *Ibid* at 354–74.
176 *Ibid* at 411–17.
177 *Ibid* at 485–91.
178 *Ibid* at 704–9.
179 *Ibid* at 709–39. This would not be an "American-style" contingency agreement that would involve a percentage of recovery, but a modified contingency fee along the lines of option (3) as outlined in Section G, above in this chapter.
180 *Ibid* at 519–603.

In addition, the OLRC specifically rejected the concept of a publicly financed fund to assist plaintiffs in class actions, because the start-up costs would be too high and the only experience of such a fund was in Quebec, where it had been running only since 1978.[181] The attorney general invited interested parties to make submissions regarding the OLRC Report,[182] and the business community was very quick to take him up on his offer.

These groups were unanimous in their opposition to class action reform that departed from the traditional model of litigation,[183] stating that any changes should be merely to the existing Rules of Civil Procedure and not involve an entirely new statute.[184] They stated that the OLRC had acted outside the bounds of its mandate by making policy decisions.[185] Others resurrected the "legalized blackmail" epithet, stating that the social costs of class actions far outweighed their benefits.[186] They also raised fears that class actions would impact their sector specifically,

181 Stephen T Goudge, "Working Paper on Costs" (Toronto: Ontario Law Reform Commission, 1980) at 35–36, in Box No B380538, above note 43. Goudge was at the time a partner at Cameron, Brewin & Scott, along with Ian Scott, who would later oversee the introduction of class action legislation as attorney general: Scott, above note 29 at 133. In addition, two of the legal research officers who worked on the OLRC Report, Larry Fox and Ann Merritt, both ended up working on the implementation of a class actions fund once it had been recommended by the Attorney General's Advisory Committee in 1990.

182 Hansard, 24 June 1982, above note 162.

183 CMA 1982, above note 142 at 1 and 4; HJ Hemens et al, *A Discussion Memorandum on Class Actions for the Ontario Law Reform Commission*, 1978 at 56 [McMillan Binch Report], CMA File on Class Actions, 1978–1983, RG 4-40, LEG-2-24-5, Box No B381441, North York, Archives of Ontario. The McMillan Binch Report was drafted by five lawyers from McMillan Binch (essentially representing the interests of their numerous corporate clients) who had opposed the class action provisions of the proposed *Competition Act*, two of whom had also worked with the Canadian Manufacturers' Association (at 1–2). See also WA Macdonald & JW Rowley, "Ontario Class Action Reform: Business and Justice System Impacts—A Comment" (1984) 9 *Canadian Business Law Journal* 351 [Macdonald & Rowley].

184 CMA 1982, above note 142 at 4; CMA Letter 1983, above note 165 at 2; McMillan Binch Report, above note 183 at 59–65. This was a manifestation of what Marcus calls the "adjectival" conception, which holds that class actions are purely procedural and should not depart from traditional rules of civil procedure: David Marcus, "The History of the Modern Class Action, Part I: *Sturm und Drang*, 1953–1980" (2013) 90 *Washington University Law Review* 587 at 590.

185 McMillan Binch Report, above note 183 at 10.

186 Submission of the Institute of Chartered Accountants of Ontario with respect to Class Actions, enclosed with letter from JL MacInnis, ICAO president, to R McMurtry (6 May 1983) at 2–3 [CA Brief], in Box No B502275—Consultations, above note 165.

expanding liability, adding to costs, reducing competition, and leading to overly risk-averse practices.[187] Some business opponents were particularly critical of the fact that the report had been written largely by academics with little practical experience of the legal system,[188] with the CMA stating that "the Commission has departed from attempting to develop a workable procedure to address real world issues. Rather it has succumbed to some form of academic perfectionism which will not correct real world problems but only complicate them."[189]

Overall, the business groups took issue with the following recommendations of the OLRC, which ran counter to the submissions they had made to the OLRC five years previously:

- *No-way costs*: The business groups all maintained that traditional costs rules should apply to class actions,[190] and some even stated that plaintiffs' groups should be made to put up security for costs.[191]
- *Contingency fees*: These were strongly opposed by all the interest groups, largely on ethical grounds and the fact that such fees would give lawyers a financial incentive to encourage litigation.[192]
- *Opting-out*: All the business groups stated that class actions should be on a strictly opt-in basis to avoid the spectre of indeterminate classes, and to avoid binding the rights of unwilling class members.[193]
- *Aggregate damages*: The business groups unanimously opposed the OLRC's proposal to allow aggregate damages (or "fluid recovery"), on the basis that this compromised defendants' procedural rights.[194]

---

187 CA Brief, *ibid* at 4–5.

188 *Ibid* at 8–9.

189 Submission by the Canadian Manufacturers' Association to the Honourable R Roy McMurtry, QC, on Ontario Law Reform Commission Report on Class Actions (OLRC Report), September 1983 [CMA Submission 1983], in Box No B248633—General File #1, above note 142.

190 CA Brief, above note 186 at 6–8; CMA Letter 1983, above note 165 at 3; McMillan Binch Report, above note 183 at 54.

191 CMA 1982, above note 142 at 3–4; CMA Submission 1983, above note 189 at 30–36; UDI Submission, above note 153 at 2.

192 CA Brief, above note 186 at 6–8; CMA 1982, above note 142 at 2; CMA Letter 1983, above note 165 at 3; CMA Submission 1983, above note 189 at 30–36; McMillan Binch Report, above note 183 at 44–45 and 54.

193 CMA 1982, above note 142 at 1; CMA Letter 1983, above note 165 at 3; CMA Submission 1983, above note 189 at 22; McMillan Binch Report, above note 183 at 53; UDI Submission, above note 153 at 1.

194 CMA 1982, above note 142 at 2–3; CMA Letter 1983, above note 165 at 3; CMA Submission 1983, above note 189 at 36–37; UDI Submission, above note 153 at 2.

- *Common interest*: The submissions from the business groups stated that class actions should be permitted only when there was a common interest, such as identical contracts, between members of the class;[195] individual damages should be tried in individual actions.[196]
- *Certification test*: The business groups did not want certification to involve an assessment of the merits, because then they would be forced to reveal their defence strategy to the plaintiffs.[197]
- *Notice*: All of the business groups recommended mandatory post-certification notice to every member of the class, in order to enable them to opt in if they wished.[198]
- *Attorney general*: There was all-round opposition to the involvement of the attorney general in class actions, other than as an intervenor and with leave of the court.[199]

It was not only the business groups that opposed several of the OLRC's key recommendations. Even those who were sympathetic to the case for reform found the OLRC's draft legislation overly complex,[200] setting so many hurdles in the way of a prospective plaintiff as to "make it improbable that anyone in Ontario would ever commence a class action."[201] The report appeared to be the product of divided minds, a prospect that the committee itself foresaw as early as 1979.[202] In the final report, the chairman himself wrote a reservation, dissenting on significant aspects of the OLRC Report including the vital subject of costs (he opposed the no-way costs proposal and contingency fees because they treated plaintiffs and

195 CMA 1982, above note 142 at 3; McMillan Binch Report, above note 183 at 39–40, 52; UDI Submission, above note 153 at 1.

196 CMA 1982, above note 142 at 3; CMA Letter 1983, above note 165 at 2–3; CMA Submission 1983, above note 189 at 13–14; McMillan Binch Report, above note 183 at 64–65.

197 CMA Submission 1983, above note 189 at 11; McMillan Binch Report, above note 183 at 59–60.

198 CMA Letter 1983, above note 165 at 3; CMA Submission 1983, above note 189 at 17–18, 20, and 24; McMillan Binch Report, above note 183 at 61–62.

199 CMA 1982, above note 142 at 2–3; CMA Letter 1983, above note 165 at 3; CMA Submission 1983, above note 189 at 36–37.

200 Letter from OLRC Counsel to Director of Research at the Law Reform Commission of Australia (9 April 1984), in Box No B319671, above note 65.

201 Roman, "Class Actions," above note 170.

202 Letter from Richard A Bell, OLRC commissioner, to Derek Mendes da Costa, OLRC chairman (20 March 1979) re: Class Actions, in Box No B380543, above note 11: "[W]hat I suspect is that philosophically and otherwise, we are divided."

defendants unequally).[203] The commission's previous vice-chairman, George Alexander Gale, who had retired due to ill health, disagreed with the costs recommendations for the same reasons, a fact acknowledged at the very beginning of the report.[204]

The CBA/PIAC Report was particularly critical of the OLRC Report because of its equivocal nature. Yet, the CBA/PIAC were somewhat supportive of the OLRC's recommendations. They agreed that no-way costs rules were necessary in order to make class actions economically realistic for plaintiffs.[205] They therefore recommended a modified no-way costs rule, where the judge could retain discretion to award costs, but would take various factors (such as the conduct of the parties) into account in doing so.[206] They too rejected the idea of a publicly supported fund.[207] However, the CBA/PIAC also opposed some of the OLRC's proposals, stating that certification should require plaintiffs to demonstrate a "reasonable probability of success,"[208] notice should be mandatory,[209] the attorney general should have no special role in class actions,[210] and contingency fees should not be allowed on ethical grounds.[211] The submission of the Advocates' Society was similar in these respects. With regard to costs, however, the Advocates' Society rejected the OLRC's recommendations

203 OLRC Report, above note 27 at 851–54; draft OLRC Report (March 1982 Minister's Copy), "Chairman's Reservations," in Box No B380546, above note 171. Mendes da Costa also found the chapter on costs and benefits unpersuasive and unduly guided by the American experience; he disagreed with active case management and a role for the activist judge; he thought that opting-out should be a right and should not require leave of the court; he disagreed with cy-près awards; and he thought that undistributed aggregate awards should be returned to the defendant.

204 OLRC Report, above note 27, acknowledgements page.

205 CBA/PIAC Report, above note 127 at 42.

206 *Ibid* at 30–31 and 61.

207 *Ibid* at 32–37. Interestingly, the original majority report recommended traditional costs and a public fund; this was changed in order to make the report unanimous following John Holding's dissenting report: Class Action Committee Minority Report by John D Holding, QC (September 1983), in Box No B248633-CBA, above note 127. The CMA was also in support of a fund, combined with traditional costs rules: CMA Submission 1983, above note 189 at 30–36.

208 CBA/PIAC Report, above note 127 at 61.

209 *Ibid* at 62.

210 *Ibid.*

211 *Ibid* at 37–41.

on no-way costs and contingency fees, although it did support the idea of a public fund for class actions.[212]

Very few people wholeheartedly supported the OLRC's recommendations.[213] The media coverage of the report's release evinced wide public support for class action reform. However, the news articles rarely went into detail about the report's actual recommendations.[214] They focused instead on the well-known examples of mass wrongs referred to by the OLRC,[215] which had awakened the public consciousness to the concept of group injury and group litigation in previous years. These included the Re-Mor and Astra Trust investment scandal, as well as the Mississauga train derailment.[216] The Re-Mor and Astra Trust scam involved the collapse of several financial institutions, leaving more than 300 investors with losses of approximately $6 million. Legal proceedings were subsequently commenced, including several class actions, which alleged that the Ontario government had been negligent in its licensing of Re-Mor.[217]

212 Submission of the Advocates' Society on the Report of the Ontario Law Reform Commission on the Reform of Class Action Legislation in Ontario (February 1984) at 7–8 and 17–22, in Class Actions—Advisory Council to Advocates' Society Submission, in Box No B319671, above note 65. The Advocates' Society also stated that the certification test should include a consideration of the merits (at 4 and 6).

213 There is only one letter in the archival record asking the attorney general to implement the OLRC draft legislation without change: Jacob Ziegel, professor of Law at the University of Toronto (a consumer advocate who had supported the OLRC Consumer Report, above note 15) to Roy McMurtry (1 March 1983), in Box No B380537, above note 8.

214 Roseman, above note 164; R Speirs, "Ontario Report Asks for Class Action Law" *Globe and Mail* (25 June 1982) 1, in Box No B380537, above note 8. See also "Remove That Bottleneck," Editorial, *Kitchener-Waterloo Recorder* (6 July 1982); "Class Action Legislation Must Keep Up with Times," Editorial, *Guelph Daily Mercury* (28 June 1982); D Collins, "Class Action Lawsuit Process Will Never Be Perfect: Experts" *Ottawa Citizen* (26 June 1982); "Make Class Actions Easier," Editorial, *Toronto Star* (12 July 1984); all these articles can be found in Box No B380543, above note 11.

215 This is largely because those events were the focus of the Canadian Press story, which regional newspapers such as the *Hamilton Spectator* and the *London Free Press* simply reprinted or rewrote: Canadian Press (24 June 1982), in Box No B380537, above note 8.

216 It also included environmental disasters such as the mercury contamination of fish in the Wabigoon-English river system, which led to the poisoning of members of two First Nations bands in Northern Ontario. The group actions that ensued were settled for $16.6 million by way of the *Grassy Narrows and Islington Indian Bands Mercury Pollution Claims Settlement Act*, SC 1986, c 23.

217 OLRC Report, above note 27 at 97–99.

The scandal prompted numerous calls for law reform, including reform of the Ontario *Securities Act*.[218]

The Mississauga train derailment occurred on 10 November 1979, when a train carrying several tankers of explosive and flammable chemicals derailed and subsequently exploded, leading to a chlorine leak that necessitated the evacuation of 250,000 people for six days. The damages in terms of lost income and business profits were estimated at $80 to $100 million.[219] Roy McMurtry, attorney general and solicitor general at the time of the derailment and when the OLRC Report was released, was commended for his response as chair of the Emergency Response Committee.[220] The response of Canadian Pacific Railway (CP) in terms of compensating the victims, however, was not as impressive. CP made payouts to only about half the people evacuated, and those people had to sign releases in exchange for compensation, which resulted in the Law Society of Upper Canada establishing an emergency legal clinic to advise those claimants.[221] The consequent coverage in the press expressed frustration at the unwillingness of the insurance companies to pay claims and the fact that full compensation was not forthcoming from the train companies, as well as the logistics of co-ordinating the hundreds of lawsuits that were filed.[222]

---

218 Ontario, Legislative Assembly, *Official Report of Debates (Hansard)*, 32nd Parl, 2nd Sess (20 January 1983) (Jim Breithaupt), online: http://hansardindex.ontla.on.ca/hansardeissue/32-2/l187.htm. Breithaupt became chairman of the Ontario Law Reform Commission in November of the following year, serving until 1991.

219 OLRC Report, above note 27 at 91.

220 Samuel Grange, *Report of the Mississauga Railway Accident Inquiry* (Ottawa: Supply and Services Canada, 1980), cited in Roy McMurtry, *Memoirs and Reflections* (Toronto: University of Toronto Press, 2013) at 271–76.

221 OLRC Report, above note 27 at 91–92; Law Society of Upper Canada, "Legal Aid Letter" (Newsletter of the Ontario Legal Aid Plan), No 14 (January 1980) in Class Actions—General 1976–1980, in Box No B319671, above note 65; Canadian Press, "Claims to Pile Up Next as Result of Derailment" *Montreal Gazette* (19 November 1979) 7, online: Google Newspaper Archives https://bit.ly/2lLOCfo. One group of Mississauga residents retained Jeffery Lyons, the lawyer who represented the plaintiffs in the *Naken* action: D Dowling, "Mississauga Aftermath: Legal Settlements Could Take Years" *Financial Post* (November 1979), in Box No B380543, above note 11.

222 Dowling, *ibid*; P Rickwood, "Insurance Unlikely for Evacuation Losses" *Toronto Star* (1 February 1980); N Louttit, "Battle of Mississauga: The Next Step Is Up to the Courts" *Toronto Star* (undated); Z Kashmeri, "128 Firms, 735 People Suing over Derailment" *Globe and Mail* (16 April 1981) 1; Kirk Makin, "Derailment Suits to Be Heard Together" *Globe and Mail* (24 September 1982) 3; all these articles can be found in Box No B380543, above note 11.

In light of incidents such as this and the consequent delays in getting compensation to the numerous victims, the media and the public began to favour class action reform as a mechanism for addressing mass claims. However, none of the news articles shows a detailed grasp of the OLRC Report's recommendations. Given the later support for the Report of the Attorney General's Advisory Committee—which was quite different from that of the OLRC—the media would probably have supported the concept of reform even if the recommendations had been somewhat different.

Upon tabling the OLRC Report in the legislature, the attorney general stated that "[t]he government will be studying the report with interest."[223] However, apart from a couple of submissions from business groups that were met with a token response,[224] there appears to have been very little activity in the MAG for the better part of a year.[225] Finally, in February 1983, the ministry was jolted into action by a decision from the Supreme Court of Canada that effectively ended the common law evolution of class actions in Ontario.

J. *NAKEN* AND THE SUPREME COURT OF CANADA

Hopes were high for the Supreme Court of Canada's decision in *Naken*.[226] As detailed in the previous chapter, the case had moved through the lower levels of court until the Court of Appeal for Ontario decided that it could proceed. There were hopes that the Supreme Court of Canada would uphold that decision, confirming at last that class actions for damages under Rule 75 could proceed in Ontario.

Those hopes were dashed. The plaintiffs had attempted to fit their claims within the "same interest" requirement of Rule 75 by placing a flat limit on individual damages ($1,000 per class member)[227] and, in response to the judgment of the Court of Appeal, limiting the class to owners who

223 Hansard, 24 June 1982, above note 162.

224 Letter from McMurtry to DW Montgomery, CMA (18 January 1983) in Box No B502275—Consultations, above note 165.

225 Jennifer Bankier, one of the researchers for the OLRC Report, stated in an article on 25 February 1983 that the report had virtually been ignored in Canada and that Ontario's attorney general had yet to respond: S Thorne, "Court Decision Undermines Use of Class Action Suits" *Halifax Mail Star* (25 February 1983) 14, in Class Actions—Correspondence 1981–1984, in Box No B319671, above note 65.

226 *General Motors of Canada Ltd v Naken*, [1983] 1 SCR 72 [*Naken* SCC].

227 *Ibid* at 76.

responded to and relied on GM's advertisements.[228] Justice Estey, writing for the Court, held that this was insufficient to enable the action to be conducted under Rule 75. He held that the class members had varying contractual arrangements with the defendant, giving rise to different claims in contract. These differences meant that the "same interest" requirement was not met even though some of the contracts were similar and they all related to the same model of car (that is, the 1971–1972 Firenzas).[229]

Justice Estey stated that the differences between class members meant that they would each have to prove that they had entered a unilateral contract with the defendant, and each would have to prove the damages arising from the breach of that contract.[230] This would involve a long and complex procedure and a "new and distinct method of proceeding" that was simply beyond the scope of Rule 75, or indeed any of the Rules of Civil Procedure.[231] There were numerous procedural considerations for which Rule 75 did not provide, including the assessment of damages arising from different circumstances; costs, especially with respect to non-parties; the involvement of non-parties in pre-trial procedures; the effect of a class action on class members' own rights of action; and the effect of the *Statute of Limitations* on class and individual proceedings.[232]

Justice Estey referred to the detailed and comprehensive legislation that allowed for class actions in other jurisdictions, and compared it with the sparseness of Rule 75.[233] He also picked up on the comments in the OLRC Report regarding the procedural inadequacy and "skeletal nature" of Rule 75,[234] as well as the comments from the Court of Appeal for Ontario to the same effect.[235] Reviewing the jurisprudence, Estey J concluded that

228 *Ibid* at 77. However, no amended statement of claim had yet been delivered, despite the Court of Appeal's order: *General Motors of Canada Ltd v Naken et al* (Factum of the Appellant at para 7), *Naken* Records, Supreme Court of Canada Archives [*Naken*, Appellant's Factum].

229 *Naken* SCC, above note 226 at 103–4. See also *General Motors of Canada Ltd v Naken et al* (Factum of the Respondent at paras 10–14), *Naken* Records, Supreme Court of Canada Archives.

230 *Naken* SCC, above note 226 at 104; *Naken*, Appellant's Factum, above note 228 at paras 14–15.

231 *Naken* SCC, above note 226 at 104.

232 *Ibid* at 93–94, 96–102, and 104–5.

233 *Ibid* at 78 and 88–92.

234 *Ibid* at 93, citing the OLRC Report, above note 27 at 76.

235 *Naken* SCC, above note 226.

previous actions under Rule 75 had been permitted because either they claimed damages as a class (that is, damages that could be awarded to the entire class without the need for individual assessments), or claimed a common interest in a statutory right.[236]

He concluded that the *Naken* action could not be framed as a class action under Rule 75, but had to proceed as a joined action involving the named plaintiffs.[237] Justice Estey further concluded that "the rule, consisting as it does of one sentence of some thirty words, is totally inadequate for employment as the base from which to launch an action of the complexity and uncertainty of this one."[238] While class actions might be a desirable device in the modern marketplace, "[t]hese ... are matters of policy more fittingly the subject of scrutiny in the legislative rather than the judicial chamber."[239]

In its judgment in *Naken*, the Supreme Court of Canada clearly stated that class actions could not proceed under Rule 75 and that, if such actions were to be allowed in Ontario, they would instead have to be permitted by legislation.[240] The ball was back in the court of the MAG. The attorney general was subsequently quoted in several news reports stating that class actions were a priority for his ministry,[241] that there was now a stronger impetus to introduce class action legislation,[242] and that he hoped it would be possible to bring forward legislative proposals

236 *Ibid* at 79–88, 94–96, and 98. The jurisprudence on class actions reviewed in *Naken* is covered in Chapter 2.

237 *Ibid* at 105.

238 *Ibid.*

239 *Ibid* at 102.

240 As a result, very few class actions were litigated in Ontario in the decade between the *Naken* decision and the proclamation into force of the *CPA* on 1 January 1993. For a list of those actions, see WA Bogart, "Questioning Litigation's Role," above note 42 at 683–84 and accompanying notes. The cases that distinguished *Naken* and allowed class actions to proceed were, for the most part, either those involving a common fund (for example, *Swift Canadian Co Ltd v Alberta Pork Producers Marketing Board*, 1984 ABCA 175) or those involving a statutory right (for example, *Sparling et al v Royal Trustco Ltd et al*, 1984 CanLII 2040 (Ont CA)).

241 Ontario, Legislative Assembly, *Official Report of Debates (Hansard)*, 32nd Parl, 3rd Sess (17 June 1983) (Standing Committee on Administration of Justice, Estimates, Ministry of the Attorney General), J-173, Ontario Law Reform Commission files, Nov 1976–Dec 1982, Project name: class actions, RG 4-66, BA77, Box No B380537, North York, Archives of Ontario [Hansard, 17 June 1983].

242 Marina Strauss, "Supreme Court Bars Firenza Buyers from Launching a Class-Action Suit" *Globe and Mail* (9 February 1983) 1–2, in Box No B380537, above note 8.

within the next year.[243] This was also the hope of the general public as expressed in the media. Newspaper reports expressed disappointment in the Supreme Court's judgment, and particularly focused on the injustice of the fact that large groups of consumers and other wronged groups (such as victims of the Mississauga train derailment) would now have little recourse.[244] Some suspected that the government's hesitancy to act on the OLRC Report was due to the influence of big business.[245]

The MAG began consulting with interested groups on the same day that *Naken* was released. Simon Chester, counsel to the Policy Development Division at the MAG, met with the CMA on 8 February 1983,[246] rightfully acknowledging that the *Naken* decision "may . . . heighten public awareness of the class action issue."[247] While the CMA was in favour of a "balanced mechanism" to enable class actions, they were of the position that this could be achieved by an amendment to the Rules of Civil Procedure; yet they also told the MAG that class actions would entail substantive changes that would dramatically affect the economy of the province. Chester saw this position as inconsistent, because substantive changes to the law could not be made by the Rules Committee.[248] Furthermore, the CMA's position that class actions should be allowed only on an opt-in basis and where damages were identical, with discovery rights and

243 Letter from Simon Chester to DW Montgomery, director, Government Relations and Legislation, CMA (9 February 1983) [Chester to CMA February 1983], in Box No B502275—Consultations, above note 165; Andrew Roman, "Class Action Reform: Notes for an Address to the Canadian Bar Association (Ontario) Council" Public Interest Advocacy Centre (10 June 1983) at 3, in Box No B248633-CBA, above note 127.

244 Strauss, above note 242 at 2; Jacob Ziegel, "Class Action Dealt a Legal Blow" *Globe and Mail* (29 March 1983) 7; "10 Years Is Enough," Editorial, *Kitchener-Waterloo Record* (March 1983); "We Need Class-Action Suits," Editorial, *Toronto Star* (10 February 1983); all these articles can be found in Box No B380537, above note 8. See also Thorne, above note 225; "Make Class Actions Easier," Editorial, *Toronto Star* (12 July 1984), in Box No B380543, above note 11.

245 Ziegel, above note 244.

246 Chester to CMA February 1983, above note 243; Norm Stewart, who would later sit on the Attorney General's Advisory Committee as CMA representative, was at this meeting.

247 *Ibid.*

248 *Ibid*, citing the case of *Circosta v Lilly*, [1967] 1 OR 398 (CA); Bernhardt Memo February 11, above note 165 at 1; Memorandum to Simon Chester, counsel, from Peter Bernhardt, student-at-law re: Assessment of the preliminary brief on class actions from the Canadian Manufacturers' Association (14 February 1983) at 1 [Bernhardt Memo 14 February], in Box No B502275—Consultations, above note 165.

the requirement for security for costs from all class members,[249] was, by its own admission, "unduly restrictive"[250] and "little more than a system of 'permissive joinder.'"[251] By the MAG's assessment, the CMA's proposals on costs and discovery were "even more prohibitive than the procedures presently in place,"[252] and the other proposals differed little from the current law, with a prohibition on individual damages and separate contracts.[253] This first meeting with the CMA on the subject of class action reform was not promising; essentially the CMA was acknowledging the need for limited reform while being resistant to the changes such reform would entail.

Following the *Naken* decision, however, the MAG had to make some formal announcement about reform in response to the Supreme Court's hint that legislation was required to bring about class actions in Ontario. McMurtry made this announcement on 17 June 1983.[254] He regarded class action reform as "a high priority" and stated that he "would expect to be discussing these issues . . . with [his] cabinet colleagues in the early autumn, with a view to possibly bringing first reading legislation before the House by the end of the year."[255] McMurtry expressed his commitment to reform and to "develop[ing] progressive and effective legislation."[256] The only issue was the form this legislation would take.[257]

In the wake of this announcement, the Ministry of the Attorney General next turned to the CBA, anticipating (correctly) that it might be somewhat more open to class action reform than the CMA,[258] given its

249 The CMA also articulated its position in an article on the *Naken* decision dated 15 April 1983; Jeffery Lyons, counsel for the plaintiffs in *Naken*, put forward the "pro" position in the same article: "Ineffective Class-Action Legislation Must Be Updated . . . But Comprehensive Reform Draws Some Opposition" *Ottawa Citizen* (15 April 1983), in Class Actions—General II 1981–1984, in Box No B319671, above note 65.

250 Bernhardt Memo 14 February, above note 248 at 1.

251 Bernhardt Memo 11 February, above note 165 at 2; Bernhardt Memo 14 February, above note 248 at 4.

252 Bernhardt Memo 14 February, *ibid.*

253 *Ibid* at 2.

254 Hansard, 17 June 1983, above note 241.

255 *Ibid*, J-173.

256 *Ibid*, J-175.

257 *Ibid.*

258 For some reason, the MAG was not as responsive to the Institute of Chartered Accountants of Ontario regarding its CA Brief (above note 186), possibly because the MAG suspected the meetings with that group would be similar to the meetings with the CMA: Letter from Roy McMurtry to JL MacInnis, president, ICAO (9 June 1983), and letter from A Skinner to Roy McMurtry (7 July 1983), both of which can be found in Box No B502275—Consultations, above note 165.

positive take on the class proceeding provisions of the ill-fated *Competition Act*.[259] Chester's invitation to the CBA to comment on the OLRC Report,[260] coupled with McMurtry's formal announcement, led to the release of the joint report between the CBA and the PIAC, detailed above.[261] This report, while critical of many of the OLRC's recommendations, was supportive of class action reform in general. The CBA and the PIAC supported the MAG in its view that specific legislation, rather than a mere tinkering with the rules, was necessary for reform.[262] They were also of the view that class actions were economically incompatible with the traditional costs rules in Ontario.[263] The release of the CBA/PIAC Report in December 1983 was accompanied by a fair amount of publicity in favour of class action reform.[264] The MAG was successfully shoring up its position, and was creating a climate in which it could potentially introduce class action legislation.

However, it never actually did so. In fact, there was very little activity in the MAG following the release of the CBA/PIAC Report. There was, however, some discussion of class actions in the business and academic communities.[265] The Advocates' Society released its report in February

259 CBA Competition Submission, above note 78.

260 Letter from Simon Chester to GDE Adair, chair, Litigation Committee of the Canadian Bar Association (Ontario) (18 March 1983) in Box No B248633-CBA, above note 127.

261 CBA/PIAC Report, above note 127.

262 Roman, "Address," above note 243 at 2; Interview of Andrew Roman by Stan Carew (13 December 1983) on *Metro Morning, CBC Radio* [Roman interview], in Box No B248633-CBA, above note 127.

263 Roman, "Address," above note 243 at 8 and 11; Roman interview, above note 262. This view became more widespread with the news of various costs awards against plaintiffs who had tried to bring class actions and failed: see, for example, *Palmer v Nova Scotia Forest Industries* (1983), 2 DLR (4th) 397 (NSSCTD), in which approximately $250,000 in costs was awarded against the fifteen plaintiffs: "Ruling Shakes Spray Plaintiffs" *Halifax Mail-Star* (16 September 1983) 1. Both the judgment and the news article are cited in JK Bankier, "The Future of Class Actions in Canada: Cases, Courts and Confusion" (1984) 9 *Canadian Business Law Journal* 260 at 278.

264 Roman interview, above note 262; P Chisholm, "A-G Planning Class Action Statute" *Ontario Lawyers' Weekly* (12 December 1983) in Policy Development Division Counsel correspondence files, Class Actions—Draft Policy Submission file #2, 1982–1985, RG 4-40, Box No B248501, North York, Archives of Ontario [Box No B248501—Draft Policy Submission file #2].

265 Numerous articles by academics and practitioners were published in scholarly journals following the *Naken* decision. For example, in 1984, the *Canadian Business Law Journal* devoted a special edition (volume 9) to class actions.

1984 that, as noted above, strongly opposed the OLRC's recommendations on no-way costs and contingency fees. There was some discussion the following month between Chester and his direct superior, Doug Ewart (director of the Policy Development Division at the MAG) regarding the CBA/PIAC Report,[266] and Chester also began drafting a policy submission that was 90 percent complete by June 1985.[267] The MAG was by no means the sole advocate for reform at this time, and there was talk in the legislature of enacting statutes that would enable certain groups—namely, employees seeking pay equity[268] and members of defamed groups[269]—to bring class actions. However, the attorney general made no further formal statements on the OLRC Report, and no class action legislation was introduced. Indeed, in the debates on the pay equity legislation, certain MPPs complained about the "long wait for class action legislation by the Attorney General"[270] and stated they had little confidence that the government would ever enact such legislation.[271]

The delay may have been caused by business groups' strong opposition to class action legislation in the form put forward by the OLRC, which would have stymied any political will on the part of the Conservative government to implement the OLRC draft Act. More likely, both these factors delayed the introduction of any legislation, following which Premier Bill Davis announced in October 1984 that he would be stepping

266 Memorandum from Simon Chester to Doug Ewart, re: Canadian Bar Association—Joint Committee on Class Actions (22 March 1984), in Box No B502275—Consultations, above note 165.

267 Simon Chester, Policy Development, Ministry of the Attorney General, Policy Submission: Class Actions Act, 26 June 1985, in Box No B248501—Draft Policy Submission file #2, above note 264.

268 Pursuant to Bill 141, *An Act to amend the Employment Standards Act*, groups of employees would be able to enforce the equal pay provisions by way of a class action. Ontario, Legislative Assembly, *Official Report of Debates (Hansard)*, 32nd Parl, 4th Sess (8 May 1984) (Marion Bryden and Richard Johnston), online: http://hansardindex.ontla.on.ca/hansardeissue/32-4/l039.htm [Hansard, 8 May 1984]. The Bill did not progress beyond second reading.

269 On 30 March 1984, the attorney general tabled the results of a study conducted by NDP MPP Patrick Lawlor on group defamation, including legal recourse for defamed groups: Ontario, Legislative Assembly, *Official Report of Debates (Hansard)*, 32nd Parl, 4th Sess (30 March 1984) (Roy McMurtry), online: http://hansardindex.ontla.on.ca/hansardeissue/32-4/l009.htm; Lawlor, *Defamation*, above note 117. Lawlor had attempted to introduce class actions in 1977 and 1980 by way of two private member's bills: above notes 116 to 118.

270 Hansard, 8 May 1984, above note 268 (Richard Johnston).

271 *Ibid* (Marion Bryden).

down after more than a decade in office. This announcement led to the short-lived premiership of Frank Stuart Miller and, eventually, to a general election in May 1985. Following that election, the minority Conservative government was defeated in a no-confidence motion by an unofficial Liberal–NDP alliance on 26 June 1985. This saw the entry into power of a government that was much more sympathetic to class actions, and in time, would show itself to have the political will to bring about reform.

K. CONCLUSION

In 1970, class actions were virtually unknown in Ontario. A decade and a half later, they had become firmly implanted in the legal and political culture, as well as in the public consciousness. They did not win favour with everyone, and there was controversy over precisely what form they would take. However, the rise of consumer and environmental activism, the debate over the *Competition Act*, and the enactment of class action legislation in Quebec meant that, by the early 1980s, they were actively under discussion and no longer seen as a uniquely American device. This process was accelerated by the release of the OLRC Report and the *Naken* decision. While the report heightened public awareness of class actions and indicated to lawyers, politicians, and the public at large that class actions in Ontario were possible and even perhaps desirable, *Naken* sent a strong message that reform could come about only through legislation.

This put pressure on the MAG to introduce such legislation. The fact that it never did was a wasted opportunity. Perhaps the conditions were not quite right: the labyrinthine provisions and unrealistic recommendations of the OLRC Report, the staunch opposition to contingency fees, and the fact that the *Charter* had not yet permeated the legal culture meant that the ground was not ready for the seed and vice versa. With the change of government, however, there was appointed an attorney general who had a strong commitment to access to justice combined with unsurpassed political savvy. Perhaps more than any other factor, class actions came about in Ontario when they did because of Ian Scott.

Chapter 4

THE REPORT OF THE ATTORNEY GENERAL'S ADVISORY COMMITTEE ON CLASS ACTION REFORM (1985–1993)

A. IAN SCOTT'S EARLY YEARS AS ATTORNEY GENERAL (1985–1988)

On 18 June 1985, after more than four decades in power, the provincial Progressive Conservative government was defeated in a vote of no confidence. In its place and with the support of the NDP, David Peterson's Liberals formed a minority government.[1] When the government was sworn in on 26 June, Ian Scott was appointed attorney general. Scott had helped to negotiate the accord with the NDP that made the Liberal victory possible and was one of Peterson's right-hand ministers, part of an inner circle that had an important influence on the premier.[2]

Peterson ran his Cabinet informally, often bypassing formal channels of communication and allowing his ministers to make submissions to Cabinet without prior approval.[3] He respected Scott and trusted him implicitly, describing him to this day as "arguably the finest Attorney General this country has ever produced."[4] He gave Scott a free hand in

1 The Liberals and the NDP agreed to co-operate for a two-year period, during which the Liberals promised not to call an election, and the NDP promised not to treat a defeat in the House as a confidence measure. The two parties also agreed on a list of policies that had been in both their manifestos: Ian Scott with Neil McCormick, *To Make a Difference: A Memoir* (Toronto: Stoddart, 2001) at 121 [Scott].

2 *Ibid* at 120 and 143–44.

3 *Ibid* at 129 and 143.

4 Interview of David Peterson (24 July 2017) [Peterson interview].

running the Ministry of the Attorney General (MAG)[5] and supported all of his major decisions.[6] Peterson was a delegator and gave his ministers "as much line as they could take . . . the strong [ministers] could always get themselves out of trouble. Ian was a strong one."[7] Scott had been a practising litigator and Peterson therefore deferred to his knowledge on civil justice reform issues such as class actions.

Driven, ambitious, and a master tactician,[8] Scott would be instrumental in implementing the government's reform agenda. He had a disproportionate influence on the government's work,[9] regularly reviewing the Cabinet submissions of other ministries and putting forward his views on them, or requiring Cabinet colleagues to consult with him before publicly opining on certain subjects.[10] He believed "that an independent attorney general should have . . . a very special role to play (apart from his litigation role) in the policy-making process of government."[11]

As Peterson states, "there was no issue that came before Cabinet that [Scott] wasn't prepared for or had an opinion on. He was a very forceful and aggressive guy and would use any trick to win an argument."[12] Scott was a fearsome debater who never lost the cross-examination style he had developed as counsel.[13] He was good at getting his own way, which, despite the premier's trust in him, led to some very serious confrontations between the two on certain issues.[14] Disagreeing with him was not a pleasant experience, and he used this power of persuasion to get his policies through Cabinet.[15]

5 Scott, above note 1 at 140 and 203; Peterson interview, *ibid.*
6 Scott, above note 1 at 126 and 203.
7 Peterson interview, above note 4.
8 Interview of Advisory Committee member (13 April 2016) [AC member interview]
9 Interview of Michael Cochrane (21 April 2016) [Cochrane interview 1].
10 *Ibid*; Scott, above note 1 at 144 and 156; interview of Douglas Ewart, then director of the Policy Development Division (and Michael Cochrane's direct superior) at the Ministry of the Attorney General (26 April 2016) [Ewart interview].
11 Ian Scott, "Law, Policy, and the Role of the Attorney-General: Constancy and Change in the 1980s" (1989) 39 *University of Toronto Law Journal* 109 at 109.
12 Peterson interview, above note 4.
13 Ewart interview, above note 10; interview of Peter Woolford, representative of the Retail Council of Canada on the Attorney General's Advisory Committee (29 April 2016) [Woolford interview 1]; Scott, above note 1 at 79.
14 Peterson interview, above note 4.
15 Ewart interview, above note 10; Woolford interview 1, above note 13.

At his right hand[16] stood Michael Cochrane, a young lawyer in the Policy Development Division (PDD), one of the chief sections of the MAG.[17] Called to the bar just five years previously, Cochrane had arrived at the ministry a couple of weeks before Scott. The two men equalled each other in energy, ambition, and a desire to bring about law reform in numerous areas. Both possessed the key to any successful career in law: a seemingly endless capacity for work. Scott and Cochrane demonstrated an uncanny ability to persuade and, where persuasion failed, to get people where they wanted them through swift manoeuvring, political *savoir faire*, and sleights of hand at the negotiating table. Cochrane made full use of Scott's openness to policy ideas and his desire to rapidly advance the government's progressive agenda, often drafting statutes over the course of a weekend so they could be introduced as soon as possible.[18] Cochrane facilitated Scott's reform agenda in areas such as consumer rights and environmental protection, but one of his greatest achievements was class action reform.

Despite Cochrane's statements to the contrary,[19] class actions do not seem to have been high on the agenda of the new attorney general.[20] This is not surprising: in their first term of office, the Liberals were also busy bringing in full funding for Catholic schools; banning extra billing by Ontario's doctors; approving the Darlington nuclear power plant; introducing pay equity; addressing the rights of Indigenous peoples; dealing with the issues of abortion and abortion clinics; and participating in the Meech Lake Accord,[21] among numerous other changes. Class action reform had been effectively in limbo since the Supreme Court's decision in *Naken*, and continued to be so for a few years after the change of government. In fact, the MAG did not take any public action on the issue until the middle of 1988.

Nevertheless, Cochrane began working in the background as soon as Scott was appointed. On that same day in June 1985, Cochrane received

---

16 AC member interview, above note 8.

17 Scott, above note 1 at 130.

18 *Ibid* at 128–29 and 134; Cochrane interview 1, above note 9; interview of Michael Cochrane (28 June 2016) [Cochrane interview 2].

19 Letter from Cochrane to Julian Polika, director, Crown Law Office—Civil (8 August 1985) stating that a class action bill is one of Ian Scott's priorities for the upcoming session of the legislature, in Policy Development Division Counsel correspondence files, Class Actions—General—File #1, 1985–1987, RG 4-40, in Box No B248633, North York, Archives of Ontario [Box No B248633—General File #1].

20 Ewart interview, above note 10; Peterson interview, above note 4.

21 Scott, above note 1 at 145.

a draft policy submission drafted by his predecessor, Simon Chester. That submission laid out the various options for class action reform, and provided the basis for Cochrane's early work on the issue. Chester's submission considered the Ontario Law Reform Commission (OLRC) Report and its most controversial recommendations. He observed, and Cochrane was to find out before long, that the thorniest issue in bringing about any kind of consensus on class actions was the issue of costs. Chester summarized the conclusions of many commentators when he noted that reform would be futile if traditional costs rules continued to apply.[22] However, while the submission touched on the OLRC recommendation of a no-way costs rule, as well as contingency fee arrangements and assisting plaintiffs with their costs by way of a government-financed fund, it stopped short of making any recommendations on the issue.

Using this draft policy submission as a basis, Cochrane began to conduct his own research into class actions.[23] He emphasized what he saw as a "consensus" that the existing rules of procedure were defective with regard to class actions, from the Williston Committee that noted the "disrepair" in the state of the jurisprudence, to the Supreme Court in *Naken*, which stated that Rule 75 could not be read to permit class proceedings in Ontario. This emphasis on consensus, and the minimization of the novel and controversial nature of class actions, were to be recurring themes in Cochrane's writing and discussions on the subject.

Nevertheless, Cochrane could not deny that an attempt to change the status quo would be met with opposition from several camps. Outlining the positions of the Canadian Manufacturers' Association (CMA) and the Institute of Chartered Accountants (who opposed significant reform), as well as that of the Canadian Bar Association and Public Interest Research Centre[24]

22 Simon Chester, Policy Development, Ministry of the Attorney General, Policy Submission: Class Actions Act (26 June 1985) at 32, in Policy Development Division Counsel correspondence files, Class Actions—Draft Policy Submission file #2, 1982–1985, RG 4-40, in Box No B248501, North York, Archives of Ontario.

23 While the PDD was originally tasked with drafting a class action bill, Cochrane was instead asked to draft a policy submission presenting various options: letter from Cochrane to Doug Ewart and Craig Perkins (8 August 1985) with handwritten notes (undated) from Ewart regarding the policy submission, B248633—General File #1, above note 19.

24 The Public Interest Research Centre (PIRC) was at this time the research arm of the Public Interest Advocacy Centre (PIAC): PIAC, *25 Years Representing the Public Interest* (Ottawa: PIAC, 2001) at 10, online: www.piac.ca/wp-content/uploads/2014/11/25years.pdf.

(who wanted reform, but on different terms than outlined in the OLRC Report), Cochrane found that there was no common ground between the interest groups, and that change in any form would offend at least some of them.[25] Nevertheless, because Scott considered access to justice a priority, some change had to happen.[26] Cochrane's commitment to change was further exemplified in his drafting, in 1985 or early 1986, of what would eventually become the *Class Proceedings Act* (*CPA*).[27] The amount of opposition he faced, however, meant he had his work cut out for him.

The CMA reiterated its opposition shortly after Scott became attorney general. Norman Stewart, director of Government Relations for General Motors Canada and chair of the CMA Subcommittee that submitted its earlier report to Roy McMurtry, wrote to Scott on 7 November 1985. Stewart was the business community's most vocal and active opponent of class actions, and remained the major voice of those interests even as he later sat on the Attorney General's Advisory Committee, influencing the considerations of other members of the committee and ensuring that the reform was as conservative as possible. In 1990, in the middle of the Advisory Committee's drafting process, Stewart was to become vice-president of Government Relations and general counsel at Ford Canada. As detailed above, both GM and Ford had been the subject of class actions in Ontario for alleged manufacturing defects in their vehicles.

In his letter to Scott, Stewart pointed out that all of the submissions he had seen concluded that the OLRC's draft legislation should not form the basis for a statute. He offered to discuss the OLRC Report, but hoped that Scott had no intention of introducing class action legislation.[28] Scott agreed that there was very little common ground among the groups that submitted briefs, and that Rule 12[29] was inadequate for the purposes of

25 Cochrane handwritten notes (28 August 1985) at 18 [Cochrane handwritten notes] in Box No B248633—General File #1, above note 19.

26 *Ibid* at 19.

27 "Master Redraft: Class Actions" is a photocopy of the OLRC draft Act, with Cochrane's handwritten annotations. According to those annotations, the draft Act was to come into force in 1986. Policy Development Division Counsel correspondence files, Class Actions—Background Papers 1, 1983–1990, RG 4-40, in Box No B501822, North York, Archives of Ontario [Box No B501822—Background Papers].

28 Letter from Stewart to Scott (7 November 1985) in Box No B248633—General File #1, above note 19.

29 Previously, Rule 75 of the Rules of Practice of the Supreme Court of Ontario stated: "[w]here there are numerous persons having the same interest, one or more may sue or be sued or may be authorized by the court to defend on behalf of, or for the benefit of, all."

a class action.[30] For the time being, however, he was keeping the issue under review.[31] In the meantime, Cochrane continued to look into the possibility of reform.

The main battleground, as far as Cochrane could see, was the issue of costs. He knew that the OLRC and other observers had found costs to be the most serious and the most controversial single issue confronting class actions reformers.[32] However, without costs reform, class action legislation would be pointless.[33] Cochrane noted the dilemma whereby traditional costs rules could deter plaintiffs with meritorious suits, but the absence of such rules would be unfair to successful defendants. Scott also acknowledged that the issue of costs was a significant barrier to class action reform.[34]

The various interest groups also had widely diverging views on this issue.[35] As noted in Chapter 3, the representatives of corporate interests, as well as the Advocates' Society, opposed no-way costs, while most interest groups rejected the concept of contingency fees. The CBA/PIAC favoured a modified costs rule, but did not support a public fund for class actions (while the Advocates' Society did support such a fund). Opinions on costs differed not only between the various groups, but also were in stark contrast to the OLRC recommendations of no-way costs, contingency fees, and no public funding. If class action reform were to take place at all, Cochrane had to find a compromise between these positions that would be palatable to all concerned.

---

30 Letter from Scott to Stewart (26 November 1985) in Box No B248633—General File #1, above note 19.

31 *Ibid.* More than a year later, in December 1986, Scott told the House that he had "been looking at the class action problem," but did not anticipate that a solution would be available for the House's consideration before the late spring of 1987: Ontario, Legislative Assembly, *Official Report of Debates (Hansard)*, 33rd Parl, 2nd Sess (3 December 1986) (Ian Scott), online: http://hansardindex.ontla.on.ca/hansardeissue/33-2/l074.htm.

32 Cochrane handwritten notes, above note 25 at 14.

33 Memorandum from Cochrane to Scott (5 March 1986) at 14, in Box No B248633—General File #1, above note 19.

34 Letter from Allan Hutchinson to Scott (24 March 1986) and letter from Scott to Hutchinson (2 April 1986), both in Box No B248633—General File #1, *ibid.*

35 They laid out these views in briefs that they had previously submitted to Roy McMurtry (and resubmitted to Ian Scott when he became attorney general), which were summarized in a 23 April 1986 research memo to Cochrane, Policy Development Division Counsel correspondence files, Class Actions—Consultations, 1983–1988, CA226, RG 4-40, in Box No B502275, North York, Archives of Ontario [Box No B502275—Consultations].

By June 1986, Cochrane's review of the class action debate was largely complete.[36] However, despite his observations on costs,[37] he made no recommendations on this issue—with one exception. The submission did recommend that a fund be established for public financing of class action litigation, along the lines of the *Fonds d'aide aux recours collectifs* in Quebec.[38] This was an important development, as the OLRC Report had rejected this idea, and little further exploration had been done on the issue. Cochrane's recommendation showed that the fund was once again among the range of options open to the MAG,[39] and it would later prove to be an important tool in orchestrating a compromise. For now, however, Ewart told Cochrane that he had significant difficulties with the concept of a fund, and wanted to leave that question open for the attorney general's consideration.[40]

Despite the completion of its review, progress at the MAG on the issue of class actions continued to be sluggish. Class actions received some attention in the legislature in December 1986, when a private member's bill was introduced, calling for an environmental bill of rights that included the right of citizens to sue on a class basis for environmental pollution.[41] However, this bill was not passed until 1993, after the *Class Proceedings Act*.

There was also a brief flurry of activity at the beginning of 1987 when Cochrane learned, in a call from Arthur Stone (head of the Uniform Law

36 AG Policy Development Submission (8 June 1986) in Box No B248633—General File #1, above note 19. The submission appears to have been finalized on 6 August 1986. Cochrane's submission borrowed heavily from Chester's. An exception is Chester's recommendation that the court screen counsel for adequacy of representation; Cochrane rejected such an approach on the basis that it raised numerous awkward questions, and also that the court could sanction counsel by awarding costs against them personally under Rule 57.07. In addition, the plaintiff would have recourse against his own counsel through a professional negligence action.

37 AG Policy Development Submission (8 June 1986), *ibid* at 47.

38 *Ibid* at 59. Cochrane was later in touch with Yves Lauzon, director general of the Fonds in Quebec, regarding the details of the Fonds: letter from Lauzon to Cochrane (7 August 1986) and letter from Cochrane to Lauzon (21 August 1986), both in Box No B248633—General File #1, above note 19.

39 See also Memorandum from Cochrane to Scott (5 March 1986) at 15–16 in Box No B248633—General File #1, *ibid.*

40 Draft policy submission from Cochrane to Ewart (1 May 1986), with handwritten note (undated) from Ewart, stating his concerns regarding the fund, in Box No B248633—General File #1, *ibid.*

41 Ontario, Legislative Assembly, *Official Report of Debates (Hansard)*, 33rd Parl, 2nd Sess (10 December 1986) (Ruth Grier), online: http://hansardindex.ontla.on.ca/hansardeissue/33-2/l078.htm.

Conference of Canada (ULCC)), that New Brunswick was considering introducing class action legislation.[42] Encouraged by the fact that reform was gaining traction elsewhere in Canada, Cochrane sought to have class actions put on the agenda of the 1987 ULCC conference. He also wrote to Basil Stapleton, head of New Brunswick's Law Reform Commission and provincial PDD (and, that year, chairman of the Uniform Law section of the ULCC), to discuss the push for reform.[43] However, despite Cochrane's expressed intentions,[44] he did not present a paper. The ULCC's discussion of class actions was delayed until the summer of the following year,[45] when the Ontario MAG's activity on the issue would begin to accelerate significantly following the general election.[46]

Until then, there were two further developments that informed the debate on reform, although neither of them was due to action on the attorney general's part.[47] The first, in July 1987, was the Legislative Review Project (LRP) of the Ministry of Consumer and Commercial Relations.[48] The LRP reviewed existing consumer protection mechanisms with a view to drafting a comprehensive Consumer Protection Code. In its section on

42 Memo to File from Michael Cochrane (15 January 1987), in Policy Development Division Counsel correspondence files, Class Actions—Draft Policy Submission file # 1, 1986–1989, RG 4-40, in Box No B248501, North York, Archives of Ontario [Box No B248501—Draft Policy Submission File #1].

43 Letter from Cochrane to Stapleton (16 January 1987) (not in file, but referred to in letter from Stapleton to Cochrane (11 February 1987) in Box No B248633—General File #1, above note 19).

44 Letter from Cochrane to Stapleton (18 February 1987) in Box No B248633—General File #1, *ibid.*

45 "Proceedings of the Sixty-Ninth Annual Meeting" (Uniform Law Conference of Canada, Victoria, British Columbia, August 1987) at 27 and 316–17, online: www.ulcc.ca/images/stories/Past_Proceedings_PDF/1987ULCC0069.pdf. Cochrane was one of the Ontario commissioners from 1985 to 1989: see Michael G Cochrane, "Class Action Reform in Ontario: A Breakthrough" (July 1989) at 1 [Cochrane, "Breakthrough"], in Policy Development Division Counsel correspondence files, Class Actions—Articles by Cochrane, 1988–1989, CA226, RG 4-40, in Box No B248633, North York, Archives of Ontario [Box No B248633—Cochrane articles].

46 The Liberal-NDP accord expired at the end of May 1987, and the Liberals called an election at the end of July: Scott, above note 1 at 170.

47 In a letter to Ewart dated 6 August 1987, Andrew Roman reminded Ewart of the briefs he had sent to the attorney general on behalf of the CBA/PIAC, and observed, "[s]ince that time, everything appears to have stalled," in Box No B248633—General File #1, above note 19.

48 G Crossman, *Consumer Remedies and Government Redress* (Toronto: Legislative Review Project, Ministry of the Attorney General, 1987) [LRP Report].

"Procedural Mechanisms," the report addressed class actions. It noted the strength and divergence of opinions on the issue; developments in other jurisdictions, such as the United States and Quebec; and the history of the debate in Ontario. It noted the pros and cons of class action reform in Ontario before specifically recommending that class actions be made available. It further recommended that contingency fees be allowed in order to facilitate class actions and other procedural remedies.[49]

Various interest groups responded to the report by submitting briefs to the Ministry of Consumer and Commercial Relations. The submissions were overwhelmingly from the business community, a pattern that would be continued into later consultations on class action reform, and which likely reflected the fact that these organizations were better resourced than those on the other side of the debate. The only brief from the pro-consumer side of the debate was from the Consumers' Association of Canada, which enthusiastically supported the introduction of class actions.[50] The other briefs from the business community objected to the LRP Report's recommendations on costs. They opposed the introduction of contingency fees on the basis that such fees would encourage litigation and line lawyers' pockets.[51] There was also opposition to any change to the traditional costs rules, which were seen as performing a gatekeeping function to screen out unmeritorious actions.[52]

There was some concession among the business interests that minor changes were needed to the current Rules in order to allow for more class actions[53] as long as successful defendants would be able to recover their costs.[54] However, those groups were generally against broad-based reform.[55] They stated that more consultations were needed before introducing consumer protection legislation containing a class actions mechanism,[56]

49 *Ibid* at 15–23.

50 Brief of the Consumers' Association of Canada on the LRP Report at 32–33, in Box No B501822—Background Papers, above note 27.

51 Letter from the Canadian Advertising Foundation on the LRP Report at 3–4; brief of the Canadian Federation of Independent Business on the LRP Report at 13 [CFIB Brief]. Both briefs are in Box No B501822—Background Papers, *ibid.*

52 Submission of the Canadian Manufacturers' Association on the LRP Report at 23 [CMA Brief]; brief of the Retail Council of Canada at 10 [RCC Brief]. Both briefs are in Box No B501822—Background Papers, *ibid.* See also CFIB Brief, above note 51 at 14.

53 CMA Brief, above note 52 at 23; RCC Brief, above note 52 at 10.

54 RCC Brief, *ibid* at 10.

55 CMA Brief, above note 52 at 23.

56 CFIB Brief, above note 51 at 15.

because there was still no consensus regarding class action reform in Ontario.[57] There was clearly significant opposition to overcome in any effort towards such reform. When Scott began consultations the following year, it was agreed that the previous LRP work on class actions would be overtaken by the work of the Ministry of the Attorney General.[58]

The second development related to contingency fees. As many observers had already noted, change was needed on the issue of costs if class proceedings legislation were to be useful; contingency fees were a key part of this. Until the late 1980s, and as can be seen from the above-noted submissions to Roy McMurtry and the briefs on the Legislative Review Project, contingency fees were opposed by many (if not most) lawyers in Ontario as unethical and as an encouragement of unnecessary litigation.[59] Public opinion perceived the concept as an American import that would enable greedy lawyers to line their pockets at the expense of litigants.[60]

However, in May 1988, after studying the issue for just over a year, the Law Society of Upper Canada's Special Committee on Contingency Fees reported to Convocation.[61] They recommended the adoption of contingency fees, primarily because they would increase access to justice for the middle class. The Special Committee found that contingency fees were permitted in every province except Ontario, with no instances of abuse reported to the provincial law societies, and with contingency fees being used very little in those provinces (except for British Columbia and Alberta). The committee found no evidence that those provinces

57 Submission of the Board of Trade of Metropolitan Toronto (now the Toronto Region Board of Trade) on the LRP Report (at 13) in Box No B501822—Background Papers, above note 27.

58 Class Actions: Meeting with Business Interests (preparation note from Cochrane to Scott) (23 March 1989) at 2, in Policy Development Division Counsel correspondence files, Class Actions—Briefing Note, 1983–1990, CA226, RG 4-40, in Box No B501822, North York, Archives of Ontario [Box No B501822—Briefing Note].

59 See, for example, Canadian Bar Association (Ontario) and Public Interest Research Centre, *Report on Class Actions*, Submission to the Hon Roy McMurtry, QC, attorney general of Ontario (November 1983) at 37 [CBA/PIAC Report], in Policy Development Division Counsel correspondence files, Class Actions—Canadian Bar Association—brief—File #1, 1982–1991, RG 4-40, CA226, in Box No B248633, North York, Archives of Ontario.

60 The debate on contingency fees is covered in detail in Chapter 3.

61 Minutes of Convocation of the Law Society of Upper Canada (27 May 1988), in Policy Development Division Counsel correspondence files, LSUC Contingency Fees—Report of the Sub-committee, 1988, CA226, RG 4-40, in Box No B449218, North York, Archives of Ontario.

had seen an increase in unmeritorious lawsuits since the introduction of contingency fees. They further concluded that the system was already in de facto use in many instances in Ontario. The Special Committee recommended to Convocation that it approve in principle the introduction of contingency fees in Ontario, and the attorney general was asked to amend the *Solicitors Act* accordingly.[62]

A major point of controversy on the costs issue was now much less controversial.[63] With the recommendation from the Law Society, class action reformers could now support the idea of contingency fees without looking like they were trying to import yet another American concept.[64] Yet numerous controversies, especially on the issue of costs, remained. Even as the LSUC considered the issue of contingency fees, Scott, Cochrane, and the MAG were working behind the scenes on a plan to bring about consensus on those other issues.

B. PREPARING THE WAY FOR REFORM

The Ontario general election on 10 September 1987 saw the Liberals return to power with their first majority government in half a century. With this resounding mandate, Scott and his ministry could begin work on class action reform in earnest. Shortly before the election, Ewart wrote to Richard Chaloner, deputy attorney general, asking him to review Cochrane's draft policy submission in order to have it approved by the

62 Kirk Makin, "Ontario Law Society Withdraws Opposition to Contingency Fees" *Globe and Mail* (22 June 1988) A1–2, in Policy Development Division Counsel correspondence files, Contingency Fees—Consumers' Association of Canada, 1988, RG 4-40, in Box No B827067, North York, Archives of Ontario.

63 Some members of the legal profession were skeptical of the Law Society's recommendation, however. Terrence O'Sullivan, member of the later Attorney General's Advisory Committee on Class Action Reform, described the report as "a treatise on gravy written by a Labrador" (Interview of Terrence O'Sullivan (21 June 2017) [O'Sullivan interview]). However, it should be noted that O'Sullivan later intervened for the Advocates' Society in a case in support of the trial judge's declaration that contingency fee arrangements were not illegal in Ontario: *McIntyre Estate v Ontario (Attorney General)*, 2002 CanLII 45046 (Ont CA). The Court of Appeal upheld the trial judge's decision, paving the way for the use of contingency fee agreements outside the class actions context.

64 For example, in his later "Path to Reform" paper presented to the Uniform Law Conference in August 1988, Cochrane stated that "[t]he Law Society of Upper Canada is expected to release a report favouring contingency fees in the near future" (at 82) in Box No B248501—Draft Policy Submission File #1, above note 42.

Ministerial Cabinet Committee, and then submit a draft to Scott for consideration for the fall legislative agenda.[65]

Before any kind of consensus could even begin to build, however, the legal profession and the wider public had to be reintroduced to the concept of class actions. The OLRC Report had been released six years previously, but the sheer length of the report meant that it had not been widely read nor had its specific recommendations been commented upon.[66] Any momentum that it had built had long since dissipated. Even the *Naken* decision was five years old. The Australian Law Reform Commission (ALRC) had released a report in June 1988 that recommended class action reform, including the unusual recommendation that there be no certification requirement whatsoever (it stated that frivolous suits would instead be discouraged through the maintenance of traditional costs rules).[67] However, that report does not seem to have had much immediate impact on the debate in Canada.[68] In the summer of 1988, the MAG therefore had to start preparing the ground for a debate on class actions.

There was still a wide variety of opinions and many misconceptions about class actions in the legal and business communities.[69] To suddenly

65 Memorandum from Ewart to Chaloner (4 September 1987), in Policy Development Division Counsel correspondence files, Class Proceedings—Bill 28 and 29, 1990–1993, CR, RG 4-40, in Box No B703283, North York, Archives of Ontario [Box No B703283—Bill 28 and 29].

66 Letter from Stewart to Scott (7 November 1985), in Policy Development Division Counsel correspondence files, Class Actions—Miscellaneous Material, 1977–1981, RG 4-40, CA226, in Box No B248633, North York, Archives of Ontario [Box No B248633—Miscellaneous Material].

67 Australian Law Reform Commission Report No 46, *Grouped Proceedings in the Federal Court* (Canberra: Government of Australia Publishing Service, 1988), online: www.alrc.gov.au/sites/default/files/pdfs/publications/alrc46_Summary.pdf [ALRC Report].

68 The ALRC Report was later considered by the Attorney General's Advisory Committee, as one of its members, Andrew Roman of the CBA/PIAC, had been a consultant to the ALRC. Roman referred frequently to the ALRC Report in his submissions to the committee and elsewhere. See, for example, Andrew J Roman, "Class Actions in Canada: The Path to Reform?" (Paper delivered at the Uniform Law Conference of Canada (ULCC), Toronto, Ontario, August 1988) 97 at 97–105, online: www.ulcc.ca/images/stories/Past_Proceedings_PDF/1988ULCC0070.pdf [Roman, ULCC 1988]. The ALRC Report was also considered in the briefing documents that Cochrane wrote for the initial consultations with stakeholders in December 1988: in Box No B248633—Miscellaneous Material, above note 66.

69 Cochrane briefing note (9 September 1987), in Policy Development Division Counsel correspondence files, Class Actions—Background Papers 2, 1981–1989, RG 4-40, in Box No B502275, North York, Archives of Ontario.

announce an intention to introduce legislation, as Roy McMurtry had done following the release of the OLRC Report, would be to encounter the same inertia and outright resistance. Scott therefore broke the ground at an Access to Justice Conference in June 1988, held in Toronto and organized by the attorney general. The conference took place over three days, with the workshop on "Group Claims/Collective Rights" being last on the agenda.[70] Nevertheless, the workshop was a significant first step in the fight for reform.

The chair was Jacques Dufour of the Quebec Fonds (an acknowledgement that costs was to be a central issue in the reform debate). The panelists were Basil Stapleton of the New Brunswick Law Reform Commission (who had already expressed his commitment to reform) and Kevin Doucette of the Consumers' Association of Canada (a natural ally of the class action cause, as exhibited in his presentation at the workshop). The only panelist who represented the case against wide-ranging reform was Margaret McNee, a young lawyer from McMillan Binch.[71] However, even McNee acknowledged that the possibilities of bringing a class action were severely constrained by the existing Rules of Civil Procedure and caselaw, and her presentation implied that some reform was needed.

The discussion, which was largely about the funding of class actions, ended with the following conclusion:

> The workshop formed a consensus that class actions should be more readily available in appropriate cases. Similarly, public funding of class actions should be provided where meritorious claims might otherwise be commenced.[72]

The word "consensus" should be regarded with caution. Scott and Cochrane were to use the word throughout the class actions consultation

70 Ministry of the Attorney General, *Conference on Access to Civil Justice: June 20–22, 1988* (Toronto: Ministry of the Attorney General, 1988).

71 *Ibid*; Access to Justice Workshop Report (21 June 1988), Group Claims/Collective Rights [Access to Justice Workshop Report], in Policy Development Division Counsel correspondence files, Class Actions—Access to Justice Conference, 1988, RG 4-40, in Box No B502275, North York, Archives of Ontario. McMillan Binch had submitted a brief to Roy McMurtry, and subsequently Ian Scott, on the OLRC Report: HJ Hemens et al, *A Discussion Memorandum on Class Actions for the Ontario Law Reform Commission* (1978) at 56 [McMillan Binch Report], CMA File on Class Actions, 1978–1983, RG 4-40, LEG-2-24-5, in Box No B381441, North York, Archives of Ontario.

72 Access to Justice Workshop Report, above note 71 at 4.

process, even when little or no consensus actually existed.[73] In addition, both men were later to report the conclusions of this workshop as being resoundingly in favour of wholesale reform, when this was not the case[74] (even though the vast majority of attendees were from organizations that would have held a pro-class actions stance).[75] Nevertheless, it is apparent that some common ground had begun to take shape on the subject.

The next step was to get the buy-in of the other provinces by way of the Uniform Law Conference of Canada, a process that Cochrane had begun the previous year (although in fact the ULCC had been discussing the subject of class action reform for many years before that). Cochrane was due to present at the conference in early August 1988, and as the basis of this presentation he used his policy development submission from 6 August 1986.[76] Where Cochrane's submission recommended that class action reform be undertaken, however, he changed the first draft of his ULCC paper to appear somewhat more neutral so that, for example, all language on "recommendations" was removed.[77] Cochrane also inserted a disclosure that the views expressed were his own and not those of the Government of Ontario.[78] Nevertheless, the paper still contained Cochrane's conclusion that "the case for class action reform has been made."[79]

This was not acceptable for Doug Ewart, director of the PDD at the MAG. Putting forward the option of class action reform at the ULCC was one thing; stating that reform was a foregone conclusion was quite another. The debate had only just begun again publicly, and it was too

73 See, for example, letter from the head of the Canadian Bar Association—Ontario to Scott (21 January 1989): "Michael Cochrane has indicated that there has been a consensus but as far as C.B.A.O. is concerned there is not," in Policy Development Division Counsel correspondence files, Class Actions—Correspondence, RG 4-40, CA226, in Box No B248633, North York, Archives of Ontario [Box No B248633 Correspondence].

74 Ontario, Legislative Assembly, *Official Report of Debates (Hansard)*, 34th Parl, 2nd Sess (29 June 1989) (Ian Scott), online: http://hansardindex.ontla.on.ca/hansardeissue/34-2/l034.htm; Michael G Cochrane, *Class Actions: A Guide to the Class Proceedings Act, 1992* (Aurora, ON: Canada Law Book Inc, 1993) at 2. It should be noted, however, that Cochrane was not actually in attendance at this conference.

75 Ministry of the Attorney General, *Conference on Access to Civil Justice: June 20–22, 1988*, above note 70, list of attendees at workshop on Group Claims/Collective Rights.

76 AG Policy Development Submission (6 August 1986) in Box No B248501—Draft Policy Submission File #1, above note 42.

77 Michael G Cochrane, "Class Actions: A Discussion Paper," in Box No B248501—Draft Policy Submission File #1, *ibid*.

78 Cochrane, "Class Actions: A Discussion Paper," *ibid* at cover page.

79 *Ibid* at 86.

soon to risk any perception that the MAG had already made up its mind. Ewart stated as much in his handwritten changes to the first draft of Cochrane's ULCC paper:[80]

> Particularly near the beginning there are a number of conclusions and/or statements of opinion. I feel that these should be deleted before the paper goes out. Even with your disclosure the press could still [find] that a policy advisor to the AG had concluded that class action reform was essential etc. etc. The ULC is not worth the risk.

As a result of Ewart's comments, the final draft of the ULCC paper contained no pro-reform conclusions. Nevertheless, the title of the paper ("A Path to Reform") made Cochrane's sympathies clear. Once the ULCC conference was over, Cochrane created a further version of his "Path to Reform" paper in January 1989,[81] which was essentially identical to the first draft, and included the original conclusion that "the case for class action reform has been made." This was clearly Cochrane's own personal conviction, if not a wider conviction throughout the MAG.[82]

The case for reform was also articulated at the ULCC conference by Andrew Roman of the Public Interest Advocacy Centre, who had acted as a consultant to the Australian Law Reform Commission in formulating its draft class action bill. Roman's key recommendations stemmed from the content of the ALRC draft bill: no certification requirement, and public funding of class actions. He argued that these represented a less radical departure from traditional litigation than the US or Quebec model.[83]

As a result of Cochrane's and Roman's papers, the ULCC referred the matter back to the Ontario commissioners for a further report and to draft an act for discussion the next year.[84] Again, however, this conclusion was

80 *Ibid* at cover page.

81 Michael Cochrane, "A Path to Reform" (30 January 1989) in Box No B248501—Draft Policy Submission File #1, above note 42.

82 Scott's sympathies were also for reform at this time. He stated to the ULCC that class action reform was a topic "close to [his] heart": The Honourable Ian Scott, Attorney General of Ontario, "Notes for Remarks" (Closing banquet, 1988 Uniform Law Conference Meeting, 11 August 1988) at 10 [Scott, "Notes" ULCC], in Policy Development Division Counsel correspondence files, Class Actions—Communications Plan, 1988–1990, MGC, RG 4-40, in Box No B501822, North York, Archives of Ontario [Box No B501822—Communications Plan].

83 Roman, ULCC 1988, above note 68 at 103.

84 Proceedings, Uniform Law Conference of Canada (ULCC), Toronto, Ontario, August 1988) at 28, online: www.ulcc.ca/images/stories/Past_Proceedings_PDF/1988ULCC0070.pdf.

much less resounding than Cochrane later reported it to be. In a Cabinet submission the following year, Cochrane stated that the 1988 ULCC had approved a detailed set of proposals for class action reform, and that the proposed remedy would provide a model suitable for adoption by other Canadian provinces.[85] Given that the Ontario commissioners had not yet even produced a further report or draft act, let alone had it approved by the ULCC, one wonders precisely what "proposed remedy" Cochrane had in mind.[86] Certainly his own paper articulated numerous different proposals, and Roman's paper sharply disagreed with Cochrane's suggestion on certification. Even Ian Scott acknowledged the preliminary state of the ULCC's discussions on class actions in his closing remarks to the conference.[87] Once again, Cochrane painted a picture of consensus and certainty where little existed.

Nevertheless, the ULCC and Access to Justice conferences were important events that began building a momentum towards reform, or at least a discussion about reform. Although Cochrane painted an overly optimistic picture of the conclusions reached at these conferences, they did serve as a signal to the bar, business interests, and the public that class actions were firmly on the attorney general's agenda.

C. INITIAL CONSULTATIONS (1988–1989)

The attorney general built on this momentum by conducting initial consultations with those who would be most affected by reform. These consultations began in earnest on 2 December 1988, when Ian Scott met with representatives of numerous organizations to brief them on the possibility of class action legislation.[88] The documents circulated to these organizations show that the attorney general had made up his mind on

85 Cabinet submission (20 March 1989) [Cabinet submission, 20 March 1989], in Policy Development Division Counsel correspondence files, Class Actions—Final Cabinet submissions, 1989, CA226, RG 4-40, in Box No B248633, North York, Archives of Ontario.

86 In fact, the ULCC did not adopt a model *Uniform Class Proceedings Act* until 1996: ULCC Proceedings of the Seventy-Eighth Annual Meeting, Ottawa, Ontario, August 1996, online: www.ulcc.ca/en/annual-meetings/412-1996-ottawa-annual/civil-section-documents/1907-uniform-class-proceedings-act-1992.

87 Scott, "Notes ULCC," above note 82 at 10.

88 Letter from the Gang of Four to Scott (20 January 1989) at 1 in Box No B248633 Correspondence, above note 73. Cochrane does not appear to have been at this meeting, because he did not meet Stewart (who was at the meeting) until 22 December: letter

the need for reform, and that the only question now was the shape that reform would take.

A second consultation took place on 22 December, when Cochrane met with various stakeholders,[89] including the Consumers' Association of Canada (CAC), the Advocates' Society, and the group known colloquially in Queen's Park as the "Gang of Four."[90] The "Gang of Four" consisted of the Canadian Manufacturers' Association (CMA), the Retail Council of Canada (RCC), the Ontario Chamber of Commerce (OCC), and the Canadian Federation of Independent Business (CFIB). The CMA was a policy, lobbying, and public relations group for manufacturers across Canada. It was arguably the biggest of the four, with seven regional divisions, thirty-three local branches, and a full-time staff of more than 100. Its members represented approximately 75 percent of Canada's manufacturing output.[91]

The RCC represented grocery and general merchandise retail stores in Canada. It existed to inform the government on the latter's policy objectives, and played more of a technical advisory role than a lobbying role.[92] Its spokesperson for the class action consultations with the MAG was Peter Woolford, who was responsible for government relations and public policy at the RCC. Woolford had just joined the RCC, having been a senior public servant in economic and fiscal policy for the federal government, and knew very little about class actions.[93]

from Stewart to Cochrane (7 December 1988) in Box No B502275—Consultations, above note 35.

89 Meeting between Cochrane and stakeholders (22 December 1988), handwritten minutes by Michael Cochrane [Meeting, 22 Dec 1988] in Box No B502275—Consultations, *ibid.* Additional groups were also consulted informally: Briefing note by Michael Cochrane (6 January 1989) at 1, and attached list [Briefing note, 6 Jan 1989] (in Box No B502275—Consultations, *ibid*), which lists the same groups to which the 10 January 1989 materials were circulated (see below, note 116).

90 The original Gang of Four was a political faction of four officials from the Chinese Communist Party, that came to prominence during the Cultural Revolution and controlled the major organs of the Communist Party during the last years of the revolution. Clearly, the use of this epithet for the major business interests at Queen's Park was not entirely respectful. Nevertheless, it will be used as a convenient shorthand for the group for the remainder of this book.

91 Letter from WL Hetherington, chairman, Ontario Division of the Canadian Manufacturers' Association, to the Honourable R Roy McMurtry, QC (15 September 1983) at 1 [CMA Letter 1983].

92 Interview of Peter Woolford (27 September 2016) [Woolford interview 2].

93 *Ibid.*

The third member of the four, the OCC, lobbied on behalf of tens of thousands of business people throughout Ontario,[94] and it was represented in the class action consultations process by Robert Anderson. Anderson was general counsel at Procter & Gamble Inc,[95] and he collaborated with Stewart and Woolford on other consultations after the Attorney General's Advisory Committee had concluded its work.[96]

The fourth member of the Gang of Four was the CFIB, which represented small businesses across Canada[97] and regularly polled its members in order to formulate positions on which to lobby the government.[98] Its representative in the consultation process was Judith Andrew, director of Provincial Affairs and later director of Provincial Policy at the CFIB,[99] who had previously pursued a management career in the banking industry.[100] All of the Gang of Four representatives had worked together earlier that year, meeting weekly on government consultations involving revisions to

94 Website of the Ontario Chamber of Commerce, online: www.occ.ca.

95 Letter from Anderson to Cochrane (18 January 1990) in Box No B248633, above note 73 [Anderson Letter].

96 Jocelyn David, *The Public Consultations of the Competition Bureau: Building Bridges to Consumers* (Montréal: Option consommateurs, 2003) at 8, online: Option consommateurs http://option-consommateurs.org/documents/principal/fr/File/rapports/competition/concurr_eng_oc0603.pdf.

97 The CFIB currently represents 109,000 small business owners across Canada, although there is little information in the archival record regarding its status at the time of the class actions consultations: website of the Canadian Federation of Independent Business, online: www.cfib-fcei.ca/english/about-us/canada/178-about-us.html.

98 CFIB, Registration with Office of the Commissioner of Lobbying of Canada, online: OCLC https://lobbycanada.gc.ca/app/secure/ocl/lrs/do/vwRg;jsessionid=IpiW6Gs41UQJ9McNjQ6Yme5W.app-ocl-01?regId=500543&cno=4590. In January 1989, the CFIB conducted a poll of its members, asking "[s]hould the justice system in Canada allow for 'class action' law suits?" Of 142 respondents, 54 percent said "yes," while a further 18 percent was "undecided": CFIB Mandate, January 1989 [CFIB Poll], in Policy Development Division Counsel correspondence files, Class Actions—Cabinet submission, 1987–1990, CA226, RG 4-40, in Box No B501822, North York, Archives of Ontario [Box No B501822—Cabinet submission].

99 Ontario, Ministry of the Attorney General (MAG), Policy Development Division, *Report of the Attorney General's Advisory Committee on Class Action Reform* (Toronto: Ministry of the Attorney General, 1990) at 3 [Advisory Committee Report].

100 Government of Canada, Canada Employment Insurance Commission (CEIC), Commissioner for Employers: Judith Andrew, online: CEIC www.canada.ca/en/employment-social-development/corporate/portfolio/ei-commission/commisioner-employers.html.

the Ontario *Consumer Protection Act*.[101] They therefore had a close working relationship and went into the class action consultations as a fairly tightly knit unit on behalf of the business community.[102]

In advance of the 22 December meeting, Stewart forwarded to Cochrane a copy of the CMA brief that he had submitted to Roy McMurtry in 1983.[103] This brief illustrated some of the points of overlap and contention between the various parties at the consultation table. According to the brief, the CMA favoured "opt-in" class actions.[104] At the 22 December meeting, on the other hand, the CAC and the Advocates' Society made clear that they favoured the "opt-out" option.[105] The Gang of Four appears to have been willing to consider the opt-out route, provided it remained within the court's discretion, and provided that the court could narrow the class and concretize damage claims at an early stage.[106] There was also agreement between the parties regarding post-certification notice (in favour) and the role of the attorney general (no special role).[107]

Various options for cy-près distribution and costs were also discussed on 22 December, but no agreement was reached.[108] Nevertheless, the simple act of sitting around a table and talking to each other, as well as the points of tentative agreement that were reached, led to further understanding between the various factions that was to come in useful during the meetings of the Attorney General's Advisory Committee that would take place the following year: indeed, the same parties and, for the most

---

101 Woolford interview 2, above note 92. The revised Act was eventually passed in 1990: *Consumer Protection Act*, RSO 1990, c C.31.

102 Interestingly, however, Peter Woolford states that it was more of a "Gang of Three," with Judith Andrew remaining something of an outsider due to the "political" nature of the CFIB and the personality dynamics of the group: Woolford interview 2, above note 92.

103 Letter from Stewart to Cochrane (7 December 1988) in Box No B502275—Consultations, above note 35.

104 Meeting, 22 Dec 1988, above note 89 at 1, in Box No B502275—Consultations, *ibid.* For a definition of "opt-in" and "opt-out" class actions, see the appendix to this book.

105 Meeting, 22 Dec 1988, above note 89 at 1.

106 *Ibid* at 2.

107 *Ibid* at 3. Scott appears to have accepted this submission despite the fact that he had personally intervened in numerous actions throughout his tenure as attorney general: see the terms of reference for the Attorney General's Advisory Committee, below note 206, which explicitly state that there will be no special role for the attorney general in class actions. However, the attorney general would still be able to apply for intervenor status as in a normal action.

108 Meeting, 22 Dec 1988, *ibid* at 3–4.

part, the same people, were involved in both. This was an encouragement to Scott and Cochrane, as were concurrent developments in other provinces[109] and the rising tide of public opinion.[110]

True to form, however, Cochrane overestimated the goodwill that had been built up by these meetings. On 4 January 1989, he wrote to the various interest groups in order to confirm what was discussed at the December 1988 meeting, and stated that, if further consultations were not possible before the introduction of a bill, he would welcome their comments on any proposed draft legislation.[111] He observed shortly afterwards in a briefing note that the stakeholders were willing to talk about the shape of reform, instead of whether reform itself was desirable.[112] Cochrane enthused that "[t]his is the closest Ontario has ever come to having a concensus [*sic*] among major interest groups on what class action reform should look like,"[113] although he noted that the group had not come to a specific conclusion with respect to costs.[114] This last issue was to prove a major sticking point, both in getting the groups to the table for further negotiations, and in coming to any kind of eventual consensus.

Cochrane's over-optimism with regard to these consultations is in stark contrast to the stakeholders' perception of them. Just the day before

---

109 In January 1989, Alberta's Committee on Fair Dealing in Consumer Savings and Investments released its report titled *A Blueprint for Fairness* (Edmonton: Consumer and Corporate Affairs Alberta, 1989), online: https://archive.org/details/blueprint-forfairooalbe [*Blueprint*]. This report was a response to the collapse of various financial institutions in Alberta throughout the 1980s. It recommended the creation of a Consumer Savings and Investment Information Act, which would include a civil right of action on a class basis for breaches of the Act, with government allowed to participate (at 55). The report's recommendations were never implemented, although it did receive some coverage in the media: M Fisher, "Alberta Urged to Read the Riot Act to Reeling Financial Services Industry" *Globe and Mail* (17 January 1989) B1 and B4, in Box No B248501—Draft Policy Submission File #1, above note 42. Michael Cochrane also mentioned the *Blueprint* in his later Cabinet submission, although this was simply to note that the *Blueprint* had recommended class action reform for consumers: Cabinet submission, 20 March 1989, above note 85.

110 CFIB Poll, above note 98.

111 Letter from Cochrane to Class Action Consultation Members (4 January 1989) [Letter, 4 Jan 1989], in Policy Development Division Counsel correspondence files, Class Actions—Business Consultation, 1989, CA226, RG 4-40, in Box No B501822, North York, Archives of Ontario [Box No B501822—Business Consultation].

112 Briefing note, 6 Jan 1989, above note 89 at 1.

113 *Ibid* at 3.

114 *Ibid* at 2.

he wrote his briefing note, the Gang of Four met with the premier in regard to the Legislative Review Project and told him that they did not want class action legislation introduced.[115] Five days after that, Cochrane wrote to the "Class Action Consultation Members," again asking them to confirm their "consensus" on the basic structure of a class actions remedy.[116] In response, the Gang of Four voiced their discontent directly to Ian Scott,[117] stating that Cochrane was mistaken in assuming they were supportive of a new class action law.[118] They criticized the consultative process as unfocused and incapable of leading to workable legislation,[119] stating that it was premature because they saw no current need for class action reform.[120] While they expressed willingness to take part in appropriate consultations, as well as the possibility and need for consensus, they listed several questions that had to be answered as a condition of their participation. These largely related to the need or demand for class action legislation in Ontario given the alternatives available; whether the MAG was prepared to make it a priority relative to its numerous other initiatives; and the costs of the new law and by whom those costs would be borne.

The other stakeholders clearly shared the concerns of the Four. They wasted no time in writing to Cochrane to set the record straight, and

115 Letter from Gang of Four to Scott (15 March 1989) at 1, in Policy Development Division Counsel correspondence files, Class Proceedings—Correspondence, 1990, CA226, RG 4-40, in Box No B248501, North York, Archives of Ontario [Box No B248501—Correspondence].

116 Letter from Cochrane to Class Action Consultation Members (10 January 1989) in Box No B248633, above note 73. Cochrane's ULCC 1988 paper was enclosed with this letter, as was a "Class Action Consultation Paper" that he had authored, setting out the various viewpoints on class actions as well as the experience of other jurisdictions. The consultation paper concluded: "the case for reform has been made . . . . The real question for consideration is which model is best suited to the needs of litigants in Ontario" (at 12). The letter was sent to all the members of the future Attorney General's Advisory Committee, as well as Robert Prichard (the dean of the University of Toronto Faculty of Law), Jim O'Grady (of the Ontario Federation of Labour), Susan Ursel at Mary Cornish & Associates (for the Women's Legal Education and Action Fund (LEAF)), Jim Breithaupt (chair of the Ontario Law Reform Commission), and Raj Anand (chair of the Ontario Human Rights Commission and previously a colleague of Ian Scott's at the law firm of Cameron, Brewin & Scott).

117 Letter from Gang of Four to Scott (20 January 1989) at 2, in Box No B248633, above note 73.

118 *Ibid* at 4.

119 *Ibid.*

120 *Ibid* at 1.

their responses indicated that the consensus he sought was still a long way off. Janet Yale, general counsel at the CAC,[121] disagreed strongly that unsuccessful plaintiffs should pay the costs of notice (her recollection was that a public fund would pay the costs of notice up front, and a review of Cochrane's notes from the 22 December meeting shows her to be correct).[122] She further wrote that she had not agreed on the return of unclaimed damages awards to the defendant[123] (this issue was to be a major bone of contention that would almost prevent the formation of the Advisory Committee), and that, as Cochrane had previously observed, no-way costs were essential to encouraging meritorious class actions.[124]

On the same date, Andrew Roman of the Public Interest Advocacy Centre (who had not been able to attend the December 1988 meetings) wrote to Cochrane and Scott to question why such "non-issues" as opting-in/opting-out had been put before the consultation members as the focus for discussion.[125] Roman stated that there were only two issues to discuss: the economic barriers to class actions (costs) and the legal barriers (certification), both of which had to be removed to facilitate class actions.[126] He urged Cochrane not to tell Scott that there was a consensus on the basic structure of a class actions remedy.[127]

Similarly, JD Grenkie, the president of the Canadian Bar Association —Ontario (CBA), wrote to Scott on 21 January 1989, stating that his organization was pleased that class action reform was back on the ministry's agenda. The MAG saw the CBA as one of the natural representatives of the legal profession,[128] and had been in touch with it regarding class actions since the late 1970s when the *Competition Act* was being debated. As the CBA had noted in its previous submissions to the Ontario government, it wanted to make its views known before that government became committed to a policy on class actions, especially given the possibility that other provinces could follow Ontario's lead on the issue.[129] The CBA

121 Letter from Yale to Cochrane (13 January 1989) at 1 [Yale Letter], in Box No B502275—Consultations, above note 35.

122 Meeting, 22 Dec 1988, above note 89 at 3.

123 Yale Letter, above note 121 at 1; Letter, 4 Jan 1989, above note 111 at 4.

124 Yale Letter, above note 121 at 2.

125 Letter from Roman to Cochrane (13 January 1989) at 1–2 [Roman Letter], in Box No B501822—Business Consultation, above note 111.

126 Roman Letter, above note 125 at 2.

127 *Ibid.*

128 Interview of Michael Cochrane (26 September 2016) [Cochrane interview 3].

129 CBA/PIAC Report, above note 59 at 3.

was therefore eager to take part in the resurrected consultations. However, it disagreed strongly with Cochrane's indication that there was a consensus.[130] Grenkie also felt that further study and consultation was required before any bill could be prepared.

A couple of weeks later, and also in response to Cochrane's 10 January letter, Rino Stradiotto of the Advocates' Society (TAS) also expressed concern about the consultation process.[131] He stated that the views he had expressed to date were solely his own, and that the TAS view could only be obtained by having one of its committees review draft legislation and then report to the Board of Directors, who would then canvass the TAS membership before providing the MAG with input.[132] Again, the MAG was keen to obtain the views of TAS, seeing it as another strong representative of the legal profession[133] that had previously made submissions on the class actions issue.[134] TAS would eventually appoint a member to sit on the Advisory Committee on its behalf, in the form of its vice-president, Terrence O'Sullivan.[135]

The only point of consensus appeared to be that further consultations were required. There was certainly no general agreement that the case for reform had been made, as Cochrane seemed to imply. Nevertheless, Scott decided that the time for debate on the reform question was over: he wanted stakeholders to move on and discuss the shape of a class actions remedy that was going to become law whether they liked it or not.

130 Letter from CBA president to Scott (21 January 1989) in Box No B248633, above note 73.

131 Letter from Stradiotto to Cochrane (7 February 1989) in Box No B248633, *ibid.* Stradiotto was a well-known and widely respected insurance defence litigator.

132 Geoffrey Adair of the CBA wrote to Cochrane saying essentially the same thing: letter from Adair to Cochrane (18 January 1989) in Box No B501822—Business Consultation, above note 111.

133 Cochrane interview 3, above note 128.

134 Submission of the Advocates' Society on the Report of the Ontario Law Reform Commission on the Reform of Class Action Legislation in Ontario (February 1984), in Class Actions—Advisory Council to Advocates' Society Submission, in Ontario Law Reform Commission files, Class Actions—General 1976–1980, RG 4-66, in Box No B319671, North York, Archives of Ontario. The Advocates' Society also stated that the certification test should include a consideration of the merits (at 4 and 6).

135 O'Sullivan was a partner at McMillan Binch, which had previously submitted a brief to the Ontario Law Reform Commission that took a very restrictive view of class actions [McMillan Binch Report, above note 71]. O'Sullivan has stated that he did not agree with this brief and was not influenced by it in his work with the Advisory Committee: O'Sullivan interview, above note 63.

He replied to Grenkie and the Gang of Four by stating that a powerful case for reform had already been made by the Supreme Court's decision in *Naken*, the OLRC Report, and the recent experience in Quebec and the United States, as well as mass incidents such as the Mississauga train derailment.[136] He reiterated Cochrane's position that there was a general consensus on the direction of reform, although further consultations were likely to take place. It was time to "seriously apply [their] minds to the shape of the reform."[137]

The message from Scott was clear: you cannot stop reform from happening, but you can help determine its shape. This was even more alarming to the Gang of Four than Cochrane's 10 January letter. They told Scott that his personal support for class action reform contradicted the premier's statement to them that he did not want any initiatives that would encourage litigation.[138] They criticized Scott's reliance on the OLRC Report, saying that a number of groups (including the CMA) had been critical of its conclusions, which at any rate were now seven years old. Finally, they demanded answers to their previous questions before they would be willing to take part in further consultations.[139]

Scott and Cochrane faced an uphill battle in getting the various interest groups together to discuss the shape of reform, and there were issues that would prove contentious on all sides. It was the Gang of Four, however, who would be the most difficult to persuade. Simply to get them to the table, Scott and Cochrane made significant compromises that would have long-term effects for class actions in Ontario.

D. BUILDING THE ATTORNEY GENERAL'S ADVISORY COMMITTEE

Following the initial round of consultations, Cochrane prepared a Cabinet submission.[140] Although it was signed by Scott, it was based heavily upon Cochrane's earlier policy development submission of June 1986.

136 Letter from Scott to Grenkie (21 February 1989) [Letter, 21 Feb 1989] and letter from Scott to Gang of Four (23 February 1989) [Letter, 23 Feb 1989]; both letters are in Box No B248633, above note 73.

137 Letter, 21 Feb 1989, and Letter, 23 Feb 1989, *ibid*.

138 Letter from Gang of Four to Scott (15 March 1989) at 1, in Box No B248501—Correspondence, above note 115.

139 *Ibid* at 1.

140 Cabinet submission, 20 March 1989, above note 85.

This later version was updated with developments such as the ULCC conference of 1988 (where class action legislation was discussed, and the Ontario commissioners were asked to draft an act and a further report for discussion the following year) and the Law Society's approval of contingency fees, as well as the results of the initial consultations. Cochrane provided a characteristically overly optimistic description of these results, stating that there was widespread agreement that reform was needed,[141] and that consensus was possible along the lines recommended in the submission.[142] Of course, there was no agreement of the sort, and it was certainly not clear that a consensus was possible according to Cochrane's proposals.[143] The feedback from the consultations demonstrated that the following recommendations were particularly controversial:[144]

- Class actions should require court approval before they proceed (certification), with the certification test including a preliminary merits assessment;
- The traditional costs rules should be amended to provide:
  - » A no-way cost rule (because the role of normal costs rules in discouraging improperly brought actions would instead be performed by the threshold test at the certification stage);[145]
  - » A modified, court-supervised contingency fee arrangement; and
  - » Cost-sharing among successful class members, whereby fees and disbursements owed to class counsel would be deducted from any class recovery.[146]

The aim of Cochrane's submission was to secure Cabinet approval for consultation with the Attorney General's Advisory Committee, as well as the terms of reference for that consultation (as listed in the proposal and recommendation section).[147] Given that major stakeholders such as the Gang of Four had not yet agreed to further consultations, let alone the terms of that consultation, a Cabinet submission was almost certainly

141 *Ibid* at 1.

142 *Ibid* at 3.

143 *Ibid.*

144 *Ibid* at 4.

145 *Ibid* at 17.

146 Interestingly, the proposal and recommendation section makes no mention of the fund, even though it had been discussed during initial consultations.

147 The idea of negotiating the content of the legislation by way of a committee of stakeholders with predetermined terms of reference was an idea that Cochrane says he put to Scott: Cochrane interview 2, above note 18.

premature. Indeed, the next three months would see a number of changes that would render the proposal and recommendation section (and therefore the terms of reference) inaccurate.[148]

These changes were made primarily to get the Gang of Four onto the Attorney General's Advisory Committee. Scott and Cochrane met with the representatives of the Four on 23 March 1989.[149] At that meeting, Scott made it clear to the Four that class action reform was going to take place, in all likelihood according to the five terms of reference that he presented to the group[150] (these terms essentially mirrored the proposal and recommendation section of the 20 March Cabinet submission, and included the provision on no-way costs).[151] The draft terms of reference were left with the Gang of Four for their consideration.[152] A few days later, however, they made their response quite clear when the president and general manager of GM Canada, George Peapples, met with the premier.[153] He stated that the questions posed by the Gang of Four in its 20 January letter to Scott had not been answered, and that therefore, he could not support the introduction of class action legislation. He urged Peterson not to allow Scott to publicly announce his intention to introduce such legislation.[154]

148 Despite these changes, the Cabinet minutes of 21 June 1989 [Cabinet minutes], which approved consultation with the Attorney General's Advisory Committee, reproduced Cochrane's proposal and recommendation section verbatim: in minutes of Cabinet Meetings, 1989, 1/89 to 45/89, RG 75-14, in Box No B834837, North York, Archives of Ontario.

149 Class Action Consultation Advisory Committee: Agenda and Draft Terms of Reference (23 March 1989) [Terms of Reference, 23 March 1989]. This meeting is also referred to in a letter from Cochrane to the Gang of Four (28 March 1989) [Letter, 28 March 1989]. Both documents can be found in Policy Development Division Counsel correspondence files, Class Actions—Advisory Committee minutes and notes, 1989–1990, MGC, RG 4-40, in Box No B502275, North York, Archives of Ontario [Box No B502275—AGAC minutes].

150 Terms of Reference, 23 March 1989, above note 149; Letter, 28 March 1989, above note 149; Class Actions: Meeting with Business Interests (preparation note from Cochrane to Scott) (23 March 1989) at 2, in Box No B501822—Business Consultation, above note 111.

151 Cabinet submission, 20 March 1989, above note 85 at 3.

152 Letter, 28 March 1989, above note 149 at 3.

153 This meeting is mentioned in a subsequent letter from Peapples to the premier (31 March 1989), on which Scott was copied [Peapples Letter, 31 March 1989], in Box No B502275—AGAC minutes, above note 149.

154 Peapples Letter, 31 March 1989, above note 153 at 2.

The Gang of Four were clearly not in favour of the terms proposed by Scott and Cochrane on 23 March, or of the general idea of reform at all. Nevertheless, less than a week later, Scott was putting those very same terms before the Cabinet Committee on Justice (CCJ), stating that all parties to the consultations had generally endorsed them.[155] He further told the CCJ that he intended to announce, by the end of May, the introduction of class action legislation based on those terms, with a committee to advise on the drafting.

It is unclear quite what Scott and Cochrane were hoping to achieve in overstating the support for class actions in this way. They may well have been hoping that, by the end of May, the Gang of Four would be persuaded to come to the table, either because they genuinely wanted reform, or because events would otherwise move ahead without them (Scott's indication that he wanted to make a public announcement[156] may also have been intended to force the Four's hand). It does seem apparent that Scott was prepared to move forward with class action reform no matter what the outcome of the consultations.

The Gang of Four, however, continued to show their reluctance on the issue of reform. They wrote to Scott on 11 April 1989, expressing a willingness to continue discussions focused on a set of agreed-upon principles, such as the five terms of reference that were discussed at the 23 March meeting. However, they insisted that further consultations were necessary so they could better understand the potential impact of reform,[157] and that, before such consultations were completed, they were unable to publicly reject or support the introduction of a class actions remedy.[158] Cochrane still had a long way to go in achieving the consensus for which he was aiming.

---

155 Cabinet Committee on Justice, Report, Meeting No J6/89 (6 April 1989) at 7, in Box No B502275—AGAC minutes, above note 149. Cochrane was also present at the meeting, and at all the other Cabinet committee meetings at which class actions were discussed. This was very unusual: interview of John D Gregory, general counsel from 1985 to 2016 in the Justice Policy Development Branch, Ministry of the Attorney General (Ontario) (24 July 2017) [Gregory interview]. It is an indication of Cochrane's close working relationship with Scott and the central role he played in the development of the legislation.

156 Peapples Letter, 31 March 1989, above note 153 at 2.

157 Letter from Gang of Four to Scott (11 April 1989) in Box No B502275—AGAC minutes, above note 149.

158 *Ibid.*

He acknowledged as such in a briefing note drafted in response to the Gang of Four's 11 April letter.[159] The note details the requests made in that letter (no rejection or support of a class actions remedy; continuation of consultations with the MAG, with the five terms of reference as the possible focus; and suspension of other class action initiatives, such as those contained in the *Environmental Bill of Rights* and the ULCC model legislation), as well as what the MAG itself wanted (the Gang of Four's endorsement of the five principles, or at least their neutrality; and their participation in the Attorney General's Advisory Committee).[160] Cochrane then demonstrated the mediation skills that were to prove so useful in breaking the logjam on class action reform. He suggested a way out of the impasse: the MAG would announce class action reform along the lines of the five principles, with the Gang of Four joining the Advisory Committee; in return, the Four could remain neutral on the need for reform, and the ULCC draft legislation (as well as the class actions remedy in Bill 13—the *Environmental Bill of Rights*) would be suspended pending further consultations.[161] Cochrane drafted a press release incorporating this possible solution,[162] which is very close to what eventually happened—with one important exception. Later changes to the press release reflect changes to the five terms of reference, with the provision for no-way costs disappearing entirely.

In the meantime, the Gang of Four was not the only group that needed to be brought on side. Around the middle of April 1989, the environmental and consumer groups began expressing their frustration at the compromises that appeared to have been made. In particular, they wanted the content of the certification test and the issue of unallocated damages awards to be open for discussion (while the business groups wanted these issues to be determined in advance of any further consultations, and indeed felt they had a specific commitment from the attorney

159 It is unclear whether the briefing note was directed to Ewart, Scott, or both. Cochrane briefing note, April 1989 [Briefing note, April 1989], in Box No B502275—AGAC minutes, above note 149.

160 This is one of the earliest documents in which the term "Advisory Committee" is used. Briefing note, April 1989, *ibid.*

161 *Ibid.*

162 Draft press release dated 13 April 1989. Another draft of this press release, which is substantially similar but with minor wording changes, is dated 17 April 1989. Both documents can be found in Box No B502275—AGAC minutes, above note 149.

general in this regard).[163] This had created an impasse that prevented the announcement on reform and the beginning of consultations.[164]

Cochrane suggested a number of options to break this new impasse, including maintaining the commitment to the business interests and beginning consultations without the environmental groups, or conducting the consultations without any private groups at all (their views would instead be represented by the relevant ministries, such as the Ministry of the Environment). The preference was clearly to maintain the commitment to the business groups while giving a concession to the environmental groups. Cochrane recommended that Scott make one final offer to all the groups on a "take it or leave it" basis, stating that there would be a presumption that unclaimed damages awards would be returned to defendants, with the consultation group to discuss any exceptions to this rule (for example, in environmental cases). Consultations would begin immediately.[165] This is the option that the MAG ultimately pursued, and Cochrane communicated it to the consultation group on 18 April 1989.[166] Clearly there was some urgency to the matter, because the Gang of Four informed Cochrane immediately that they would have a response to him by 21 April.[167]

Once again, however, Scott and Cochrane overplayed their hand. Before any of the consultation groups had a chance to respond to the 18 April letter, the attorney general (with Cochrane) appeared before the Cabinet Committee on Economic Policy (CCEP) to discuss the

163 Michael G Cochrane, "Class Actions Consultation—Options" [Cochrane, "Options"], in Box No B502275—AGAC minutes, *ibid*. This is undated, but it appears to have been written in mid-April 1989 because it mentions the suspension of the class actions remedies in the *Environmental Bill of Rights* and the ULCC draft legislation, which occurred at the beginning of April. Consumer groups also did not agree to the return of unclaimed monies to the defendants, as evidenced by Janet Yale's letter to Cochrane, above note 121 at 1.

164 Cochrane, "Options," above note 163. It is not entirely clear when the attorney general was supposed to have made the commitment to the business groups on the content of the certification test and undistributed damages awards; there is no other documentation of this in the archival record.

165 *Ibid* at 2.

166 This letter does not appear to be in the archival record, but is mentioned in a letter from the Gang of Four to Premier Peterson, dated 21 April 1989 [Peterson Letter, 21 April 1989], in Box No B502275—AGAC minutes, above note 149.

167 Peterson Letter, 21 April 1989, above note 166 at 1.

Cabinet submission of 20 March 1989.[168] Scott announced before the Cabinet Committee that the Gang of Four would co-operate with a public announcement on new class action legislation.[169] On the basis of Scott's representations, the CCEP agreed to recommend to Cabinet (concurrently with the CCJ Report of 6 April 1989)[170] that class actions should be brought about in Ontario, in the manner outlined in the Cabinet submission of 20 March and the five principles put to the Gang of Four on 23 March (including the provision for no-way costs).[171]

Of course, the Gang of Four had never indicated that they would co-operate with an announcement on class action reform. The Four heard about Scott's announcement before the CCEP and immediately wrote to Premier Peterson, copying all other Cabinet ministers (presumably to draw their attention to the inaccuracy of Scott's representations to them). They expressed their "dismay" at this recent development,[172] and tersely stated that Scott should have waited for their response to Cochrane's 18 April letter.[173] Frustrated with Scott's attempts to force them into his consultation process, they reiterated their previous reservations about class action reform. They flatly denied that they supported the establishment of a process to develop class action legislation, that their negotiations with Scott had been concluded, or that they were prepared to publicly support the introduction of legislation.[174]

The Four further objected to Scott's actions and his proposed consultation process as a whole, stating that it was highly unusual. Technically, there was no formalized consultation process for legislation in Ontario; the process was, and still is today, within the discretion of the minister and subject to Cabinet approval.[175] Nevertheless, the Four were accustomed to pre-legislative consultation processes such as the one they were

168 Cabinet Committee on Economic Policy, Report, Meeting No E7/89, 20 April 1989 [CCEP, 20 April 1989], in Box No B502275—AGAC minutes, above note 149; Cabinet submission, 20 March 1989, above note 85.

169 CCEP, 20 April 1989, above note 168 at 2.

170 Cabinet Committee on Justice, Report, Meeting No J6/89, 6 April 1989, in Box No B502275—AGAC minutes, above note 149.

171 CCEP, 20 April 1989, above note 168 at 2–3.

172 Peterson Letter, 21 April 1989, above note 166.

173 *Ibid* at 1.

174 *Ibid.*

175 Legislative Research Service, *How an Ontario Bill Becomes Law: A Guide for Legislators and the Public* (Government of Ontario: Legislative Assembly of Ontario, 2011) at 8 and 12, online: www.ola.org/sites/default/files/common/how-bills-become-law-en.pdf.

involved in with the Ministry of Consumer and Commercial Relations, regarding the Legislative Review Project (LRP),[176] whereby groups would meet and discuss, sometimes around pre-agreed terms of reference. The Four pointed out that there was no precedent for Scott's proposed consultation process,[177] which involved the following:

- An up-front public announcement that reform would be taking place;
- The public announcement would name a group of organizations which would be discussing the shape of reform; and
- The announcement would include the key terms of reference, not up for negotiation, around which discussions would focus.[178]

Such a process would not allow the Four to negotiate on the subject of reform itself, and would leave them with limited flexibility on the shape of that reform, having made a public commitment that would imply their support for a number of highly contentious issues that had not yet been resolved. They would be unable publicly to criticize a bill that would result from any process in which they had taken part. In other words, they would be backed into a corner. The Four described this approach as "totally unreasonable."[179]

Nevertheless, as the Gang of Four had previously stated, they were willing to continue discussions with various interested groups (just as they were doing with the LRP) and senior MAG staff, on the need for class action reform in Ontario, provided there would be no public announcement.[180] Following those discussions, if the participants agreed, then further consultations would take place around key terms of reference. The Gang of Four stated that some of the terms of reference put forward by Scott and Cochrane at their meeting on 23 March (other than the certification requirement and no special role for the attorney general) "would require some amendment in order for us to agree to begin a consultative process."[181]

The Four and the MAG were still quite far apart. However, on 25 April 1989, the two parties met. Although there are no minutes of this meeting, the correspondence exchanged by the parties afterwards shows

---

176 Peterson Letter, 21 April 1989, above note 166 at 2.

177 *Ibid.*

178 *Ibid.*

179 *Ibid.* This was, of course, Scott's intention in pursuing a consensus for reform.

180 *Ibid.*

181 *Ibid.*

that significant concessions were made on both sides.[182] Scott and Cochrane got their public announcement that consultations would take place around certain key terms of reference. However, those key terms changed from those contained in the Cabinet submission of 20 March and the five principles put to the Gang of Four on 23 March. The major concession made by Scott and Cochrane to the business interests was on the issue of costs.

The five terms of reference previously put to the Four, and approved by the CCEP and CCJ, stated that the ordinary rules with respect to costs would be replaced with a no-way costs rule.[183] However, in a letter to Scott on 11 May 1989, the Gang of Four refused to allow the issue of costs to be included in the terms of reference, stating that the attorney general's public announcements on class actions should be silent on the issue.[184] The Four strongly reiterated their position that existing costs rules should be retained for class actions, as no-way costs rules would encourage frivolous suits.[185] Dropping the issue of costs from the terms of reference was a significant concession by the MAG. Without a public acknowledgement that any class actions remedy would include a no-way costs rule, the Attorney General's Advisory Committee was free to come to any conclusion it wished. This would be an issue on which the business interests would eventually win, and having it removed from the terms of reference was a crucial first step.

The Four also made an important suggestion as to what the consultation process would look like. Having protested in their 21 April letter that there was no precedent for Scott's consulting mechanism, the Four made a suggestion of their own that was also very unusual. They proposed that if the participants reached a consensus, then they should take

182 Letter from Gang of Four to Scott (11 May 1989) [Scott Letter, 11 May 1989], in Box No B502275—AGAC minutes, above note 149.

183 Terms of Reference, 23 March 1989, above note 149; Cabinet submission, 20 March 1989, above note 85.

184 Scott Letter, 11 May 1989, above note 182 at 2. In fact, an earlier draft of this press release, dated 27 April 1989, explicitly states that "[t]he remedy will include . . . existing cost rules" (draft press release from Gang of Four to Scott, 27 April 1989). Given that this draft press release was found in Cochrane's papers (in Box No B502275—AGAC minutes, above note 149), it is safe to assume that the Four had sent the press release to Cochrane for his comments, and Cochrane had taken out the provision on existing costs rules, recommending, as a middle way, that the press release remain silent on the issue.

185 Scott Letter, 11 May 1989, above note 182 at 6–8.

part in the drafting of the legislation.[186] It was unusual for participants in pre-legislative consultations to be actively involved in the drafting of any eventual bill. Normally, legislative counsel would draft the bill, using the Advisory Committee report as only one of many guidance documents.[187] The Four were asking for a level of control over the drafting process that was virtually unprecedented. They used Scott's desire for consensus to secure that level of control—if they gave Scott his consensus, they wanted to make sure that it would be reflected in the legislation.

While the Gang of Four was meeting with the ministry to discuss its terms for consultation, Cochrane was also trying to keep the consumer and environmental groups happy. On 1 May 1989, Cochrane wrote to Rollie Thompson, chair of the Regulated Industries Program at the Consumers' Association of Canada, to finalize the terms of reference with him.[188] These terms contained no mention of costs—presumably the result of Scott and Cochrane's meeting with the Gang of Four a few days prior. This proved less of a concern for the CAC than the issues of a high bar at certification and the return of undistributed damages awards to defendants. Although Thompson eventually signed off on the finalized press release and terms of reference,[189] he implied that the CAC's "serious misgivings" about those issues could lead it to leave the committee altogether.[190]

---

186 *Ibid* at 3.

187 Memo from Donald Revell, chief legislative counsel, to Ewart (27 February 1990) [Revell Memo], in Policy Development Division Counsel Correspondence Files, Class Actions—Drafting Instructions, 1989–1990, MGC, RG 4-40, in Box No B248633, North York, Archives of Ontario [Box No B248633—Drafting Instructions].

188 Letter from Cochrane to Thompson (1 May 1989) in Box No B502275—AGAC minutes, above note 149. In the end, Thompson was unable to sit on the Attorney General's Advisory Committee due to cuts to CAC funding. In July 1989, a few days before the first meeting of the committee, the CAC asked Edward Belobaba to represent them. Belobaba had worked with Ian Scott when he was in private practice at Cameron, Brewin & Scott (which in 1983 merged into Gowling, Strathy & Henderson), the firm to which Scott returned after retiring from the legislature in 1992. The two appeared on several cases together, including *Bhinder v Canadian National Railway Co*, [1985] 2 SCR 561; *Giouroukos v Cadillac Fairview Corp*, [1986] 2 SCR 707, leave information online: www.scc-csc.ca/case-dossier/info/dock-regi-eng.aspx?cas=18182; and *Crocker v Sundance Northwest Resorts Ltd*, 1985 CanLII 2182 (Ont CA).

189 Letter from Scott to Attorney General's Advisory Committee (12 May 1989) in Box No B502275—AGAC minutes, above note 149.

190 Letter from Thompson to Scott (17 May 1989) in Box No B502275—AGAC minutes, *ibid*.

The representatives of the environmental groups had similar concerns. The Canadian Environmental Law Association (CELA), which Scott had acted for in several cases,[191] was represented by its in-house counsel Richard Lindgren. Energy Probe was represented by Toronto lawyer David Poch, who had worked with Scott on a prior case involving intervenor funding.[192] While CELA accepted Scott's invitation to take part in the Attorney General's Advisory Committee, it did so only on certain conditions—including that certification must be discussed in the most general terms possible, and that the issue of unallocated funds was to be left open for discussion. CELA also expressed concern about costs and funding, saying that both issues should be open for discussion by the Attorney General's Advisory Committee.[193]

However, it was the issue of the return of undistributed damage awards to the defendants that was the deal breaker for the environmental groups, because they did not want to see unclaimed damages awards (a fairly likely scenario in the environmental context, where damages were often widespread but difficult to document, or awards too small to bother claiming) revert to the defendants, thereby unjustly enriching them after they had already been found liable.[194] The dispute on this point had been threatening the entire idea of the Attorney General's Advisory Committee since at least early April 1989.[195] On 5 May 1989, Cochrane again met with CELA and Energy Probe representatives to try to break the impasse.[196] He confirmed that the only real sticking point for them was the return of undistributed damages awards.[197] Cochrane reiterated that the business groups felt they had a commitment from the attorney general on this

191 *Re Canadian Environmental Law Association et al and Pitura*, 1981 CanLII 1679 (Ont CA); *Re Regional Municipality of Hamilton-Wentworth and Hamilton-Wentworth Save the Valley Committee, Inc et al*, 1985 CanLII 1957 (Ont Div Ct) [*Save the Valley*].

192 *Save the Valley*, *ibid*. Interestingly, Andrew Roman (who represented the Canadian Bar Association on the Attorney General's Advisory Committee) was counsel for the Ontario Energy Board on this case.

193 Memo from Moffet (executive assistant to Ian Scott) to Ewart (2 May 1989); motion of the CELA Board of Directors, 2 May 1989. Both documents are in Box No B502275—AGAC minutes, above note 149.

194 Letter from Poch to Cochrane (8 May 1989) [Poch Letter, 8 May 1989], in Box No B502275—AGAC minutes, above note 149.

195 Cochrane, "Options," above note 163.

196 This meeting is documented in a letter from Cochrane to the CELA/Energy Probe representatives (8 May 1989) [CELA Letter], in Box No B502275—AGAC minutes, above note 149.

197 CELA Letter, *ibid* at 1.

point and were unlikely to back down.[198] Cochrane, however, could not persuade the environmental groups to change their position. On 8 May, Poch wrote to Cochrane to inform him that they had already conceded that certification would be part of any class actions remedy; they were unwilling to back down on the issue of unclaimed damages.[199] At some point, Cochrane must have taken this issue back to the Gang of Four to see if they were willing to compromise in any way. Fortunately, they were willing to consider, for environmental cases, an exception to the principle of returning unclaimed damages awards to the defendants.[200] The consultation process was back on track.

On 12 May 1989, Scott wrote to the members of what was to become the Attorney General's Advisory Committee: the Canadian Federation of Independent Business, the Canadian Manufacturers' Association, the Retail Council of Canada, the Ontario Chamber of Commerce,[201] the Consumers' Association of Canada, the Canadian Environmental Law Association, the Advocates' Society, the Canadian Bar Association, Energy Probe, and the Insurance Bureau of Canada. It is unclear why women's groups such as the Legal Education and Action Fund (LEAF) were not invited to sit on the committee. Cochrane had written to numerous women's groups in March 1989, asking them for their opinions on the use of a potential class actions remedy for advancing the rights of women.[202] Naomi Alboim, the assistant deputy minister of the Ontario Women's Directorate, wrote to Deputy Attorney General Richard Chaloner around the same time, stating that she was in favour of no-way costs as this would ensure that women (who generally had a lower income) could access class actions on the same footing as men.[203] However, the issue of costs was quietly dropped from the terms of reference just over a month later.

198 *Ibid* at 1–2.

199 Poch Letter, 8 May 1989, above note 194.

200 Scott Letter, 11 May 1989, above note 182 at 2.

201 As noted previously, these four organizations were colloquially referred to at Queen's Park as the "Gang of Four."

202 Letters from Cochrane to Sherene Razack (professor at University of Toronto), Mary Lou Fassell (counsel for the Barbra Schlifer Clinic, a women's legal clinic), and Joan Bercovitch (legal policy analyst at the Status of Women Canada) (16 March 1989), in Policy Development Division Counsel Correspondence Files, Class Actions—Women's Interests, 1987–1989, CA226, RG 4-40, in Box No B248501, North York, Archives of Ontario.

203 Letter from Naomi Alboim, assistant deputy minister, Ontario Women's Directorate, to Richard Chaloner (29 March 1989) in Box No B501822—Cabinet submission, above note 98.

A member of the committee later reported that they had been receiving calls from women's groups who felt their interests were not represented. In response, Cochrane noted that he had offered to meet with members of LEAF "but nothing had come of it."[204] Whether it was inertia on the part of women's groups, skepticism on their part that they would be truly heard, or the committee's unwillingness to include them as full members, is unknown. It may be that women's groups were not invited because the business interests had asked Scott in their 11 May 1989 letter that the committee be restricted to the ten organizations listed above, "particularly as [the committee] already represents a diversity of interests."[205] It seems that many women later disagreed that the committee was truly that diverse.

In writing to the members of the committee, Scott confirmed that "a consensus has been reached concerning the basic parameters of the consultation" and that Cochrane was to chair the group.[206] The terms of reference listed in Scott's letter and in the enclosed draft press release reflected the outcome of months of negotiation between the ministry and the various groups:

1) The remedy was to have a structured certification procedure, although the precise content of that procedure (such as a preliminary consideration of the merits of the case) was open for discussion.
2) The remedy would be an "opt-out" model whereby class members who did not opt out of the action would be automatically bound by it.
3) Notice would be given after certification, unless the court otherwise ordered.
4) There would be a controlled contingency fee arrangement.
5) There would be no special role for the attorney general.
6) Undistributed damage awards would be returned to defendants, with the possible exception of environmental cases.
7) The remedy should treat plaintiffs and defendants in a fair and equitable manner, and impose no unnecessary burdens on the courts.[207]

---

204 Minutes of the Attorney General's Advisory Committee on Class Action Reform (23 November 1989) at 16 [AGAC minutes, 23 Nov 1989], in Box No B502275—AGAC minutes, above note 149.

205 Scott Letter, 11 May 1989, above note 182 at 9; Cochrane interview 1, above note 9.

206 Letter from Scott to Attorney General's Advisory Committee (AGAC) (12 May 1989) at 1 [Scott Letter, 12 May 1989], in Box No B502275—AGAC minutes, above note 149.

207 Scott Letter, 12 May 1989, *ibid* at 2.

Although this list contained some important concessions from the business groups (such as the use of contingency fees and the opt-out model), those groups also prevailed on important issues such as a certification test, no special role for the attorney general, and the return of undistributed damages awards. In the ensuing discussions of the Attorney General's Advisory Committee and the subsequent hammering out of the legislation, it was the voice of the Gang of Four that was to prevail over that of the consumer and environmental groups.

The attorney general's 12 May letter stated that any participant was free to leave the consultation if dissatisfied with the process.[208] However, at some point it was made clear to the members of the committee that their conclusions had to be unanimous in order for their recommendations to be carried forward into legislation.[209] As if to emphasize the requirement for consensus, Scott asked the prospective members of his Advisory Committee for their sign-off to indicate their acceptance of the terms of reference and the draft press release.[210] Most of the committee members signed off without substantive comment.[211] However, as noted above, the CAC signed off on the terms of reference and press release, while indicating its "serious misgivings" on the issues of a high bar at certification and the return of undistributed damages awards to defendants in non-environmental cases.[212] Even after agreement on the terms of reference, unanimity between the committee members seemed a long way off.

None of these issues were reflected in the Cabinet minute of 21 June 1989 that authorized the attorney general to continue consultations on the subject of class action reform.[213] That minute contained exactly the same terms of reference that had been listed in Cochrane's 20 March Cabinet submission. It had not been amended to reflect the agreements that had since been reached between the parties—there was no mention in the Cabinet minute of the return of undistributed damages awards. The Cabinet minute was specific on the elements of the certification

208 *Ibid* at 3.

209 Cochrane interview 1, above note 9; AC member interview, above note 8.

210 Scott Letter, 12 May 1989, above note 206 at 4.

211 For example, Rino Stradiotto of the Advocates' Society simply informed Scott that the TAS representative on the committee would be its vice-president, Terrence O'Sullivan of McMillan Binch. Letter from Stradiotto to Scott (15 May 1989) in Box No B502275—AGAC minutes, above note 149.

212 Letter from Thompson to Scott (17 May 1989) in Box No B502275—AGAC minutes, *ibid*.

213 Cabinet minutes, above note 148, signed by RD Carman, secretary of the Cabinet.

test (including a preliminary merits assessment), while the agreement between the parties was clearly to keep the elements of certification open for discussion.[214] There was no indication in the Cabinet minute that other class action initiatives, such as that contained in the ULCC model legislation, would be suspended.[215] Finally, on the issue of costs, the parties had agreed to publicly remain silent on that issue.[216] In the minute, however, Cabinet explicitly stated that the ordinary rules with respect to costs should be replaced with a no-way costs rule.[217] The instructions from Cabinet were directly at odds with the agreements the attorney general had made with the various interest groups with whom he had consulted. In announcing the establishment of the Attorney General's Advisory Committee on 29 June 1989, along with its terms of reference, Scott was acting outside the bounds of his Cabinet mandate.

The Cabinet minute was also much more equivocal on the manner in which the new remedy would be implemented. Whereas Cochrane's 20 March submission stated that the new class actions remedy should be provided by statute,[218] the Cabinet simply agreed that, once the consultations were concluded, the report should be brought forward for approval and further consideration as to how to incorporate it in statutory form.[219] The Cabinet minute contained no agreement that legislation would be introduced following the completion of the report of the Attorney General's Advisory Committee.

Scott's statement to the legislature and in the press on 29 June that a consultation process was about to take place, and that the government would introduce legislation at the end of that process,[220] was, therefore, another step too far.[221] The secretary of the Cabinet, Robert Carman,

---

214 Scott Letter, 12 May 1989, above note 206 at 2.

215 *Ibid* at 3.

216 Scott Letter, 11 May 1989, above note 182 at 8. See also Ministry of the Attorney General, News Release, "Attorney General Announces Class Action Reform" (29 June 1989) [News Release, 29 June 1989], which contains no mention of costs rules: in Box No B248633—Cochrane articles, above note 45.

217 Cabinet minutes, above note 148 at 1–2.

218 Cabinet submission, 20 March 1989, above note 85 at 3.

219 Cabinet minutes, above note 148 at 3.

220 News Release, 29 June 1989, above note 216. See also Ontario, Legislative Assembly, *Official Report of Debates (Hansard)*, 34th Parl, 2nd Sess (29 June 1989) (Ian Scott), online: http://hansardindex.ontla.on.ca/hansardeissue/34-2/l034.htm.

221 Michael Cochrane made the same overstep in Cochrane, "Breakthrough," above note 45, which appears to have been written shortly after Scott's statement to the legislature.

pointed out this inconsistency to Richard Chaloner, the deputy attorney general. Carman stated that the Cabinet minute deliberately did not include the recommendation of the CCJ that a new comprehensive class actions remedy be implemented by statute, as the minute "reflects the different views held respecting the introduction of class action legislation."[222] Scott's announcement that legislation would be introduced therefore went beyond the bounds of the Cabinet minute.[223]

Carman urged Chaloner to ensure that, once the Attorney General's Advisory Committee had completed its work, its report should be discussed in the CCJ and the Cabinet for approval before proceeding to the Cabinet Committee on Legislation.[224] In other words, any report produced by the Advisory Committee could not immediately go to legislative counsel for drafting a bill. It would have to go through a second round of Cabinet approval in order to ensure that the report complied with the Cabinet's instructions (as reflected in the minute of 21 June 1989), and to determine whether, and in what form, the provincial government wanted to introduce a draft bill.

This is what eventually happened,[225] but thanks to the work of Scott and Cochrane who wanted to see the Advisory Committee's Report changed as little as possible prior to introduction as a draft bill, the process was largely a formality. In the meantime, Chaloner defended Scott's actions by stating that the only way the MAG could secure the support of the business groups was by promising that class actions would only be available through one comprehensive statute—so that in that regard, there would be nothing to fear from potential consumer or environmental legislation.[226] This was clearly not anticipated by the Cabinet minute. However, Chaloner assured Carman that any draft legislation

222 Memorandum from Carman to Chaloner (25 July 1989) at 1 [Carman Memo], in Policy Development Division Counsel correspondence files, Class Proceedings Cabinet minutes & submissions 1990, 1989–1990, MGC, RG 4-40, in Box No B248501, North York, Archives of Ontario [Box No B248501—Cabinet minutes].

223 Carman Memo, *ibid* at 2.

224 *Ibid* at 2.

225 See "Briefing Note: Class Action Reform," drafted by Cochrane at the end of October 1989, in Box No B501822—Briefing Note, above note 58. This note acknowledged that the attorney general had to bring the AGAC Report back before Cabinet for specific authorization to draft legislation (at 1).

226 Memorandum from Chaloner to Carman (22 August 1989) at 2, in Box No B248501—Cabinet minutes, above note 222.

would be put to the appropriate Cabinet committees and the Cabinet for review.

While this is not quite what Carman was looking for, he seems to have been placated by Chaloner's assurances because the two men do not appear to have corresponded further on the subject. The matter was not taken further because of Scott's relationship with Premier Peterson. Because Cabinet minutes are simply the decision of the Cabinet and do not have any legal status, any overstep such as this would be for the Cabinet to sanction, and no sanctions would have occurred without the premier's say-so.[227] Peterson trusted Scott; although he was unaware that Scott had stepped outside his Cabinet mandate, he would not have imposed sanctions even if he had known.[228] As noted below, the Cabinet does not even seem to have noticed. In this way, Scott's influence and sleights of hand enabled him to surreptitiously change the Advisory Committee's terms of reference.

The work of the Attorney General's Advisory Committee on Class Action Reform therefore proceeded as planned, with Cochrane as chair. Informally at least, the mandate of the committee was to come up with a unanimous report regarding the shape of a class actions remedy for Ontario, which had to comply with the terms of reference to which the committee members had agreed.[229] In order to secure this unanimity, significant concessions would be made affecting class actions in Ontario for decades to come.

E. THE REPORT OF THE ATTORNEY GENERAL'S ADVISORY COMMITTEE

The committee met for the first time on 18 July 1989. It met approximately every two to three weeks up to December 1989, when it began finalizing its report, and then on numerous occasions thereafter. The committee members spent much of their time together hammering out the relatively non-controversial parts of an Act that had been drafted by Michael Cochrane and the MAG staff.[230] The discussions did not revolve around

227 Gregory interview, above note 155.

228 Peterson interview, above note 4.

229 Cochrane interview 1, above note 9; AC Member interview, above note 8.

230 Minutes of the Attorney General's Advisory Committee on Class Action Reform (AGAC) (7 September 1989) at 11 [AGAC minutes, 7 Sept 1989]; AC Member interview, above note 8. Andrew Roman's draft Act was also considered by the committee.

whether class action reform was desirable—the terms of reference made clear that such reform would definitely take place—but its shape. As a result, there was little if any discussion of developments that had swayed government and public opinion towards the enactment of reform over the past decade, such as the Mississauga train derailment and other events that gave rise to mass claims.[231] The focus instead was on precedents in other jurisdictions (particularly Quebec), the briefs submitted to the government by various committee members, and how much the Ontario bill should borrow from those sources.

There were several points of sharp disagreement between the committee members, largely on the issues of costs and certification.[232] With regard to both issues, CBA representative Andrew Roman[233] had certain materials circulated a few days after the initial meeting. These included his draft bill prepared for Consumer and Corporate Affairs Canada (which did not include a certification requirement), and the joint CBA/PIAC brief (which argued for a departure from the traditional costs rules).[234] On the other side of the debate, the law firm of McMillan Binch submitted a memo to the committee articulating the business community's negative perception of the current government and its pursuit of "social

While these draft acts are not contained in the archival record, they are likely based on Cochrane and Roman's papers from the 1988 Uniform Law Conference of Canada (ULCC) 1988 conference, "Proceedings of the Seventieth Annual Meeting" (Toronto, Ontario, August 1988), online: www.ulcc.ca/images/stories/Past_Proceedings_PDF/1988ULCC0070.pdf; Cochrane's ULCC paper had been circulated as "Class Action Reform in Ontario: A Breakthrough" to committee members before they met (above note 45).

231 Cochrane interview 3, above note 128; email correspondence with Advisory Committee member (26 September 2016); Woolford interview 2, above note 92. Other events giving rise to potential mass claims included the investment scandals that plagued the financial industry throughout the 1980s, such as those involving the Crown, Seaway, and Greymac trusts. Surprisingly, given the pervasiveness of securities class actions for misrepresentation in Ontario today, the committee members interviewed state that these scandals were not even mentioned in their discussions.

232 Although all the minutes of the July–December 1989 meetings (other than the first meeting) are in the archival record, only those minutes discussing the more controversial points will be referred to.

233 Roman was not only general counsel to the PIAC, but he had also been chair of the CBA's Special Committee on Class Actions, which had produced the CBA/PIAC Report, above note 59 at 4.

234 Letters from Roman to Cochrane, with enclosures (21 July 1989 and 9 August 1989). Both these letters can be found in Box No B501822—Business Consultation, above note 111.

advance."[235] The memo also argued against any departure from traditional costs rules.[236] As in the United States, the philosophical divide was between those who saw class actions as advancing social good (such as stronger consumer and environmental rights), and those who saw class actions as merely a procedural device that should not depart from established rules of court.[237] Clearly, the two sides were still very much divided on crucial issues.

The initial meeting appears to have consisted of a general discussion of the terms of reference, as well as setting an agenda for the remainder of the committee's work.[238] However, this work had barely begun when an article in the *Financial Post* threatened to derail the participation of the business groups. The 28 August article implied that the business interests were in support of a class actions remedy, an impression that the Gang of Four had tried very hard to avoid giving.[239] Norm Stewart, on behalf of the CMA and the Gang of Four, clearly believed that Cochrane had something to do with the article, because he wrote to him later that week to express his discontent at what he perceived as "posturing" in the media.[240] He was disturbed to see that Cochrane himself, on behalf of the minister, believed that "the goal is to write legislation that is less restrictive than that of Quebec."[241] He stated

235 Discussion Memo re: Ontario Class Action Consultative Process (16 August 1989) at 1 [McMillan Binch Memo], in Box No B501822—Business Consultation, above note 111. The memo was written by WA Macdonald and JW Rowley, who had written an article in 1984 criticizing the OLRC Report, while recommending conservative reforms to the current Rules to permit certain class actions: WA Macdonald & JW Rowley, "Ontario Class Action Reform: Business and Justice System Impacts—A Comment" (1984) 9 *Canadian Business Law Journal* 351.

236 McMillan Binch Memo, above note 235 at 6.

237 David Marcus, "The History of the Modern Class Action, Part I: *Sturm und Drang*, 1953–1980" (2013) 90 *Washington University Law Review* 587 at 590–96 [Marcus].

238 Letter from Cochrane to AGAC members (13 July 1989) in Box No B502275—AGAC minutes, above note 149. The archival record appears to contain no minutes of this initial meeting.

239 A Willis, "Businesses, Public Welcome Ontario Move to Class Action" *Financial Post* (28 August 1989) [Willis, "Businesses"], in Policy Development Division Counsel Correspondence Files, Class Actions—Media 1990, 1989–1990, CA226, RG 4-40, in Box No B248501, North York, Archives of Ontario [Box No B248501—Media]. The article identified Cochrane as "Scott's policy director." Although Doug Ewart was actually the director of the Policy Development Division, this epithet may have been a more accurate reflection of Cochrane's role with regard to class actions.

240 Letter from Stewart to Cochrane (1 September 1989) at 1 [Stewart Letter, 1 Sept 1989], in Box No B502275—AGAC minutes, above note 149.

241 Stewart Letter, 1 Sept 1989, *ibid.* See also Willis, "Businesses," above note 239.

that the article made it very difficult to approach the consultations with an open mind, and that it could cause business interests to "unnecessarily fear that we are about to create a litigation monster."[242] Stewart therefore asked that committee participants restrict their contact with the media.[243] This was to be the first in a long series of letters from Stewart to Cochrane, in which the former (as the voice of the Gang of Four) persistently attempted to control the outcome of the committee's deliberations.

These attempts were largely successful, with Cochrane paying more heed to Stewart's input than perhaps any other member of the committee. This is demonstrated in the fact that, just a few weeks after Stewart's letter, the attorney general personally addressed the CMA regarding class actions. This appears to be the only member organization of the Advisory Committee that Scott personally addressed. Scott attempted to put CMA members' minds at ease, not about class action reform as a whole or even certain elements of it, but about the consultation process itself.[244] Not only did he attempt to persuade the CMA that the consultation process was beneficial to them because it ensured their interests were accommodated, but that, in taking part, they were helping to design a remedy that in reality they had not yet even agreed to, at least publicly.[245] It was the persuasive genius of Scott to thank the CMA for support it had not yet given. The speech, as an attempt to keep the CMA in the consultation process and reassure other business interests, appears to have been successful as the business groups remained on the Advisory Committee.

Those groups continued to be influential in the committee's deliberations. For example, at the committee's second meeting on 7 September, Stewart's concerns with the media were the first issue to be raised by Cochrane, with the latter concluding that all future committee meetings

242 Stewart Letter, 1 Sept 1989, above note 240 at 1–2.

243 *Ibid* at 2. Stewart's reference to the non-public nature of the LRP discussions with the Ministry of Consumer and Commercial Relations implied that he wished the same for the committee.

244 "Notes for Remarks by the Honourable Ian Scott, Attorney General" (Delivered at the Luncheon Meeting of the Canadian Manufacturers' Association, 19 September 1989) at 2, speeches and notes for remarks by Ian Scott, F 4339-1, in Box No B222612, North York, Archives of Ontario.

245 *Ibid* at 8–9. Even as late as November 1989, members of the Attorney General's Advisory Committee were asking Cochrane whether they were discussing wholesale reform by way of legislation, or simply through an amendment to the Rules. Cochrane said he would get back to them on that point, but his response is not noted in the remaining minutes: minutes of AGAC (8 November 1989) at 1–2 [AGAC minutes, 8 Nov 1989], in Box No B502275—AGAC minutes, above note 149.

would be confidential.[246] This point was later taken even further, when the committee decided that minutes would no longer be attributable to individual members.[247]

However, one of the most controversial issues among the committee members was costs, on which the committee was more divided than any other issue.[248] It was a consumer advocate who first articulated a possible compromise on this point. At their second meeting, the committee discussed certification, with business interests advocating a stringent test and members such as Andrew Roman (for the CBA) wanting a simpler and less onerous test.[249] In the middle of this discussion, Edward Belobaba, for the Consumers' Association of Canada, stated that he too would prefer less onerous certification requirements.[250] He then articulated the link between certification and costs:

> E.B. added that if Committee wished to constrain class actions it should be accomplished up front with costs and symmetrical appeal rules ... E.B. suggested that if we need a structured criteria [for certification] it would do to eliminate ... anything to do with merits (and to instead use cost rules).[251]

This was one of the first articulations of the connected functions of costs and certification.[252] Both were a way of weeding out unmeritorious actions. Up until this point, the business interests had been pressing for

246 AGAC minutes, 7 Sept 1989, above note 230 at 1–2. In a follow-up letter to the AGAC dated 14 September 1989 (in Box No B502275—AGAC minutes, *ibid*), Cochrane referred to a recent submission from the Chartered Accountants' Institute, which does not appear to be in the archival record.

247 AGAC minutes, 21 September 1989 at 9, in Box No B502275—AGAC minutes, *ibid*. From the meeting of 21 September onwards, minutes were no longer attributable to individual members.

248 AGAC minutes, 8 Nov 1989, above note 245 at 10. This observation was made by Cochrane himself.

249 AGAC minutes, 7 Sept 1989, above note 230 at 5–6.

250 *Ibid* at 6.

251 *Ibid*. "Symmetrical appeal rules" meant that both plaintiffs and defendants would have the same rights of appeal from any order in a class proceeding. In fact, the *Class Proceedings Act* [*CPA*] ended up having asymmetrical rights of appeal, whereby plaintiffs can appeal certification orders as of right, but defendants must seek leave: *CPA*, SO 1992, c 6, ss 30(1) & (2).

252 This point had not been articulated in the discussion paper on certification provided to the Advisory Committee: Class Action Reform Discussion Paper Re: Certification Procedure, undated, in Box No B501822—Background Papers, above note 27.

traditional costs rules and a stringent test at certification. The consumer and environmental groups had been advocating for no-way costs and limited or no certification requirements. Belobaba's suggested compromise meant that both groups could get something of what they wanted, while balancing the goals of consumer/environmental groups (access to justice) and those of business (traditional rules of fairness).[253] In addition, it meant that class actions adhered as closely as possible to the traditional model of litigation, another goal of the business groups.[254] It was a brilliant solution at the time, and one that was ultimately to become part of the *Class Proceedings Act*. Unfortunately, it would not work so well in practice, and Edward Belobaba would come to regret his suggestion.[255]

The issue of costs dominated the later meetings of the committee. On 8 November, the members once again discussed the link between certification and costs, with most of the committee discerning this link to be fairly strong. The business community in particular felt that if the certification standard were lowered, the normal cost rules should not be changed,[256] as current cost rules were essential in deterring frivolous litigation.[257] On the other side, the consumer and environmental representatives felt that contingency fees were a major step towards removing the financial obstacles to class actions. However, more needed to be done to help plaintiffs with costs, or "the integrity of the Attorney General and the government's commitment to class actions would be put in doubt."[258] The discussion became so heated that Cochrane "noted that the Committee was more divisive on this point than any other issue."[259]

---

253 AGAC minutes, 7 Sept 1989, above note 230 at 5.

254 *Ibid.*

255 Now a sitting class actions judge, Belobaba J wrote the following in his decision in *Rosen v BMO Nesbitt Burns Inc*, 2013 ONSC 6356 at para 2:

> Most members of the class action bar, whether acting for plaintiffs or defendants, agree that a "no costs" rule would be much more sensible. Like them, I also wish that the recommendations on costs as set out in the Ontario Law Reform Commission's *Report on Class Actions* had been accepted. Instead, the provincial legislature decided to adopt the views of the Attorney-General's Advisory Committee and continue the "costs follow the event" convention for the very different world of class actions as well. I was a member of that Advisory Committee. I now realize that I was wrong and that the OLRC was right.

256 AGAC minutes, 8 Nov 1989, above note 245 at 9 and 12.

257 *Ibid* at 10.

258 *Ibid* at 9–10.

259 *Ibid*; Cochrane interview 1, above note 9.

With little movement from the business interests on traditional cost rules, and the consumer and environmental groups insisting that more needed to be done for plaintiffs than just a simpler certification test and contingency fees, a middle way was needed to break the deadlock. Various alternatives were suggested, such as no-way costs until certification and traditional cost rules thereafter.[260]

However, public funding, along the lines of the Fonds in Quebec, was the most promising middle way. The issue had been raised previously,[261] but the committee now began discussing it in earnest in order to find a consensus on the costs issue. There was some pushback on the establishment of a fund for disbursements and payment of legal costs. However, many members stated that such a fund would remove the barrier to class actions faced by representative plaintiffs, who would otherwise be faced with carrying the costs and disbursements of an entire class (with very little ultimate financial benefit, because they could only pursue damages for their own individual claims).[262] While a no-way costs rule would perform essentially the same function, it was acknowledged that "defendants would object to this idea."[263] The choice therefore seemed to be between a fund with traditional costs rules, or no fund with a no-way costs rule.[264] However, the committee noted that such a fund could be politically controversial and could jeopardize the entire Act.[265] The decision was therefore made to ask the attorney general if the idea of a fund was acceptable to the government.[266] This was the only question that was formally put to the attorney general throughout the committee's deliberations, and the fact that the committee did so showed the importance of the funding question with respect to breaking the stalemate on costs.

Subsequent meetings saw discussions on costs that were just as heated. In the 23 November meeting, certain members noted that they felt uncomfortable with bending the costs rules for class actions, which

260 AGAC minutes, 8 Nov 1989, above note 245 at 13–14.

261 AGAC minutes, 26 October 1989, at 6, in Box No B502275—AGAC minutes, above note 149.

262 AGAC minutes, 8 Nov 1989, above note 245 at 3.

263 *Ibid.*

264 *Ibid.* This was the same choice that faced the CBA/PIAC in formulating its report, with the original majority report calling for traditional costs and a fund, and the final CBA/PIAC Report (incorporating the view of the minority) calling for no-way costs and no fund: above note 59.

265 AGAC minutes, 8 Nov 1989, above note 245 at 4.

266 *Ibid* at 14.

"was removing the original fairness of the British justice system."[267] Others stated that if the committee members did their job right, "the incremental costs of a class action to the point of certification should be minimal."[268] At this point, the subject of a fund came up again, because it would prevent the financial disincentive to class actions caused by traditional costs rules.[269]

In the alternative, if the government was not willing to establish such a fund, the committee suggested that traditional costs rules could instead apply only at certain stages, such as after certification or after the common issues trial.[270] This option was discussed on 30 November, where the committee agreed that normal costs rules should apply at the individual issues stage, and considered the CBA proposal that there be no costs up to and including certification.[271] Additionally, the CBA proposed that trial judges also have discretion to refrain from awarding costs, based on as yet unspecified factors.[272]

The committee outlined other options, several of them heavily contingent on the existence of a class actions fund:

- Having traditional costs rules apply;
- Settling on the issue of a fund, because that would remove or reduce the problems with traditional costs rules;
- Present a "take it or leave it" option to the government: retain a traditional costs regime premised on the existence of a fund, because otherwise there would be no consensus on the entire issue of class actions; or
- Present two options to the government: the CBA proposal, or traditional costs rules with a fund.[273]

267 AGAC minutes, 23 Nov 1989, above note 204 at 4.

268 *Ibid.* Anyone familiar with the current state of class actions in Ontario, where certification costs easily run to hundreds of thousands of dollars, will know that this hope was in vain.

269 *Ibid.*

270 AGAC minutes, 8 Nov 1989, above note 245 at 13–14.

271 AGAC minutes, 30 November 1989, at 6 [AGAC minutes, 30 Nov 1989], in Box No B502275—AGAC minutes, above note 149. The "CBA proposal" refers to the CBA/PIAC Report, above note 59, although there was also a CBA meeting on costs shortly before the AGAC meeting of 30 November 1989. The minutes of the CBA meeting are not in the archival record.

272 AGAC minutes, 30 Nov 1989, above note 271 at 7.

273 *Ibid.*

The committee eventually settled on the third option. It was clear that business groups wanted traditional costs rules to apply, but consumer and environmental groups would not agree to a class actions remedy that would rarely be used because of the financial barriers that plaintiffs would face. The fund was the key to the consensus between the two camps.[274]

The attorney general was initially pessimistic on this subject. In answer to the question posed to him on 8 November, Scott stated that he could not guarantee a government-financed or even a government-seeded fund.[275] He could not answer the committee's question, but did say that "[t]he Treasury will not cough-up a lot of money to make this sort of litigation available."[276] In that same message, however, Scott made it clear that he required a consensus report.[277] The committee knew that one of the only ways that consensus could be secured was through the provision of a fund. It therefore decided to ask the government to put its money where its mouth was—in other words, if it wanted a consensus, it would have to pay for it. This is made clear in the final report, in which "[t]he Committee concluded that if the Government is committed to reform in this area and committed to increasing access to justice it will provide whatever assistance it can to establish the fund, adequately endowed, to assist class litigants."[278]

The committee would also have been aware of Scott's personal sympathies towards government funding of public interest litigation. Scott himself had granted $1 million of funding to LEAF in 1988,[279] was a firm supporter of legal clinic funding,[280] and had overseen the introduction of the *Intervenor Funding Project Act*,[281] which provided qualified intervenors

---

274 As the committee stated in its Advisory Report, "[t]he Committee's retention of the existing costs regime for class actions was based in part on a number of considerations, including . . . that the Government . . . should establish a fund to assist parties to class proceedings": Advisory Committee Report, above note 99 at 57. See also Cochrane interview 1, above note 9.

275 "Government financed" meant that the government would supply the money to be distributed by the fund. "Government seeded" meant that the government would provide "seed money" to start the fund, which would eventually become self-financing and thereafter pay back the seed money.

276 AGAC minutes, 30 Nov 1989, above note 271 at 8.

277 *Ibid.*

278 Advisory Committee Report, above note 99 at 59–60.

279 Scott, above note 1 at 134–35.

280 *Ibid* at 175.

281 SO 1988, c 71.

with advanced funding.[282] These projects were in fact used as examples of government funding in the final report of the Advisory Committee.[283]

At the next meeting, on 15 December 1989, the committee discussed the various models for financing the fund. It was unanimously decided that a fund should be part of any class actions remedy,[284] and that it should consist of a self-funding assistance program, with seed money from a variety of sources including the government.[285] While the CBA option was discussed as a possible alternative,[286] Cochrane's handwritten notes on the issue of the fund state, "[n]o alternative."[287]

The committee was getting close to unanimity on the controversial issue of costs. By the 15 December meeting, a consensus had already been reached on the availability of contingency fees; that such fees should be court supervised;[288] and that traditional costs rules should apply to individual proceedings, to certification, and to common issues trials (provided a fund was put in place).[289] The court would also have discretion to not award costs against unsuccessful plaintiffs if the proceeding was a test case, raised a novel point of law, or was otherwise in the public interest.[290]

Consensus was close, but it had not yet been reached. Business groups continued to be reticent, as evidenced by a *Canadian Business* article in which several of the committee members were quoted.[291] Nevertheless,

282 Jamie Benidickson, "From Empire Ontario to California North: Law and Legal Institutions in Twentieth-Century Ontario" in DeLloyd J Guth & WW Pue, eds, *Canada's Legal Inheritances* (Winnipeg: Canadian Legal History Project, Faculty of Law, University of Manitoba, 2001) at 652.

283 Advisory Committee Report, above note 99 at 63–65; memorandum from Doug Ewart to Scott, 1 February 1990, in Box No B703283—Bill 28 and 29, above note 65.

284 Cochrane's handwritten minutes of the AGAC meeting (15 December 1989) at 3 [AGAC minutes, 15 Dec 1989], in Box No B502275—AGAC minutes, above note 149.

285 AGAC minutes, 15 Dec 1989, above note 284 at 3; handwritten notes by Daniel Jazvac, law student, of the AGAC meeting, 15 December 1989, at 4 [Jazvac handwritten notes], in Box No B502275—AGAC minutes, *ibid*.

286 AGAC minutes, 15 Dec 1989, above note 284.

287 *Ibid* at 4. See also Advisory Committee Report, above note 99 at 72, where the committee declined to make alternative recommendations to its funding proposals.

288 Jazvac handwritten notes, above note 285 at 1–2.

289 *Ibid* at 3–4.

290 *Ibid* at 3. These criteria were based on class actions practice in California and New York (*ibid* at 3), and the point was first raised in the AGAC minutes, 8 Nov 1989, above note 245 at 12.

291 C Allard, "Issues: Class War" *Canadian Business* (December 1989) 123, in Policy Development Division Counsel correspondence files, Class Actions—Media, 1988–1990, CA226, RG 4-40, in Box No B248633, North York, Archives of Ontario

on 2 January 1990, Cochrane wrote to Ewart to tell him that the committee had completed its work and was finalizing the report, which was "unanimous."[292] Once again, Cochrane was trumpeting consensus when it had not yet come about. The Gang of Four had further comments on the draft report, and would contact Cochrane with numerous other substantive changes while the legislation was being drafted. For example, just days after Cochrane's letter to Ewart, Norm Stewart suggested changes to section 33 of the draft Act, regarding the use of a multiplier to determine lawyer's fees (Stewart stated that the "risk" the multiplier was intended to reflect was the risk incurred at various stages throughout the proceeding, not simply as assessed at the outset), and to the "Related Matters and Recommendations" section, regarding the percentage contribution to the fund to be levied against damages awards (Stewart wanted to make it clear that the levy would be taken out of the damages award, not a separate cost the defendant would have to pay).[293] Apart from these changes, however, Stewart approved of the draft report.[294]

Other committee members also had concerns about funding. In January 1990, Cochrane asked the committee to make recommendations on how the fund should be created and maintained.[295] Several members responded with consternation. Robert Anderson, for the Ontario Chamber of Commerce, said that, although a fund was crucial to the report, it would actually weaken the whole proposal unless experts considered its implementation.[296] Terry O'Sullivan, for the Advocates' Society, was concerned that Scott's enthusiasm for the fund would override the committee's recommendation that a separate committee look at the best way to set it up.[297] Norm Stewart also stated that the specifics should be left to a

[Box No B248633—Media]. The article referred to the Mississauga train derailment, an event that had occurred a decade previously, showing the influence that such mass disasters had on the public debate about class actions.

292 Memorandum from Cochrane to Ewart (2 January 1990) in Box No B502275—AGAC minutes, above note 149.

293 Letter from Stewart to Cochrane (8 January 1990) [Stewart Letter, 8 Jan 1990], in Box No B248633, above note 73.

294 Stewart Letter, 8 Jan 1990, above note 293.

295 This letter does not appear to be in the archival record, but is mentioned in the subsequent letters of Anderson (January 18) and O'Sullivan (January 25) [O'Sullivan Letter, 25 Jan 1990], both of which can be found in Box No B248633 Correspondence, above note 73.

296 Anderson Letter, above note 95.

297 O'Sullivan Letter, 25 Jan 1990, above note 295 at 3; letter from O'Sullivan to Cochrane, 16 January 1990, in Box No B248633, above note 73.

task force of actuaries and funding experts.[298] Both O'Sullivan and Stewart disliked the fact that the draft report did not mention that defendants would also be able to use the fund.[299] In O'Sullivan's opinion, this left that section with a distinctly "pro-plaintiff" flavour.[300] Edward Belobaba, for the Consumers' Association of Canada, was more concerned with the representation on the board that would make funding decisions. He asked that there be representation from a diversity of community groups, which should make decisions according to publicly accountable guidelines.[301]

The committee met with Cochrane again on 26 January 1990.[302] Stewart seems to have put forward further concerns about the fund at this point, stating that the attorney general should provide different options for funding from which the committee could choose. He was opposed to a specific level of financing for the fund, and agreed with the other members that actuarial assistance was needed in setting it up.[303] Cochrane was able to accommodate most of Stewart's concerns, but felt that some of them were beyond the scope of the consensus (specifically, changes to the modified contingency fee that would explicitly forbid lawyers from seeking a percentage of recovery).[304]

Cochrane wrote to the committee on 14 February 1990, mediating between them and Stewart in an effort to maintain the fragile consensus that was essential for the draft Act to see the light of day. He stated that Scott was striving to make the group's recommendations work at a political level, but that he needed a final unanimous report. In order to bring Stewart on side, he offered the committee's support in "selling the

298 Letter from Stewart to Cochrane (19 January 1990) in Box No B703283—Bill 28 and 29, above note 65.

299 *Ibid* at 2.

300 O'Sullivan Letter, 25 Jan 1990, above note 295 at 3.

301 Letter from Belobaba to Cochrane (25 January 1990) at 1, in Box No B248633 Correspondence, above note 73.

302 While the minutes for this meeting do not appear to be in the archival record, Cochrane made handwritten notes of the committee members' concerns about the fund [AGAC minutes, 26 Jan 1990], in Box No B248633 Correspondence, *ibid.*

303 AGAC minutes, 26 Jan 1990, above note 302 at 1; letter from Stewart to Cochrane, 19 February 1990 [Stewart Letter, 19 Feb 1990] at 2, in Box No B248633 Correspondence, *ibid.*

304 Letter from Cochrane to AGAC (14 February 1990) [Cochrane Letter, 14 Feb 1990], in Policy Development Division Counsel correspondence files, Class Actions—Class Proceedings Fund, 1988–1990, MGC, RG 4-40, in Box No B501822, North York, Archives of Ontario [Box No B501822—CPF].

consensus to his members," noting that the consensus was a compromise in which no one group had its way completely.[305] Cochrane's message was clear: Stewart had to pull his weight by supporting the fragile consensus, or the committee's work would be for nothing. At the same time, there was public awareness of the report and mounting pressure to release it, both from business interests and the pro-consumer camp.[306]

Nevertheless, Stewart was willing to gamble on the consensus in order to have further changes made. He wrote to Cochrane again a few weeks later with more detailed concerns regarding the section on the costs assistance fund.[307] He was concerned about the presumptions the draft report was making regarding the shape of the fund.[308] Stewart ended his letter by reassuring Cochrane that all of his suggestions were made to ensure that the report was consistent with the group's consensus.[309] Stewart knew that Scott and Cochrane wanted a consensus, and even at this late stage, he was willing to try and make further tweaks to the draft report by appealing to that desire. This pattern was to continue even after the report was finalized, and well into the legislative drafting stage.

Stewart's efforts were mirrored by O'Sullivan. O'Sullivan was personally persuaded of the need for class action legislation, having worked on the litigation arising from the Air India bombing and seeing first-hand the difficulties of processing multiple claims in the context of such a tragedy.[310] However, his constituency, the Advocates' Society, had misgivings about percentage contingency fees. The Advocates' Society felt it was "safer to use a multiplier that reflected a premium on the effort expended, subject to court review, as an introduction until we felt more comfortable with percentages."[311] Terry O'Sullivan therefore wrote to Cochrane two

---

305 Cochrane Letter, 14 Feb 1990, above note 304 at 1.

306 Allan Hutchinson & Kent Roach, "Legislation Needed to Increase Access to Class-Action Suits" *Financial Post* (24 February 1990) at 15; W Macdonald & W Rowley, "Reforming Ontario Class Action Procedures" *Financial Post* (20–22 January 1990) 21; Allan Hutchinson, "Should the Province Expand Class Action Suits? Yes" *Law Times* (12 March 1990) 7; W Macdonald & W Rowley, "Should the Province Expand Class Action Suits? No" *Law Times* (12 March 1990) 8. All these articles can be found in Box No B248501—Media, above note 239.

307 Advisory Committee Report, above note 99 at 56.

308 Stewart Letter, 19 Feb 1990, above note 303 at 1–2.

309 *Ibid* at 3.

310 O'Sullivan interview, above note 63. The bombing of Air India Flight 182 took place on 23 June 1985. It killed 329 people and was the deadliest terror attack in Canadian history.

311 *Ibid.*

days after Stewart did so, with comments that were essentially identical (including the changes to the modified contingency fee that Cochrane had already stated went beyond the scope of the consensus).[312] Cochrane and other MAG officials observed that the two men were working together to bring about the changes they wanted. Upon receiving O'Sullivan's letter, Shawn Scromeda, an articling student with the ministry, forwarded the letter to Cochrane with a note saying that O'Sullivan's comments were "very similar to those 'suggested' by Norm Stewart."[313] Stewart was to make many more "suggestions" before the draft legislation was finalized.

While there appears to be no further correspondence between Stewart or O'Sullivan and Cochrane in February 1990, Cochrane must have spoken to the two men to assuage their concerns, because by late February 1990, all the committee members had signed off on the report and it was presented to Scott.[314] Obtaining something of a consensus among such diverse interests was a huge achievement. However, the committee's recommendations still had to find their way onto the statute books.

F. DRAFTING THE LEGISLATION

Scott and Cochrane had worked hard to get the members of the committee to agree on the shape of reform.[315] A fragile consensus had been reached that complied with the attorney general's terms of reference. Specifically, the fund was the glue that held the positions of the various parties together, and the committee's report made it clear that the class actions remedy was contingent on the fund. In fact, it refused to make alternative recommendations on a class actions remedy should the government refuse to implement a fund, stating that to do so "would jeopardize the unanimity of the Committee and undercut the value of the

312 Letter from O'Sullivan to Scromeda (21 February 1990) in Box No B248633, above note 73.

313 Note from Scromeda to Cochrane (21 February 1990) in Box No B248633, *ibid.*

314 Letter from AGAC to Scott (February 1990) in Box No B502275—AGAC minutes, above note 149.

315 Cochrane was well aware of his achievement: on 28 February 1990, he wrote to Ralph Nader, champion of the US consumer and a person Cochrane clearly admired, to tell him about the committee's unanimous report. Letter from Cochrane to Nader (28 February 1990) in Box No B501822—Communications Plan, above note 82.

recommendations."[316] The certification test, costs regime, and fund were therefore interdependent.

Having worked so hard to secure unanimity, Scott and Cochrane were not about to let the consensus be jeopardized by the tinkering of the Cabinet committees and the drafting process. They were certainly not about to subject the report (and the draft Act that it contained) to a public consultation process, which would delay the Act's introduction and possibly change the Advisory Committee's model.[317] The *Class Proceedings Act* that eventually became law therefore looks remarkably like the draft Act put forward by the committee, except for a few minor changes. There is little doubt that this was the result of Scott's iron hand over the process, as well as Cochrane's ability to negotiate with the various parties to ensure that the consensus held together while the draft Act was given life.

In fact, the report and draft Act passed through inter-ministerial consultation and the various Cabinet committees remarkably smoothly, largely due to the emphasis (in Cochrane's Cabinet submission[318] and consultations with the various ministries)[319] on the unanimous nature of the committee's recommendations. While certain ministers had concerns about the fund (primarily whether it would divert resources away from Legal Aid)[320] and others had concerns that enabling class actions would

316 Advisory Committee Report, above note 99 at 72. See also memorandum from Cochrane to Scott (28 May 1990) at 2 [Cochrane memorandum, 28 May 1990], in Box No B248633—Drafting Instructions, above note 187.

317 "Briefing Note: Class Action Reform," drafted by Cochrane at the end of October 1989 (at 2) in Box No B501822—Communications Plan, above note 82. This was a departure from Scott's usual style, which was to conduct public consultations before making major policy decisions: Scott, above note 1 at 144.

318 Cabinet submission, 20 March 1990; an earlier draft version, dated 8 March 1990, has much less emphasis on the consensus of the committee. It is not clear who made the changes to the draft, but it was clearly felt that emphasizing the consensus would assist with the draft bill's passage through the committee stages. Both documents can be found in Box No B248501—Cabinet minutes, above note 222.

319 Memorandum from Chaloner (Deputy Attorney General) to all deputy ministers (27 March 1990); report of the deputy ministers' Committee on Economic and Environmental Policy (E&E 4/90), 12 April 1990 at 2. Both documents can be found in Policy Development Division Counsel correspondence files, Class Actions—Inter-Ministry Consultation, 1989, CA226, RG 4-40, in Box No B248501, North York, Archives of Ontario [Box No B248501—Inter-ministry consultation].

320 Report of the deputy ministers' Committee on Justice (DCJ 4/90), 12 April 1990. The Ministry of Industry, Trade and Technology raised the same concerns noted by some committee members, that the fund needed to be set up and monitored with the help of actuarial experts: letter from the deputy minister to Chaloner (9

mean more lawsuits against the government,[321] all had their concerns assuaged[322] and all eventually indicated their assent to the draft Act.[323]

Neither the CCJ nor the Cabinet Committee on Economic and Environmental Policy seems to have noticed that the draft Act departed from the Cabinet minute of 21 June 1989 (which authorized the establishment of the Advisory Committee) in one significant respect: costs. A variance memorandum should have highlighted where the draft Act differed from the Cabinet minute, but no such document seems to have been submitted.[324] Both committees recommended to the Cabinet that the *CPA* be adopted along the lines laid out in the draft bill, and explicitly approved the principle that "normal costs rules apply and continue to be in the court's discretion."[325] Cabinet followed this recommendation. It did not change its mind on the issue of costs; it was simply never informed of the change. Even if it had been informed, Cabinet would have found it fairly difficult and politically inexpedient to contest a costs mechanism

April 1990). These documents, as well as other correspondence from the various deputy ministers raising concerns about funding, can be found in Box No B248501—Inter-ministry consultation, *ibid.*

321 Internal electronic message from Ewart to Cochrane (8 April 1990) re: questions from Graham Stoodley of Legal Services, Human Resources Secretariat. Ewart stated that "the government could occasionally be exposed to an embarrassing lawsuit . . . but it would probably be more embarrassing to put a provision in the legislation to exempt the Crown from class actions." This document, as well as other correspondence from the various deputy ministers raising concerns about increased litigation against the government, can be found in Box No B248501—Inter-ministry consultation, *ibid.*

322 Letter from Chaloner to various deputy ministers (12 April 1990) addressing their concerns about the fund, in Box No B501822—Cabinet submission, above note 98.

323 Cabinet approval of *CPA* and *Law Society Amendment Act* for introduction, signed by Secretary of the Cabinet Peter Barnes, 30 May 1990, in Cabinet Submissions, CS6990/90 to CS7047/90, 1986–1996, CA61, RG 75-18-1, in Box No B861458, North York, Archives of Ontario.

324 On 28 May 1990, Cochrane wrote to the members of the Legislation Committee to draw their attention to changes that had been made in the draft legislation from the draft that had been circulated the previous week (Memorandum from Cochrane to members of Legislation Committee, re: *Class Proceedings Act* 1990 new draft bill, dated 28 May 1990, in B703283). However, there is no record of any variance memorandum showing the points of departure from the Cabinet minute.

325 Report of the Cabinet Committee on Economic and Environmental Policy (E&E 4/90), 19 April 1990, at 4; report of the Cabinet Committee on Justice (J 5/90), 19 April 1990, at 8. Cabinet did adopt the *CPA* along those lines: Cabinet minute (13-13/90), 2 May 1990. All these documents can be found in Box No B248501—Cabinet minutes, above note 222.

that had received the unanimous support of a diversity of stakeholders, and upon which the entire class actions remedy hinged.[326]

In the meantime, Cochrane attempted to control the drafting of the actual legislation. Days after the committee submitted its report, Cochrane asked legislative counsel Cornelia Schuh to draft a bill for introduction in May 1990. He agreed with Doug Ewart that Schuh had the most talent for drafting the bill and stated that "[t]he only delicate issue is the Committee's touchiness about their own drafting."[327] Of course, it was not Cochrane's job to decide which counsel had "the most talent" to draft the legislation.[328]

It was also highly unusual for consultation groups to have detailed input into the drafting process after submitting their report, let alone a veto as Cochrane was implying.[329] Normally, a report or draft bill would be prepared and given to the minister, who would then take the report to the Cabinet Committee on Justice and thereafter the Cabinet, which would develop parameters for the legislation by way of a Cabinet minute. Legislative counsel would then draft the legislation, using the report or draft bill as only one of many guidance documents, and would also consult with the relevant ministry officials. The draft would then be examined by the Legislation and Regulations Committee to see if it was in accordance with the Cabinet minute, and, if it was, the legislation would then be approved for introduction.[330] This is very similar to the process that was followed when the regulations under the *Law Society Amendment Act* were drafted, dealing with the Class Proceedings Fund.[331] By

---

326 In fact, some deputy ministers congratulated Cochrane on his success in bringing together so many disparate viewpoints: letter from deputy minister of financial institutions to J Johnson, acting deputy attorney general (17 April 1990) in Box No B501822—CPF, above note 304.

327 Handwritten note from Cochrane to Cornelia Schuh (legislative counsel) and Craig Perkins (director of the Court Reform Task Force and the Rules Committee at the MAG) (26 February 1990) in Box No B248633—Drafting Instructions, above note 187.

328 *Ibid.*

329 Gregory interview, above note 155.

330 Cochrane interview 1, above note 9; Revell Memo, above note 187.

331 Letter from Laura Hopkins, legislative counsel, to Carmen Rogers, MAG counsel, re: Regulations under the *Law Society Act* (3 December 1992) [Hopkins Letter], in Policy Development Division Counsel correspondence files, CPA—Regulations, 1992–1993, CR, RG 4-40, in Box No B703283, North York, Archives of Ontario [Box No B703283—*CPA* Regulations]. By this time, Cochrane had left the MAG for private practice.

contrast, Cochrane's approach, in surrendering the drafting process to the Advisory Committee, was virtually unprecedented.[332]

Chief legislative counsel Donald Revell quickly attempted to put Cochrane in his place, writing a disgruntled memorandum the next day to Cochrane's superior, Doug Ewart:

> First, I do not think that it is your role or the role of Mike Cochrane to run my office by deciding who has "the most talent" to work on your projects ... If Mr. Cochrane understood the policy then I am sure that, given proper instruction, any of my counsel could do an appropriate job.
>
> ...
>
> Secondly, I am surprised that an advisory committee chaired by a member of your office would get into a drafting exercise on some understanding that the committee and not the Legislative Counsel would draft the bill. This is the first time that I can recall that a member of your staff has been involved in such an action ... In the past, when committee's [*sic*] have been involved in drafting, it was always on the understanding that the committee's draft would be only one more document to be considered by us in drafting the bill. To say that we have a "delicate issue" because of "the Committee's touchiness about their own drafting" is like a threat to this Office to leave the draft as it appears in the report.[333]

Although it was a little over-zealous to characterize Cochrane's note as a "threat," in fact it was precisely his intention (and that of Scott) that the final legislation resemble the committee's draft Act as closely as possible. Revell stated that he did "not intend to compromise the standards of the Office because of the 'touchiness' of a committee,"[334] and finished his letter by stating that he would not assign counsel to the project until his concerns were addressed.

There is no other correspondence between Revell and Ewart (or Cochrane) in the archival record. Nevertheless, it appears that Revell's

332 There have been other examples of close involvement of outside groups in drafting, although they did not involve quite the veto power that the Advisory Committee had with regard to the *CPA*. They generally involved areas where a number of competing forces had to be accommodated, and where any change to the legislative wording could affect the consensus that had been reached between the groups. Examples include legislation on construction liens, limitations reform, and accountancy licensing (Gregory interview, above note 155).

333 Revell Memo, above note 187.

334 *Ibid* at 2.

concerns were addressed, because counsel was at some point assigned to the project. Just over two months later, Cochrane received a complete first draft of the *CPA* from legislative counsel Marilyn Leitman.[335] Even though Leitman was formally appointed by Revell,[336] it appears that she was subsequently co-opted into going along with the committee's wishes. According to Cochrane, he met with Leitman informally and explained to her that the committee members wanted to be directly involved in the drafting of the legislation. She was reportedly very reluctant to go along with this but agreed to meet with the committee anyway, and subsequently drafted the legislation in direct and repeated consultation with them.[337]

Cochrane has confirmed that this process was completely unprecedented, and that, when the committee asked to be involved in this manner, he told them as much. Leitman reportedly assured the committee that she would consider their opinions when drafting, but the members insisted on having control over the actual wording of the statute. Each provision of the draft *CPA*, therefore, was drafted after consultation with the committee, and then run past them again to make sure each provision reflected their consensus.[338] This is reflected in the letters from Leitman to Cochrane of 9 and 18 May 1990, with which she enclosed the preliminary and complete first drafts of the *CPA*.[339] Leitman referred repeatedly to sections and subsections of the "AC," meaning the provisions of the Advisory Committee draft Act.[340] She justified why certain sections of the AC draft Act had not been included (because they had been covered elsewhere, either in the draft statute or in other legislation),[341] and asked for

335 Letter from Leitman to Cochrane, enclosing first draft of the *Class Proceedings Act* (18 May 1990) in Box No B248633—Drafting Instructions, above note 187. Shortly after the passage of the *CPA*, Leitman changed her first name to Mariam. She went on to become deputy chief legislative counsel and also acting chief legislative counsel.

336 Cochrane interview 1, above note 9.

337 *Ibid.*

338 *Ibid*; Woolford interview 1, above note 13.

339 Letter from Leitman to Cochrane (9 May 1990) (enclosing preliminary first draft of *CPA*) in Box No B703283—Bill 28 and 29, above note 65; letter from Leitman to Cochrane, 18 May 1990 (enclosing complete first draft of *CPA*) [Leitman Letter, 18 May 1990], in Box No B248633—Drafting Instructions, above note 187.

340 Leitman Letter, 18 May 1990, above note 339. An annotated copy of the draft Act, forwarded on the same day to the committee on Cochrane's behalf, clarifies that "AC = Advisory Committee."

341 *Ibid*, notes section at 1–2 (regarding section 38 of the report), 3 (regarding appeal rights), and 4 (regarding costs of notice, offers to settle, and the rules of court).

clarification on other sections (for example, on contingency fee agreements).[342] Clearly, her aim was to reflect the provisions of the AC draft Act as faithfully as possible, within the confines of coherence, consistency, and the current law.

When Cochrane received Leitman's draft Act, he immediately forwarded it to the committee for their review. The Act was annotated with Cochrane's handwritten notes in red pen, showing exactly how the provisions of Leitman's draft Act corresponded with the provisions of the AC draft Act.[343] Where sections of the latter had been changed or deleted, Cochrane justified those changes or deletions. For example, on page 4 of the annotated Act, Cochrane wrote that section 6(5) was "[n]ew but needed," and on the top of that page he wrote, "[n]ote AC 4(6) onus eliminated as unnecessary."[344] In doing this, Cochrane was mediating once more—this time between legislative counsel, who was improving the legislation while keeping it faithful to the AC draft Act, and the committee members, who wanted the drafting as far as possible to be in their own words.

On 25 May 1990, the committee met to discuss the first draft of the bill.[345] At that meeting, Cochrane produced a second version of the draft bill,[346] which incorporated some prior suggestions from the group,[347] all of which were acceptable to the committee.[348] They also made further changes, including the reinsertion of section 28(1), which suspended the running of applicable limitation periods upon the commencement of a class action.[349] The majority of the changes to the draft bill appear to have been made by Norm Stewart. He had significant concerns about sections 24 (aggregate damages), 25 (individual issues), and 26 (judgment distribution). His changes meant, in part, that a court had to consider whether

342 *Ibid*, notes section at 3 & 4.

343 Cochrane handwritten annotations to draft Act, faxed by his assistant to committee members on 18 May 1990 [Cochrane notes draft *CPA*], in Box No B248633—Drafting Instructions, above note 187. Cochrane was in Washington at the time, on secondment to the National Association of Attorneys General.

344 Cochrane notes draft *CPA*, above note 343 at 4.

345 The minutes of this meeting do not appear to be in the archival record, but the meeting is referred to in Cochrane memorandum, 28 May 1990, above note 316.

346 Leitman had sent this to Cochrane the previous day: letter from Leitman to Cochrane (24 May 1990) in Box No B703283—Bill 28 and 29, above note 65.

347 Letter from Stewart to O'Sullivan (29 May 1990) at 2 [Stewart Letter, 29 May 1990], in Box No B248633—Drafting Instructions, above note 187.

348 Stewart Letter, 29 May 1990, above note 347.

349 *Ibid.*

individual damages awards were impractical prior to awarding an aggregate damages award; and that unclaimed amounts under both aggregate awards and individual assessments would be returned to the defendants after a certain amount of time.[350] Interestingly, there is no mention in any draft of the Act (including the AC draft Act) of an exception for environmental cases as was originally suggested (but not required) by the attorney general's terms of reference. The environmental groups appear to have conceded on this point, in exchange for a provision on cy-près distribution of awards, which is dealt with in the same section of the *CPA*.[351]

Stewart brought up his concerns at the 25 May meeting. He was clearly the dominant force in the committee's review of the draft bill. Despite the fact that the other members of the committee, including Cochrane, had not identified any issues with sections 24 to 26 during their review, they agreed with Stewart.[352] In addition, Stewart strongly objected to a provision inserted into the second draft that would allow agreements that contingency fees be paid based on percentage of recovery. While he insisted that the provision be replaced by section 33(3) of the AC draft Act that expressly prohibited such agreements, the most he could get was the group's agreement to delete the objectionable provision.[353] Stewart's attempt to impose his will on the committee was successful only to a certain extent.

However, it is clear that Stewart was able to persuade Cochrane to make most of his changes because a few days after the meeting, Cochrane reported to the attorney general that "several of the changes incorporated into the most recent version of the Bill were necessary to obtain some of the above signatures" (which included Stewart's and the signatures of two other representatives of the Gang of Four).[354] Many of the changes reflected Stewart's comments.[355] The other committee members who had not yet signed were unable to attend the 25 May meeting, one of them being O'Sullivan, representing the Advocates' Society.[356] Stewart filled

---

350 *Ibid* at 1–2.

351 *CPA*, above note 251, ss 26(4)–(6); interview of David Poch (24 July 2017) [Poch interview].

352 Stewart Letter, 29 May 1990, above note 347 at 1.

353 *Ibid* at 3.

354 Leitman had sent the most recent version of the draft bill to Ewart earlier that day: memorandum from Leitman to Ewart (28 May 1990) in Box No B703283—Bill 28 and 29, above note 65; Cochrane memorandum, 28 May 1990, above note 316 at 1.

355 Memorandum from Cochrane to Legislation Committee (28 May 1990) in Box No B703283—Bill 28 and 29, above note 65.

356 Cochrane memorandum, 28 May 1990, above note 316.

O'Sullivan in on the discussions that had taken place on 25 May, and also offered to advise him on the timing of the bill's introduction in the legislature.[357] The two continued to meet after Cochrane sent out the third draft of the bill on 31 May.[358] O'Sullivan thereafter wrote to Cochrane to advise him that he was in agreement with all the changes suggested by Stewart[359] and that he particularly agreed with Stewart's objections on the contingency fee issue.[360]

Stewart, with O'Sullivan's help, continued to pressure Cochrane regarding the changes he had requested. In the first week of June, he wrote to Cochrane twice to remind him that one of the changes (on aggregate damages) he had mentioned at the 25 May meeting had not been incorporated into the third draft of the bill.[361] In doing so, he appealed once again to both Cochrane and Scott's desire for consensus and the committee's desire to remain true to its own draft Act. Stewart informed Cochrane that O'Sullivan shared his concerns and demanded that Cochrane fax, to both him and O'Sullivan, copies of the final bill incorporating the amendments they had requested by noon the next day.[362]

Cochrane responded quickly, making handwritten annotations to Stewart's letter in order to communicate the changes to others on the committee. The annotations are addressed to "David"[363]—likely David Poch of Energy Probe, whose constituents would be especially affected by changes stating that unclaimed damages awards would be returned to defendants, and whose sign-off would be essential. The first reading of

357 *Ibid.*

358 Letter from O'Sullivan to Cochrane (1 June 1990) [O'Sullivan Letter, 1 June 1990], in Box No B248633—Drafting Instructions, above note 187. Leitman had sent the third draft of the bill to Cochrane on 31 May 1990: memorandum from Leitman to Cochrane (31 May 1990) in Box No B703283—Bill 28 and 29, above note 65.

359 O'Sullivan Letter, 1 June 1990, above note 358.

360 *Ibid* at 2.

361 Letter from Stewart to Cochrane (1 June 1990); letter from Stewart to Cochrane (4 June 1990) (copying O'Sullivan) [Stewart Letter, 4 June 1990]. By this time, Stewart had moved from GM Canada to become general counsel and secretary of Ford Motor Company of Canada, Ltd. Both documents can be found in Box No B248633—Drafting Instructions, above note 187.

362 Stewart Letter, 4 June 1990, above note 361. O'Sullivan followed up with a letter to Cochrane on 5 June, signing off on the draft bill on the condition that Stewart's changes would be made: letter from O'Sullivan to Cochrane (5 June 1990) in Box No B248501—Correspondence, above note 115.

363 Stewart Letter, 4 June 1990, above note 361 at 2.

the *CPA* was just days away, and Cochrane was working to hold the consensus together.

In the final event, however, there was not enough time to make the changes; they would instead have to be addressed after first reading.[364] By 5 June 1990, all the committee members had signed off on the draft bill as consistent with their report (some of them, such as Stewart and O'Sullivan, on the condition that their changes would be made).[365] Cochrane wrote to the committee to inform them that the *CPA* would receive its first reading on 7 June 1990, along with the *Law Society Amendment Act* creating the Class Proceedings Fund.[366] He further confirmed Scott's commitment to get the legislation through committee without substantive changes, stating that "[t]he Attorney General is committed to our Bill and we can continue to polish it without jeopardizing the consensus."[367]

On 12 June 1990, the *Class Proceedings Act* and the *Law Society Amendment Act* received their first reading in the Ontario legislature.[368] In speaking to the House, Scott referred to the unanimous recommendations of the committee members, many of whom were sitting in the gallery.[369] While Scott stated that traditional costs rules would apply to class actions, he also pointed to contingency-fee arrangements and the fund as a counterbalance to this.[370] The goal was to get the legislation passed as soon as possible.[371]

---

364 Letter from Cochrane to AGAC (5 June 1990) [Cochrane Letter, 5 June 1990], in Box No B248501—Correspondence, above note 115.

365 Memorandum from AGAC to Scott, in Box No B248501—Correspondence, *ibid.* Although this memo is dated 22 May 1990, it is clear from subsequent correspondence that the sign-off was not actually obtained from all parties until late May or early June 1990: Cochrane memorandum, 28 May 1990, above note 316. It is therefore likely that the final memorandum, signed by all parties, indicated sign-off on the final draft bill prior to first reading (which took place on 12 June 1990). The version of the memorandum signed by all parties does not appear to be in the archival record.

366 Cochrane Letter, 5 June 1990, above note 364.

367 *Ibid.*

368 Ontario, Legislative Assembly, *Official Report of Debates (Hansard)*, 34th Parl, 2nd Sess (12 June 1990) (Ian Scott), online: http://hansardindex.ontla.on.ca/hansard espeaker/34-2/l045_90-22.html [Hansard, 12 June]. The *CPA* and the *LSAA* were companion bills, and from this point onwards, reference to the *CPA* includes the *LSAA*.

369 Hansard, 12 June, *ibid.*

370 *Ibid.*

371 *Ibid.* See also memorandum from Ewart to the communications branch (31 May 1990), making changes to Scott's draft statement to the legislature because "[i]t's *important* that we signal a desire for early passage" [emphasis in original], in Box No B501822—Communications Plan, above note 82.

To this end, Cochrane proposed to the Advisory Committee that the bill go to a Committee of the Whole House and be passed without amendment by 28 June; the attorney general would then give a written undertaking that the changes requested by Stewart and O'Sullivan would be contained in an amending bill in the fall of 1990, prior to royal proclamation of the *CPA*.[372] However, Stewart and O'Sullivan both felt that they could not accept this approach, as too many intervening events that would be beyond Scott's control could take place.[373] They insisted instead that their amendments be made prior to second reading.[374] In addition, Stewart reminded Cochrane of the attorney general's promise that the *CPA* would be the only class actions mechanism available in Ontario; the *Environmental Bill of Rights* was still before the legislature, and it still contained a class actions remedy.[375]

Scott would never get the chance to implement the changes requested by his committee. The attorney general wrote to the committee on 16 July 1990,[376] saying there was a high degree of consensus in the House regarding the *CPA*, and he did not anticipate any problems with its passage. However, it had not been possible to pass the legislation before the House rose at the end of June, and it would therefore have to be reintroduced in the fall. Before that could happen, the "intervening events" anticipated by Stewart came to pass, in a way that very few could have predicted. On 1 October 1990, the Ontario provincial election saw David Peterson's Liberal government voted out of power. Ian Scott did not lose his seat, but he lost his job as attorney general and was replaced by Howard Hampton. The NDP assumed the mantle of government, and the *CPA* was left in legislative limbo.

372 Letter from Stewart to Cochrane (copied to O'Sullivan) (25 June 1990) in Box No B248633—Drafting Instructions, above note 187.

373 *Ibid* at 2.

374 *Ibid.*

375 Letter from Stewart to Cochrane (29 June 1990) in Box No B248633—Drafting Instructions, above note 187. Stewart had also reminded Cochrane of this provision in the *Environmental Bill of Rights* in the fall of 1989: letter from Stewart to Cochrane (26 October 1989) in Box No B502275—AGAC minutes, above note 149.

376 Letter from Scott to the AGAC (16 July 1990) in Box No B248501—Correspondence, above note 115.

G. REINTRODUCTION OF THE *CPA*

The members of the Attorney General's Advisory Committee had seen what happened when a draft act got stuck in no-man's land.[377] The OLRC draft Act was never even introduced as a bill and had gathered dust for about six years before consultations on the subject of reform began again. Cochrane and the committee had worked hard to bring about a consensus and see legislation drafted, and they were not about to let the momentum slow down. They had to act quickly to get the *CPA* reintroduced.

The Consumers' Association of Canada was the first to write to Hampton, just days after his appointment as attorney general, to express support for reintroduction of the bill.[378] Early in November, the committee met in order to discuss a strategy for reintroduction of the *CPA* (now Bill 213), and also to discuss the amendments on aggregate damages requested by Stewart and O'Sullivan on 4 and 25 June 1990.[379] Fortunately for the committee, Cochrane indicated that the new attorney general was in favour of reintroduction, as well as any agreed technical amendments.[380] Indeed, it would have been strange if Hampton wasn't supportive: the previous year, he had criticized the Liberal government for not including class actions in the *Courts of Justice Amendment Act*, arguing passionately that aggrieved consumers needed access to justice.[381]

The committee agreed to make almost all of Stewart and O'Sullivan's changes, and also agreed that they should send a joint letter to the attorney general in support of an early reintroduction of Bill 213.[382] The committee knew that unanimity was crucial to the bill's passage, and that any doubt regarding the consensus would cause delay. Their best strategy would be to present a united front. As a result, Cochrane was careful to note the unanimous nature of the committee's recommendations in

377 Cochrane interview 1, above note 9.

378 Letter from Joan Huzar, president, Consumers' Association of Canada, to Hampton (12 October 1990) in Box No B248501—Correspondence, above note 115.

379 Fax from Norm Stewart to the AGAC (12 November 1990) detailing the committee's discussions when it met on 8 November 1990 [Stewart fax, 12 Nov 1990], in Box No B248501—Correspondence, *ibid.*

380 Stewart fax, 12 Nov 1990, above note 379 at 1.

381 Ontario, Legislative Assembly, *Official Report of Debates (Hansard)*, 34th Parl, 2nd Sess (14 June 1989) (Howard Hampton), online: http://hansardindex.ontla.on.ca/hansardeissue/34-2/l025.htm.

382 Stewart fax, 12 Nov 1990, above note 379 at 1–2.

his communications with his superiors.[383] In November 1990, Cochrane sent Ewart a copy of the finished bills,[384] stating that they were ready for consideration by the Policy & Planning and Legislation committees,[385] and enclosing a note in support of reintroduction, which stated that the Advisory Committee continued to unanimously urge reintroduction of the bills.[386]

True to his word, Hampton put the bills on the fall legislative program, to be considered for early reintroduction.[387] As the MAG tried to get the bills through committee, Cochrane's note in support of reintroduction made the rounds. At the end of November, Hampton submitted Cochrane's note to the Cabinet Committee on Justice in his efforts to have the bills reintroduced.[388] Around the same time, the deputy attorney general wrote to the deputy ministers, also enclosing Cochrane's note and emphasizing the unanimous and non-controversial nature of the committee's recommendations.[389] The MAG's ability to claim that the *CPA* was "non-controversial," when just two years previously it had provoked bitter debate among the various interest groups, shows how valuable the committee's consensus really was. As one of the committee members has stated, "Scott was nobody's fool. He knew that to get this through the House, he would have to come in waving a report and say, 'we've talked to everybody, they've signed off, why are you complaining?' Otherwise there would be no legislation for another ten years."[390] This was essentially

383 Memorandum from Cochrane to Ewart (14 November 1990) in Box No B703283—Bill 28 and 29, above note 65.

384 That is, the *CPA* and the *LSAA*, at this time known as bills 213 and 214, respectively.

385 Memorandum from Cochrane to Ewart (22 November 1990) [Cochrane memorandum, 22 Nov 1990], in Box No B248633—Drafting Instructions, above note 187. As they had done previously, the committee members reviewed and signed off on these updated bills. See, for example, letter from Stewart to Cochrane, 3 December 1990, in Box No B248633—Miscellaneous Material, above note 66.

386 Cochrane memorandum, 22 Nov 1990, above note 385.

387 Memo from Ewart to Hampton (23 November 1990), in Policy Development Division Counsel correspondence files, Legislation 1990–91, CA226, RG 4-40, in Box No B807794, North York, Archives of Ontario [Box No B807794—Legislation 1990–91].

388 Memo from Hampton to Cabinet Committee on Justice (30 November 1990) in Cabinet Submissions, CS417/90 to CS7076/90, 1990, CA61, RG 75-18-1, in Box No B861459, North York, Archives of Ontario [Box No B861459—Cabinet Submissions].

389 Letter from Chaloner to deputy ministers (29 November 1990) in Ministry of the A-G acts & regs files, Proposed Legislation 1990, 1100, RG 4-143, in Box No B827937, North York, Archives of Ontario [Box No B827937—Acts & Regs].

390 AC member interview, above note 8.

the position put forward by Cochrane when he briefed all the ministries about the reintroduction on 4 December 1990.[391]

This is almost certainly why the bills passed through the committee stage so easily. It would have been difficult to take issue with legislation that was not only based on a unanimous report by many of the major players, but that had also been drafted and signed off on by those same players. As one committee member put it, "it was pre-ordained to be acceptable."[392] This point can clearly be seen in the correspondence from the ministries regarding the reintroduced bills. Some of them had concerns regarding the potential for increased litigation against the government that could affect their ministries. However, they nevertheless indicated their assent for the consultation record because of the Advisory Committee's unanimous support for the legislation. This struck them as "unusual"[393] and was powerful enough to overcome their hesitation.

The MAG's goal was to have the legislation reintroduced as quickly as possible, with the first reading occurring before 19 December and the second reading in January 1991,[394] and initially this plan was on track.[395] On 17 December, bills 213 and 214 were reintroduced in the legislature.[396] The MAG press release put out the same day once again emphasized the consensus reached by the Advisory Committee.[397] It also downplayed the

391 Memo from Suzanne Harrington, counsel, to Rita Burak, deputy minister of Agriculture and Food (5 December 1990) [Harrington Memo], in Box No B827937—Acts & Regs, above note 389.

392 AC member interview, above note 8.

393 Harrington Memo, above note 391; similar responses from deputy ministers in other ministries can be found in Box No B248633—Miscellaneous Material, above note 66.

394 Memo to Hampton from Ewart (3 December 1990) re: fall legislative program, in Box No B807794—Legislation 1990–91, above note 387.

395 The bills were approved by the Cabinet Committee on Justice on 6 December, by the Priorities & Planning Committee on 12 December, and by the Legislation & Regulations Committee on 13 December: Memo to Hampton from Ewart (14 December 1990) re: fall legislative program, in Box No B807794—Legislation 1990–91, *ibid.* Cabinet approved reintroduction of the bills shortly thereafter: Cabinet minute of 19 December 1990, 17-11A/90, in Box No B861459—Cabinet Submissions, above note 388.

396 Ontario, Legislative Assembly, *Official Report of Debates (Hansard)*, 35th Parl, 1st Sess (17 December 1990) (Howard Hampton), online: http://hansardindex.ontla.on.ca/hansardeissue/35-1/l071_90.htm.

397 Ministry of the Attorney General, Press Release, "*Class Proceedings Act* Introduced by Attorney General" (17 December 1990) [*CPA* Introduction Press Release], in Policy Development Division Counsel correspondence files, Class Proceedings—Communications, 1992–1993, CA226, RG 4-40, in Box No B703283, North York, Archives of Ontario.

innovative nature of the bills by stating that they would support the government's work on environmental rights and the law of standing.[398] A few days previously, Minister of the Environment Ruth Grier had announced in the legislature that the government intended to introduce an *Environmental Bill of Rights*, that an advisory committee had been established for this purpose, and that the MAG was working on the questions of legal standing and class actions that would complement the bill.[399] While previous drafts of the *Bill of Rights* had included a class actions remedy, this had been removed at the request of the business members of the Attorney General's Advisory Committee.[400] The passage of the *Bill of Rights* was therefore dependent on the passage of the *CPA*, because only the latter provided a remedy for breach of the rights enshrined in the former.

The *Bill of Rights* and the *CPA* were also connected in other ways. The advisory committee mentioned by Grier was eventually modelled on the Attorney General's Advisory Committee on Class Action Reform. Cochrane recalls that, following his success with the *CPA*, Grier asked him for his assistance when the consultation process for her bill went off the rails: "She had an unholy war on her hands about the *Environmental Bill of Rights*—I was told that the [consultation] process was out of control. People were standing on tables yelling at each other."[401] A similar process was therefore set up for the *Bill of Rights*, with many of the same players. Cochrane was appointed co-chair of the Task Force on the Ontario *Environmental Bill of Rights*.[402] This task force operated according to terms of reference that were agreed in advance, and the understanding

398 *CPA* Introduction Press Release, *ibid* at 1. The press release was not widely picked up in the media, and the newspapers that did cover the story did so fairly uncritically: R Mackie, "Class Action Legislation Revived in Ontario" *Globe and Mail* (18 December 1990) A5; unknown author, "NDP OK's Group Suits" *Toronto Sun* (18 December 1990) 19; P Todd, "Ontario Plans Fund to Help Cover Cost of Class-Action Suits" *Toronto Star* (18 December 1990) A13. All these articles can be found in Box No B248633—Media, above note 291.

399 Ontario, Legislative Assembly, Official Report of Debates (Hansard), 35th Parl, 1st Sess (13 December 1990) (Ruth Grier), online: http://hansardindex.ontla.on.ca/hansardeissue/35-1/l070_90.htm.

400 Letter from Stewart to Cochrane (29 June 1990) in Box No B248633—Drafting Instructions, above note 187; letter from Stewart to Cochrane (26 October 1989) in Box No B502275—AGAC minutes, above note 149.

401 Cochrane interview 1, above note 9.

402 Letter from Cochrane to Dave Cooke, government House Leader (29 October 1991) [Cochrane Letter, 29 Oct 1991], in Box No B248633—Miscellaneous Material, above note 66.

was the same as for the Advisory Committee on Class Action Reform: if the task force produced a unanimous report, the government would have to run with it and enact legislation accordingly. When the legislation was ready to be drafted, Leitman was once more brought in to do the drafting according to the task force's instructions.[403]

This legislation could not be passed, however, until the *CPA* was passed. While the original plan was to pass the *CPA* as quickly as possible, there was a delay of almost a year between first reading (on 17 December 1990) and second reading (18 November 1991). There is little to explain this delay,[404] although the Rae government may well have been distracted by the severe difficulties it faced in its first year and thereafter, as well as the deepening recession in Ontario. At the end of October 1991, Cochrane grew tired of waiting and wrote to the leader of the House to ask him that the *CPA* receive second reading before the end of the session, highlighting again the unanimous nature of the Advisory Committee's recommendations.[405] In doing so, he referred to the Task Force on the Ontario *Environmental Bill of Rights*, stating that its terms of reference were formed on the assumption that redress for breaches of that bill would be available through the *CPA*. If the *CPA* did not pass, the work of the task force would be jeopardized.[406]

It is unclear why Cochrane was alone in urging swift passage of the *CPA*. There appear to be no follow-up letters from the Advisory Committee, either to Cochrane or to any other government representative. It is curious that a group that was so keen on having the legislation passed just one year before subsequently lost interest. Given the reaction of business groups to the Rae government, the Gang of Four may have been happy to let the possibility of class action reform lie dormant. As Cochrane recalls, "[t]he business community was horrified that there was an NDP government. The Gang of Four was on high alert for all policy development."[407]

Nevertheless, Cochrane's letter appears to have worked. Just a few weeks later, the *CPA* received second reading in the legislature. MPPs

403 Cochrane interview 1, above note 9.

404 This same question was asked when the *CPA* received its second reading: Ontario, Legislative Assembly, *Official Report of Debates (Hansard)*, 35th Parl, 1st Sess (18 November 1991) (Robert Chiarelli), online: http://hansardindex.ontla.on.ca/hansardeissue/35-1/l083.htm: "I ask, what could possibly have taken this Attorney General almost a full year to bring these bills forward?" [Hansard, 18 Nov].

405 Cochrane Letter, 29 Oct 1991, above note 402.

406 *Ibid.*

407 Cochrane interview 1, above note 9.

noted the consensus that the Advisory Committee had reached,[408] as well as the unusual nature of the consultation process, which they felt should be used more widely:

> Of interest about this bill is [that it] was based not just on consultation but collaboration, something this government should learn ... their definition of consulting is to make a decision and tell people about it afterwards but not ask for their input or opinion. This bill should teach this government a lesson ... that if it wants to get a good piece of legislation before this Legislature, it should not just consult after the fact but make people the real players ... part of a collaboration process.[409]

The *CPA* received widespread support in the House, with the only criticisms being that the government took almost a year to get the legislation to second reading,[410] and that some of its provisions were not more widely available (for example, intervenor funding).[411] It passed second reading and went to the standing committee stage.[412]

It was at this point that the fears of the Gang of Four were almost realized. The submissions of two groups to the Standing Committee threatened to upset the consensus that had been reached. The Advisory Committee members had made it clear that if substantive changes were made to the legislation as it passed through the readings, then they might no longer be able to support it.[413]

Parkdale Community Legal Services was the first to make submissions to the Standing Committee.[414] Their main request was that the *CPA* be amended so that tenants could bring class actions (the *CPA* did not apply to them pursuant to section 37, because they could bring representative actions under the *Landlord and Tenant Act*).[415] The Tenant Advocacy

408 Hansard, 18 Nov, above note 404 (David Winninger on behalf of Howard Hampton).

409 *Ibid* (Charles Harnick).

410 *Ibid* (Robert Chiarelli).

411 *Ibid* (Robert Chiarelli and Charles Harnick).

412 Ontario, Legislative Assembly, *Official Report of Debates (Hansard)*, 35th Parl, 1st Sess (2 December 1991), Standing Committee on Administration of Justice, *Class Proceedings Act, 1990*, *Law Society Amendment Act (Class Proceedings Funding), 1990* [Standing Committee on Administration of Justice], in Box No B703283—Bill 28 and 29, above note 65. Michael Cochrane was in attendance.

413 Cochrane interview 1, above note 9.

414 Standing Committee on Administration of Justice, above note 412 at J-1603–J-1606.

415 Parkdale Community Legal Services had represented tenant groups in a number of applications pursuant to the *Landlord and Tenant Act*. See, for example, *Re Quann et al and Pajelle Investments Limited*, 1975 CanLII 388 (Ont Co Ct). Such applications

Group (TAG) had made similar submissions to the MAG earlier that year and had even met with the attorney general to discuss their concerns.[416] Cochrane had drafted a briefing note for the attorney general regarding possible responses.[417] He recommended that Hampton tell the groups that a delicate consensus existed on class proceedings that the ministry was reluctant to jeopardize. To allow the "traditional power struggle between landlords and tenants to spill over into class actions" would be to endanger access to justice for all other litigants in the province.[418] Hampton's responses to the tenants' rights groups had clearly not been as effective as had been hoped, as demonstrated by the opposition that the legislation faced at Standing Committee.

Another group that voiced its opposition consisted of labour lawyers who represented trade unions. Speaking on their behalf to the Standing Committee was Toronto lawyer Mark Zigler.[419] Their main concern was that the *CPA* should be amended to allow for injunctions and also to allow unions and other unincorporated associations to sue.[420] This terrified the Gang of Four and triggered their "high alert." Cochrane had told the Advisory Committee that he would take responsibility for making sure the

presented difficulties due to lack of funding and the fact that each tenant had an individual contract with the landlord. These were some of the reasons why tenants' rights groups wanted to be able to utilize the *CPA*: Letter from AR Keating, staff lawyer, TAG, to B Holman, PDD, MAG, 18 February 1991 (re: meeting with Howard Hampton, 21 February 1991), with enclosed brief [Keating brief], in Policy Development Division Counsel correspondence files, Class Actions—Landlord-Tenant Representative Proceedings, 1991, CA226, RG 4-40, in Box No B248633, North York, Archives of Ontario [Box No B248633—Landlord-Tenant].

416 Keating brief, above note 415 at 7–9.

417 MG Cochrane, "Briefing Note: Class Proceedings and Group Tenant Applications," 19 February 1991 [Tenant briefing note], in Box No B248633—Landlord-Tenant, above note 415.

418 Tenant briefing note, above note 417 at 3.

419 Standing Committee on Administration of Justice, above note 412 at J-1606–J-1607. Zigler was (and still is) a lawyer at the firm of Koskie Minsky LLP. He also submitted his points in the form of a memo: Mark Zigler to "Ontario Legislature Justice Committee" re: *An Act Respecting Class Proceedings*, 2 December 1991 [Zigler], in Box No B248633—Miscellaneous Material, above note 66.

420 Zigler, above note 419. Unions wanted to be able to use the *CPA* regarding issues that were common to the unions' membership (for example, pension plans and group benefits), and issues regarding union members' rights in a common fund (such as a trust fund). The latter were already available at common law, but the *CPA* would provide additional benefits such as the ability to apply to the Class Proceedings Fund.

CPA was passed without any substantive changes,[421] and now it looked as if the fragile consensus was in jeopardy. He recalls that precarious time:

> [A] rumour went around that the government was going to move for an amendment to allow the *CPA* to be used by unions. That was a pretty tough moment—I told the Attorney General at the time that, "you're going to lose the whole thing." He said, "okay, I'll get back to you." Next thing we knew they didn't propose the amendment and the *CPA* was passed intact.[422]

Presumably the attorney general took the same action with regard to the tenants' rights groups, because their requested amendments were not made either. The Standing Committee reported the *CPA* and the *LSAA* (now known as bills 28 and 29, respectively) without amendment, and they were ordered for third reading.[423]

Another five months passed before the bills received third reading in the legislature, despite the Opposition's request that third reading and royal assent take place in December 1991.[424] During that time, the legal profession was busy preparing for the *CPA*[425] and further objections to the bills rolled in. These objections were dealt with summarily: with the bills based on unanimous recommendations from the major stakeholders, and having passed the Standing Committee stage without amendment, there was very little stopping them now. The first objection was from Courts Administration, stating that little thought or discussion had

421 Cochrane interview 1, above note 9.

422 *Ibid.*

423 Ontario, Legislative Assembly, *Official Report of Debates (Hansard)*, 35th Parl, 1st Sess (3 December 1991) (Gord Mills), online: http://hansardindex.ontla.on.ca/hansardeissue/35-1/l092.htm.

424 Ontario, Legislative Assembly, *Official Report of Debates (Hansard)*, 35th Parl, 2nd Sess (27 April 1992) (Robert Chiarelli), online: http://hansardindex.ontla.on.ca/hansardeissue/35-2/l012.htm [Hansard, 27 April].

425 Law Society of Upper Canada Continuing Professional Development Program, "Ontario's New *Class Proceedings Act*: Are You Prepared?" (Michael Cochrane, Chair), (18 February 1992), in Policy Development Division Counsel correspondence files, Class Proceedings—LSUC program February 1992, CA226, RG 4-40, in Box No B248501, North York, Archives of Ontario [Box No B248501—LSUC]; Canadian Institute Program, "Righting Mass Wrongs: Ontario's New *Class Proceedings Act*" (Andrew Roman, Chair), (3 March 1992), in Policy Development Division Counsel correspondence files, Class Proceedings—Canadian Institute Conference March 1992, CA226, RG 4-40, in Box No B248501, North York, Archives of Ontario [Box No B248501—CI].

been directed towards the impact of the bills on the court system.[426] That objection appears to have been dealt with by a simple phone call.[427] The second was directed to the premier himself. Bernard Wilson, a chartered accountant at Price Waterhouse, told Bob Rae that class action legislation would have an adverse impact on Ontario's economic competitiveness and would open the Pandora's box of frivolous litigation.[428] Given that the Gang of Four had signed off on the legislation long ago, however, this was too little, too late. It is also strange that Wilson objected on behalf of an Ontario Chamber of Commerce committee, given the fact that the Ontario Chamber of Commerce was part of the Gang of Four. Rae did not even respond to Wilson's letter until after the bills had received royal assent, and even then he got his attorney general to respond.[429]

The bills received third reading on 27 April 1992.[430] Again, they received widespread support and there was very little debate about the substantive details of the bills or the concept of reform. The major controversy regarded the significant delay in the passage of the bills, with Hampton announcing for the first time that his government needed six months from royal assent to take the several steps necessary for the bills to come into force. Several MPPs asked, justifiably, why none of these steps had been taken when the government was fairly confident that the

426 Letter from Jill Bell, acting manager, operations support, courts administration, to Ann Merritt, deputy director, PDD at the MAG (24 March 1992) [Bell Letter], in Policy Development Division Counsel correspondence files, Class Proceedings—Courts Administration, 1992, CA226, RG 4-40, in Box No B703283, North York, Archives of Ontario.

427 Bell Letter, *ibid*, handwritten note (unknown author), that states, "Called Jill March 31/92 to discuss." There appears to be no further correspondence to or from Courts Administration in the archival record.

428 Letter from Wilson to Rae (15 April 1992) copied to all members of the Ontario Business Advisory Council (a committee of the Ontario Chamber of Commerce) in Box No B703283—Bill 28 and 29, above note 65.

429 Letter from Hampton to Wilson (7 July 1992) in Box No B703283—Bill 28 and 29, *ibid*. Hampton once again emphasized the unanimous nature of the Advisory Committee's recommendations (at 2), and reassured Wilson about the gatekeeping function of traditional costs rules (at 4). He also made clear that economic competitiveness had to be balanced with the government's commitment to access to justice (at 5).

430 Hansard, 27 April, above note 424 (Howard Hampton). The debate was adjourned until 4 May 1992 (David Winninger, on behalf of Howard Hampton), online: http://hansardindex.ontla.on.ca/hansardeissue/35-2/l016.htm [Hansard, 4 May].

legislation would be passed.[431] In the end result, the bills passed third reading and received royal assent on 25 June 1992.[432]

As Hampton had noted, numerous tasks needed to be completed before the *CPA* and the *LSAA* were proclaimed into force.[433] First, the Class Proceedings Fund had to be designed and funds put in place so the CPF would be ready to receive applications. Second, the rules of civil procedure needed to be adapted to accommodate class actions. Third, the Law Society of Upper Canada needed to be consulted on whether changes to the Rules of Professional Conduct were necessary to take into account various ethical concerns. Fourth, the judiciary, lawyers, and the public needed to be educated on the impact of the new legislation. In addition, Courts Administration had to be prepared for the tracking and registry of class proceedings.[434]

All these tasks had to be completed following considerable turnover at the PDD. Cochrane left the MAG in mid-March 1992. With his work on class action reform (and other projects such as the *Environmental Bill of Rights*) largely completed, Cochrane decided to leave government for private practice.[435] Carmen Rogers and Larry Fox would continue his work in the PDD. Fox had been a legal research officer at the Ontario Law Reform Commission and had done considerable work on its report on class actions, particularly with regard to costs. Another former OLRC

---

431 Hansard, 27 April, above note 424 (Robert Chiarelli; Steven Offer; Chris Stockwell; Charles Harnick); Hansard, 4 May, *ibid* (Robert Chiarelli; Elinor Caplan).

432 Ontario, Legislative Assembly, *Official Report of Debates (Hansard)*, 35th Parl, 2nd Sess (25 June 1992) (Deborah Deller), online: http://hansardindex.ontla.on.ca/hansardeissue/35-2/l043b.htm.

433 Hansard, 27 April, above note 424 (Howard Hampton); Larry Fox, PDD counsel, briefing note re: Implementation of bills 28 and 29 (9 April 1992), in Policy Development Division Counsel correspondence files, Class Proceedings—Briefing Notes, 1992, CR, RG 4-40, in Box No B703283, North York, Archives of Ontario [Box No B703283—briefing notes].

434 This was taken care of fairly easily, with the preparation of a supplement to the court procedures manual that was finalized in December 1992. The manual also addressed the collection of statistical data on class proceedings: Briefing note prepared by Carmen Rogers and Larry Fox (17 November 1992) at 1, in Box No B703283—briefing notes, *ibid.*

435 Bell Letter, above note 426. Although he went to Scott & Aylen, Ian Scott's family firm, Cochrane's decision to do so had nothing to do with Scott (the firm was at that time run by David Scott, Ian's brother): email correspondence with Michael Cochrane (6 July 2016). Ian Scott returned to his previous firm of Gowling, Strathy & Henderson upon his retirement from the legislature at the end of April 1992. He also began teaching at Osgoode Hall Law School: Scott, above note 1 at 207.

legal research officer, Ann Merritt, became deputy director of the PDD. Therefore, although there was a changing of the guard at the PDD, the new faces were very experienced in class actions policy and reform.

The major task facing the MAG was the issue of funding. A deal had been struck whereby the Law Foundation of Ontario would contribute $500,000 as seed money for the CPF and would also administer it.[436] However, an advisory committee still had to be set up to develop the structure, administration, and procedures for the fund; regulations had to be written and enacted; and a class proceedings committee had to be established to process applications for funding.[437]

This process was complex and extensive.[438] What is particularly notable, however, is that the advisory committee process was deliberately different from that used with the *CPA*. The PDD acknowledged that it would be useful to have some of the representatives of the Attorney General's Advisory Committee on the Fund Advisory Committee;[439] however, they did not want to simply "use the old group,"[440] because that would increase the risk that the AGAC would expect the same consultation process to be used for the fund.[441] This time, there would be no promise of a public report; the Fund Advisory Committee "was structured as an advisory committee only,"[442] simply providing advice to the attorney general.[443] Members were not asked to reach consensus on issues, and no "sign-off" was requested.[444]

436 Hansard, 12 June, above note 368 (Ian Scott).

437 Hansard, 27 April, above note 424 (Howard Hampton).

438 Full details on the administration of the fund and applications for financial assistance are provided in the report to the attorney general re: Implementation of Bill 29 (the *LSAA*), 29 November 1992 [Fund Report], in Box No B703283—*CPA* Regulations, above note 331. The fund covered plaintiffs' disbursements and indemnified them against adverse costs awards, but it did not cover the fees of plaintiffs' counsel.

439 Larry Fox, briefing note on Class Proceedings Fund, 27 April 1992 [Fund briefing note], in Box No B703283—briefing notes, above note 433. Two of the AGAC members (Terry O'Sullivan for the Advocates' Society and Edward Belobaba for the Consumers' Association of Canada) sat on the Fund Advisory Committee: Fund Report, above note 438.

440 Annotation by Doug Ewart on letter to him from Chris Happel, legislative assistant to the attorney general, re: Advisory Committee for Fund (31 March 1992), in Policy Development Division Counsel correspondence files, Class Proceedings Committee, 1992–1993, CR, RG 4-40, in Box No B703283, North York, Archives of Ontario.

441 Fund briefing note, above note 439.

442 Fund Report, above note 438.

443 Fund briefing note, above note 439.

444 Fund Report, above note 438; Fund briefing note, above note 439.

As the PDD explicitly stated in its final report to the attorney general on the CPF, the report was not a "committee" report as the Advisory Committee Report had been, but was prepared by the PDD and simply drew on the advice of the committee members.[445] In this second process, the PDD therefore gave much less power to the parties with whom it consulted. The *CPA* had by this time received its third reading,[446] and the PDD was only too familiar with the control that had been exerted over that legislation, particularly by the business interests. Consultations on the fund—a mechanism constructed specifically for plaintiffs—were different.

In addition to the fund, changes also had to be made to the rules of civil procedure in order to reflect the new legislation. Fortunately, relatively little work was needed on this front.[447] Rule 12 needed to be revoked and replaced with a rule that took into account class proceedings in order to do the following: to allow for court staff to identify and register class proceedings; to clarify aspects of the discovery of class members other than the representative plaintiffs; to allow the Law Foundation to make submissions to the court on the issue of costs in funded cases; to remove the costs consequences of offers to settle where the case was funded; and to require that any judgment or settlement approval order of a funded case deal with how the Law Foundation's levy would be paid.[448] The Rules Committee reviewed these recommended changes on 24 November 1992,[449] and six weeks later the new Rule 12 came into force.[450]

The ethical issues arising from class actions also had to be considered. On 18 August 1992, Larry Fox wrote to the senior counsel for professional conduct at the Law Society of Upper Canada on the subject of whether the professional conduct handbook should be amended to accommodate the

445 Fund Report, above note 438; Fund briefing note, above note 439.

446 Hansard, 27 April, above note 424.

447 Letter from Larry Fox to the Honourable Mr Justice RS Montgomery, Ontario Court (General Division), Civil Rules Committee (22 October 1992) [Letter from Fox to Montgomery], in Policy Development Division Counsel correspondence files, Class Proceedings—Rules of Court, 1992–1993, CA226, RG 4-40, in Box No B703283, North York, Archives of Ontario [Box No B703283—Rules].

448 Memorandum of the Civil Rules Secretariat re: Rules to fit with the *Class Proceedings Act, 1992* (22 October 1992) (enclosure to Letter from Fox to Montgomery, above note 447) in Box No B703283—Rules, *ibid.*

449 Letter from Fox to Montgomery, above note 447.

450 Ontario Gazette, Vol 126-1, Reg 770/92, 2 January 1993 at 20–21 [*CPA* proclaimed into force], in Box No B703283—Rules, above note 447.

ethical issues arising from class proceedings.[451] These included the duty of class counsel to represent the interests of both the representative plaintiff and class members, and where conflicts of interest could arise; sharing information among class members and whether that would breach the duty of confidentiality; whether special written retainers were required in order to clarify the duties of class counsel; the use of contingency fees; advertising to class members; and making public statements. The LSUC decided not to amend the Rules of Professional Conduct, but instead issued a set of guidelines titled, *The Challenges of Class Proceedings for Civil Litigators*.[452]

That left the issue of education. Numerous conferences had been held in order to educate lawyers and the judiciary,[453] and the MAG had also corresponded with other ministries and provinces on the subject.[454] However, the public also needed to be informed about the effects of the new legislation. The MAG had already released a backgrounder with the details of the *CPA* and the *LSAA*,[455] and in November 1992 it also developed a communications plan.[456] This plan noted that, despite the unanimous

451 Fox to Stephen Traviss, senior counsel, professional conduct, LSUC (18 August 1992), in Policy Development Division Counsel correspondence files, Class Proceedings—Ethics, 1992, CA226, RG 4-40, in Box No B7703283, North York, Archives of Ontario [Box No B7703283—Ethics].

452 Law Society of Upper Canada, *The Challenges of Class Proceedings for Civil Litigators* (Toronto: LSUC, 1992). These guidelines were mentioned in an LSUC circular (Vol 2, No 2; November 1992), which in turn was attached to a letter from Traviss to Rogers (18 November 1992) in Box No B7703283—Ethics, *ibid.* Traviss stated in this letter that Michael Cochrane was drafting the guidelines, which indicates that Cochrane continued to be involved in the work of finalizing the *CPA* even after leaving his role in the government. A change to the Rules of Professional Conduct would have been preferable to guidelines, given the numerous ethical challenges that have since arisen in the context of class actions in Ontario.

453 Box No B248501—LSUC and Box No B248501—CI, above note 425.

454 See, for example, memorandum to Larry Fox from Christopher Ferguson, policy analyst, Ministry of Consumer and Commercial Relations, re: Class Proceedings in Ontario (26 October 1992), in Policy Development Division Counsel correspondence files, Class Proceedings—Miscellaneous, 1989–1992, CR, RG 4-40, in Box No B7703283, North York, Archives of Ontario. Ferguson wanted information for use by his deputy minister at a federal-provincial deputy ministers' conference on class actions, which took place in Victoria, British Columbia, on 12–13 November 1992. Ferguson particularly wanted to know why the legislation had not yet been proclaimed into force.

455 MG Cochrane, *Class Proceedings in Ontario: Backgrounder* (Toronto: Ministry of the Attorney General, 1990) in Box No B248633—Miscellaneous Material, above note 66.

456 Class Proceedings Communications Plan, MAG Communications Division [MAG communications plan], in Box No B248633—Miscellaneous Material, *ibid.* This document is undated but appears to have been prepared in November 1992.

nature of the Advisory Committee's recommendations, the *CPA* was still controversial among some groups (particularly business interests).[457] However, other sections of the population, particularly consumer groups, had greeted the legislation with enthusiasm,[458] and some even praised the collaborative nature of the Attorney General's Advisory Committee and its consensus.[459] Through its communications plan, the MAG also took pains to emphasize this consensus, as well as the access to justice dimensions of the new statutes.[460] Overall, the news articles published around the time of third reading and proclamation reveal a high level of awareness about the legislation. The release of the Attorney General's Advisory Committee Report, as well as high-profile cases such as *General Motors of Canada Ltd v Naken*,[461] appear to have made an impression on the public consciousness.[462]

On 1 January 1993, the *CPA* and *LSAA* came into force.[463] A MAG news release put out shortly thereafter explained the basics of the *CPA* and the fund, and provided information to the public on how to start a class action lawsuit.[464] It did not take long for the public to do so, with the first lawsuit under the *CPA* being issued less than two weeks later.[465] Canadian

457 MAG communications plan, above note 456 at 3. See also D Best, "Coming Soon: Legal Excess, US-Style" *Financial Times of Canada* (9 March 1992), referred to in MAG communications plan (*ibid* at 3). Best's article states that class actions and contingency fees will lead to a major change in the way Canadian courts do business by moving towards the more litigious US model.

458 MAG communications plan, *ibid* at 2–3. See also T Williams, "Class Action Suits: Laws Are Welcome News for Consumers" *Toronto Sun* (7 November 1992) 77, in the Ministry of the Attorney General Policy Development Division (PDD) Counsel correspondence files, Class Proceedings—Media, RG 4-40, in Box No B703283, North York, Archives of Ontario [PDD Media].

459 C Bernstein, "Proposed New Class Action Law Shows How Rules Should Be Made" *Toronto Star* (5 May 1991) F6, in PDD Media, *ibid.*

460 MAG communications plan, above note 456 at 4.

461 [1983] 1 SCR 72.

462 See, for example, Brad Evenson, "The Lemon Car Legacy" *Ottawa Citizen* (26 July 1992) A4. This article outlines the events leading up to the *Naken* decision, and the effect that decision had on the movement for class action reform.

463 *CPA* proclaimed into force, above note 450.

464 Ontario Ministry of the Attorney General, News Release, "Class Proceedings Legislation Expands Access to Justice" (7 January 1993), with backgrounder, in Policy Development Division Counsel correspondence files, Legislation 1992–1993, CA226, RG 4-40, in Box No B807794, North York, Archives of Ontario.

465 The Borrowers Action Society, Press Release, "Credit Card Class Action Seeks $800 Million Plus Interest" (18 January 1993) [Canadian Tire Class Action], in PDD Media, above note 458.

Tire credit card holders alleged that their agreements with Canadian Tire were in violation of section 4 of the federal *Interest Act*, and sought $800 million in interest plus damages.[466] The lawsuit garnered extensive news coverage,[467] which provided further awareness of the new legislation and the manner in which it could be used by consumers and others.

However, the first class action under the *CPA* also served as a warning to the others that would follow. It was dismissed on a Rule 20 motion, with Winkler J for the Ontario Divisional Court finding that the credit card agreements were not in violation of the *Interest Act* on a plain reading of that statute.[468] A subsequent judgment on the issue of costs found that there had been serious improprieties akin to champerty or maintenance, with a non-party conducting and basically profiting from the proceedings, and promising a reward that was not available under the *CPA*.[469] The non-party, Larry Whaley, had set up a corporation called the Borrowers Action Society to solicit contributions from credit card holders towards the costs of this and other class proceedings against credit card companies.[470] The "investors" were promised between 10 and 30 percent of any settlement or judgment in favour of the society. While a different representative plaintiff was put forward in order to shield Whaley from an adverse costs award, he personally gained from the lawsuit by paying himself a salary from the society.[471] Justice Winkler awarded costs on a solicitor–client basis[472] against Whaley and the society, holding that

---

466 Canadian Tire Class Action, *ibid.*

467 See, for example, J Heinzl, "Canadian Tire Faces Lawsuit: Borrowers Dispute Interest Charges" *Globe and Mail* (9 January 1993) B3; and L Ainsworth, "Ontario's Class Action Laws Face First Test" *Toronto Star* (16 January 1993) A14. Both articles can be found in PDD Media, above note 458.

468 *Smith v Canadian Tire Acceptance Ltd*, 1994 CanLII 7298 (Ont Ct Gen Div), aff'd 1995 CanLII 3152 (Ont CA).

469 *Smith v Canadian Tire Acceptance Ltd*, 1995 CanLII 7163 (Ont Ct Gen Div) [*Smith* 1995].

470 D Carlson, "Ontario's Class-Action Law to Get Its First Test" *Law Times* (January–February 1993); L Ainsworth, "Class Action Suit Filed Against Canadian Tire" *Toronto Star* (16 March 1993) PC1. Both articles can be found in PDD Media, above note 458. Both reported that Whaley was soliciting contributions from class members, and the *Star* article reports that class members had to pay a fee to register their credit cards with the Borrowers Action Society.

471 *Smith* 1995, above note 469. See also The Honourable Chief Justice Warren K Winkler, "Caught in a Trap—Ethical Considerations for the Plaintiff's Lawyer in Class Proceedings," online: www.ontariocourts.on.ca/coa/en/ps/speeches/caught.htm [Winkler speech].

472 Known today as substantial indemnity costs.

they were the "real" plaintiffs who had instigated the action. The financial consequences would have been devastating, given that the plaintiffs subsequently appealed the costs judgment and sought leave to appeal to the Supreme Court of Canada (which was denied with costs).[473]

This case had a chilling effect on entrepreneurial lawyers who might have been tempted to use the costs provisions of the *CPA* to generate a profit.[474] Class actions were not as easy to bring as many in the business community had previously thought, and, while the *CPA* aimed to level the playing field for plaintiffs in terms of costs, it was neither a boon to avaricious lawyers nor a tool for promoting litigation.[475] It was to be many years, and indeed the turn of the millennium, before the *CPA* began to be used on anything like a widespread basis. The fears that it would open the floodgates of litigation have never been realized, and in fact the certification requirement has become burdensome for plaintiffs far beyond that envisaged by the members of the Attorney General's Advisory Committee.[476] Twenty-five years later, the *CPA* is now under review by the Law Commission of Ontario due to various issues that have arisen—including those related to costs—that were never foreseen by its authors.

H. CONCLUSION

In the literature on the history of class proceedings, the dominant view has been that the *CPA* was enacted for a public interest purpose. Scholars such as Bill Bogart and Shaun Finn have focused on consumers and the environment, seeing class action legislation as a counterbalance to the exploitation of both.[477] Public interest theory posits that legislation is enacted to correct

473 *Smith v Canadian Tire Acceptance Ltd*, 1995 CanLII 2281 (Ont CA), leave to appeal to SCC refused with costs, [1996] SCCA No 12. It is unlikely that the fund would have paid these costs, given that its role was to indemnify plaintiffs for adverse cost awards, not lawyers personally.

474 Winkler speech, above note 471.

475 *Smith* 1995, above note 469.

476 AC member interview, above note 8.

477 Shaun Finn, "In a Class All Its Own: The Advent of the Modern Class Action and Its Changing Legal and Social Mission" (2005) 2:2 *Canadian Class Action Review* 333; Shaun Finn, *Étude d'un recours évolutif: redéfinir la procédure sui generis du recours collectif Québécois* (LLM Thesis, Faculté de Droit, Université Laval, 2011) [unpublished]; WA Bogart, Jasminka Kalajdzic, & Ian Matthews, "Class Actions in Canada: A National Procedure in a Multi-jurisdictional Society?" (Report for the Globalization of Class Actions Conference, Oxford University, December 2007).

market failures (in that small claims are not litigated because they are not individually economically viable),[478] to protect vulnerable groups, or to ensure resources are distributed fairly (aggregating individual claims to prevent the unjust enrichment of the corporation at the cost of the consumer).[479]

However, the genesis of class actions in Ontario reveals that private interests were just as important, if not more, in the creation of the legislation. The historical record demonstrates that, while Scott and Cochrane intended class action legislation to serve a public interest purpose, in fact the legislative process was co-opted or "captured" by private interests, notably the Gang of Four and other business groups.[480]

Anthony Ogus and other scholars of law and economics[481] have articulated this "capture" theory. Essentially, regulatory agencies are stymied in meeting their public interest goals because they have been subverted by pressure and influence to protect the interests of those who were the subjects of the regulation.[482] This is particularly so in circumstances when such agencies conduct their work away from the public gaze; when certain information required by the agency is only obtainable from the regulated industries; when the agency must rely on the expertise of officials from those industries; and when those industries have the power to exercise some kind of veto or ability to obstruct the agency's work.[483] The historical record shows that these circumstances were in play when class proceedings legislation was being considered in Ontario:

1) The Attorney General's Advisory Committee conducted its work away from the public gaze. Its terms of reference and its report were public, but the deliberations of its members were confidential, leaving room for influence by corporate representatives.

---

478 Anthony Ogus, *Regulation: Legal Form and Economic Theory* (Oxford: Hart, 1994) at 55.

479 *Ibid* at 46–54.

480 Interestingly, this "capture" theory also includes legislators' private interests, which can include a desire to make an imprint on history (Ogus, *ibid* at 67). This could well have been one of Scott's primary motives. Scott stated in his memoirs that "the legislation allowing class actions may be the most important legacy of my time as attorney general" (Scott, above note 1 at 182). Ogus also applies this analysis to bureaucrats (Ogus, above note 478 at 68), and Cochrane very likely had similar motives. As Peter Woolford of the Retail Council of Canada put it, "[t]hey were trying to get legislation for the ages" (Woolford interview 1, above note 13).

481 See, for example, George Stigler, "Theory of Economic Regulation" (1971) 2:1 *Bell Journal of Economics and Management Science* 3.

482 Ogus, above note 478 at 57.

483 *Ibid* at 57–58.

2) Scott and Cochrane needed the Gang of Four, not only for the information they could provide as to how class actions would affect corporate interests (a perspective that had been sorely lacking from the OLRC Report), but also for their ability to represent the views of their constituents. The membership network of the CMA alone, for example, accounted for approximately 75 percent of all Canadian manufacturing production.[484]
3) The Gang of Four had the power to stop the work of the Attorney General's Advisory Committee. Without their sign-off, there would have been no consensus, and therefore no *CPA*. Cochrane explicitly stated that the business groups had a veto over class action reform,[485] and this enabled them to disproportionately influence the work of the Advisory Committee.

The circumstances articulated above, however, applied equally to both the corporate and the consumer/environmental groups. What would enable the former to exercise more sway than the latter? And why did the latter not advance their position on class actions in Ontario as forcefully as they might have done? According to public choice theory that has expanded on the above analysis, there are two types of interest groups: those representing particular sectional interests (such as manufacturers or retailers), and those representing causes or ideologies (such as environmentalists or consumers).[486]

Each group is subject to the "free rider" problem, in that their members will benefit from the activities of the group even if they have not participated in those activities. The group will be less subject to this problem, however, if it is well organized and able to exercise control over its members, which in turn will be made easier if the members' interests are homogeneous. Effectiveness will be maximized where the group has a strong leadership that can require financial contributions and has the power to speak for the members. Sectional interests (such as the CMA and the Retail Council of Canada) fit this description; consumer and environmental groups (such as the Consumers' Association of Canada and Energy Probe), whose memberships tend to be much more diffuse, numerous, and disparate in interest, and who rarely require financial contributions, do not. The pressure for a particular measure will be greater from a homogeneous

484 CMA Letter 1983, above note 91.

485 Cochrane interview 1, above note 9.

486 Ogus, above note 478 at 70.

group whose members are heavily invested in and will derive direct benefits from the measure, than from a diffuse group whose members may or may not experience benefits and have little invested in the result.

As Ogus points out, therefore, this theory predicts that groups representing producers are likely to exert a greater influence on legislation than those representing consumers and other "public" interests, such as the environment.[487] This also explains the central thesis of the work of Richard Posner and George Stigler, that "as a rule, regulation is acquired by the industry and is designed and operated primarily for its benefit."[488]

The irony of this scenario will not be lost on anyone familiar with the economics of class actions. Class actions are needed, ostensibly, because the interests of consumers and other citizens are diffuse, and the impact of corporate misbehaviour on each individual is relatively light. As a result, it is not financially viable to bring an individual action, and neither is it possible to join those diffuse interests in one lawsuit without incurring huge transaction costs.[489] The same factors that necessitate class action legislation, however, also ensure that consumers and other citizens have less influence on the shape of that legislation.

Ontario was no exception to this theory. Business interests with well-organized and well-resourced constituencies were successful, first in delaying class action reform and, when reform appeared inevitable, shaping that reform to be as conservative as possible, particularly regarding costs. The disproportionate nature of this influence was made possible by the informal and non-public nature of the Advisory Committee's deliberations. The results changed the shape of the *CPA* and continue to be felt by class actions lawyers to this day.

---

487 *Ibid* at 71; Sophie Harnay & Alain Marciano, "Collective Litigation Versus Legislation: A Rent-Seeking Approach to Class Actions" in Jürgen G Backhaus et al, eds, *The Law and Economics of Class Actions in Europe: Lessons from America* (Cheltenham, UK: Edward Elgar, 2012) at 221. See also Poch interview, above note 351, where Poch acknowledges that "lobbying by the Gang of Four etc is always present and impactful whereas consumer and environmental groups usually have less influence, so the process [of the Attorney General's Advisory Committee] at least gave us a seat at the table."

488 Stigler, above note 481 at 3; Richard A Posner, *Theories of Economic Regulation* (New York: National Bureau of Economic Research, 1974), online: www.nber.org/papers/w0041.pdf.

489 Thomas S Ulen, "The Economics of Class Action Litigation" in Backhaus et al, eds, above note 487 at 79–81.

Chapter 5

COMPARING THE REPORTS OF THE ONTARIO LAW REFORM COMMISSION AND THE ATTORNEY GENERAL'S ADVISORY COMMITTEE

The history of the *Class Proceedings Act* provides significant insights into the ways in which law reform can be brought about effectively. In this regard, the contrast between the Ontario Law Reform Commission (OLRC) Report and that of the Attorney General's Advisory Committee (Advisory Committee) is striking. Many factors, both internal to the legislative process and external as part of the wider culture, ensured that the Advisory Committee Report would be successful in bringing about reform where its predecessor failed.

A. WIDER SOCIAL AND CULTURAL CONTEXT

Several changes had taken place in the wider culture by the time the OLRC Report was tabled in the legislature in June 1982. For example, consumer and environmental rights had come to the forefront of the public consciousness, with reports being released throughout the 1970s promoting consumer rights in general and class actions in particular, as well as a number of environmental disasters raising awareness of the fragile state of the planet. The closely related issue of standing was the subject of several court decisions in the 1970s and 1980s, which gave public interest litigants standing in certain circumstances. In the same vein, the *Charter* became part of Canadian law in 1982, giving citizens certain rights against the power of the state. The *Charter* would also see an increasing amount of power taken out of the hands of the legislature and given to judges, who would play more of an activist role in public interest litigation. These developments, which challenged the traditional two-party model of litigation and allowed judges a more active role in the cases before them, were to prove positive for the advent of class actions.[1]

In addition, by the time the OLRC Report was released, Ontario had the examples of the United States and Quebec on which to rely. The two jurisdictions were referred to extensively in both the OLRC and the Advisory Committee reports,[2] with reformers using various statistics to combat the argument that class actions would open the floodgates of litigation in the province. The findings of the Williston Report, which concluded that "the present procedure respecting class actions is in a very serious state of disrepair,"[3] were also a boost to proponents of class actions. The Supreme Court's judgment in *General Motors of Canada Ltd v Naken*[4]—that legislation was needed in order to enable class actions in Ontario—also seemed to be a victory for those pushing for reform.

However, the opponents of class actions remained intransigent in the face of the *Naken* decision, as evidenced by the submissions of business groups and the bar to the Ministry of the Attorney General (MAG). The OLRC Report and *Naken* brought the divisions on the subject of class action reform to the fore, but did nothing to heal them. This was likely the primary reason why Roy McMurtry did not subsequently introduce class action legislation—because the issue was simply too contentious—and it is not surprising that a government on the eve of an election would want to avoid it.

By contrast, by the time Ian Scott was setting up consultations on class action reform in the late 1980s, the Liberal government was in a very strong position. It had been in power for two years with the help of the NDP (a party that was also sympathetic to the case for reform), and ostensibly had years ahead of it. In addition, the factors that had been favourable to the movement for reform in the early 1980s were now more mature and arguably more encouraging: there was the example of Quebec (and, to a

---

1 Interview of WA Bogart (1 April 2016) [Bogart interview].

2 Ontario Law Reform Commission, *Report on Class Actions* (Toronto: Ministry of the Attorney General, 1982) at 50–69, 70–75, 214–78 [OLRC Report]; Ontario, Ministry of the Attorney General (MAG), Policy Development Division, *Report of the Attorney General's Advisory Committee on Class Action Reform* (Toronto: Ministry of the Attorney General, 1990) at 56–73 and Part II [Advisory Committee Report].

3 Walter B Williston, *Report of the Civil Procedure Revision Committee* (Toronto: Ministry of the Attorney General, 1980) at 16.

4 [1983] 1 SCR 72 [*Naken*].

lesser extent, of the United States); and the influence of the *Charter*, which had undergone several years of litigation and had made lawyers and the public more comfortable with the concept of judicial activism, collective rights, and public interest standing. The OLRC Report's recommendation that contingency fees be allowed was quite contentious; by the time the Attorney General's Advisory Committee was discussing reform, however, contingency fees had been approved by the Law Society of Upper Canada and were receiving cautious acceptance among members of the bar. It was therefore easier for the Advisory Committee to recommend a court-supervised contingency fee, and thereby remove another major obstacle in the way of class actions (because few representative plaintiffs would choose to bear the financial burden of the class while having no greater an entitlement to any eventual damages award).

Nevertheless, conditions were not entirely favourable for the Advisory Committee. There were still fears of US-style excesses,[5] and business groups continued in their opposition to various aspects of reform, a fact noted by Michael Cochrane.[6] These obstacles were faced by the authors of both the OLRC and the Advisory Committee reports. However, there were other key differences between the reports that explained the success of the latter where the former had failed. Scott and Cochrane ensured that interest groups were prepared for the prospect of reform by organizing the Access to Justice Conference and attending the Uniform Law Conference of Canada (ULCC) Conference, both in the summer of 1988. The OLRC, by contrast, conducted virtually no consultations before releasing its report in 1982, long after the attorney general had referred the question of class actions to them and interested groups had submitted briefs. Most importantly, Scott and Cochrane oversaw a unique consultation process that mediated between the various interest groups and drew together their positions so that compromise on reform was possible.

5 Class Proceedings Communications Plan, MAG Communications Division [MAG communications plan], in Policy Development Division Counsel correspondence files, Class Actions—Miscellaneous Material, 1977–1981, RG 4-40, CA226, in Box No B248633, North York, Archives of Ontario. This document is undated but appears to have been prepared in November 1992. See also D Best, "Coming Soon: Legal Excess, US-Style" *Financial Times of Canada* (9 March 1992), referred to in MAG communications plan (above in this note at 3).

6 Cochrane handwritten notes (28 August 1985) at 18, in Policy Development Division Counsel correspondence files, Class Actions—General—File #1, 1985–1987, RG 4-40, in Box No B248633, North York, Archives of Ontario [Box No B248633—General File #1].

B. THE CONSULTATION PROCESS

More than anything else, it was Scott and Cochrane's unique consultation process that led to class action reform in Ontario. While the initial consultations in December 1988 and the following months may seem cursory, in comparison to the usual lengthy and formal consultation processes engaged in by governments, they were still more substantial than the OLRC's almost non-existent process. It was not until after the OLRC Report was released, to heavy criticism from many quarters, that the attorney general himself formally invited submissions from interested groups.

By contrast, Scott and Cochrane began their consultation process almost a year and a half before the Advisory Committee Report was released. Better yet, the parties with whom the government was consulting were also the authors of the report. Scott was well aware of the fate of the OLRC Report and the hackles it had raised in the business community; that was why he didn't simply introduce the OLRC's draft Act in the legislature upon becoming attorney general. Instead, he was willing to drop the controversial OLRC draft Act, start from scratch, and have a new act drafted by the interest groups themselves.[7] In negotiating with these groups, Scott and Cochrane often overreached and concluded that consensus had been reached or aspects of reform had been agreed to when in fact they hadn't, and Scott even stepped outside the bounds of his Cabinet mandate. Nevertheless, this "pushing" was never quite enough to drive away the interest groups (although at times it came close), and it arguably speeded up the consultation process and made the groups realize that reform was going to happen, whether they liked it or not.

The "pushiness" of Scott and Cochrane was combined with a willingness to mediate and compromise in order to reach an agreement on the terms of reference of the Advisory Committee. These terms of reference were key to the success of the report.[8] The MAG's initial consultations were aimed at securing the interest groups' commitment to reform around the terms of reference so that a public announcement could be made stating

---

7 Michael Cochrane encouraged Environment Minister Ruth Grier to do the same with the *Environmental Bill of Rights*—in other words, to drop the draft Act as detailed in her private member's bill, and bring the various interest groups to the negotiating table with entirely new terms of reference: Interview of Michael Cochrane (21 April 2016) [Cochrane interview 1].

8 Michael G Cochrane, "The Process of Principled Negotiation of Public Policy: An Overview" (unpublished, on file with the author) at 6 [Cochrane, "Principled Negotiation"].

that (1) reform would be taking place, (2) certain widely representative groups would be discussing the shape of that reform, and (3) the discussions would revolve around fixed terms of reference, which were not up for negotiation. To a certain extent, the shape of reform had been decided even before the Advisory Committee had its first meeting. The terms of reference meant the interest groups were publicly committed to reform[9] and could not leave the negotiating table without appearing to go back on their word. In exchange for agreeing to these terms of reference, Scott promised the members of the committee that he would carry forward their recommendations to Cabinet. This was important to the committee, who knew that their efforts would not be wasted.[10]

The process by which the Advisory Committee deliberated was also unique. It reflected a method that Cochrane dubbed the "principled negotiation of public policy."[11] The discussions of the committee were interest based rather than positional: for example, business groups did not approach the negotiating table simply stating that "class actions are bad for business," but instead negotiated the various aspects of reform in ways that would benefit business.[12] Because consumer and environmental groups did the same, the final product was a compromise that would benefit all groups to some degree. In addition, abandoning a positional approach meant that the groups at the table were more likely to listen to each other on the various aspects of reform, so that, for example,

9 *Ibid.*

10 *Ibid* at 2 and 6.

11 Cochrane's process is unique in that it has rarely been attempted outside of a certain number of contexts: namely, the *Class Proceedings Act*, the Attorney General's Advisory Committee on Mediation in Family Law, and the *Environmental Bill of Rights*. Cochrane spoke to Bob Rae about using the process for labour legislation, but this never materialized: Cochrane interview 1, above note 7. A similar process had been used for amendments to the *Labour Relations Act* between the 1960s and the 1980s, but by the 1990s, the government's approach had become much more restrictive: KM Burkett, "The Politicization of the Ontario Labour Relations Framework in the 1990s" (1998) 6 *Canadian Labour and Employment Law Journal* 161. There is evidence that a similar process was used for amendments to the *Competition Act*, which came into force in March 1999: Bill C-20, *An Act to amend the Competition Act and to make consequential and related amendments to other Acts*, Minutes of Proceedings and Evidence of the House of Commons Standing Committee on Industry (6 May 1998) (Norman Stewart and Peter Woolford), online: Parliament of Canada www.parl.gc.ca/HousePublications/Publication.aspx?DocId=1038689&Language=E&Mode=1&Parl=36&Ses=1 [*Competition Act* amendment—oral hearing].

12 Cochrane, "Principled Negotiation," above note 8 at 3–4 and 6–7.

consumer groups could see why business groups would want to retain the traditional costs rules.[13] The unique nature of this process was noted and appreciated by several members of the committee. This included Norm Stewart who, when making submissions to a Standing Committee nearly a decade later with regard to changes to competition legislation, stated that the process was ideal for framework legislation such as the *CPA*:

> They also work well when you have a contentious issue, where there is or has been some opposing views by various groups in society, and there's a need to legislate. Where you can bring those groups together in a strong framework, strong terms of reference, and with a careful chairperson to guide the process, you can reach a consensus you wouldn't ordinarily reach . . . [It] worked well in Ontario with their *Class Proceedings Act* and their *Environmental Bill of Rights Act* . . .[14]

David Poch, for Energy Probe (and as a director of the Canadian Environmental Law Association), also stated that because of the opportunity to educate and be educated, and to share goodwill with one's opponents, the process "was quite different from the usual multi-stakeholder consultation in which opposing viewpoints are presented to government with no resolution to the debate except by fiat."[15] Several other members of the committee have praised the "principled negotiation" concept in similar terms.[16]

Through this mediation-style process, the groups could reach a consensus and come up with unanimous recommendations for reform. According to the principled negotiation model, such unanimity eliminates the political risk for the minister concerned because it demonstrates

13 *Ibid* at 6–7; Cochrane interview 1, above note 7.

14 *Competition Act* amendment—oral hearing, above note 11.

15 Letter from Poch to Cochrane (10 January 1990), in Policy Development Division Counsel correspondence files, RG 4-40, in Box No B248633, North York, Archives of Ontario, at 1–2 [Poch Letter, 10 Jan 1990]. Poch added a few cautions, noting first that not every constituency was represented at the table, and that less well-financed groups would benefit from government funding to remedy this; second, that the government should avoid viewpoints that were too polarized, but at the same time should not paper over differences in opinion; and finally, that the success of any such consultation depended upon knowledgeable support from within the ministry (as happened here) and the political will to follow through with any recommendations.

16 Interview of Peter Woolford, representative of the Retail Council of Canada on the Attorney General's Advisory Committee (29 April 2016) [Woolford interview]; interview of Peter Woolford (27 September 2016) [Woolford interview 2]; interview of Advisory Committee member (13 April 2016) [AC member interview]; interview of Terrence O'Sullivan (21 June 2017).

a broad base of support. In exchange, the minister agrees to use their authority to promote the recommended reforms.[17] This is exactly what happened with the *Class Proceedings Act*: the Advisory Committee reached consensus on their recommendations, and Scott and Cochrane ensured that they were enacted, unchanged, into legislation.

The principled negotiation approach is a combination of a strong point of American politics (the very active involvement of interest groups and stakeholders in policy development) and a strength of Canadian politics (powerful Cabinet ministers who can single-handedly make reform happen in certain circumstances).[18] In the case of class action reform, the members of the Advisory Committee were motivated to reach a consensus because they knew that it would result in legislation that would be pushed through by Scott. Scott was not just any Cabinet minister; he had the force of personality and the political adroitness to push through class reform, and the unanimity of the Advisory Committee Report enabled him to do just that.

The consensus of the Advisory Committee stands in stark contrast to the divided nature of the OLRC Report. However reasonable it was, the dissent of OLRC chairman, Derek Mendes da Costa, substantially undermined the strength of the report. He dissented not only on the crucial issue of costs, but also on five other major issues.[19] Even supporters of class action reform observed that "[t]he proposals appear to be the product of different minds and sets of values."[20] The divisions and philosophical inconsistencies apparent in the OLRC Report are undoubtedly one of the reasons why McMurtry never introduced the draft Act as legislation. If the OLRC itself could not come to agreement, what hope was there for the massively divided stakeholders?

By contrast, Scott's insistence that the Advisory Committee reach a consensus meant that he could present the legislature and any opponents with a united front—it would be very difficult to oppose a report on which most of the key stakeholders had signed off.[21] In this way, Scott was able to pull together the many divergent interests and break the logjam on class action reform. Scott's strength of personality and his skills as

17 Cochrane, "Principled Negotiation," above note 8 at 5.

18 *Ibid* at 4.

19 OLRC Report, above note 2 at 851–54.

20 Andrew J Roman, "Class Actions in Canada: The Path to Reform?" (1988) 7 *Advocates' Society Journal* 28 at 1.

21 AC member interview, above note 16.

a minister, combined with the principled negotiation approach, are the main reasons why the Advisory Committee Report succeeded where the OLRC Report did not.

C. THE RECOMMENDATIONS

It was not only the unanimous nature of the Advisory Committee's recommendations that made its report so influential; it was also the nature and timing of its recommendations. The Advisory Committee Report departed as little as possible from the established rules of civil procedure, because each step away from the established rules would lead to more opposition.[22] That is one of the reasons why the report did not depart from the traditional costs rules—not only did the business interests strongly oppose such a change, but Cochrane, as well as the consumer and environmental representatives, knew that this departure would undermine the unanimity of the draft Act and make it much more difficult to "sell." The Advisory Committee Report had to chart a course between the desire of consumer and environmental groups to use class actions to enforce and advance their rights, and the desire of the business groups to adhere to the traditional rules of court and not change the substantive law.[23]

The OLRC Report, on the other hand, departed quite drastically from the established rules. Not only did it recommend that traditional costs rules not apply to class actions, it recommended that the attorney general have a right to intervene in private civil litigation; it would allow courts to enquire as to the competence of plaintiffs' counsel, and it would make class members take part in litigation unless the court gave them leave to opt out. Such recommendations indeed gave the OLRC Report an unrealistic air; a sense that these proposals would put an unacceptable burden on the civil litigation system.

This may have been a product of the authors of the report, very few of whom were actively involved in litigation at the time of writing. The OLRC did have an advisory committee on which several practising lawyers sat; however, this committee never met, and it does not appear

22 Bogart interview, above note 1.

23 Faced with the same situation in the United States, Marcus wrote that "decision-makers [have] muddle[d] through without picking sides," enabling the two desires to coexist by maintaining an ambiguity in the interpretation of class action doctrine: David Marcus, "The History of the Modern Class Action, Part I: *Sturm und Drang*, 1953–1980" (2013) 90 *Washington University Law Review* 587 at 597.

as if any of its members were ever consulted with regard to the OLRC Report.[24] This factor left the report open to accusations of "academic perfectionism" and a failure to "correct real-world problems."[25] It might also explain the length of the report, which, at nearly 900 pages, was read by very few people with more pressing things to do. The OLRC Report was repetitive and meandering. It read like a series of largely unedited essays by several different people; indeed, that is exactly what it was. This, in turn, would explain the length of time it took to write the report. Additionally, the timing of the OLRC Report was very poor. The fact that it took six years to write meant that any momentum the movement for reform might have had in 1976, when McMurtry wrote his reference, had long since dissipated by 1982. If it had not been for the *Naken* decision and the fact that Scott picked up the cause of class action reform later in the decade, the OLRC Report might have disappeared into obscurity entirely.

The Attorney General's Advisory Committee was very different in composition to the group that authored the OLRC Report. More than half of the committee were practising lawyers; where they were not lawyers, they were representatives with significant experience in their area of industry.[26] They were not only knowledgeable, but also representative of a fairly wide cross-section of the groups that would be affected by the *CPA*.[27] They knew from everyday experience how class actions would interact with the courts, the legal profession, and business. Furthermore, the forte of their recommendations was not their length (the Advisory Committee Report can be comfortably read in an hour), but rather their simplicity and their unanimity. As one of the members of the committee has put it, "[t]he unanimity of the product was essential. You don't even have to read the Report. It was unanimous."[28]

The timing of the Advisory Committee Report was also the result of political mastery. The Advisory Committee met over the course of

24 Letters from Derek Mendes da Costa to members of the OLRC Advisory Committee on Class Actions (7 July 1982), in Ontario Law Reform Commission files, Nov 1976–Dec 1982, Project name: class actions, RG 4-66, BA77, in Box No B380543, North York, Archives of Ontario.

25 Submission by the Canadian Manufacturers' Association to the Honourable R Roy McMurtry, QC, on Ontario Law Reform Commission Report on Class Actions (OLRC Report), September 1983, in Box No B248633—General File #1, above note 6.

26 Cochrane interview 1, above note 7.

27 Cochrane, "Principled Negotiation," above note 8 at 6.

28 AC member interview, above note 16.

at least six months, which enabled them to become educated about the other interests at the table and bring them closer to a compromise. It also allowed them to consult with their various constituencies to ensure that the consensus that was eventually reached was truly representative of those constituencies.[29] However, the process did not last much longer than that. The attorney general made his statement to the legislature regarding the consultation process at the end of June 1989, and the *CPA* received its first reading less than a year later. This meant that the attorney general could capitalize on the momentum that he had successfully built up with the various conferences on class actions as well as the consultation process.[30] He introduced legislation based on a unanimous report to a house that was well informed and very supportive of reform. In light of this, it is no surprise that the only real controversy in the legislature, when the bill was debated, was why it had taken so long to progress through its various readings.

D. POLITICAL WILL

Another secret to the success of the Advisory Committee Report was the political will behind it. The principled negotiation method advocated by Cochrane dictates that the unanimity of a committee's recommendations must be matched with the political will to implement them.[31] This was certainly true for the Advisory Committee Report, which Scott had the will and the ability to carry through into legislation. Both Scott and Cochrane made commitments to the Attorney General's Advisory Committee to get their draft legislation enacted without substantive changes,[32] and this is indeed what happened, despite the submissions of unions and tenants' groups that the *CPA* be amended to include those very groups.

Of course, Scott was part of a reformist government that had been largely sympathetic to his other changes, such as court reform and no-fault auto insurance. The NDP government that succeeded the Liberals in September 1990 was also sympathetic to the cause of class action

29 Cochrane, "Principled Negotiation," above note 8 at 7.

30 *Ibid.*

31 *Ibid* at 5.

32 Letter from Cochrane to AGAC (5 June 1990), in Policy Development Division Counsel correspondence files, Class Proceedings—Correspondence, 1990, CA226, RG 4-40, in Box No B248501, North York, Archives of Ontario; Cochrane interview 1, above note 7; AC member interview, above note 16.

reform. Politically, therefore, circumstances were in Scott's favour. It was his use of those circumstances, however, that led to the passage of the *CPA*. He knew that he needed to get the right people to the table and get them to agree on the shape of reform. Cochrane's negotiating skills and training as a mediator were also crucial in bringing the Advisory Committee to agreement. Once agreement was reached, Scott (and Cochrane) also had the determination and the ability to manoeuvre the unanimous report through the legislature without substantive changes.

The members of the Advisory Committee, as well as Cochrane himself and his superior, Doug Ewart, agree that Scott's personality was crucial to the successful enactment of class action reform.[33] Peter Woolford, who attended the committee meetings on behalf of the Retail Council of Canada (which was part of the Gang of Four), put it this way:

> I don't think the *CPA* would have happened without Mr. Scott. He was the driver, he was determined and had a brilliant legal mind. Everyone was deeply respectful of him and his skill and knowledge. Another Minister would not have had the credibility to get [the *CPA*] through. He was a very powerful Minister who clearly had the confidence of the Premier, and there was also the force of his personality. No Ian, no Act.[34]

Members of the Advisory Committee praise Scott as a masterful tactician[35] who provided the leadership that class action reform needed, and that few other attorneys general could have shown.[36] He was not an average attorney general—he not only ran his own ministry without interference, but was very influential and had a significant role in the work of other ministries.[37] Ewart recalls that Scott was "rhetorically adept. He never really lost that cross-examination style. He had the power of persuasion to get things through Cabinet. He was a lovely man but you didn't want to get into an argument with him."[38] Scott's determination did not mean that he was unprincipled; in fact, he strongly believed that it was his job as attorney general to ensure that matters of principle remained

---

33 AC member interview, *ibid.*

34 Woolford interview, above note 16; Bogart interview, above note 1.

35 AC member interview, above note 16.

36 Cochrane interview 1, above note 7; interview of David Poch (24 July 2017).

37 Interview of Douglas Ewart, then director of the Policy Development Division (and Michael Cochrane's direct superior) at the Ministry of the Attorney General (26 April 2016).

38 *Ibid.*

central to policy-making.[39] It did mean, however, that he was more interested in turning the right policies into law, than in how those policies became law, and this was exemplified in the class proceedings context.

The political determination of Ian Scott, combined with the unanimous support of the major stakeholders and the work of Cochrane, meant that the *CPA* saw the light of day after decades of debate on class action reform,[40] thereby leading the way for class action legislation throughout the rest of common law Canada.[41]

The political will behind the OLRC Report, by contrast, was clearly lukewarm at best. This was not due to any antipathy on McMurtry's part towards law reform in general: in fact, McMurtry was a very active attorney general for whom reform was a major priority. During his tenure, he introduced fifty-nine statutes that were passed by the Ontario legislature.[42] However, this enthusiasm did not extend to class actions. Following the release of the OLRC Report, the attorney general did not introduce class action legislation, despite the fact that the *Naken* court implicitly asked him to do so. It is not surprising that a certain amount of "criticism and cynicism set in as [the] government used [the consultation process] to delay, rather than develop, reform,"[43] as the OLRC had not reported for six years and, even after that, there was no government commitment to implement its recommendations.[44] If Scott had not broken the logjam,[45] class actions in Ontario could have stagnated for another decade,[46] which is what happened in New Brunswick and British Columbia.

---

39 Ian Scott, "Law, Policy, and the Role of the Attorney-General: Constancy and Change in the 1980s" (1989) 39 *University of Toronto Law Journal* 109 at 112.

40 AC member interview, above note 16.

41 The only province without class action legislation is Prince Edward Island. Even here, a class action can be brought pursuant to the common law following the Supreme Court of Canada's decision in *Western Canadian Shopping Centres Inc v Dutton*, 2001 SCC 46, which effectively overturned *Naken*.

42 Roy McMurtry, *Memoirs and Reflections* (Toronto: University of Toronto Press, 2013) at 198.

43 Cochrane, "Principled Negotiation," above note 8 at 1.

44 *Ibid.*

45 WA Bogart, Jasminka Kalajdzic, & Ian Matthews, "Class Actions in Canada: A National Procedure in a Multi-jurisdictional Society?" (Report for the Globalization of Class Actions Conference, Oxford University, December 2007) at 3.

46 AC member interview, above note 16.

E. FLAWS IN THE ADVISORY COMMITTEE PROCESS

The principled negotiation method by which Scott and Cochrane successfully brought about class action reform was well received by almost all who observed it. It was praised in the legislature as "a collaboration process [that] make[s] people the real players."[47] Members of the Advisory Committee also said that the method "was quite different from the usual multi-stakeholder consultation ... Here it seemed possible to obtain a result that satisfied everyone. One reason is the opportunity to educate one's enemy and be educated in turn. Another is due to the goodwill shared by all the participants."[48] The process engendered a great deal of goodwill and was ultimately successful in bringing about class action reform. However, it was not without its flaws.

The main charge against the principled negotiation process is that it is anti-democratic. The process worked in the case of the *CPA* because the members of the Advisory Committee reached a consensus in exchange for Scott's promise to get the legislation through the House unamended. In Cochrane's words, "[i]t is essentially an almost contractual relationship between the political forces in Cabinet and the public as represented by these key stakeholders."[49] But who is party to that contract? This question raises two problems from the perspective of democracy.

The first is that there is no guarantee that the "key stakeholders" are truly representative of the public. Scott selected the Attorney General's Advisory Committee based on people and organizations with whom he had worked previously.[50] The assumption was that these organizations had the power to "veto" class action reform if they were not consulted.[51] Once the committee had been selected, the powerful business interests ensured that no additional groups were invited to the table on the basis that the process would be unworkable.[52] The fact that one man, or a

47 Ontario, Legislative Assembly, *Official Report of Debates (Hansard)*, 35th Parl, 1st Sess (18 November 1991) (Charles Harnick), online: http://hansardindex.ontla.on.ca/hansardeissue/35-1/l083.htm.

48 Poch Letter, 10 Jan 1990, above note 15.

49 Cochrane, "Principled Negotiation," above note 8 at 5.

50 Woolford interview, above note 16.

51 Cochrane, "Principled Negotiation," above note 8 at 6.

52 Letter from Gang of Four to Scott (11 May 1989) at 9, in Policy Development Division Counsel correspondence files, Class Actions—Advisory Committee minutes and notes, 1989–1990, MGC, RG 4-40, in Box No B502275, North York, Archives of

small group of men, could decide who would sit at the negotiating table, does not seem especially democratic.[53] Women's groups, especially, felt that they were not sufficiently represented in the debate on class action reform.[54] If the basis of the principled negotiation process is that the key stakeholders represent the public, the Attorney General's Advisory Committee arguably failed in this respect.[55]

The representative nature of the committee may also have been compromised by the fact that lobbying the government is expensive. Briefs need to be researched and written, meetings attended, vast amounts of material read. This all takes time and money. Groups with more resources are therefore more likely to lobby the government on certain issues, and, when it comes to selecting an advisory committee, are more likely to be chosen because the minister involved knows who they are. They can also afford to send a representative for monthly or weekly meetings. Once on the committee, groups with more resources will have the time and money to be better prepared and better informed. As a result, financially less advantaged groups will be drowned out. This was arguably the case with the Attorney General's Advisory Committee. For example, Rollie Thompson, representative of the Consumers' Association of Canada (CAC), was unable to sit on the committee due to cuts to CAC funding.[56] The environmental and consumer representatives missed more committee meetings than any other members, in all likelihood due to time and resource constraints.[57] The Retail Council of Canada, on the other hand, had numerous lawyers and marketing experts at its disposal.[58]

Ontario [Box No B502275—AGAC minutes]. See also Cochrane, "Principled Negotiation," above note 8 at 6: "The negotiating table can only accommodate so many voices."

53 This is ironic, given Scott's self-avowed commitment to broad-based consultations on major policy decisions: see Ian Scott with Neil McCormick, *To Make a Difference: A Memoir* (Toronto: Stoddart, 2001) at 144.

54 Minutes of the Attorney General's Advisory Committee on Class Action Reform (23 November 1989) at 16 [AGAC minutes, 23 Nov 1989], in Box No B502275—AGAC minutes, above note 52.

55 Poch Letter, 10 Jan 1990, above note 15: "not every constituency was represented at the table." Poch did not refer to any constituencies specifically.

56 Letter from Cochrane to Thompson (1 May 1989) in Box No B502275—AGAC minutes, above note 52.

57 The representatives of the CAC and the Canadian Environmental Law Association missed four of the ten meetings. This was twice as many meetings as were missed by Helen Gagné and Robert Anderson (both members of the Gang of Four; the other members of the Four only missed one meeting).

58 Woolford interview 2, above note 16.

As David Poch, representative of Energy Probe and a director of the Canadian Environmental Law Association, pointed out:

> [T]he wealthier interests will always be able to pay for good representation in the consultation process. The situation is analogous to that of class actions—improved access is only valuable if you can also afford to get involved. Environmental groups, minority groups and other special interests that do not have a direct pecuniary interest or who are relatively poorer need both access and funding.[59]

Cochrane also admitted that funding would be required in order to make the principled negotiation process truly representative.[60] The ability of better-resourced groups to make stronger and more frequent submissions was not unique to the Advisory Committee; this was also the case with the submissions on the Legislative Review Project, the OLRC Report, and before that, the debate on the *Competition Act*.[61]

The second problem with the principled negotiation process is the implied promise by the ministers involved that they will carry through the draft Act into legislation. In the case of class action reform, this effectively meant that the unanimous recommendations of the committee were enacted into legislation without any meaningful democratic oversight by the legislature. As noted in Chapter 4, the committee agreed upon a draft Act, and then undertook a clause-by-clause review of the legislative counsel's work to ensure that it complied with their draft and their consensus. Once this bill was drafted, Scott and Cochrane ensured

---

59 Poch Letter, 10 Jan 1990, above note 15 at 1. See also interview of Michael Cochrane (28 June 2016).

60 Cochrane, "Principled Negotiation," above note 8 at 7. On the funding of public participation in consultations, Ian Scott was of the same view: Ian Scott & Raj Anand, "Financing Public Participation in Environmental Decision Making" (1982) 60 *Canadian Bar Review* 81.

61 This was also true for the Law Commission of Ontario's current review of the *CPA*: Law Commission of Ontario, *Review of Class Actions in Ontario: Issues to Be Considered* (Toronto: Law Commission of Ontario, 2013), online: www.lco-cdo.org/wp-content/uploads/2014/01/class-actions-issues-to-be-considered.pdf [LCO 2013]. See also "Class Actions: Objectives, Experience and Reforms," announcement online: www.lco-cdo.org/wp-content/uploads/2013/04/CA-Press-Release-FINAL-Sept-22-2017.pdf; Law Commission of Ontario, *Class Actions: Objectives, Experiences and Reforms: Consultation Paper* (Toronto: Law Commission of Ontario, 2018) [LCO 2018]. Defence counsel have already established committees to monitor and develop submissions. See, for example, the International Association of Defense Counsel's Canadian Class Actions Project Task Force.

that it passed through the legislature without substantive amendment, over and above the submissions of unions and tenant groups, as well as some expressions of concern by various ministers.

The lack of democratic oversight also meant that there was nothing stopping the more powerful representatives (that is, the business groups) from exerting an undue amount of influence on the creation of the *CPA*. These private interests used their influence to make the *CPA* as conservative as possible, especially regarding costs. This began even before the Advisory Committee's first meeting. Due to the Gang of Four's influence, Scott exceeded the terms of the Cabinet minute authorizing consultations by dropping the no-way costs requirement from the terms of reference.

This was a politicization of the process that Scott was virtually powerless to stop if he wanted a consensus. The Gang of Four held a veto power over class action reform[62]—Scott needed their support in order to obtain his unanimous report, but if they did not support reform, it was very likely that it simply would not happen (which would be just fine from the business groups' standpoint). He had much more to lose from a failure to bring about reform (having announced publicly that it would happen) than did the business groups. They could therefore play on Scott's desire for consensus. The group also did this with regard to the fund, telling Scott that if he wanted class action reform, his government would have to pay for it. Scott's need for unanimity meant that he was willing to compromise, even against the terms of his government mandate.

F. COMPROMISES MADE IN THE ADVISORY COMMITTEE PROCESS

The fact that there was little accountability to the consultation process also meant that compromises were made against the wishes of the legislature. As noted in Chapter 4, Scott stepped outside the bounds of his Cabinet mandate by agreeing to terms of reference that were not reflected in the Cabinet minute of 21 June 1989. This included dropping the term of reference that specifically mandated no-way costs. While the secretary of the Cabinet picked up on the fact that Scott's public commitment to a new statute was beyond the bounds of his mandate, the other

62 Scott was of the view that if the business groups did not agree to class action reform, it simply wouldn't happen: Cochrane interview 1, above note 7.

transgressions seem to have slipped by unnoticed. The government's public commitment to no-way costs, therefore, was simply dropped. Having been dropped as a public commitment, it was much easier to drop as part of the discussions of the Advisory Committee.

The consumer and environmental advocates were willing to back down on no-way costs in exchange for a no-merits certification test. In addition, plaintiffs would also be able to make use of contingency fee agreements, and could also apply to the fund for financial assistance. The intent of the Advisory Committee was that plaintiffs would not have to pay up-front fees (their lawyers would assume these under a contingency fee agreement), and would be protected from any adverse cost awards by the fund.[63] In certain circumstances (for example, public interest cases), the court could also exercise its discretion not to award costs against the plaintiffs. The end result would be essentially the same as no-way costs, without departing too far from traditional costs rules.[64] The expectation was also that a no-merits certification process would be fairly straightforward and consume relatively little time and few resources.[65]

Unfortunately, however, the practice of class actions has not reflected the hopes of the Advisory Committee. Although the committee made it clear that its recommendations on certification were closely intertwined with its recommendations on the fund, contingency fees, and traditional costs rules,[66] there is serious doubt as to whether those recommendations are functioning as intended.[67] Given that other provinces such as British Columbia, Manitoba, Saskatchewan, and Newfoundland and Labrador have the no-way costs rule,[68] the Law Commission of Ontario has stated that "[a] comparative analysis of the way in which adverse costs alter the landscape of class actions in Canada would assist to paint a clearer picture of its impact."[69] Such a study has not been conducted to date,[70] and

63 Advisory Committee Report, above note 2 at 49–51 and 58–61.

64 *Ibid* at 56–61.

65 AGAC minutes, 23 Nov 1989, above note 54 at 4; Advisory Committee Report, above note 2 at 31.

66 Advisory Committee Report, *ibid* at 72; see also memorandum from Cochrane to Scott (28 May 1990) at 2, in Policy Development Division Counsel correspondence files, Class Actions—Drafting Instructions, 1989–1990, MGC, RG 4-40, in Box No B248633, North York, Archives of Ontario.

67 LCO 2013, above note 61 at 9.

68 *Ibid.*

69 *Ibid* at 10. See also LCO 2018, above note 61 at 22.

70 Correspondence from the Law Commission of Ontario (14 July 2016).

would prove a fruitful avenue for future research. For now, however, it is clear that the costs provisions of the *CPA* are not functioning quite as the Advisory Committee intended, and may even be obstructing the goal of access to justice underlying the Act.[71]

G. CONCLUSION

The Attorney General's Advisory Committee succeeded where the OLRC failed. The committee's success owed a great deal to the personality of Ian Scott, and the innovative consultation process that he set up with the help of Michael Cochrane. The collaborative nature of the Advisory Committee Report and the political will with which it was carried forward into legislation explains its success. However, this success was not entirely democratic.[72] The consensus of the Advisory Committee was admirable, but many groups remained shut out of this process, and the political "contract" that Ian Scott made with the committee meant that the *CPA* was not subject to meaningful democratic oversight. In addition, the compromises that had to be made in order to reach unanimity were not without consequences. Class actions came about in Ontario when they did because Scott knew that consensus was the key, and that consensus involved negotiation and compromise. The compromises made for the sake of reform, however, are still being felt among class actions lawyers nearly a quarter of a century later.

71 LCO 2013, above note 61 at 9.

72 However, Scott and his colleagues in the Ontario government learned the hard way that highly democratic and consultative processes can have less-than-happy endings. The Meech Lake Accord failed around the time the Attorney General's Advisory Committee began to meet, and this experience may have taught Scott that a less-than-democratic success was better than a highly democratic failure.

Chapter 6

CLASS ACTIONS TWENTY-FIVE YEARS ON

To bring about the *Class Proceedings Act* (*CPA*), the Attorney General's Advisory Committee (Advisory Committee) made a number of compromises in order to secure a consensus in an area that "has been the subject of controversy and debate."[1] Consumer and environmental representatives compromised on the issue of costs, while the business interests compromised on the issue of contingency fees and a no-merits certification test. Both groups looked to the government to establish the Class Proceedings Fund (CPF) to provide further financial assistance to litigants.

While the result led to the advent of class proceedings in Ontario, and thereafter in the rest of common law Canada, the underlying controversies remained. The issue of costs was front and centre in the first action brought under the *CPA*. In *Smith v Canadian Tire Acceptance Ltd*,[2] as detailed in the previous chapter, Larry Whaley attempted to shield himself from an adverse costs award by putting forward a "straw man" plaintiff. Although the court quickly thwarted this attempt, the case raised the hackles of many who were already apprehensive of the new legislation.[3]

1 Ontario, Ministry of the Attorney General (MAG), Policy Development Division, *Report of the Attorney General's Advisory Committee on Class Action Reform* (Toronto: Ministry of the Attorney General, 1990) at 24–25 [Advisory Committee Report].

2 1995 CanLII 7163 (Ont Ct Gen Div).

3 Jean-Marc Leclerc, "'The Sport of Kings: Financing Class Actions in Ontario" (2012) 8:1 *Canadian Class Action Review* 121 at 129–31.

Twenty-five years later, the controversies continue. Some were envisaged by the Advisory Committee, such as the intertwined issues of costs, funding, and certification. Other issues have arisen because they were not sufficiently addressed by the committee or by other bodies such as the Law Society of Upper Canada, namely, the issue of ethics in class actions. Still other controversies, such as carriage motions and overlapping class actions, barely crossed the drafters' minds, but today threaten to undermine the very purposes of the *CPA*.

Given the controversial nature of the Act, as well as the dearth of precedents on which its drafters could rely (after the United States and Quebec, Ontario was one of the first jurisdictions in the world to enact class proceedings legislation), it is scarcely surprising that such issues have arisen. The nature of the Act's framework papered over many of these controversies and left much to the discretion of judges. For example, while traditional costs rules continue to apply, courts have the discretion to make no order as to costs pursuant to section 31; the certification test under section 5(1) is silent regarding the evidentiary burden on the plaintiff; and the Act makes no mention of carriage motions or national class actions, which have been managed under the court's residual power to determine the conduct of its own proceeding under section 12, as well as its ability to stay related proceedings under section 13. The caselaw arising from such broad-brush provisions has given rise to uncertainty and inefficiency as the concept of class proceedings has matured and expanded to other Canadian jurisdictions.

This is why the Law Commission of Ontario (LCO) commenced a review of the *CPA* in 2013, stating "[i]t is unclear whether the *CPA* is working as intended and many unforeseen challenges associated with it have become fodder for discussion in conferences, academic papers, professional associations, social media and other commentary."[4] This chapter will review several of these class actions controversies, which stem from the manner in which the *CPA* was drafted and passed, as well as the Act's

4 Law Commission of Ontario, *Review of Class Actions in Ontario: Issues to Be Considered* (Toronto: Law Commission of Ontario, 2013) at 9, online: www.lco-cdo.org/wp-content/uploads/2014/01/class-actions-issues-to-be-considered.pdf [LCO 2013]. After stalling for some time, this project was relaunched in 2017 and renamed "Class Actions: Objectives, Experience and Reforms," announcement online: www.lco-cdo.org/wp-content/uploads/2013/04/CA-Press-Release-FINAL-Sept-22-2017.pdf. See also Law Commission of Ontario, *Class Actions: Objectives, Experiences and Reforms: Consultation Paper* (Toronto: Law Commission of Ontario, 2018) [LCO 2018].

various lacunae. The central issues that will be addressed include costs and funding; the certification process; ethics; and overlapping actions, including carriage motions. These issues are crucial to the operation of the *CPA* and remain contentious despite a quarter of a century of caselaw.

A. COSTS AND FUNDING

The Advisory Committee recognized that the application of traditional costs rules to class actions would expose a representative plaintiff to a potentially enormous adverse costs award, far in excess of that plaintiff's interest in the proceeding. That is why the committee explicitly stated that the class actions remedy was contingent on a public fund to indemnify representative plaintiffs.[5] Neither the Ontario Law Reform Commission (OLRC) nor the Advisory Committee reports foresaw the development of third party litigation funding;[6] however, the Advisory Committee, at least, recognized the underlying necessity of such funding.[7] Subsequent caselaw also noted the "grim reality" posed by the traditional costs rules:

> [N]o person in their right mind would accept the role of representative plaintiff if he or she were at risk of losing everything they own. No one, no matter how altruistic, would risk such a loss over a modest claim. Indeed, no rational person would risk an adverse costs award of several million dollars to recover several thousand dollars or even several tens of thousand dollars.[8]

Funding, whether by the CPF or by a third party funder, is therefore essential in order to remove a barrier to access to justice: "the prospect of a crushing costs award to be borne by the representative plaintiff or counsel."[9] Such arrangements are a reality of the committee's recommendation that the traditional costs rules apply to class actions.

---

5 Advisory Committee Report, above note 1 at 72. See also David Gourlay, "A Class Act Comes of Age: Costs and Certification as the OLRC Report Turns Twenty" (2004) 1:2 *Canadian Class Action Review* 273 at 280.

6 Jon Bricker, "Ontario's Class Proceedings Fund: A Good (If Less Than Perfect) Class Action Costs Model" (2008) 4:2 *Canadian Class Action Review* 399 at 417.

7 Advisory Committee Report, above note 1 at 56–59.

8 *Dugal v Manulife Financial Corp*, 2011 ONSC 1785 at para 28 [*Dugal*].

9 *Ibid* at para 33. While an indemnification by class counsel would serve the same purpose as an indemnification by a funder, this brings with it its own problems that will be addressed further below.

The committee established two mechanisms to cushion the impact of this reality for certain types of cases. First, section 31(1) of the *CPA* invites courts, when exercising their discretion to award costs, to consider whether the class proceeding is a test case, raises a novel point of law, or involves a matter of public interest. If the case falls into any of these categories, the plaintiff or defendant may be relieved from any obligation to pay costs (or may be subject to a reduced costs award). Second, the CPF was designed to provide funding to plaintiffs for disbursements and any adverse costs, in meritorious cases or proceedings that affect the public interest.[10] Both mechanisms were intended to provide relief from traditional costs rules, such that the effect would be similar to that of a no-way costs regime. In practice, however, the result has been rather different.[11]

With regard to the courts' discretion not to award costs against unsuccessful plaintiffs pursuant to section 31, this was used fairly widely until the mid-2000s.[12] Where costs were awarded against plaintiffs, the quantum tended to be fairly low, in the range of $5,000 to $15,000.[13] Subsequently, however, courts began to make much larger adverse costs awards, in the hundreds of thousands of dollars, and to exercise their discretion under section 31 much more sparingly.[14] In 2007, the Supreme Court of Canada found the unsuccessful plaintiff in *Kerr v Danier Leather Inc*[15] liable for the defendants' costs, estimated to be in excess of $1 million,[16] despite the plaintiff's submission that the case involved a matter of public interest. A decade later, an unsuccessful certification motion in a class action involving the Rana Plaza factory collapse led to an award of more than $2.3

10 *Class Proceedings*, O Reg 771/92, s 5 [Funding Regulations].

11 Gourlay, above note 5 at 292.

12 See, for example, *Ciano v York University*, [2000] OJ No 681 (SCJ), aff'd 2000 CarswellOnt 3248 (CA); *Williams v Mutual Life Assurance Co of Canada*, [2001] OJ No 445 (SCJ); *Vennell v Barnado's*, 2004 CanLII 33357 (Ont SCJ), all cases cited in Bricker, above note 6 at 404.

13 Bricker, above note 6; Gourlay, above note 5 at 298–99.

14 Bricker, above note 6 at 403–8; Gourlay, above note 5 at 298–99 and 301–2; Michael PA Carabash, "Ethical Conduct for Class Counsel in Ontario" (2006) 3:2 *Canadian Class Action Review* 617 at 626–27.

15 2007 SCC 44 [*Danier Leather*]. See also *McCracken v Canadian National Railway Co*, 2012 ONSC 6838 [*McCracken*].

16 Bricker, above note 6 at 405; a premium of $1 million was awarded to the successful plaintiffs at trial: 2005 CanLII 16619 (Ont SCJ). There is no reported costs decision following the Supreme Court of Canada's judgment, and it therefore appears as if the costs issue was settled between the parties.

million against the plaintiffs.[17] Such decisions have demonstrated that the courts interpret section 31 permissively, and are not necessarily obligated to discount costs simply because the litigation involves the public interest.[18] They have also placed something of a chill on ostensibly novel or public interest cases, with a fair amount of unpredictability that plaintiffs' counsel will be absolved from paying costs.[19]

The courts' varying interpretations of the terms "test case," "novel point of law," and "public interest" have exacerbated this uncertainty. While "test case" is the term that is best defined in the jurisprudence, courts have been wary about using it to shield plaintiffs from adverse costs.[20] "Novel point of law" has been used much more often, but its definition is much more nebulous and uncertain.[21] The term "public interest" has also been subject to various interpretations, with different criteria applied in different cases.[22]

In recent years, it has become relatively rare for a court to exercise its discretion not to award costs against an unsuccessful plaintiff.[23] As Binnie J stated in *Danier Leather*, general concerns about access to justice do not necessarily warrant a departure from the usual costs consequences: "it should not be assumed that class proceedings invariably engage access to justice concerns to an extent sufficient to justify withholding costs from the successful party . . . caution must be exercised not to stereotype class proceedings."[24] Courts have also found that section 31 can be used to deny plaintiffs their costs when they succeed on a certification motion (that is, the provision can be used in favour of defendants).[25] In certain instances, judges have even found that section 31 adds nothing to the considerations

17 *Das v George Weston Ltd*, 2017 ONSC 5583 [*Das*].

18 LCO 2013, above note 4 at 9; LCO 2018, above note 4 at 22; *Das, ibid* at paras 49–50.

19 LCO 2013, above note 4 at 9; LCO 2018, above note 4 at 22; Bricker, above note 6 at 425.

20 Bricker, *ibid* at 405–6.

21 *Ibid* at 406; *McCracken*, above note 15 at para 80.

22 Bricker, above note 6 at 407; *McCracken*, above note 15 at paras 78–79.

23 Edwin G Upenieks & Angela H Kwok, "Costs in Class Actions" (Presentation delivered to the Advocates' Society, 9 May 2017, at 7), online: www.lawrences.com/docs/default-source/publications/costs-in-class-actions.pdf?sfvrsn=5.

24 *Danier Leather*, above note 15 at para 69.

25 Matthew Fleming & Ara Basmadjian, "Costs Awards in Class Actions: Equal Treatment for Plaintiffs and Defendants" (30 June 2015), online: International Law Office www.dentons.com/en/~/media/e9abfafe25904b9987f3a846afdd2e3e.ashx, referring to the costs decision in *Fischer v IG Investment Management Ltd*, 2014 ONSC 6260, leave to appeal refused, 2015 ONSC 2491.

courts have always taken into account when awarding costs.[26] This has provided even more uncertainty, and has made it even more unlikely that plaintiffs will proceed with litigation on the chance that they will be insulated from costs under section 31 of the *CPA*.[27]

With regard to the CPF, a number of factors have deterred plaintiffs' counsel from making applications to the Class Proceedings Committee, which administers the fund. First, the committee has proven quite conservative in its willingness to fund cases, and has only approved about two-thirds of applications to date.[28] By contrast, the Quebec *Fonds* has an approval rate of 91 percent and covers the applicant's own legal fees.[29] The committee's risk-averse approach that assesses the merits of the case and its chances of being certified[30] has given rise to a general perception that it will only fund cases that are "sure bets." As a result, some commentators have suggested that most claims fall into one of two groups: those that are so risky that the committee will not fund them; and those with much less risk that class counsel are willing to fund themselves (or submit to a third party funder for a lower premium, as will be discussed further below).[31] This may be an oversimplification of the matter, because the committee does not simply look at a case's chance of success—it also looks at other factors, such as a case's importance as a matter of public interest. The committee has therefore funded several cases in this category that are also very risky or novel.[32] Nevertheless, although the CPF is not motivated by profit, it is sustained by the levies it obtains on

26 Gourlay, above note 5 at 298–300, and cases cited therein.

27 *Ibid* at 293.

28 Law Foundation of Ontario, *Class Proceedings Fund: 20 Years in Review*, online: www.lawfoundation.on.ca/wp-content/uploads/CPF-Brochure-2013.pdf at 7 and 14 [CPF Review]. This figure does not include applications for funding that were withdrawn and in which no funding decision was required. Between 1992 and 2009, only 52 percent of applications were approved: Leclerc, above note 3 at 128.

29 Janet Walker et al, *Class Actions in Canada: Cases, Notes and Materials* (Toronto: Emond Montgomery, 2013) at 232; Gourlay, above note 5 at 296–97.

30 "Implementation of Bill 29 (the *LSAA*)" (29 November 1992), in Policy Development Division Counsel correspondence files, CPA—Regulations, 1992–1993, CR, RG 4-40, in Box No B703283, North York, Archives of Ontario.

31 Bricker, above note 6 at 422–23; Gourlay, above note 5 at 294.

32 Gina Papageorgiou, "Ontario's Class Proceedings Fund: Separating Fact from Fiction" (2015) 10:1 *Canadian Class Action Review* 81 at 92. By way of example, the committee approved funding for the Rana Plaza class action: see *Das*, above note 17 at para 2.

successful cases. It cannot therefore fund too many risky cases if it is to remain solvent.[33]

Second, the application process for funding is quite labour intensive, taking up time that many counsel would prefer to spend on preparing for the certification motion; and there are also ongoing reporting obligations.[34] Third and most significantly, the premium on funding is disproportionately high, especially in very successful cases.[35] The plaintiff must pay to the fund a levy of 10 percent of any award or settlement funds to which class members are entitled.[36] This amount cannot be negotiated and remains the same regardless of the anticipated costs or disbursements; it also reduces the amount that is ultimately paid to class members.[37]

While there are some advantages of applying to the fund (for example, it reduces the risk that the funder will attempt to control the course of the litigation, which is a potential danger with third party funding), there are also significant drawbacks. As a result, the majority of plaintiff lawyers simply choose not to make an application to the CPF.[38] Without an application to the fund, the barrier to representative plaintiffs remains: they are faced with a potentially enormous adverse costs award. Historically, in order to remove this barrier, plaintiff counsel offered to indemnify their clients against such an award.[39] Because counsel had much more to gain from the proceeding than a representative plaintiff, offering to indemnify the client became not only acceptable but the ethical thing to do.[40] The practice became so widespread that courts openly acknowledged that representative plaintiffs "are only fictionally affected by costs

33 Papageorgiou, above note 32 at 96–97; Gourlay, above note 5 at 294; interview of David Poch (24 July 2017).

34 Walker et al, above note 29 at 233; Bricker, above note 6 at 421.

35 Walker et al, above note 29 at 233; Bricker, above note 6; Leclerc, above note 3 at 128; Carabash, above note 14 at 624.

36 Funding Regulations, above note 10, s 10.

37 Leclerc, above note 3 at 128–29; Paul Perell, "Class Proceedings and Lawyers' Conflicts of Interest" (2009) 35 *Advocates' Quarterly* 202 at 208.

38 CPF Review, above note 28 at 1 (only 10 percent of all class actions in Ontario to date have received funding). This was predicted by Kent Roach in his review of Michael Cochrane's book (Michael G Cochrane, *Class Actions: A Guide to the Class Proceedings Act, 1992* (Aurora, ON: Canada Law Book, 1993)), in "Book Reviews" (1994) 23 *Canadian Business Law Journal* 156 at 159. See also Bricker, above note 6 at 420; Carabash, above note 14 at 624; Gourlay, above note 5 at 280 and 293.

39 *Bayens v Kinross Gold Corporation*, 2013 ONSC 4974 at para 29 [*Bayens*].

40 *Ibid* at para 30; Perell, above note 37 at 208–9.

awards."[41] In certain cases, courts have even found that counsel's failure to provide an indemnity affects the plaintiff's suitability to act as a representative for the class.[42]

Indemnities by class counsel come with their own hazards, however. Because the financial risk is entirely on the lawyers in such circumstances, cases are likely to be selected not on the basis of merit, but because they can be litigated for less money.[43] Class actions will be litigated by a small number of firms that are prepared to take such a risk, and have the resources and expertise to do so.[44] In addition, representative plaintiffs with a very small potential claim are unlikely to be in a position to question the litigation decisions of lawyers that are bearing all the risk. This can be problematic where conflicts of interest arise.[45] Finally, class counsel providing an indemnity are likely to be much more risk-averse, not only in their selection of cases but their conduct of them, potentially to the detriment of the class.[46] For example, counsel providing an indemnity will be tempted to accept settlements that do not provide fair compensation to the class, but that do provide a swift legal fee that allows the lawyers to move on to more lucrative cases. Alternatively, lawyers can delay settlement if they decide that their fees are not high enough.[47] Because lawyers who provide an indemnity are invested in their cases to such a significant degree, they may be tempted to compromise the interests of the class.[48]

The practice of providing indemnities began to wane as the quantum of adverse costs awards began to increase exponentially. Costs awards

---

41 *McCracken v Canadian National Railway Co*, 2010 ONSC 6026 at paras 7 and 9.

42 *Poulin v Ford Motor Company of Canada Limited*, 2007 CanLII 56490 at para 51 (Ont SCJ).

43 Bricker, above note 6 at 413.

44 *Ibid* at 414. Bricker predicts that, should indemnification by counsel become the norm, "there is some risk that the class action bar would quickly become a fairly cloistered world" (*ibid*). Most members of the class action bar would acknowledge that this risk has now become a reality. See also Perell J's comments in *Houle v St Jude Medical Inc*, 2017 ONSC 5129 at para 79 [*Houle*].

45 Jasminka Kalajdzic, "Self-Interest, Public Interest, and the Interests of the Absent Client: Legal Ethics and Class Action Praxis" (2011) 49 *Osgoode Hall Law Journal* 1 at 11 [Kalajdzic, "Self-Interest"]. See also the Honourable Chief Justice Warren K Winkler, "Caught in a Trap—Ethical Considerations for the Plaintiff's Lawyer in Class Proceedings," online: www.ontariocourts.on.ca/coa/en/ps/speeches/caught.htm [Winkler speech].

46 Bricker, above note 6 at 414–15.

47 Leclerc, above note 3 at 151.

48 These and other ethical questions will be addressed later in this chapter.

against plaintiffs following unsuccessful certification motions were fairly low in the early years of class proceedings.[49] However, from at least 2009, adverse costs awards began to balloon, and such awards can now easily amount to half a million dollars or more.[50] Class counsel became increasingly unwilling to provide indemnities for such potentially astronomical costs awards. With an application to the fund proving equally unattractive, counsel were drawn towards third party litigation funding.[51]

Third party funding first made an appearance in Canada in 2009, when the court approved a private funding arrangement in an Alberta class action, *Hobsbawn v ATCO Gas and Pipelines Ltd*.[52] They came to Ontario the same year. In *Metzler Investment GMBH v Gildan Activewear Inc*,[53] the court denied a funding arrangement on the grounds that there was no cap on the amount the funder would receive in the event of settlement or judgment.[54] While the court held that third party funding agreements are not inherently champertous,[55] it also held that they could become so in certain circumstances, for example, where the funder is able to control the conduct of the litigation by attending settlement discussions or withdrawing financial support at short notice.[56]

Two years later, a third party funding agreement was approved in Ontario for the first time in *Dugal v Manulife Financial Corp*.[57] In this case, the agreement included a cap on the compensation the funder would receive, an explicit acknowledgement that class counsel's duties were to the plaintiffs and not the funder, and a provision whereby funding could only be withdrawn if the plaintiffs breached their obligations under the agreement.[58] The arrangement was therefore found not to be champertous

49 Walker et al, above note 29 at 230.

50 *Ibid* at 226 and 230; Bricker, above note 6 at 425: Papageorgiou, above note 32 at 86–88. For a summary of costs awards prior to 2010, see *Singer v Schering-Plough Canada Inc*, 2010 ONSC 1737 at para 10.

51 *Bayens*, above note 39 at paras 33–34; Jasminka Kalajdzic et al, "Justice for Profit: A Comparative Analysis of Australian, Canadian and US Third Party Litigation Funding" (2013) 61:1 *American Journal of Comparative Law* 93 at 118 [Kalajdzic et al, "Justice"].

52 (14 May 2009), 0101-04999 (Alta QB), cited in Walker et al, above note 29 at 238, and Leclerc, above note 3 at 131.

53 (2009), 81 CPC (6th) 384 (Ont SCJ) [*Metzler*].

54 *Ibid* at paras 71–73.

55 *Ibid* at para 63. See also *Bayens*, above note 39 at para 41.

56 *Metzler*, above note 53 at paras 58–60.

57 *Dugal*, above note 8.

58 *Ibid* at para 6.

and was approved, although the court required that the third party funder (who had no assets in Ontario) post security for costs.[59] A similar agreement was approved later that year in *Fehr v Sun Life Assurance Co of Canada*,[60] where Perell J held that third party funding agreements must be disclosed promptly to the court and would require court approval in order to protect against interference with the administration of justice.[61]

More recently, in *Houle*, Perell J confirmed that courts must be enabled to scrutinize the third party funding agreement,[62] and that third party funding must be both necessary and sufficient for enabling meaningful access to justice and discouraging or deterring wrongdoing.[63] In that particular case, however, Perell J noted the same concerns that the court had remarked upon in *Metzler*: that the third party funder would be overcompensated, and that the agreement would enable the funder to interfere in the conduct of the litigation.[64] Unlike in *Metzler*, however, Perell J simply ordered the agreement amended, instead of denying it altogether.[65] This is an indication that courts are becoming more confident in their ability to monitor third party funding agreements, and more comfortable with the principle of such funding in general.

---

59 *Ibid* at paras 35–37.

60 2012 ONSC 2715.

61 *Ibid* at para 89. See also *Bayens*, above note 39 at para 41. "Promptly," according to the caselaw, means prior to certification or before a leave motion under Part XXIII.1 of the *Securities Act*, RSO 1990, c S.5: Aaron Dantowitz, "Commercial Third Party Funding of Class Actions in Ontario: Eight Early Lessons" (Presentation to the Advocates' Society, Second Annual Securities Litigation Practice Group Symposium, 13 September 2012) at 19–21.

62 The factors that must be satisfied are as follows: (1) the plaintiffs must receive independent legal advice; (2) the retainer and third party funding agreements must be disclosed to the court; (3) the retainer and third party funding agreements must be disclosed to the defendant; (4) there must be appropriate confidentiality provisions in the third party funding agreement; (5) the third party funder must be willing and able to post security for costs; (6) evidence of the background factual circumstances must be proffered; and (7) the affected parties (including the defendants and third party funder) must be given notice and an opportunity to be heard (*Houle*, above note 44 at para 74).

63 *Ibid* at paras 75 and 78.

64 *Ibid* at paras 80–99.

65 Justice Perell preapproved the funder's compensation in the amount of 10 percent (that is, the amount that would be levied in other cases by the CPF), with the remainder to be approved following the conclusion of the case (*ibid* at para 87); and the provisions of the funding agreement that would allow the funder to interfere in the litigation were ordered deleted and replaced (*ibid* at paras 93 and 99).

Despite their potential for increasing access to justice,[66] however, third party funding arrangements carry similar ethical risks as indemnities by counsel. For example, they can lead to self-dealing as the interests of plaintiffs' counsel are more closely aligned with the funder than with the class or even the client.[67] Justice Perell also recognized in *Bayens* and *Houle* that third party arrangements carry risks of their own:[68] they can diminish the representative plaintiff's rights to instruct counsel and control the litigation;[69] and where the plaintiff has a minimal stake and is carrying none of the risk, they can also become indifferent and lose interest in controlling the litigation to the point where they defer to counsel's decisions even if they are not in the best interests of the class.[70] Justice Perell noted that third party funding agreements can potentially overcompensate the funder for assuming the risks of an adverse costs award.[71] Finally, His Honour noted that third party funders are precluded from disclosing any confidential or privileged information, and are bound by the deemed undertaking rule.[72]

Third party funding agreements are currently unregulated by statute.[73] In 2006, the Law Society of Upper Canada investigated third party funding generally (not just in the class action context), and identified some of the risks enumerated above, but it ultimately decided to take a "wait and see" approach.[74] In addition to these ethical risks, defence counsel also have concerns about the lack of a direct right of action against a third party funder in the case of an adverse costs award against the representative plaintiff.[75] Defendants are not party to such agreements and therefore have no basis on which to sue third party funders; they would have to pursue the representative plaintiff, who would then have to pursue the funder. The issues with collecting adverse costs awards are

66 *Dugal*, above note 8 at para 33.

67 LCO 2013, above note 4 at 8; LCO 2018, above note 4 at 14; *Bayens*, above note 39 at para 41.

68 *Bayens*, *ibid* at para 41; *Houle*, above note 44 at paras 64–65.

69 Kalajdzic et al, "Justice," above note 51 at 121–22; Dantowitz, above note 61 at 12–14.

70 *Bayens*, above note 39 at para 41; Kalajdzic et al, "Justice," above note 51 at 126.

71 *Bayens*, above note 39 at para 41; Kalajdzic et al, "Justice," above note 51 at 122.

72 *Bayens*, above note 39 at para 41; Kalajdzic et al, "Justice," above note 51 at 125; Dantowitz, above note 61 at 14.

73 S Gordon McKee & Nicole Henderson, "Class Action Reform: The Law Commission of Ontario Review of the *Class Proceedings Act*" (2016) 83 *Defense Counsel Journal* 32 at 41.

74 Kalajdzic et al, "Justice," above note 51 at 122, citing Law Society of Upper Canada, Access to Justice Committee, Report to Convocation (23 November 2006) at 3.

75 Kalajdzic et al, "Justice," above note 51.

compounded by the fact that many third party funders have no assets in Ontario. As a result, courts have occasionally ordered that funders post security for costs, or such security has been required as a condition of the funding agreement.[76]

There are other questions regarding third party funding that have not yet been addressed by the courts; for example, whether a funder has a right (as the CPF currently does) to make submissions at a costs hearing in the event of an adverse costs award.[77] It is clear, however, that such funding arrangements were not envisaged by the Advisory Committee when it drafted the *CPA*, and that further legislative intervention may be required to clarify this evolving area of class actions practice. As Perell J stated in *Bayens*:

> It may be wise for the Legislature to revisit whether any of this is what it intended when it rejected the Law Reform Commission's recommendation that class actions not be governed by the loser pays principle. In the meantime, the court is now challenged with developing the jurisdiction to determine when third party funding should be approved for a particular case.[78]

Given the inconsistent application of section 31 of the *CPA*, the drawbacks of applying to the CPF, and the ethical and other risks inherent in counsel indemnities and third party funding, many commentators have come to believe that traditional costs rules should no longer apply to class proceedings in Ontario. This includes one of the most prominent judges on Toronto's class actions panel. In *Rosen v BMO Nesbitt Burns Inc*,[79] Belobaba J stated that certification motions are being over-litigated, leading to astronomical costs awards, and making access to justice too expensive:

> Most members of the class action bar, whether acting for plaintiffs or defendants, agree that a "no costs" rule would be much more sensible. Like them, I also wish that the recommendations on costs as set out in the Ontario Law Reform Commission's *Report on Class Actions* had been accepted.[80]

---

76 See, for example, *Dugal*, above note 8 at para 35; *Bayens*, above note 39 at para 41; *Labourers' Pension Fund of Central and Eastern Canada (Trustees of) v Sino-Forest Corp*, 2012 ONSC 2937 at para 13; Dantowitz, above note 61 at 15.

77 Dantowitz, *ibid* at 23–24.

78 Above note 39 at para 35.

79 2013 ONSC 6356 at para 1.

80 *Ibid* at para 2.

Another judge on the class actions panel, Perell J, has not called for a complete abolition of the traditional costs rules regarding class actions, but has stated that disproportionately high costs awards are having an adverse effect on access to justice. In *McCracken*,[81] His Honour noted that these effects include the following:

> [T]he court's response to arguments about costs has been inconsistent, and the outcome of costs determinations is uncertain and unpredictable. Another very serious consequence is that the number of new class actions appears to be declining, and small but possibly meritorious class actions are disappearing as class counsel warily select the cases that they will prosecute. The risk of grotesque adverse costs awards is a serious disincentive to law firms being prepared to take on class actions and serve the public's demand for access to justice.[82]

Some commentators have called the traditional costs rules "impractical and repugnant to the [*CPA*'s] objectives; as such, it should be abrogated and repealed by a general rule providing that no costs may be awarded to either party at any stage of a class action."[83] Indeed, this was the recommendation of the OLRC, and one of the original terms of reference of the Attorney General's Advisory Committee. Other provinces have departed from the traditional rule: British Columbia, Manitoba, and Newfoundland and Labrador have no-way costs, and Quebec only has minimal costs at a small claims court level.[84]

Other commentators, however, have questioned whether abandoning the "loser pays" rule would address the issues outlined above. Jasminka Kalajdzic states that eliminating costs would do little for access to justice, because it would deny class counsel their ability to recoup costs in the event of success, and such funds are often used to finance ongoing litigation. She further argues that the unavailability of costs is unlikely to reduce the amount of time and resources spent on certification motions, because wealthy defendants will still be able to conduct a war of attrition (which, presumably, plaintiffs' counsel will have to match if they hope to win). Most notably, Kalajdzic points out that there is no evidence that Ontario's class action regime is any less robust or thriving than those of

81 Above note 15.

82 *Ibid* at para 113.

83 Carabash, above note 14 at 636–37.

84 Walker et al, above note 29 at 35.

provinces with no-costs regimes.[85] Indeed, Saskatchewan was a no-costs province until 2015, when it aligned its class action costs rules more closely with the traditional costs model.[86] If anything, then, the national trend seems to be away from no-way costs.

Finally, given the interdependent nature of costs, the CPF, and certification,[87] the obvious corollary of abolishing the traditional costs rules is that the CPF would no longer exist (or would exist in a substantially modified form), and the certification test would have to be recalibrated. The choice facing the Advisory Committee was a no-merits certification test with traditional costs rules, or a merits-based certification test with no costs. If the "loser-pays" rule no longer applied to class actions, then the certification test would likely have to be reworked to include a consideration of the merits. This has the potential to make certification motions even longer and more expensive. It is to the question of certification that the discussion will now turn.

B. CERTIFICATION

The Advisory Committee predicted that "the incremental costs of a class action to the point of certification should be minimal."[88] The committee saw certification, especially without a merits test, as a simple procedural step—the real costs would be incurred at trial. The practice of class actions, however, has turned out rather differently. As the British Columbia Supreme Court put it, "[o]ne probably unintended consequence of class proceedings statutes has been the transformation of certification

85 Jasminka Kalajdzic, "It's Complicated: Access to Justice & Cost Shifting in Class Actions" (24 November 2013) (blog), online: *Slaw* www.slaw.ca/2013/11/24/its-complicated-access-to-justice-cost-shifting-in-class-actions.

86 In 2015, amendments were made to *The Class Actions Act*, SS 2001, c C-12.01, s 40. Saskatchewan courts now have the right to make any order of costs the court considers appropriate with respect to any application, action, or appeal under the Act. The changes have retroactive force. However, Saskatchewan costs awards continue to be much more modest than in other provinces.

87 Gourlay, above note 5 at 275.

88 Minutes of the Attorney General's Advisory Committee on Class Action Reform (23 November 1989), in Policy Development Division Counsel correspondence files, Class Actions—Advisory Committee minutes and notes, 1989–1990, MGC, RG 4-40, in Box No B502275, North York, Archives of Ontario.

proceedings from preliminary step to battleground; in some senses, the certification proceeding is the trial."[89]

The stakes on a certification motion are extremely high for both parties, because success dramatically increases the potential recovery for the plaintiffs, as well as the potential liability of the defendants. By their very nature, class proceedings often involve numerous individually non-viable claims, so a denial of certification generally means the end of the action. As such, the certification motion is a zero-sum game into which both plaintiff and defence counsel pour vast amounts of time and resources.

Certification motions routinely involve delay and are rarely brought within the ninety-day deadline stipulated in section 2(3) of the *CPA*. In fact, the time between the commencement of the action and the hearing of the certification motion has stretched anywhere from two years to seven years or longer.[90] Such delays have a significant impact on counsel's ability to effectively litigate or settle a case.[91] Some class counsel "park" cases—commencing them, and then failing to move them forward in the hope that they can piggyback on settlements in other jurisdictions.[92] This is not the only cause of the delays, however. Pressure on court resources and scheduling difficulties, as well as an increasing number of pre-certification motions, increase costs and prolong the time before the certification motion can be heard.[93]

Furthermore, because both sides file voluminous certification motion material often going to the merits of the case, the certification hearings themselves can last several days. In addition, expert witnesses must file primary and reply evidence, and be cross-examined, which adds to the delay and expense. This improper focus on the merits, despite section 5(5) of the *CPA*, which states that "[a]n order certifying a class proceeding is not a determination of the merits of the proceeding," increases scheduling complications and consumes more time and resources.[94]

---

89 *Consumers' Assn of Canada v Coca-Cola Bottling Co*, 2006 BCSC 863 at para 35, cited in Vince Morabito & Jane Caruana, "Can Class Action Regimes Operate Satisfactorily Without a Certification Device? Empirical Insights from the Federal Court of Australia" (2013) 61 *American Journal of Comparative Law* 579 at 580.

90 Warren Winkler et al, "Has the Time Come to Amend Section 2(3) (the "Ninety-Day Rule") of the *Class Proceedings Act, 1992*?" (7 March 2013), online: www.siskinds.com/has-the-time-come-to-amend-section at 2–3 [Winkler et al, "Amend"].

91 *Ibid* at 3.

92 This phenomenon will be addressed further in Section D, below in this chapter.

93 Winkler et al, "Amend," above note 90 at 3–5.

94 *Ibid* at 5–6.

As a result, and as discussed earlier in this chapter, adverse costs awards against plaintiffs can be in the hundreds of thousands of dollars, especially if appeals are involved. Because of the potential for large costs awards, class actions lawyers "show no restraint in their approach to prosecuting or defending the certification motion. The parties roll the dice that they will be the successful party, show no restraint in running up costs, but hope to recover an enormous award of costs."[95] Where plaintiffs are on the wrong side of such a costs award, they can be motivated to abandon any rights of appeal in exchange for a discount on costs, thereby compromising the rights of the class for reasons having nothing to do with the merits of the case.[96] Where appeal rights are not abandoned, they can add years to the process, as certification decisions are frequently appealed to the Divisional Court, Court of Appeal, and sometimes even the Supreme Court of Canada.[97] The potential for crippling costs awards on certification motions has made class actions the "sport of kings in the sense that only kings or equivalent can afford it."[98] This has obvious implications for access to justice, as well as judicial economy, two of the main objectives of the *CPA*.

The Advisory Committee recommended that traditional costs rules apply because they envisaged a fairly straightforward procedural motion that would not involve a consideration of the merits.[99] In the first decade of class actions in Ontario, the certification test was fairly stringent and arguably imported a merits assessment, while adverse costs awards remained very low.[100] Since then, the reverse has become true: costs awards began climbing from the mid-2000s, and in 2013 the Supreme Court of Canada reiterated the no-merits certification test in *Pro-Sys Consultants Ltd v Microsoft Corporation*.[101] Justice Rothstein for the Court stated that the standard of proof on a certification motion is not the balance of probabilities, as the defendants in *Pro-Sys* and other cases had

95 *McCracken*, above note 15 at para 113.

96 LCO 2013, above note 4 at 10.

97 Neil Finkelstein et al, "Summary Judgment Prior to Certification in Class Actions: How *Microsoft* and *Hryniak* Have Changed the Landscape" (2015) 44 *Advocates' Quarterly* 229 at 243–44.

98 *Danier Leather*, above note 15 at para 63.

99 Gourlay, above note 5 at 279.

100 See Section A, above in this chapter. See also Gourlay, *ibid* at 280–81.

101 2013 SCC 57 [*Pro-Sys*].

argued, but the *Hollick* standard of "some basis in fact" for each of the certification criteria except section 5(1)(a):[102]

> The certification stage does not involve an assessment of the merits of the claim and is not intended to be a pronouncement on the viability or strength of the action; "rather, [it] focuses on the form of the action in order to determine whether the action can appropriately go forward as a class proceeding."[103]

Despite the Supreme Court's finding in *Pro-Sys* and its two sister cases,[104] certification motions remain protracted, time-consuming, and expensive. Counsel on both sides continue to submit evidence that goes to the merits of the action, and pre-certification motions appear to be increasing in number. Following the Supreme Court of Canada's judgment in *Hryniak v Mauldin*,[105] defence counsel have started to bring summary judgment motions either prior to, or at the same time as, the certification motion.[106] As will be discussed further below, other pre-certification motions such as carriage motions are also on the rise.

In light of these developments, there are several options for reform. If the current costs regime in Ontario is to be maintained, then courts should refocus on the procedural nature of the certification motion itself in order to decrease expense and delay, thereby enhancing judicial economy and access to justice.[107] Pre-certification motions should continue to be kept to a minimum[108] or heard at the same time as the certification motion, which should be heard within a certain time period after the Statement of Claim has been served.[109]

---

102 *Ibid* at para 102; *Hollick v Toronto (City)*, 2001 SCC 68 at para 25. Section 5(1)(a) of the *CPA*, SO 1992, c 6, requires that "the pleadings or the notice of application discloses a cause of action," and this criterion is subject to the same test as on a motion to strike under Rule 21: whether it is "plain and obvious" that the plaintiff's statement of claim discloses no reasonable cause of action (*Hunt v Carey Canada Inc*, [1990] 2 SCR 959).

103 *Pro-Sys*, above note 101 at para 102.

104 *Sun-Rype Products Ltd v Archer Daniels Midland Company*, 2013 SCC 58, and *Infineon Technologies AG v Option consommateurs*, 2013 SCC 59.

105 2014 SCC 7.

106 Finkelstein et al, above note 97 at 229, 233–37, and 242.

107 Winkler et al, "Amend," above note 90 at 6.

108 The Supreme Court of Canada has discouraged such "litigation by instalments": *Garland v Consumers' Gas Co*, 2004 SCC 25 at para 90.

109 Winkler et al, "Amend," above note 90, in which the authors suggest a six-month time frame.

If traditional costs rules are abolished for class actions, then the certification test will have to be reconsidered. Some defence-side lawyers have already recommended that if a no-way costs regime is put in place, a merits test be added to the certification threshold.[110] Another less controversial suggestion is that the certification test should include "a rigorous analysis of the evidence relevant to the certification criteria and that the plaintiff demonstrate that those criteria have been met on a balance of probabilities."[111] Although not quite a full-blown review of the merits of the action, this would, as articulated above, be a more stringent test than the current "some basis in fact" standard. Defence counsel have also called for the abolition of the current asymmetrical rights of appeal, whereby plaintiffs can appeal certification orders as of right, but defendants must seek leave.[112]

The Advisory Committee envisaged the class action regime as a carefully calibrated balance between a low certification threshold, the "loser-pays" costs rule, and the CPF. Any changes to the certification test would therefore involve changes to the costs rule (and vice versa) and potentially other parts of the *CPA*, as well as the CPF.

Although costs and certification were two of the most controversial issues facing the Advisory Committee, this at least meant that a great deal of thought was given to those issues, which will likely facilitate any future reform efforts. Other areas of class action practice, however, did not receive as much attention. Ethics in class actions seems to have been something of an afterthought to the Advisory Committee, as well as to the OLRC before it. As a result, class action practice has become an ethical minefield that counsel have had to navigate without a map.

C. ETHICS

The Advisory Committee foresaw numerous ethical pitfalls in the practice of class actions, as did the OLRC. Both reports discuss potential issues such as conflicts of interest when representing the plaintiff and class members; solicitation and advertising to class members; and the role of the lawyer in financing the class action.[113] The Advisory Committee recommended

110 McKee & Henderson, above note 73 at 37.

111 *Ibid.*

112 *Ibid* at 38; *CPA*, above note 102, ss 30(1) & (2).

113 Advisory Committee Report, above note 1 at 32; Ontario Law Reform Commission, *Report on Class Actions* (Toronto: Ministry of the Attorney General, 1982) at 201–2

"that the Law Society of Upper Canada consider changes to the Rules of Professional Conduct to resolve potential conflicts between the lawyer's respective obligations to the representative plaintiff and members of the class."[114] The OLRC made the same recommendation.[115]

Contrary to these recommendations, however, the Law Society instead issued a set of guidelines titled *The Challenges of Class Proceedings for Civil Litigators*,[116] which was released on the eve of the passage of the *CPA*. Even to this day, the Law Society has not amended the Rules of Professional Conduct to accommodate class actions.[117] This state of affairs is puzzling, given the numerous ethical controversies that have arisen since the *CPA* was passed.

As the Advisory Committee predicted, conflicts of interest have become a major concern in class actions practice. The Rules of Professional Conduct address conflicts of interest,[118] but the unique lawyer-plaintiff-class relationship can result in conflicts that are not present in individual litigation. There are two aspects to the lawyer-client relationship that are unique to class actions.

First, the representative plaintiff is generally not as involved in the litigation as the individual client.[119] Clients in individual litigation bring their claim to the law firm of their choice, and, except in the smallest cases, their stake is larger than any fee to which counsel will be entitled. In class actions, however, representative plaintiffs are often recruited by counsel. This does not necessarily mean they have no genuine interest in the case;[120] it is rare that courts find that the representative plaintiff is "a mere benchwarmer or a puppet manipulated by counsel."[121] Nevertheless,

[OLRC Report]; Fox to Stephen Traviss, senior counsel, Professional Conduct, LSUC (18 August 1992), in Policy Development Division Counsel correspondence files, Class Proceedings—Ethics, 1992, CA226, RG 4-40, in Box No B703283, Archives of Ontario.

114 Advisory Committee Report, above note 1 at 32.

115 OLRC Report, above note 113 at 201–2.

116 Law Society of Upper Canada, *The Challenges of Class Proceedings for Civil Litigators* (Toronto: LSUC, 1992) [LSUC Guidelines].

117 Kalajdzic, "Self-Interest," above note 45 at 3 and 27.

118 Law Society of Upper Canada, *Rules of Professional Conduct*, section 3.4, online: LSUC www.lsuc.on.ca/lawyer-conduct-rules [LSUC Rules].

119 Kalajdzic, "Self-Interest," above note 45 at 10. See also Winkler speech, above note 45.

120 *Fantl v Transamerica Life Canada*, 2008 CanLII 17304 at para 63 (Ont SCJ), Perell J [*Fantl*]. See also Perell, above note 37 at 204–5.

121 *Singer v Schering-Plough Canada Inc*, 2010 ONSC 42 at para 216. See also *Sondhi v Deloitte Management Services LP*, 2017 ONSC 2122.

a client that is invited to be part of an action will generally be less motivated and more passive than a client that takes the initiative.[122]

More importantly, however, a representative plaintiff's financial interest in the class action will be much smaller than their lawyer's. Representative plaintiffs typically have a very small potential claim; even where their damages are in the tens of thousands of dollars, class counsel's potential fee award will be much higher.[123] Class actions are almost always prosecuted on a contingency fee basis, which means that a representative plaintiff has no up-front expenses to pay. Where plaintiffs have also been indemnified by their lawyer against adverse costs, they bear none of the risk. All financial risk and reward is borne by the lawyer,[124] who also has most of the expertise and does most of the work. There is a real danger, therefore, that representative plaintiffs will fail to direct class counsel or question their decisions, even when those decisions might prejudice the interests of the class.[125]

Second, class counsel act not only for the representative plaintiff, but also for the class. The relationship between the lawyer and the class varies according to the stage of the proceeding. According to caselaw, prior to certification there is a *sui generis* relationship between the lawyer and the class.[126] Class members are usually not regarded as the lawyer's clients, not least because the identity of each class member is often unknown before certification;[127] at the same time, however, the *CPA* requires that

122 Certain judges have referred to the "client fiction" that is the representative plaintiff: "[They are] not clients in the normal sense. They can't be. The lawyers are the driving force." Interview of retired judge (13 July 2017) [Judge interview].

123 Perell, above note 37 at 206–8.

124 Perell, *ibid* at 208–11, 216; *Fantl*, above note 120 at paras 49, 52, and 60; Kaitlyn MacDonell, "Ethics of Class Counsel: Is There a Need for Restrictions on Investigating Class Claims?" (2011) University of Toronto Faculty of Law Centre for the Legal Profession, online: CLP http://clp.law.utoronto.ca/sites/clp.law.utoronto.ca/files/documents/Ethics-of-Class-Counsel.pdf at 5 [MacDonell].

125 Kalajdzic, "Self-Interest," above note 45 at 10–11; Notes for Remarks of The Honourable Frank Iacobucci, "Class Actions and IRS Settlement" (2007) *The Cambridge Lectures* [unpublished, on file with the author] at 24 [Iacobucci, "IRS"].

126 *Fantl*, above note 120 at paras 78–80; *Heron v Guidant Corp*, [2007] OJ No 3823 at para 10 (SCJ), leave to appeal refused, [2008] OJ No 48 (Div Ct); Perell, above note 37 at 212; Carabash, above note 14 at 639–42; Michael P Abdelkerim, "Class Counsel's Ethical Obligations" (2004) 18 *Windsor Review of Legal & Social Issues* 105 at 113 [Abdelkerim]; Catherine Piché, "The Class Action Settlement Actors: Who Protects Whom?" (2011) 53 *Supreme Court Law Review* (2d) 57 at 58–59 [Piché, "Settlement Actors"].

127 Perell, above note 37 at 211–12; Abdelkerim, above note 126 at 114–15.

the lawyer and the representative fairly and adequately represent the interests of the class.[128] After certification, class members are considered to be the lawyer's clients,[129] and the lawyer essentially has a joint retainer between the representative plaintiff and the class.[130]

At all stages of the proceeding, class counsel have a duty to avoid conflicts of interest between themselves, the representative plaintiff, and the class members.[131] However, the very nature of the lawyer-class relationship means that the risk of such conflicts is ever-present. Conflicts between the representative plaintiff and the class can occur where a settlement favours some or all class members over the representative plaintiff (as in *Richard v British Columbia*),[132] or vice versa (as in *Burnett Estate v St. Jude Medical, Inc*).[133] Wherever the representative plaintiff or the class members (or both) are "absent" from the litigation (and that is invariably the case in class actions), there is a risk that their interests will be overlooked.[134] If a representative plaintiff is actively involved in the litigation, there is a danger that counsel and the plaintiff will prefer their interests above those of some or all of the class; if a representative plaintiff is not particularly concerned with the litigation, there is a danger that counsel will make decisions in their own interests.

The risk of self-dealing by class counsel arises from the lawyer's financial interest in the litigation and is particularly acute in the settlement context. Lawyers generally take on class actions on a contingency

128 *CPA*, above note 102, s 5(1)(e)(i); Perell, above note 37 at 212; Abdelkerim, above note 126 at 117–20; Piché, "Settlement Actors," above note 126 at 58–59; Carabash, above note 14 at 642.

129 *Ward-Price v Mariners Haven Inc*, 2004 CanLII 13951 (Ont SCJ); *1176560 Ontario Ltd v Great Atlantic & Pacific Co of Canada*, [2003] OJ No 1016 (SCJ (Master); Perell, above note 37 at 213–14; Carabash, above note 14 at 643–51.

130 Perell, above note 37 at 220–21. Justice Perell points out (*ibid* at 222) that it would be impractical for lawyers to get class members to sign a joint retainer agreement. The rules and policies for joint retainers have therefore been supplanted by the notice and opt-out provisions of the *CPA*.

131 *CPA*, above note 102, s 5(1)(e)(i) and (iii); Carabash, above note 14 at 653.

132 2007 BCSC 1107. In that case, counsel negotiated a settlement that excluded the representative plaintiff, without the plaintiff's knowledge; the court therefore removed counsel from the record.

133 2009 BCSC 82. In that case, counsel negotiated a settlement that included the representative plaintiff and some putative class members, but that excluded other putative class members with psychological injury claims; the court therefore refused to approve the settlement.

134 Kalajdzic, "Self-Interest," above note 45 at 10–11; Carabash, above note 14 at 638.

fee basis,[135] and in many cases they will also provide the representative plaintiff with an indemnity against a potential adverse costs award. Such economic incentives for lawyers are said to increase access to justice by making litigation affordable.[136] However, where counsel carry all the risk,[137] the representative plaintiff is more likely to "take a back seat" and uncritically accept the decisions of class counsel. When it comes to settlement, a lawyer who carries all the financial risk and whose decisions are uncritically accepted will be tempted to self-deal—for example, by accepting a quick settlement that provides them with a generous fee, even if it is unfair to the class.[138]

By the time the prospect of settlement arises, a class action has usually been prosecuted for several years. Class counsel have poured large amounts of time and money into the case, paying for disbursements (including expensive expert reports), salaries, and the general costs of running the firm.[139] Their ability to pursue cases on contingency depends on the ability to make money from those cases in a timely fashion. Counsel will therefore be very interested in any overtures for settlement. At the same time, the representative plaintiff may be uninterested and the class members "absent," providing little oversight of class counsel's efforts at negotiation.[140] Where counsel has a stake in the action that is out of all proportion to any

135 Contingency fees in general are addressed by section 3.6-2 of the LSUC Rules, above note 118.

136 Minutes of Convocation of the Law Society of Upper Canada (27 May 1988) at 1 [LSUC Contingency Fees], in Policy Development Division Counsel correspondence files, LSUC Contingency Fees—Report of the Sub-committee, 1988, CA226, RG 4-40, in Box No B449218, North York, Archives of Ontario; Kalajdzic, "Self-Interest," above note 45 at 6, citing *Fantl v Transamerica Life Canada*, 2009 ONCA 377 at para 66.

137 This has led some commentators to question whether class counsel can ethically fund litigation or offer their clients an indemnity against adverse costs; however, they have also recognized that few people would become representative plaintiffs without contingency arrangements or an indemnity: Carabash, above note 14 at 633–36.

138 Perell, above note 37 at 216–17; Kalajdzic, "Self-Interest," above note 45 at 6, citing *Dabbs v Sun Life Assurance Co of Canada*, 1998 CanLII 14855 (Ont SCJ) [*Dabbs II*]; Abdelkerim, above note 126 at 109; Winkler speech, above note 45; Iacobucci, "IRS," above note 125 at 24; Frank Iacobucci, "What Is Access to Justice in the Context of Class Actions?" (2011) 53 *Supreme Court Law Review* (2d) 17 at 17–18 [Iacobucci, "Access to Justice"]; JJ Camp, "Avoiding Pitfalls and Potential Conflicts in Negotiating Class Counsel Fees and Obtaining Court Approval" in *Litigating Conspiracy: An Analysis of Competition Class Actions* (Toronto: Irwin Law, 2006) 277 at 282.

139 Cara F Zwibel, "Settling for Less? Problems and Proposals in the Settlement of Class Actions" (2004) 1:2 *Canadian Class Action Review* 165 at 168.

140 *Ibid.*

individual class member's interest,[141] and is only nominally accountable to their client and the class, there will be a very strong temptation to prefer their own interests above those of the client and the class.[142]

When contingency fees were being debated in the late 1980s, the objection that they would "line lawyers' pockets" was common.[143] One of the counter-arguments to this objection was that contingency fees would make lawyers more diligent and ethical in prosecuting the action because a return for the client would equal a return for the lawyer,[144] and there would be a close correlation between the fee paid on contingency and the value of the services performed.[145]

However, these arguments were made in the context of individual litigation, not class actions, and assumed that lawyers' recovery would always be based on a percentage of the monetary award to the class. In fact, many class action settlements (or a certain proportion of those settlements) come in the form of cy-près distributions or coupons.[146] In other cases, there will be a large monetary award, but claims by class members

141 Kalajdzic, "Self-Interest," above note 45 at 8.

142 *Ibid* at 7–8; Zwibel, above note 139 at 168–69; Iacobucci, "IRS," above note 125 at 26–27.

143 Letter from the Canadian Advertising Foundation on the LRP Report (at 3–4); brief of the Canadian Federation of Independent Business on the LRP Report (at 13). Both briefs are in Policy Development Division Counsel correspondence files, Class Actions—Background Papers 1, 1983–1990, RG 4-40, in Box No B501822, North York, Archives of Ontario. See also Walter B Williston, "The Contingent Fee in Canada" (1968) 6 *Alberta Law Review* 184 at 198–99 [Williston, "Contingent Fee"]; David W Slater, *Final Report of the Ontario Task Force on Insurance*, vol 1 (Toronto: The Task Force, 1986) at 53; Michael Trebilcock, "Our 'Legal Machine Can't Enforce Rights'" *Globe and Mail* (11 September 1972) 2, in Ontario Law Reform Commission files, Nov 1976–Dec 1982, Project name: class actions, RG 4-66, BA77, in Box No B380537, North York, Archives of Ontario; "Don't Give Lawyers a Cut," Editorial, *Toronto Star* (24 March 1980), in Ontario Law Reform Commission files, Nov 1976–Dec 1982, Project name: class actions, RG 4-66, BA77, in Box No B380543, North York, Archives of Ontario [Box No B380537]; Report of the Professional Organizations Committee of the CBA, Submission to the Ministry of the Attorney General Professional Organizations Committee (30 April 1979) at 84 and 86, in Box No B380537 (*ibid*); Larry Fox, "Ban on Contingency Fees Remains in Ontario" *Ontario Lawyers Weekly* (12 August 1983) 5, in Policy Development Division Counsel correspondence files, Class Actions, 1988–1990, RG 4-40, in Box No B502275, North York, Archives of Ontario. For a discussion of the debate on contingency fees generally, see Chapter 3.

144 Williston, "Contingent Fee," above note 143 at 200. See also Kalajdzic, "Self-Interest," above note 45 at 6.

145 LSUC Contingency Fees, above note 136 at 1.

146 Iacobucci, "IRS," above note 125 at 29.

will be minimal, so the "take-up rate" is very low.[147] In these cases, lawyers may get a fee calculated on the basis of their time (or a multiplier of their time) instead, so that their recovery will be vastly disproportionate to the recovery by class members.[148] This is especially so where counsel have inflated their time in the lead up to settlement negotiation and approval, with a view to a higher fee.[149]

Given that both settlement agreements and fee arrangements must be approved by the court pursuant to the *CPA*,[150] one would assume that this process would catch any ethical irregularities.[151] In the absence of any Rules of Professional Conduct pertaining to class actions practice, the jurisprudence on settlement and fee approval has provided some guidance.[152] However, the *CPA* leaves much to the discretion of judges in this area,[153] and while this gives courts a great deal of flexibility, it can also lead to insufficient attention to the fairness and adequacy of a settlement.[154]

The role of the court in a settlement approval hearing is to determine whether the settlement is fair, reasonable, and in the best interests of the class.[155] The difficulty with supervising the fairness of settlements is the absence of any party whose interest is adverse to those supporting the settlement.[156] Plaintiffs' counsel, as noted above, will be interested in recovering the time and disbursements that have been expended on the action. Defence counsel will be interested in terminating the action for the lowest possible figure, and may be prepared to offer plaintiffs' counsel a generous fee for their co-operation. Where the representative plaintiff and class members are either absent or insufficiently informed about the settlement, counsel on both sides will be able to collude with each other to put their interests above those of the class.[157] Even where there is no

147 MacDonell, above note 124 at 12.

148 Kalajdzic, "Self-Interest," above note 45 at 6–7; Iacobucci, "IRS," above note 125 at 29; Walker et al, above note 29 at 247.

149 Iacobucci, "IRS," above note 125 at 26 and 30.

150 *CPA*, above note 102, ss 29(2) & (3), and s 32, respectively.

151 *Dabbs v Sun Life Assurance Co of Canada*, 1997 CanLII 12294 (Ont SCJ) [*Dabbs*].

152 Perell, above note 37 at 218.

153 Kalajdzic, "Self-Interest," above note 45 at 30; Judge interview, above note 122.

154 Zwibel, above note 139 at 180–81.

155 *Dabbs II*, above note 138.

156 Judge interview, above note 122; *Bancroft-Snell v Visa Canada Corp*, 2016 ONCA 896 at para 30 [*Bancroft-Snell*]; *Smith Estate v National Money Mart Co*, 2011 ONCA 233 at paras 36–39.

157 Jasminka Kalajdzic calls this the "adversarial void" problem: Kalajdzic, "Self-Interest," above note 45 at 9–10. See also Iacobucci, "IRS," above note 125 at 28; Winkler

collusion, once plaintiff and defence counsel have reached a settlement, they will both have a strong interest in having the settlement approved even if it is less than optimal.

With no adverse parties before the court, there will be no check on whether counsel are providing full disclosure of all material facts to the court, as they are required to do.[158] There may be objectors to the settlement; however, objectors are not considered parties to the settlement approval proceedings and have very limited rights of discovery and cross-examination.[159] They therefore lack the information needed to challenge counsel's submissions. Furthermore, because they are not considered parties, objectors cannot appeal the settlement approval order, foreclosing any further review.[160]

Judges are also constrained in terms of time and resources. They are therefore more likely to prefer the submissions of experienced counsel, with extensive knowledge of the case and its settlement, over the submissions of a few objectors (who are usually self-represented).[161] Judges are unable to act as advocates for the class or become inquisitors if they question the *bona fides* of counsel; they are institutionally unsuited for these roles due to the usual nature of court proceedings that involve two or more parties who are adverse in interest.[162] In fact, constraints of time and resources in the court system as a whole have led to an institutional preference for settlement, something that is encouraged by the current Rules of Professional Conduct.[163] Judges may therefore be tempted to approve settlements even if they have some concerns.[164] Lack of information at the settlement stage—for example, regarding the valuation of the

speech, above note 45; Camp, above note 138 at 282; Zwibel, above note 139 at 169; Walker et al, above note 29 at 250–51.

158 *McCarthy v Canadian Red Cross Society* (2001), 8 CPC (5th) 341 (Ont SCJ) [*McCarthy*].

159 *Burnett Estate v St Jude Medical, Inc*, 2008 BCSC 1163.

160 Zwibel, above note 139 at 184, citing *Dabbs*, above note 151.

161 Zwibel, above note 139 at 170–71. However, where the representative plaintiff objects or where objectors are numerous, a settlement is unlikely to be approved. See, for example, Gloria Galloway, "Sixties Scoop Deal in Jeopardy as More Potential Claimants Object" *Globe and Mail* (5 March 2018), online: www.theglobeandmail.com/news/politics/sixties-scoop-deal-in-jeopardy-as-more-potential-claimants-object/article38216223.

162 Kalajdzic, "Self-Interest," above note 45 at 9, citing *Smith Estate v National Money Mart Co* (2010), 94 CPC (6th) 126 at para 33 (Ont SCJ); Iacobucci, "IRS," above note 125 at 27; *McCarthy*, above note 158 at para 21.

163 LSUC Rules, above note 118, s 3.2-4.

164 Zwibel, above note 139 at 170–71.

settlement or the size of the class—may force judges to approve settlements without all of the necessary information.[165]

These difficulties have led to a number of judge-made solutions, such as structured payouts of counsel fees, so that lawyers are accountable for the speed and manner in which the settlement is administered;[166] and the appointment of court experts to assist the judge in determining the reasonableness of a settlement.[167] Caselaw has already held that settlement of the action cannot be contingent upon approval of class counsel's fee.[168] Even with these solutions, however, it is clear that the settlement process in class actions presents significant ethical quandaries that have not yet been resolved by the caselaw.

It is quite probable that they may never be. Because the settlement approval process relies on full and frank disclosure by lawyers, judges may be seeing only the most egregious infractions committed by the most shameless counsel.[169] Outside of these examples, however, are numerous grey areas in which class counsel must make countless difficult decisions. Although rules do not automatically make lawyers ethical, they do guide lawyers who face ethical quandaries, and they also show the profession and the public what proper practice looks like. Given the numerous ethical pitfalls that are unique to the class actions context, therefore, particularly with regard to settlement, it would seem desirable to amend the Rules of Professional Conduct to specifically address these issues.[170]

165 *Ibid* at 171; Iacobucci, "IRS," above note 125 at 28.

166 Camp, above note 138 at 283–84. This was the approach taken by Cumming J in *Wilson v Servier Canada Inc*, 2005 CanLII 7128 (Ont SCJ).

167 Camp, above note 138 at 284. This was the approach taken by the Court of Appeal for Ontario in *Bancroft-Snell*, above note 156 at para 27.

168 *Garland v Enbridge Gas Distribution Inc*, 2006 CanLII 36243 at paras 16–23 (Ont SCJ) [*Garland*].

169 Examples include *McCallum-Boxe v Sony Corp*, 2015 ONSC 6896 at para 12; *Bancroft-Snell*, above note 156 at para 52; *Kutlu v Laboratorios Leon Farma, SA*, 2015 ONSC 7117 at paras 31–32 and 2016 ONSC 2127 at para 1. In response to third party reports of misconduct on the part of lawyers in western Canada with regard to the Indian Residential Schools settlement, the Canadian Bar Association issued "Guidelines for Lawyers Acting for Survivors of Aboriginal Residential Schools" in August 2000, with the Law Society of Upper Canada issuing its own guidelines in 2003, online: www.lsuc.on.ca/media/guideline_aboriginal_res.pdf, both cited in Kalajdzic, "Self-Interest," above note 45 at 5. However, only one of these thirteen guidelines touches on class actions. The guidelines address recruiting tactics, lack of competence, and unethical fee arrangements in all forms of action regarding the First Nations residential schools.

170 Carabash, above note 14 at 618.

The Law Commission of Ontario will also be reviewing the problem of self-dealing and will examine ways in which the *CPA* can give more guidance to judges and counsel in this regard.[171]

Even providing more guidance by way of an amendment to the Rules or the *CPA*, however, would not address the deeper issues with class action settlements. The problem is with the financial incentives that provide lawyers in individual cases with the incentive to obtain the optimum result for their clients but which, in class actions, provide an "almost irresistible" temptation to self-deal.[172] Where lawyers drive the litigation and assume the financial risks and rewards, they will be motivated primarily by profit in choosing cases. The profit is made when the case ends, and in class actions (as in most civil litigation), this is in settlement. Counsel will therefore choose cases that will settle the most quickly and with the least work. These are usually cases that piggyback onto US class actions and which have been subject to extensive media attention. Smaller, local cases that involve more extensive investigation will often be overlooked.[173] The current situation therefore favours entrepreneurial lawyers over access to justice, which is not what the Advisory Committee envisaged. As Perell J has noted, "The *CPA* was not enacted for the financial benefit of the legal profession."[174] Perhaps the solution is not more ethical guidelines, but to increase oversight and provide more effective sanctions for breaches of those guidelines. Where there are lacunae in the *CPA* and in associated rules and regulations, they will provide pitfalls for the unwary and opportunities for the unethical.

Regarding ethics, at least the Rules of Professional Conduct and several decades of jurisprudence have provided some guidance. Certain other issues, however, were not foreseen by the Advisory Committee at all, and did not arise in the jurisprudence until at least a decade after the *CPA* was enacted. The most notable of these are the related issues of carriage motions and national class actions.

171 LCO 2013, above note 4 at 8. See also LCO 2018, above note 4 at 13 and 21.

172 Louis W Hensler III, "Class Counsel, Self-Interest and Other People's Money" (2004) 35 *University of Memphis Law Review* 53 at 69; Kalajdzic, "Self-Interest," above note 45 at 8; LCO 2013, above note 4 at 8; LCO 2018, above note 4 at 13 and 21.

173 See *Kowalyshyn v Valeant Pharmaceuticals International Inc*, 2016 ONSC 3819 at paras 253–55 [*Kowalyshyn*], where Perell J noted the "rarity of purely local class actions" because they are less lucrative.

174 *Garland*, above note 168 at para 23.

D. OVERLAPPING ACTIONS

Because Ontario was the first common law jurisdiction in Canada to enact class proceedings legislation, the drafters of the *CPA* did not envisage a scenario in which multiple class proceedings would be commenced in multiple jurisdictions against the same defendant(s) and regarding the same issue. The OLRC foresaw the possibility of overlapping actions (at least in Ontario), but wrote only one paragraph on the issue, concluding that courts could co-ordinate related actions under their power to stay litigation.[175] The Advisory Committee, too, only discussed the potential for overlapping actions in Ontario, and then in the most cursory way. Ontario lawyers lived in a fairly insular world in the late 1980s and early 1990s. The internet had not yet come on the scene, and even interprovincial law firms were in their infancy. As a result, Ontario lawyers' horizons were largely provincial; the wider interprovincial and international issues connected with class actions simply did not occur to them.

The Advisory Committee only mentioned the issue once. In its meeting of 11 October 1989,[176] the committee discussed "what would happen if four or five different groups of victims brought similar class actions." The potential solutions that were discussed included consolidating the numerous actions; considering pre-existing actions to be "opted out" of the first action to be certified, with the option to opt in; use of Rule 17 and the concept of *forum non conveniens*; requiring defendants to disclose pre-existing actions known to them; and providing notice to plaintiffs in pre-existing actions. It was also suggested that, "if the court decides that a class action is the best vehicle[,] who goes first should not be a factor."[177]

This discussion shows how little the committee foresaw of what was to come. The members clearly saw the problem as one of enabling the consolidation of multiple actions, as well as providing notice of the various actions to the class, and giving individuals the right to proceed with their own suit apart from a class action.[178] They did not anticipate situations

175 OLRC Report, above note 113 at 455.

176 Minutes of the Attorney General's Advisory Committee (11 October 1989) at 3–4, in Policy Development Division Counsel correspondence files, Class Actions—Minutes of the Meetings, 1989, CA226, RG 4-40, in Box No B248501, North York, Archives of Ontario.

177 *Ibid* at 3. Cochrane said he would research these issues and get back to the committee, but the issue does not appear to have been discussed further.

178 *Ibid* at 4.

in which class counsel would refuse to consolidate their actions, leading to protracted and often bitter carriage motions that would add years to the proceedings. Nor did they anticipate overlapping national class actions, involving issues of jurisdiction, unfairness to defendants, abuse of process, and delays in settlement approval. The sole provision relating to the issue is section 13 of the *CPA*, which states that "[t]he court, on its own initiative or on the motion of a party or class member, may stay any proceeding related to the class proceeding before it, on such terms as it considers appropriate."[179] The provision is silent on class actions in other jurisdictions.

Overlapping actions undermine several of the *CPA*'s objectives. These include judicial economy (class actions were brought about, in part, to avoid multiple actions with potentially inconsistent results) and access to justice (because overlapping actions increase litigation costs).[180] The Law Commission of Ontario has included national and overlapping class actions in its review, recognizing the confusion and inefficiency that can result from such actions.[181] This chapter will review the issues that arise from the proliferation of carriage motions (whether solely in Ontario or across Canada), and national overlapping class actions.

1) Carriage Motions

Carriage motions have proliferated as class action firms jostle for position on the most potentially lucrative proceedings. Although litigants in individual actions are free to choose their own lawyers, courts have a supervisory function in class proceedings and want to ensure that the class members' rights are fairly and adequately prosecuted;[182] additionally,

179 Section 12 of the *CPA*, above note 102, also permits the court to determine the conduct of any class proceeding before it.

180 Fiona Hickman, "National Competing Class Proceedings: Carriage Motions, Anti-suit Injunctions, Judicial Co-operation, and Other Options" (2004) 1:2 *Canadian Class Action Review* 367 at 368–69. See also Gerald Antman, "Carriage Motions in Ontario: Inconsistent Application of an Indeterminate Test" (2018) 13:1 *Canadian Class Action Review* 101 at 127 [Antman].

181 LCO 2013, above note 4 at 16–18; LCO 2018, above note 4 at 12–13 and 27–28. This recognition is shared by many in the class actions bar, as well as some lawyers who were previously members of the Advisory Committee: Interview of Terrence O'Sullivan (21 June 2017) [O'Sullivan interview].

182 Antman, above note 180 at 104.

courts generally see a multiplicity of class proceedings as undesirable.[183] More importantly, however, as class counsel aim for the most lucrative actions with the highest prospects for settlement,[184] they will be less inclined to work co-operatively and share the spoils with other law firms.

A plaintiff firm or group of firms is therefore more likely to bring a carriage motion, asking the court to award it carriage of the class proceeding and stay other related actions. The court's power to award carriage stems from section 12 of the *CPA*, which authorizes the court to "make any order it considers appropriate respecting the conduct of a class proceeding to ensure its fair and expeditious determination," as well as its power to stay proceedings under *CPA* section 13. In addition, section 106 of the *Courts of Justice Act* states that a court may stay any proceedings "on such terms as are considered just."[185]

The overarching considerations on a carriage motion are whether the best interests of the class are met, the solution is fair to the defendants, and the policy goals and objectives of the *CPA* are advanced.[186] Pursuant to those considerations, the court will look at the following factors on a carriage motion:

1) the nature and scope of the causes of action advanced;
2) the theories advanced by counsel as being supportive of the claims advanced;
3) the state of each class action, including preparation;

183 Section 138 of the *Courts of Justice Act*, RSO 1990, c C.43, provides that, "as far as possible, multiplicity of legal proceedings shall be avoided." See also Warren K Winkler et al, *The Law of Class Actions in Canada* (Toronto: Canada Law Book, 2014) at 170 [Winkler et al, *Law*]; *Kowalyshyn*, above note 173 at para 235.

184 The issue of commencing actions purely for their potential settlement value is detailed in Section C, above in this chapter. See also *Kowalyshyn*, *ibid* at paras 253–55, in which Perell J notes that the "rarity of purely local class actions" (because they are less lucrative) means that carriage motions are often fought across jurisdictions, which serves to compound the problem.

185 These provisions are cited in *Mancinelli v Barrick Gold Corporation*, 2016 ONCA 571 at para 12 [*Barrick OCA*].

186 *Vitapharm Canada Ltd v F Hoffman-Laroche Ltd*, [2000] OJ No 4594 at paras 48–50 (SCJ) [*Vitapharm*]; *Smith v Sino-Forest Corporation*, 2012 ONSC 24 at para 16 [*Sino-Forest*]; *Setterington v Merck Frosst Canada Ltd*, 2006 CanLII 2623 at paras 9–11 (Ont SCJ) [*Setterington*]; *Sharma v Timminco Limited*, 2009 CanLII 58974 at para 14 (Ont SCJ) [*Sharma*]; *Mancinelli v Barrick Gold Corporation*, 2014 ONSC 7431 at para 13; *Barrick OCA*, above note 185 at para 13; Antman, above note 180 at 107; Timothy Morgan, "Who Takes the Reins? A Review of Carriage Decisions over the Last Decade" (2013) 9:1 *Canadian Class Action Review* 101 at 104.

4) the number, size, and extent of involvement of the proposed representative plaintiffs;
5) the relative priority of commencing the class action;
6) the resources and experience of counsel;[187]
7) the presence of any conflicts of interest;[188]
8) the presence of a funding agreement, whether by the CPF or a third party funder;
9) the class definition as pleaded in the Statement of Claim;
10) the class period as pleaded in the Statement of Claim;
11) joinder of defendants;
12) the correlation between plaintiffs and defendants;
13) prospects for certification;[189]
14) counsel's fee arrangements;[190]
15) prospect of success against the defendants; and
16) the interrelationship with class actions in other jurisdictions.[191]

This is not an exhaustive list, and courts may consider some factors determinative in some cases, but not in others.[192] Courts may also consider additional factors that could not have been predicted by the parties when the carriage motion was brought;[193] for example, factors 15 and 16 were introduced by Perell J on the *Kowalyshyn* carriage motion for the first time.[194] Finally, some factors have declined in importance over time (particularly the resources and experience of counsel as more firms gain experience

187 These six factors were articulated by Cumming J in *Vitapharm*, above note 186 at para 49. See also Antman, above note 180 at 108; Morgan, above note 186 at 103–5.

188 *Sharma*, above note 186 at para 17, Perell J. See also *Richard v British Columbia*, [2003] BCJ No 1466 at para 39 (SC); Morgan, *ibid* at 107 and 120–22; Antman, above note 180 at 108.

189 Factors 8 to 13 were articulated by Perell J in *Sino-Forest*, above note 186 at para 18. See also Morgan, above note 186 at 122; Antman, above note 180.

190 *Barrick OCA*, above note 185 at paras 18–21.

191 Factors 15 and 16 were articulated by Perell J in *Kowalyshyn*, above note 173 at para 141. See also Antman, above note 180 at 116.

192 *Barrick OCA*, above note 185 at para 17.

193 Antman, above note 180 at 117.

194 His Honour did point out that counsel could make amendments to their proposal for carriage as late as oral argument, stating, "I am not going to treat the factors for carriage as if I [were] marking a law school exam with no marks for an answer after time has expired" (*Kowalyshyn*, above note 173 at para 145). However, if the factors to be considered on carriage motions were clear in advance, they might make counsel think twice about bringing such a motion.

in class actions),[195] and there is uncertainty about others (particularly the prospect of success against the defendants, as the overwhelming weight of the caselaw states that the merits of the actions should not be considered on a carriage motion).[196] As a result, the test for carriage in Ontario is inconsistent and unpredictable.[197]

This uncertainty led the Court of Appeal for Ontario to consider the jurisprudence pertaining to carriage motions in *Mancinelli v Barrick Gold Corporation*.[198] Unfortunately, the appeal decision did little to bring more certainty to the jurisprudence, and the parties settled the carriage issue before it could be heard by the Supreme Court of Canada.[199] Until the Supreme Court has an opportunity to intervene, or the *CPA* is amended to address this issue, the confusion and uncertainty will continue, leading to further costs and delays in class proceedings.[200]

2) National Overlapping Class Actions

As noted above, where there are lacunae in the *CPA*, opportunistic lawyers will exploit them. In the carriage context, this is particularly apparent where there are numerous overlapping national class actions.[201] The *CPA* says nothing about national classes, not only because the drafters did not anticipate this issue,[202] but also because the Act is a provincial statute and any provisions relating to other provinces would arguably be *ultra vires*. National class actions were simply not an issue until the Supreme Court of Canada's *Dutton* decision in 2001, which allowed for

195 Morgan, above note 186 at 132; Antman, above note 180 at 113–14; Winkler et al, *Law*, above note 183 at 173; *Simmonds v Armtec Infrastructure Inc*, 2012 ONSC 44 at para 54. In *Quenneville v Audi AG*, 2018 ONSC 1530, Perell J condemned the "self-reverent testimonials" and the "blood sport of lawyer-bashing" inherent in carriage motions where the resources and experience of counsel are considered (at paras 2–3). However, see *Agnew-Americano v Equifax Canada Co*, 2018 ONSC 275 at paras 15, 204–7, and 211–36, where Glustein J held that the experience and past conduct of individual lawyers is relevant, and in that case was determinative.

196 *Barrick OCA*, above note 185 at para 45; Antman, above note 180 at 110–11.

197 Antman, *ibid* at 127.

198 *Barrick OCA*, above note 185.

199 *Mancinelli v Barrick Gold Corp*, 2016 CarswellOnt 17001 (Application/Notice of Appeal).

200 Antman, above note 180 at 105.

201 Although there have been some overlapping international classes (see *Silver v IMAX Corp*, 2013 ONSC 1667), this chapter focuses on overlapping national class actions, which are more common and present more troublesome issues, at least with regard to carriage.

202 *McSherry v Zimmer GMBH*, 2012 ONSC 4113 at paras 94–95.

class actions pursuant to the common law,[203] and following which, other Canadian provinces began enacting class proceedings legislation.

The courts in Ontario and other provinces have recognized that a national class action may be certified on an opt-out basis (where the class proceedings legislation of that province allows for opt-out actions),[204] provided that the court has jurisdiction to do so. The court will have jurisdiction where there is a "real and substantial connection"[205] between the subject matter of the action and the province. Even if some class members are not residents, orderly decision making and fairness will favour the litigation of all the factual issues out of one province.[206] National class actions, therefore, are not inherently unconstitutional even though they require one province to take jurisdiction over the residents of another province.[207] Provided that a real and substantial connection exists, that

203 *Western Canadian Shopping Centres Inc v Dutton*, 2001 SCC 46. See also Chris Dafoe, "A Path Through the Class Action Chaos: Selecting the Most Appropriate Jurisdiction with a National Class Action Panel" (2006) 3:2 *Canadian Class Action Review* 541 at 545; Walker et al, above note 29 at 17.

204 Ontario, Manitoba, Alberta, Saskatchewan, and Nova Scotia are "opt-out jurisdictions" that will include, within a class, resident and non-resident persons who do not opt out. British Columbia, New Brunswick, and Newfoundland and Labrador are "opt-in jurisdictions" that will include non-residents within a certified class only if they opted to participate in the proceeding: Walker et al, above note 29 at 34–35.

205 *Club Resorts Ltd v Van Breda*, 2012 SCC 17 at paras 66–100.

206 Walker et al, above note 29 at 265–67. Ontario courts have held that common issues between class members are sufficient to satisfy the "real and substantial connection" test for the purpose of inclusion of non-residents in a national class action: *McCutcheon v Cash Store Inc*, 2006 CanLII 15754 at para 57 (Ont SCJ); Ward Branch & Christopher Rhone, "Chaos or Consistency? The National Class Action Dilemma" (2004) 1:1 *Canadian Class Action Review* 3 at 4–5 [Branch]; Dafoe, above note 203 at 548–49. See also *Meeking v Cash Store Inc*, 2013 MBCA 81 at para 97 (the Supreme Court of Canada granted leave to appeal, but on 27 August 2014, granted the representative plaintiff's motion to adjourn the appeal hearing *sine die* pursuant to a stay granted as part of proceedings under the *Companies' Creditors Arrangement Act*, RSC 1985, c C-36. The appeal was discontinued entirely on 22 February 2016, online: www.scc-csc.ca/case-dossier/info/dock-regi-eng.aspx?cas=35608).

207 This issue is not without controversy. See Colin Irving & Mathieu Bouchard, "National Opt Out Class Actions, A Constitutional Assessment" (2009) 26 *National Journal of Constitutional Law* 111; Peter W Hogg & S Gordon McKee, "Are National Class Actions Constitutional?" (2010) 26 *National Journal of Constitutional Law* 279; Janet Walker, "Are National Class Actions Constitutional?: A Reply to Hogg and McKee" (2010) 48:1 *Osgoode Hall Law Journal* 95 [Walker, "National"]; Joshua Krusell, "'Are National Class Actions Constitutional?' A Reply to Walker, Hogg and McKee" (2012) 70 *University of Toronto Faculty of Law Review* 9.

non-resident class members are accorded procedural fairness including adequate notice, and that their rights are adequately represented, then a court may take jurisdiction over a national class.[208]

Where class members reside across Canada, class counsel now invariably bring national class actions; they are incentivized to ensure that the certified class covers as wide a geographical area as possible to maximize both the pressure on the defendants and the financial rewards when it comes time to settle.[209] Unfortunately, other counsel also have the same idea,[210] and they are not always willing to co-operate with each other.[211] The resulting carriage motions become much more complex due to the involvement of multiple jurisdictions.[212]

Because national class actions are permitted, but there is no comprehensive framework for regulating them, opportunistic class counsel can commence class proceedings in several jurisdictions at once, against the same defendants and regarding the same issue. Such counsel often "park" actions, commencing proceedings and then doing nothing with them, in the hopes of extorting a fee from counsel in other provinces in exchange for simply disappearing from the class action landscape.[213] This practice of commencing actions in numerous jurisdictions has been condemned as an abuse of process where it does not serve any legitimate interest of the plaintiffs.[214] As Cullity J stated in *Tiboni v Merck Frosst Canada Ltd*:

---

208 These requirements will vary according to the interests or rights at stake: *Currie v McDonald's Restaurants of Canada Ltd*, 2005 CanLII 3360 at para 25 (Ont CA); Branch, above note 206 at 10–13; Tristram Mallett & Kelly Osaka, "Alberta Adopts an Opt Out Class Proceedings Regime" (6 January 2011) at 2, online: Osler LLP www.osler.com/en/resources/regulations/2011/alberta-adopts-an-opt-out-class-proceedings-regime-en. However, a court may refuse to certify a national class where the proceeding involves provincial statutes that are materially different from each other: *McNaughton Automotive Ltd v Co-operators General Insurance Co* (2003), 66 OR (3d) 112 (SCJ).

209 Mallett & Osaka, above note 208 at 1; *Kowalyshyn*, above note 173 at 243–45; Linda Silberman, "The Role of Choice of Law in National Class Actions" (2008) 156 *University of Pennsylvania Law Review* 2001 at 2030.

210 Branch, above note 206 at 9.

211 *Ibid* at 24–25.

212 Dafoe, above note 203 at 542–43.

213 *Bancroft-Snell*, above note 156 at para 52. This "inter-counsel blackmail" was predicted by Craig Jones in "The Case for the National Class" (2004) 1:1 *Canadian Class Action Review* 29 at 33.

214 *Turner v Bell Mobility Inc*, 2016 ABCA 21; *BCE Inc v Gillis*, 2015 NSCA 32; *Duzan v GlaxoSmithKline, Inc*, 2011 SKQB 118 at paras 29–30 and 36–37; *McKay v Air Canada*, 2016 BCSC 1671 at para 16; *Bancroft-Snell*, above note 156 at 85; *Kowalyshyn*, above note 173 at paras 249 and 268; Antman, above note 180 at 117–18. Most recently, in

> The practice of rushing to commence overlapping actions in as many jurisdictions as possible in order to claim turf and secure carriage for law firms—rather than to advance the interests of a putative class—gives ambulance-chasing a good name and, in my opinion, smacks of an abuse of process.[215]

However, this practice shows no signs of abating, and it causes chaos and delay as courts across the country try to resolve the carriage issues that subsequently arise.

One notorious example is the *Setterington* carriage fight, involving the Vioxx class action.[216] In January 2006, a national consortium of nineteen law firms won carriage over the Merchant Law Group (MLG), which was found to have a conflict of interest.[217] The consortium then brought motions in British Columbia and Manitoba to enforce the Ontario carriage order; MLG opposed these motions, stating that carriage could not be decided before certification. The BC and Manitoba courts allowed the carriage motions to proceed, but before those motions could be decided, MLG obtained certification of its national class action in Saskatchewan.[218] This was subsequently overturned by the Court of Appeal.[219] In the meantime, the national consortium moved for and obtained certification of a national opt-out class action in Ontario (excluding Saskatchewan and Quebec),[220]

David v Loblaw; Breckon v Loblaw, 2018 ONSC 1298, competing class counsel characterized the practice as "predatory" (at para 33). In that carriage motion, Morgan J held the interrelationship of class actions in more than one jurisdiction to be a determinative factor (at paras 42–43).

215 2008 CanLII 37911 at para 37 (Ont SCJ), aff'd (*sub nom Mignacca v Merck Frosst Canada Ltd*) 2009 CanLII 10059 (Ont Div Ct) [*Tiboni*].

216 *Setterington*, above note 186.

217 Merchant Law Group (MLG) was prosecuting a securities class action against Merck Frosst at the same time as the product liability action, and the court found that if the securities class action were successful, it could seriously jeopardize the recovery of class members in the product liability action (*Setterington*, *ibid* at para 25).

218 Shortly after this action was certified, Saskatchewan became an opt-out province, and MLG obtained an order turning its class action into a national opt-out proceeding: *Wuttunee v Merck Frosst Canada Ltd*, 2008 SKQB 229 [*Wuttunee*]. See also Morgan, above note 186 at 113; and Walker et al, above note 29 at 29.

219 *Merck Frosst Canada Ltd v Wuttunee*, 2009 SKCA 43. See also Morgan, above note 186 at 115–16.

220 *Tiboni*, above note 215 (only the stay order was considered by the Divisional Court, leave to appeal the certification order having been denied). See also Morgan, above note 186 at 114–15; and Walker et al, above note 29 at 29.

successfully defeating the Merck defendants' motion to stay the Ontario proceedings in favour of the Saskatchewan action.[221]

Certification motions in two provinces, carriage motions in three provinces, and numerous appeals meant that a final decision certifying a national class action was delayed for nearly four years. Such delays cannot possibly be in the interests of class members, and defeat the objective of ensuring that all litigation regarding a certain issue is managed within one proceeding, as class actions were designed to do.[222] This kind of class action chaos is not unique, and it has been observed in numerous national proceedings.[223]

What, then, are the obstacles to solving this problem? The certification of national opt-out class actions does not provide a complete answer, for several reasons. First of all, certification of a national opt-out class action in one province does not necessarily preclude almost identical national opt-out class proceedings being certified in another province, as seen in the examples above.[224] Such a situation would probably lead to a carriage motion, but the successful counsel group would still have to

221 *Tiboni*, above note 215. When the Court of Appeal for Saskatchewan overturned the certification order, the Merck defendants sought to reopen in Ontario the Divisional Court's decision to deny leave to appeal the Ontario certification order. In December 2009, the Divisional Court reaffirmed its decision to deny leave to appeal in *Mignacca v Merck Frosst Canada Ltd*, [2009] OJ No 5233 (SCJ).

222 Branch, above note 206 at 8. See also O'Sullivan interview, above note 181.

223 In the Volkswagen class action, for example, Belobaba J granted carriage of a national class action to a consortium of eight law firms, stayed an Ontario action by MLG, and ordered that "no other similar class action shall be issued or be continued without leave of this Court" (order issued in Court File No CV-15-537029-00CP on 4 December 2015). Despite this order, in January 2016 MLG sent retainer agreements to 3,500 Ontario residents for their signature; Belobaba J condemned this as "reprehensible" and awarded $40,000 in substantial indemnity costs against MLG (*Quenneville v Volkswagen Group Canada Inc*, 2016 ONSC 959 at paras 16–17). Even after this decision, MLG continued to email Ontario residents, although the court held that this did not rise to the level of contempt (*Quenneville v Volkswagen Group Canada Inc*, 2016 ONSC 4607). Following the settlement of the action, sixty-six class members sought to opt out (after the deadline, and after the Administrator had ruled they had not validly opted out), so they could participate in a joinder of claims action prosecuted by MLG. The court dismissed their motion to have their opt-outs declared valid: *Quenneville v Volkswagen Group Canada Inc*, 2018 ONSC 1020. See also Dafoe, above note 203 at 546–47, discussing the settlement of the Baycol class action (*Coleman v Bayer Inc*, 2004 CanLII 8303 (Ont SCJ)), and Antman, above note 180 at 122–24, discussing the *Bancroft-Snell* case, above note 156.

224 *Tiboni*, above note 215 at para 46; Mallett & Osaka, above note 208 at 2.

enforce the order from one province in other provinces across Canada, risking the chaos that was witnessed in the Vioxx class action.

Second, jurisdictional questions remain, especially if class members not resident in the province where the class action is certified are not given sufficient notice, or do not have their rights adequately represented. This was an issue in *Canada Post Corp v Lépine*,[225] where the Supreme Court of Canada upheld the finding of the lower courts in Quebec that the notice of certification of the Ontario proceeding was inadequate and confusing to Quebec class members, which was found to contravene the fundamental principles of procedure. Justice LeBel for the Court stated that the creation of national classes raises the issue of relations between superior courts in the Canadian provinces:

> This case shows that the decisions made may sometimes cause friction between courts in different provinces. This of course often involves problems with communications or contacts between the courts and between the lawyers involved in such proceedings. However, the provincial legislatures should pay more attention to the framework for national class actions and the problems they present. More effective methods for managing jurisdictional disputes should be established in the spirit of mutual comity that is required between the courts of different provinces in the Canadian legal space.[226]

Quebec courts in particular have been sensitive to the practice of some class counsel in other jurisdictions of commencing a national class action in Quebec with a view to "parking" it in favour of a national class action elsewhere. Recent changes to the province's *Code of Civil Procedure* (CCP) provide that a court cannot stay a Quebec class action solely on the basis that Quebec residents are part of a national class.[227]

Any attempt to co-ordinate class actions on a national basis, therefore, is likely to be viewed with suspicion by some of the provinces. Scholars and other commentators have suggested various solutions, few of which are viable because of Canada's federal structure and the fact that civil procedure and the administration of justice are under provincial jurisdiction.[228]

225 2009 SCC 16.

226 *Ibid.*

227 *Code of Civil Procedure*, CQLR c C-25.01, art 577 (the new CCP came into force on 1 January 2016).

228 *Constitution Act, 1867* (UK), 30 & 31 Vict, c 3, s 92, reprinted in RSC 1985, Appendix II, No 5.

For example, establishing a federal body to oversee national class actions,[229] or giving the Federal Court jurisdiction over national class actions,[230] would be almost impossible without constitutional change (which is, in turn, almost impossible). Any serious effort to implement these proposals would go the same way as the proposals for a national securities regulator.[231]

Nevertheless, some workable solutions have been proposed "for an agreement or protocol among the superior courts that will provide for nationally accepted carriage motions and determine the jurisdiction in which such motions will be heard."[232] In 2005, the *Report of the Uniform Law Conference of Canada's Committee on the National Class and Related Interjurisdictional Issues: Background, Analysis and Recommendations*[233] (the ULCC Report) was released. The ULCC Report recommended that the first court seized of a class action should take carriage of it, subject to arguments from counsel in another Canadian jurisdiction that the class would be better served by prosecuting the action there. This would necessitate certain notice requirements, as well as improved court-to-court communications and a centralized registry.[234] The report further recommended that class proceedings legislation in all Canadian jurisdictions permit opt-out classes that include non-residents, and that the preferable procedure analysis on certification should consider the existence of class proceedings in other provinces.[235]

Certain provinces did follow the recommendations of the ULCC Report. Saskatchewan amended its legislation to permit opt-out classes

229 Dafoe, above note 203 at 557–72; *Kowalyshyn*, above note 173 at paras 252 and 256. This would be similar to the Judicial Panel on Multidistrict Litigation in the United States, which groups together multiple federal class proceedings that share common issues of fact into "multidistrict litigation" (MDL), and transfers the MDL to one federal district court.

230 Dafoe, above note 203 at 555–57; Hickman, above note 180 at 368–69.

231 *Reference re Securities Act*, 2011 SCC 66, in which the Court held that the federal government could not impose a common securities regulator on unwilling provinces. See also Branch, above note 206 at 23–24.

232 *Tiboni*, above note 215 at para 41, Cullity J.

233 (Vancouver: ULCC, 2005) [ULCC Report]. See also Janet Walker, "Coordinating Multijurisdiction Class Actions Through Existing Certification Processes" (2005) 42 *Canadian Business Law Journal* 112; Dafoe, above note 203 at 553–55; Iacobucci, "IRS," above note 125 at 22; *Kowalyshyn*, above note 173 at para 236.

234 ULCC Report, above note 233 at 2–4.

235 *Ibid.* The factors in the ULCC's recommended preferable procedure analysis are similar to the factors that courts in Ontario consider on carriage motions: Section D(1), above in this chapter.

and to include the recommended preferable procedure analysis.[236] Alberta subsequently followed suit.[237] Under both statutes, courts must now consider the following, pursuant to the preferable procedure analysis:

1) the alleged basis of liability;
2) the stage of proceedings;
3) the plan for the proposed multijurisdictional proceeding, including its viability and the resources for carrying it out;
4) the location of class members;
5) the location of evidence and witnesses;[238] and
6) the advantages and disadvantages of litigation being conducted in more than one jurisdiction.[239]

The ULCC Report and the subsequent amendments to the legislation in Saskatchewan and Alberta indicate that the problem of overlapping national class actions could be ameliorated by provinces' willingness to stay (or not certify) an action in response to proceedings elsewhere.[240] Notably, however, shortly after Saskatchewan's legislation was amended, the Court of Queen's Bench certified a national opt-out class in the Vioxx class action that conflicted with the national opt-out class that had already been certified in Ontario.[241] Also discouraging are Quebec's recent changes to its CCP, that go in the opposite direction to the ULCC's recommendations. Similarly, British Columbia, New Brunswick, and Newfoundland and Labrador continue to be "opt-in jurisdictions" where the efficiencies of the national class action cannot be utilized.[242]

This has led to additional efforts to address the national class action dilemma, namely, the Canadian Bar Association's National Task Force on Class Actions. The task force has recommended that courts adopt a

236 *The Class Actions Act*, SS 2001, c C-12.01, s 6 [Saskatchewan *CPA*]; Walker et al, above note 29 at 290–91.

237 *Class Proceedings Act*, SA 2003, c C-16.5, as amended by Bill 20, *Class Proceedings Amendment Act, 2010*, 3d Sess, 27th Leg, Alberta, 2010 (in force 1 March 2011) [Alberta *CPAA*]; Mallett & Osaka, above note 208 at 2.

238 Saskatchewan *CPA*, above note 236, s 6(3); Alberta *CPAA*, above note 237, s 5.

239 Alberta *CPAA*, *ibid*, s 5 (this criterion is not in the Saskatchewan *CPA*).

240 Hickman, above note 180 at 390. See also *Kaynes v BP, PLC*, 2014 ONCA 580 at para 52.

241 *Wuttunee*, above note 218.

242 However, the legislation in British Columbia and Newfoundland and Labrador does require the court to consider, on a certification motion, whether the class action involves claims that are the subject of proceedings in other jurisdictions. *Rules of the Supreme Court, 1986*, SNL 1986, c 42, Schedule D, Rule 7A.04; *Class Proceedings Act*, RSBC 1996, c 50, s 4(2)(c). See also Branch, above note 206 at 20.

protocol to assist in the co-ordination and management of multijurisdictional class actions, including advising class counsel when a similar class action is commenced (by way of a centralized registry), and to facilitate the co-ordination of interprovincial settlement approval hearings. It has also recommended the adoption of two further protocols of the American Bar Association that deal with notice to class members and court-to-court communications.[243] On 15 February 2018, the CBA Annual Meeting passed a resolution to adopt, as best practices, a slightly revised Class Action Judicial Protocol for cases where no settlement is proposed, and urged courts to do the same.[244] Notably, this includes a framework for communication between judges in different provinces dealing with potentially overlapping class actions, allowing them to conduct joint case management hearings.

In addition, courts across Canada have found other ways to co-ordinate the litigation and settlement of multijurisdictional class actions. A notable example is the Indian Residential Schools (IRS) settlement. In November 2005, the parties to the IRS class actions reached an agreement in principle, representing one of the largest class action settlements in history. The parties included Indigenous plaintiffs in individual and class actions, churches, Indigenous organizations (particularly the Assembly of First Nations), and the federal government.[245] The settlement included the Common Experience Payment made to all former students of Indian Residential Schools; payments made to the Aboriginal Healing Foundation; the setting up and funding of the Truth and Reconciliation Commission; and an Independent Assessment Process to handle sexual assault and serious physical abuse claims.[246]

The final settlement required court approval, pursuant to the class proceedings legislation of the various jurisdictions involved. In light of the magnitude of the individuals' claims and the geographical location of class members across Canada, and to ensure order and fairness as well

243 Council of the Canadian Bar Association, "Class Action Judicial Protocols" (Resolution 11-03-A, adopted at the annual meeting in Halifax, Nova Scotia, 13–14 August 2011), online: www.cba.org/getattachment/Our-Work/Resolutions/Resolutions/2011/Protocole-judiciaire-sur-les-recours-collectifs/11-03-A.pdf. See also Walker et al, above note 29 at 293–96; Iacobucci, "Access to Justice," above note 138 at 18–19.

244 Resolution 18-03-A, Class Action Judicial Protocols (2018), online: www.cba.org/getattachment/Our-Work/Resolutions/Resolutions/2018/Class-Action-Judicial-Protocols-(1)/18-03-A.pdf.

245 Iacobucci, "IRS," above note 125 at 6.

246 *Ibid* at 7–8.

as the enforceability of the settlement in future, approval was sought in nine jurisdictions.[247] An unprecedented notice program advised class members of the settlement approval hearings.[248] The parties agreed that the settlement would only be effective if the nine courts provided unanimous approval on terms that were, substantially, the same.[249] Four courts approved the settlement unconditionally, and five courts required further submissions before approval was granted.[250]

While the IRS settlement can be seen as exceptional in its significance and scope, similar approaches to settlement approval have been pursued in other cases.[251] Such creative remedies are encouraging, but the ultimate resolution of the problem of overlapping national class actions almost certainly lies in co-ordinated legislative amendments in each of the provinces. However, such amendments cannot be forced upon the provinces and may never voluntarily occur.

E. CONCLUSION

More than a quarter of a century after the *Class Proceedings Act* came into force, there is little doubt that the Act needs to be thoroughly reviewed. Numerous controversies have arisen, foreseen and unforeseen, surrounding costs and funding, the certification process, ethical issues, and

247 Namely, British Columbia, Alberta, Saskatchewan, Manitoba, Ontario, and Quebec, as well as the three territorial courts of Yukon, the Northwest Territories, and Nunavut: *ibid* at 9. See also Walker et al, above note 29 at 277–78.

248 Walker et al, *ibid* at 278.

249 Iacobucci, "IRS," above note 125 at 20.

250 *Ibid* at 20–22.

251 For example, counsel in the Toyota unintended acceleration class action (known in Ontario as *Hamilton v Toyota Motor Sales, USA, Inc*, 2014 ONSC 785) sought settlement approval in four courts across the country, representing class members in four geographical areas: Ontario (representing class members in Ontario, Manitoba, and the three territories), Nova Scotia (representing class members in Nova Scotia, New Brunswick, Newfoundland and Labrador, and Prince Edward Island), Quebec, and Saskatchewan (representing class members in Saskatchewan, Alberta, and British Columbia). By way of further example, in *Endean v British Columbia*, 2016 SCC 42, the Supreme Court of Canada held that judges of different provinces (in this case, British Columbia, Ontario, and Quebec) could sit together to conduct a settlement approval hearing. Finally, counsel sought settlement approval in both Ontario and Quebec in the Bextra/Celebrex class action (known in Ontario as *Voutour v Pfizer Canada Inc*, 2011 ONSC 7118) and in the Volkswagen class action (known in Ontario as *Quenneville v Volkswagen Group Canada Inc*, 2017 ONSC 2448).

overlapping actions. These controversies threaten to undermine the objectives of the *CPA*, especially judicial economy and access to justice.

A review of the *CPA* may not be sufficient, however. Many of the issues addressed in this chapter stretch beyond provincial boundaries, most notably the issue of national overlapping class actions. These issues cannot be fixed by simply amending the *CPA*. Many of them are also deeply complex and controversial, such as the issue of financial incentives for lawyers in the class actions context. They raise the question of whether class proceedings actually fit comfortably with the traditional model of litigation. Attempts by the drafters of the *CPA* to fit class actions within the traditional model have clearly run into problems, and it seems that deeper structural changes are required.

Numerous questions need to be answered. How does Canada's province-by-province litigation system fit with the modern reality of interprovincial, and even international, disputes? Should the Rules of Professional Conduct in Ontario and elsewhere be amended, and ethical breaches be more severely sanctioned? How do financial incentives for class counsel fit with the traditional costs rules? Such questions need further research and consultation, preferably on an interprovincial level, in order to thoroughly address the current hindrances to class actions practice. They would also benefit from comparative research, drawing guidance from other jurisdictions and the ways in which they have tackled similar issues.

As the Court of Appeal for British Columbia has stated in the context of national class proceedings, "new types of proceedings require reconsideration of old rules if the fundamental principles of order and fairness are to be respected."[252] Such an approach may add many years to a review that has already been significantly delayed.[253] It is necessary, however, in order to prevent further uncertainty and inefficiency, and to promote the *CPA*'s underlying objectives of judicial economy, behaviour modification, and, above all, access to justice.

---

252 *Harrington v Dow Corning Corp*, 2000 BCCA 605 at para 99. See also Dafoe, above note 203 at 572, and Walker, "National," above note 207 at 97.

253 The Law Commission of Ontario's review of the *CPA* began in the spring of 2013. As noted above, the project was relaunched in 2017: LCO, News Release, "Class Actions: Objectives, Experience and Reforms" (2 October 2017), online: www.lco-cdo.org/wp-content/uploads/2013/04/CA-Press-Release-FINAL-Sept-22-2017.pdf.

GLOSSARY

aggregate damages. Damages can sometimes be determined without reference to the individual class members' discrete claims. This can occur when the defendant's liability has been established and some or all class members are entitled to monetary relief, and it is possible to calculate the totality of the harm caused by the defendant. In this situation, an "aggregate damages" award can be made to the class as a whole, which is subsequently apportioned among the class members.

certification. Many (but not all) jurisdictions have a certification requirement for class actions, where a motion must be brought for court approval of the action as a class proceeding. Certification can be a controversial issue, as it imposes on class actions a requirement that is not imposed on ordinary proceedings. The certification stage generally requires that several criteria be met. In some jurisdictions, this includes an assessment of the merits of the action, while certification in other jurisdictions is solely a procedural hurdle.

class, class members. The group on whose behalf a class action is brought is generally defined in the statement of claim (for example, "all Canadians who ingested drug X between 2012 and 2016"), and the individuals in this group are known as "class members."

class proceeding. An action or application brought on behalf of a group of people (the class), which claims that this group has been affected by the actions of one or more defendants. For the purposes of this book, "class actions" or "class proceedings" will refer to modern-day group actions for damages, brought under Rule 75 or the *CPA* (or their equivalent in other jurisdictions), that were theoretically available to a wide variety of groups and for various causes of action.

common issues stage. If an action is certified, it will then move to a common issues trial. This is akin to an ordinary trial, except the issues to be determined are "common" across the class (for example, "did the drug ingested by the class members materially increase the risk of heart disease?").

cy-près award. In certain jurisdictions, if any part of a damages award remains unclaimed by class members after a certain amount of time, it is automatically returned to the defendant. In other situations, it may not be possible or practicable to distribute a monetary award (aggregate or otherwise) to individual class members. In that case, a cy-près award can be made, whereby the award is given to a charity or non-profit organization, or distributed in another way that can reasonably be expected to benefit class members. Cy-près is a French legal term that can be translated as "as near as possible." It originated in the law of charitable trusts.

individual issues stage. If one or more common issues are determined in favour of the class, then the action will move to the individual issues stage. This step determines issues that arise from the common questions, but cannot be determined in common—for example, individual damages. Often this step is completed through a claims process, whereby individual class members will make a claim for their damages and submit supporting documentation.

notice. Because a class action encompasses a group of individuals who are not parties, those class members must be notified of their rights at the various stages of the proceeding. This entails giving notice to the class members, which can usually be done in a number of ways, whether by direct mail, newspaper notice, or social media. In some jurisdictions, such as the United States (which has constitutional "due process" requirements), notice is mandatory for certain types of class action; in others, it is within the discretion of the court.

Notice is usually given after certification (once the proceeding has been certified as a class action), because then any subsequent judgment will bind class members. In an "opt-out" jurisdiction, if class members do not want to be bound by any subsequent judgment, they must exclude themselves within a certain period of time. Obviously, they cannot exclude themselves if they do not know about the action, which is why notice and the way in which it is given is important. Notice is also usually given after a determination of the common issues or after settlement, so class members can make claims at the individual issues stage or pursuant to any settlement agreement.

opt-in/opt-out. Depending on the jurisdiction, the class can either be "opt-in" (individuals must take steps to be included in the class, such as submitting a form) or "opt-out" (individuals captured by the class definition are automatically included in the class, unless they take steps to be excluded).

representative action. For the purposes of this book, "representative actions" refers to the actions that could be brought pursuant to a number of statutes—for example, tenants under the *Residential Tenancies Act*,[1] or shareholders under the Ontario *Securities Act*[2]—prior to the passage of the *CPA*. The term also applies to actions brought purely for injunctive, declaratory, or other equitable relief (also available before the *CPA*).

representative plaintiff. Class members are not parties to the action. They are represented by one or more representative plaintiffs, who are parties. The lawsuit is brought in the name of the representative plaintiff, who is named in the style of cause, is subject to discovery, and can be liable for costs, just like a plaintiff in an ordinary action.

1 RSO 1980, c 452.

2 RSO 1980, c 466, Part XXII.

BIBLIOGRAPHY

Legislation

Canada (Federal)

Canadian Charter of Rights and Freedoms, Part I of the *Constitution Act, 1982*, being Schedule B to the *Canada Act 1982* (UK), 1982, c 11.

Combines Investigation Act, RSC 1970, c C-23.

Companies' Creditors Arrangement Act, RSC 1985, c C-36.

Constitution Act, 1867 (UK), 30 & 31 Vict, c 3.

Grassy Narrows and Islington Indian Bands Mercury Pollution Claims Settlement Act, SC 1986, c 23.

Alberta

Class Proceedings Act, SA 2003, c C-16.5, as amended by the *Class Proceedings Amendment Act, 2010*, SA 2010, c 15.

British Columbia

Class Proceedings Act, RSBC 1996, c 50.

Trade Practice Act, RSBC 1979, c 406.

New Brunswick

Class Proceedings Act, SNB 2006, c C-5.15, since repealed and replaced by RSNB 2011, c 125.

Newfoundland and Labrador

Rules of the Supreme Court, 1986, SNL 1986, c 42, Schedule D.

Ontario

An Act Respecting Champerty, RSO 1897, c 327.
Class Proceedings Act, 1992, SO 1992, c 6.
Class Proceedings, O Reg 771/92 (under the *Law Society Act*, RSO 1990, c L.8).
Consumer Protection Act, RSO 1970, c 82.
Consumer Protection Act, RSO 1990, c C.31.
Courts of Justice Act, RSO 1990, c C.43.
Environmental Bill of Rights, 1993, SO 1993, c 28.
Law Society Amendment Act (Class Proceedings Funding), 1992, SO 1992, c 7.
The Ontario Judicature Act, 1881, 44 Vict, c 5.
Residential Tenancies Act, RSO 1980, c 452.
Rules of Court, Order XII, Rule 10, enacted as a schedule to the *Ontario Judicature Act*.
Rules of Civil Procedure, RRO 1990, Reg 194, Rule 12.
Rules of Practice and Procedure, RRO 1980, Reg 540, Rule 75.
Securities Act, RSO 1980, c 466, Part XXII.
Solicitors Act, RSO 1960, c 378, s 59.

Quebec

Code of Civil Procedure, RSQ 1977, c C-25, as enacted by SQ 1978, c 8.
Code of Civil Procedure, CQLR c C-25.01.

Saskatchewan

The Class Actions Act, SS 2001, c C-12.01.
The Department of Consumer Affairs Act, RSS 1978, c D-9.

United Kingdom

Supreme Court of Judicature Act, 1873, 36 & 37 Vict, c 66 (UK).

United States

Federal Rules of Civil Procedure, Rule 23, 383 US 1029 (1966), available online: LII www.law.cornell.edu/rules/frcp/rule_23.
Federal Rules of Civil Procedure, Rule 23, 308 US 653 (1938).

Australia

Courts and Tribunals Legislation (Miscellaneous Amendments) Act 2000 (Vict).
Federal Court of Australia Act 1976 (Cth), Part IVA.
Federal Court of Australia Amendment Act 1991 (Cth), No 181.
Supreme Court Rules 1987 (SA), Rules 34.01, 34.02, & 34.03.
Supreme Court Act 1986 (Vict), ss 34 & 35.

Primary Sources

Interviews

Advisory Committee member, oral interview, 13 April 2016; email correspondence, 26 September 2016.

Bogart, William A, oral interview, 1 April 2016.

Chester, Simon, correspondence, 4 December 2017.

Cochrane, Michael, oral interviews, 23 April, 28 June, and 26 September 2016; email correspondence, 6 July 2016.

Ewart, Doug, Ministry of the Attorney General, oral interview, 26 April 2016.

Gregory, John D, general counsel from 1985 to 2016 in the Justice Policy Development Branch, Ministry of the Attorney General (Ontario), oral interview, 24 July 2017.

Law Commission of Ontario, correspondence, 14 July 2016.

Mendes da Costa, The Honourable Derek, transcript of interview, Osgoode Society for Canadian Legal History, Oral History Collection, 2003.

O'Sullivan, Terrence, oral interview, 21 June 2017.

Parliamentary legislative assistant, oral interview, 25 August 2016.

Peterson, David, former premier of Ontario, oral interview, 24 July 2017.

Poch, David, oral interview, 24 July 2017.

Retired judge, oral interview, 13 July 2017.

Strosberg, Harvey, transcript of interview, Osgoode Society for Canadian Legal History, Oral History Collection, 2005.

Woolford, Peter, Retail Council of Canada, oral interviews, 29 April and 27 September 2016.

Government Documents

Australian Law Reform Commission Report No 46. *Grouped Proceedings in the Federal Court* (Canberra: Government of Australia Publishing Service, 1988), online: www.alrc.gov.au/sites/default/files/pdfs/publications/alrc46_Summary.pdf.

Cochrane, MG. *Class Proceedings in Ontario: Backgrounder* (Toronto: Ministry of the Attorney General, 1990).

Committee on Fair Dealing in Consumer Savings and Investments. *A Blueprint for Fairness* (Edmonton: Consumer and Corporate Affairs Alberta, 1989), online: https://archive.org/details/blueprintforfair00albe.

Crossman, G. *Consumer Remedies and Government Redress* (Toronto: Legislative Review Project, Ministry of the Attorney General, 1987).

Department of Consumer and Corporate Affairs. *Proposals for a New Competition Policy for Canada, Second Stage* (Ottawa: Supply and Services Canada, 1977).

Dore, KJ, & RW Kerr. *Third Report of the Consumer Protection Project*, vol 1 (Fredericton: New Brunswick Department of Justice, Law Reform Division, 1976).

Grange, S. *Report of the Mississauga Railway Accident Inquiry* (Ottawa: Supply and Services Canada, 1980).

Law Reform Commission of Australia. *Access to the Courts II: Class Actions* (Canberra: Government of Australia, 1979).

Law Reform Commission of Saskatchewan. *Fourth Annual Report* (Regina: Law Reform Commission of Saskatchewan, 1977).

Law Reform Committee of South Australia. *Thirty-Sixth Report Relating to Class Actions* (Adelaide: Government of South Australia, 1977).

Legislative Research Service. *How an Ontario Bill Becomes Law: A Guide for Legislators and the Public* (Toronto: Legislative Assembly of Ontario, 2011), online: https://www.ola.org/sites/default/files/common/how-bills-become-law-en.pdf.

Ministry of the Attorney General. *Conference on Access to Civil Justice: June 20–22, 1988* (Toronto: Ministry of the Attorney General, 1988).

———. Policy Development Division. *Report of the Attorney General's Advisory Committee on Class Action Reform* (Toronto: Ministry of the Attorney General, 1990).

Ontario Gazette. Vol 126-1, Reg 770/92, 2 January 1993.

Ontario Law Reform Commission. *Report on Consumer Warranties and Guarantees in the Sale of Goods* (Toronto: Ministry of the Attorney General, 1972).

———. *Fifteenth Annual Report 1981–82* (Toronto: Ministry of the Attorney General, 1982).

———. *Report on Class Actions* (Toronto: Ministry of the Attorney General, 1982).

———. *Report on the Law of Standing* (Toronto: Ministry of the Attorney General, 1989).

Lawlor, PD. *Group Defamation: Submissions to the Attorney General of Ontario* (Toronto: Ministry of the Attorney General March 1984).

Slater, DW. *Final Report of the Ontario Task Force on Insurance*, vol 1 (Toronto: Ministry of Financial Institutions, 1986).

Williams, NJ, & J Whybrow. *A Proposal for Class Actions Under Competition Policy Legislation* (Ottawa: Department of Consumer and Corporate Affairs, 1976).

WILLISTON, WB. *Report of the Civil Procedure Revision Committee* (Toronto: Ministry of the Attorney General, 1980).

Parliamentary Debates

Ontario, Legislative Assembly, *Official Report of Debates (Hansard)*, 32nd Parl, 2nd Sess (24 June 1982) (Roy McMurtry), online: http://hansardindex.ontla.on.ca/hansardeissue/32-2/l087.htm.

——, *Official Report of Debates (Hansard)*, 32nd Parl, 2nd Sess (20 January 1983) (Jim Breithaupt), online: http://hansardindex.ontla.on.ca/hansardeissue/32-2/l187.htm.

——, *Official Report of Debates (Hansard)*, 32nd Parl, 4th Sess (30 March 1984) (Roy McMurtry), online: http://hansardindex.ontla.on.ca/hansardeissue/32-4/l009.htm.

——, *Official Report of Debates (Hansard)*, 32nd Parl, 4th Sess (8 May 1984) (Marion Bryden and Richard Johnston), online: http://hansardindex.ontla.on.ca/hansardeissue/32-4/l039.htm.

——, *Official Report of Debates (Hansard)*, 33rd Parl, 2nd Sess (3 December 1986) (Ian Scott), online: http://hansardindex.ontla.on.ca/hansardeissue/33-2/l074.htm.

——, *Official Report of Debates (Hansard)*, 33rd Parl, 2nd Sess (10 December 1986) (Ruth Grier), online: http://hansardindex.ontla.on.ca/hansardeissue/33-2/l078.htm.

——, *Official Report of Debates (Hansard)*, 34th Parl, 2nd Sess (14 June 1989) (Howard Hampton), online: http://hansardindex.ontla.on.ca/hansardeissue/34-2/l025.htm.

——, *Official Report of Debates (Hansard)*, 34th Parl, 2nd Sess (29 June 1989) (Ian Scott), online: http://hansardindex.ontla.on.ca/hansardeissue/34-2/l034.htm.

——, *Official Report of Debates (Hansard)*, 34th Parl, 2nd Sess (12 June 1990) (Ian Scott), online: http://hansardindex.ontla.on.ca/hansardeissue/34-2/l045_90.htm.

——, *Official Report of Debates (Hansard)*, 35th Parl, 1st Sess (13 December 1990) (Ruth Grier), online: http://hansardindex.ontla.on.ca/hansardeissue/35-1/l070_90.htm.

——, *Official Report of Debates (Hansard)*, 35th Parl, 1st Sess (17 December 1990) (Howard Hampton), online: http://hansardindex.ontla.on.ca/hansardeissue/35-1/l071_90.htm.

——, *Official Report of Debates (Hansard)*, 35th Parl, 1st Sess (18 November 1991) (Robert Chiarelli; Charles Harnick; David Winninger on behalf of Howard Hampton), online: http://hansardindex.ontla.on.ca/hansardeissue/35-1/l083.htm.

——, *Official Report of Debates (Hansard)*, 35th Parl, 1st Sess (3 December 1991) (Gord Mills), online: http://hansardindex.ontla.on.ca/hansardeissue/35-1/l092.htm.

——, *Official Report of Debates (Hansard)*, 35th Parl, 2nd Sess (27 April 1992) (Howard Hampton; Robert Chiarelli; Steven Offer; Chris Stockwell; Charles Harnick), online: http://hansardindex.ontla.on.ca/hansardeissue/35-2/l012.htm.

——, *Official Report of Debates (Hansard)*, 35th Parl, 2nd Sess (4 May 1992) (David Winninger, on behalf of Howard Hampton; Robert Chiarelli; Elinor Caplan), online: http://hansardindex.ontla.on.ca/hansardeissue/35-2/l016.htm.

——, *Official Report of Debates (Hansard)*, 35th Parl, 2nd Sess (25 June 1992) (Deborah Deller), online: http://hansardindex.ontla.on.ca/hansardeissue/35-2/l043b.htm.

Bill C-20, *An Act to amend the Competition Act and to make consequential and related amendments to other Acts*, Minutes of Proceedings and Evidence of the House of Commons Standing Committee on Industry, 6 May 1998 (Norman Stewart and Peter Woolford), online: Parliament of Canada www.parl.gc.ca/HousePublications/Publication.aspx?DocId=1038689&Language=E&Mode=1&Parl=36&Ses=1.

Québec, Assemblée nationale, *Journal des débats,* 31ième lég, 3e sess, audition des memoires sur le project de loi no 39 (le 7 mars 1978) B-262 (Member of the National Assembly (MNA) Fernand Lalonde).

Documents of Non-governmental Organizations

Barreau du Québec. *Mémoire à la Commission parlementaire de la justice sur le projet de loi 39: Loi sur le recours collectif* (Québec: Barreau du Québec, 1978).

Belobaba, E et al. *On the Question of Consumer Advocacy: A Working Paper* (Ottawa: Canadian Consumer Council, 1972).

Canadian Bar Association. Resolution 18-03-A, Class Action Judicial Protocols (2018), online: www.cba.org/getattachment/Our-Work/Resolutions/Resolutions/2018/Class-Action-Judicial-Protocols-(1)/18-03-A.pdf.

Conseil du patronat du Québec. *Mémoire à la Commission parlementaire de la justice sur le projet de loi 39: Loi sur le recours collectif* (Québec: CPQ, 1978).

Dewees, D, J Prichard, & M Trebilcock. *Class Actions as a Regulatory Instrument* (Toronto: Ontario Economic Council, 1980).

Law Commission of Ontario. *Review of Class Actions in Ontario: Issues to Be Considered* (Toronto: Law Commission of Ontario, 2013), online: www.lco-cdo.org/wp-content/uploads/2014/01/class-actions-issues-to-be-considered.pdf.

———. *Class Actions: Objectives, Experience and Reforms* (Toronto: Law Commission of Ontario, 2017), online: www.lco-cdo.org/wp-content/uploads/2013/04/CA-Press-Release-FINAL-Sept-22-2017.pdf.

———. *Class Actions: Objectives, Experiences and Reforms: Consultation Paper* (Toronto: Law Commission of Ontario, 2018), online: www.lco-cdo.org/wp-content/uploads/2018/03/Class-Action-Consultation-Paper-FINAL1.pdf.

Law Foundation of Ontario. *Class Proceedings Fund: 20 Years in Review*, online: www.lawfoundation.on.ca/wp-content/uploads/CPF-Brochure-2013.pdf.

Law Society of Upper Canada. Access to Justice Committee. "Report to Convocation" (23 November 2006), online: www.lsuc.on.ca/convocationdisplay.aspx?id=989.

———. *Guidelines for Lawyers Acting in Cases Involving Claims of Aboriginal Residential School Abuse* (Toronto: Law Society of Upper Canada, 2003), online: www.lsuc.on.ca/media/guideline_aboriginal_res.pdf.

———. *Rules of Professional Conduct*, online: www.lsuc.on.ca/lawyer-conduct-rules.

———. *The Challenges of Class Proceedings for Civil Litigators* (Toronto: Law Society of Upper Canada, 1992).

Public Interest Advocacy Centre. *Consumer Protection in Canada and the European Union: A Comparison* (2009), online: www.piac.ca/wp-content/uploads/2014/11/piac_report_consumer_protection_in_canada_and_the_europeon_union_a_comparision.pdf.

———. *25 Years Representing the Public Interest* (Ottawa: PIAC, 2001), online: www.piac.ca/wp-content/uploads/2014/11/25years.pdf.

Trebilcock, M. *The Case for a Consumer Advocate* (Ottawa: Canadian Consumer Council, 1972).

Uniform Law Conference of Canada. *Report of the Uniform Law Conference of Canada's Committee on the National Class and Related Interjurisdictional Issues: Background, Analysis and Recommendations* (Vancouver: ULCC, 2005).

Waddell, I. *A Practical Approach to Consumer Class Actions in Civil Litigation in Canada* (Vancouver: Western Canada Institute of Legal Research and Reform, 1975).

Williams, NJ. *Consumer Class Actions in Canada: A Study Prepared for the Consumers' Association of Canada* (Ottawa: Consumers' Association of Canada, 1974).

Other Archival Documents

Insurance Bureau of Canada Archives. Legal Division Memoranda 1990, Class Actions.

Archives of Ontario. F 4339-1, Box No B222612, Speeches and Notes for Remarks by Ian Scott.

———. F 4339-2, Box No B222613, Records of Ian Scott's Political Engagement.

———. F 4339-3, Box No B222614, Ian Scott's Correspondence.

———. F 4339-5, Box Nos B738519 and B738520, Ian Scott's Research Notes and Reference Material.

———. RG 4-40, Box Nos B248501, B248633, B319671, B380614, B381441, B439607, B449217, B449218, B501822, B502275, B703283, B710273, B807794, B807806 and B827067, Policy Development Division Counsel Correspondence Files.

———. RG 4-40, Box No B381441, Canadian Manufacturing Association File on Class Actions.

———. RG 4-66, Box Nos B319671, B319672, B380536, B380537, B380538, B380543 and B380546, Ontario Law Reform Commission Files.

———. RG 4-143, Box No B827937, Ministry of the Attorney General Acts & Regulations Files.

———. RG 27-2, Box Nos B280346 and B280347, Cabinet Committee on Legislation.

———. RG 75-14, Box No B834837, Minutes of Cabinet Meetings.

———. RG 75-18-1, Box Nos B861454, B861455, B861456, B861457, B861458, B861459 and B861460, Cabinet Submissions.

Library and Archives Canada. MIKAN No 4583565, Container 1, Item 17, Jeffery Lyons Fonds.

Supreme Court of Canada Archives. Records re: *General Motors of Canada Ltd v Naken et al.*

Online Sources

Bogart, WA, J Kalajdzic, & I Matthews. "Class Actions in Canada: A National Procedure in a Multi-jurisdictional Society?" (Report prepared for Globalization of Class Actions Conference, Oxford University, December 2007), online: Global Class Actions Exchange http://globalclassactions.stanford.edu/sites/default/files/documents/Canada_National_Report.pdf.

CANADIAN BAR ASSOCIATION. Resolution 18-03-A, "Class Action Judicial Protocols" (2018), online: www.cba.org/getattachment/Our-Work/Resolutions/Resolutions/2018/Class-Action-Judicial-Protocols-(1)/18-03-A.pdf.

CANADIAN FEDERATION OF INDEPENDENT BUSINESS, ONLINE: www.cfib-fcei.ca/english/about-us/canada/178-about-us.html.

COUNCIL OF THE CANADIAN BAR ASSOCIATION. Annual Meeting in Halifax, Nova Scotia, 13–14 August 2011, Resolution 11-03-A, "Class Action Judicial Protocols," online: www.cba.org/getattachment/Our-Work/Resolutions/Resolutions/2011/Protocole-judiciaire-sur-les-recours-collectifs/11-03-A.pdf.

DAVID, JOCELYN. *The Public Consultations of the Competition Bureau: Building Bridges to Consumers* (Montréal: Option consommateurs, 2003), online: https://option-consommateurs.org/wp-content/uploads/2017/07/competition-june-2003.pdf.

DE L'ÉTOILE, VINCENT. "Quebec's Own Class Action Authorization Regime" *Canadian Lawyer* (25 April 2016), online: www.canadianlawyermag.com/6005/Quebecs-own-class-action-authorization-regime.html.

FLEMING, MATTHEW, & ARA BASMADJIAN. "Costs Awards in Class Actions: Equal Treatment for Plaintiffs and Defendants" (30 June 2015), online: International Law Office www.dentons.com/en/~/media/e9abfafe25904b9987f3a846afdd2e3e.ashx.

GLOBE AND MAIL, ONLINE: www.theglobeandmail.com/news.

GOOGLE NEWS ARCHIVE SEARCH, ONLINE: https://news.google.com/newspapers.

GOVERNMENT OF CANADA. Canada Employment Insurance Commission (CEIC). "Commissioner for Employers: Judith Andrew," online: CEIC www.esdc.gc.ca/en/ei/commissioner_employers.page.

KALAJDZIC, JASMINKA. "It's Complicated: Access to Justice & Cost Shifting in Class Actions" (24 November 2013) (blog), online: *Slaw* www.slaw.ca/2013/11/24/its-complicated-access-to-justice-cost-shifting-in-class-actions.

KAUTH, GLENN. "Bar Drops Ball on National Class Actions" *Law Times* (22 August 2011), online: www.lawtimesnews.com/201108222535/commentary/editorial-bar-drops-ball-on-national-class-actions.

MACDONELL, KAITLYN. "Ethics of Class Counsel: Is There a Need for Restrictions on Investigating Class Claims?" (2011), online: http://clp.law.

utoronto.ca/sites/clp.law.utoronto.ca/files/documents/Ethics-of-Class-Counsel.pdf.

Mallett, T, & K Osaka. "Alberta Adopts an Opt Out Class Proceedings Regime" (2011), online: Osler LLP www.osler.com/en/resources/regulations/2011/alberta-adopts-an-opt-out-class-proceedings-regime-en.

Morabito, Vince. "Group Litigation in Australia—'Desperately Seeking' Effective Class Action Regimes," National Report for Australia Prepared for the Globalisation of Class Actions Conference, Oxford University, December 2007, online: http://globalclassactions.stanford.edu/sites/default/files/documents/Australia_National_Report.pdf.

Office of the Commissioner of Lobbying of Canada. "Registration, In-House Organization," online: OCLC https://lobbycanada.gc.ca/app/secure/ocl/lrs/do/vwRg;jsessionid=IpiW6Gs41UQJ9McNjQ6Yme5W.app-ocl-01?regId=500543&cno=4590.

Ontario Chamber of Commerce, online: www.occ.ca.

Ontario Community Newspapers Collection, online: http://ink.ourdigitalworld.org/titles.

Osgoode Society for Canadian Legal History, Oral History Collection, online: www.osgoodesociety.ca/oral-history.

ProQuest Historical Newspapers, accessed through York University Libraries, online: www.proquest.com/products-services/pq-hist-news.html.

Uniform Law Conference of Canada. Proceedings of the Fifty-Ninth Annual Meeting, St Andrews, New Brunswick, August 1977, online: www.ulcc.ca/images/stories/Past_Proceedings_PDF/1977ULCC0059.pdf.

———. Proceedings of the Sixtieth Annual Meeting, St John's, Newfoundland, August 1978, online: www.ulcc.ca/images/stories/Past_Proceedings_PDF/1978ULCC0060.pdf.

———. Proceedings of the Sixty-Ninth Annual Meeting, Victoria, British Columbia, August 1987, online: www.ulcc.ca/images/stories/Past_Proceedings_PDF/1987ULCC0069.pdf.

———. Proceedings of the Seventieth Annual Meeting, Toronto, Ontario, August 1988, online: www.ulcc.ca/images/stories/Past_Proceedings_PDF/1988ULCC0070.pdf.

———. Proceedings of the Seventy-Eighth Annual Meeting, Ottawa, Ontario, August 1996, online: www.ulcc.ca/en/annual-meetings/412-1996-ottawa-annual/civil-section-documents/1907-uniform-class-proceedings-act-1992.

Winkler, The Honourable Chief Justice Warren K. "Caught in a Trap: Ethical Considerations for the Plaintiff's Lawyer in Class Proceedings," online: www.ontariocourts.on.ca/coa/en/ps/speeches/caught.htm.

——— et al. "Has the Time Come to Amend Section 2(3) (the "Ninety-Day Rule") of the *Class Proceedings Act, 1992*?" (7 March 2013), online: Siskinds LLP www.siskinds.com/has-the-time-come-to-amend-section.

Secondary Sources

Articles

Abdelkerim, MP. "Class Counsel's Ethical Obligations" (2004) 18 *Windsor Review of Legal & Social Issues* 105.

Aliverti, A. "Exploring the Function of Criminal Law in the Policing of Foreigners: The Decision to Prosecute Immigration-Related Offences" (2012) 21:4 *Social and Legal Studies* 511.

Antman, G. "Carriage Motions in Ontario: Inconsistent Application of an Indeterminate Test" (2018) 13:1 *Canadian Class Action Review* 101.

Bankier, JK. "Class Actions for Monetary Relief in Canada: Formalism or Function?" (1984) 4 *Windsor Yearbook of Access to Justice* 229.

———. "The Future of Class Actions in Canada: Cases, Courts and Confusion" (1984) 9 *Canadian Business Law Journal* 260.

Becker, GS. "A Theory of Competition Among Pressure Groups for Political Influence" (1983) 98 *Quarterly Journal of Economics* 371.

Beisner, J et al. "Class Action 'Cops': Public Servants or Private Entrepreneurs?" (2005) 57 *Stanford Law Review* 1441.

Belobaba, E. "Unfair Trade Practices Legislation: Symbolism and Substance in Consumer Protection" (1977) 15 *Osgoode Hall Law Journal* 327.

Bogart, WA. "*Naken*, the Supreme Court and What Are Our Courts For?" (1984) 9 *Canadian Business Law Journal* 280.

———. "Questioning Litigation's Role: Courts and Class Actions in Canada" (1987) 62:3 *Indiana Law Journal* 665.

Bone, RG. "Personal and Impersonal Litigative Forms: Reconceiving the History of Adjudicative Representation" (1990) 70 *Boston University Law Review* 213.

Branch, W, & C Rhone. "Chaos or Consistency? The National Class Action Dilemma" (2004) 1:1 *Canadian Class Action Review* 3.

Bricker, J. "Ontario's Class Proceedings Fund: A Good (If Less Than Perfect) Class Action Costs Model" (2008) 4:2 *Canadian Class Action Review* 399.

Burkett, KM. "The Politicization of the Ontario Labour Relations Framework in the 1990s" (1998) 6 *Canadian Labour and Employment Law Journal* 161.

Cappelletti, M. "Vindicating the Public Interest Through the Courts: A Comparativist's Contribution" (1976) 25 *Buffalo Law Review* 643.

Carabash, M. "Ethical Conduct for Class Counsel in Ontario" (2006) 3:2 *Canadian Class Action Review* 617.

Chafee, Z. "Bills of Peace with Multiple Parties" (1932) 45 *Harvard Law Review* 1297.

Chiodo, S. "Defendant Class Actions: Awkward Twin or Distant Cousin?" (2015) 10:3 *Class Action Journal* 649.

Clark, S, & C Harris. "Multi-plaintiff Litigation in Australia: A Comparative Perspective" (2001) 11 *Duke Journal of Comparative & International Law* 289.

———. "The Push to Reform Class Action Procedure in Australia: Evolution or Revolution?" (2008) 32 *Melbourne University Law Review* 775.

Cochrane, MG. "The Process of Principled Negotiation of Public Policy: An Overview" (unpublished, on file with the author).

Coffee Jr, J. "Rescuing the Private Attorney General: Why the Model of the Lawyer as Bounty Hunter Is Not Working" (1983) 42:2 *Maryland Law Review* 215.

Cromwell, T. "An Examination of the Ontario Law Reform Commission Report on Class Actions" (1983) 15 *Ottawa Law Review* 587.

Dafoe, C. "A Path Through the Class Action Chaos: Selecting the Most Appropriate Jurisdiction with a National Class Action Panel" (2006) 3:2 *Canadian Class Action Review* 541.

Dantowitz, A. "Commercial Third Party Funding of Class Actions in Ontario: Eight Early Lessons" (Paper delivered at the Advocates' Society, Second Annual Securities Litigation Practice Group Symposium, September 2012).

Dewees, DN et al. "An Economic Analysis of Cost and Fee Rules for Class Actions" (1981) 10 *Journal of Legal Studies* 155.

DuVal, B. "Book Review: Ontario Law Reform Commission *Report on Class Actions*" (1983) *American Bar Foundation Research Journal* 783.

Eizenga, MA, & E Davis. "A History of Class Actions: Modern Lessons from Deep Roots" (2011) 7 *Canadian Class Action Review* 3.

Estey, W. "Public Nuisance and Standing to Sue" (1972) 10 *Osgoode Hall Law Journal* 563.

Finkelstein, N et al. "Summary Judgment Prior to Certification in Class Actions: How *Microsoft* and *Hryniak* Have Changed the Landscape" (2015) 44 *Advocates' Quarterly* 229.

FINN, S. "In a Class All Its Own: The Advent of the Modern Class Action and Its Changing Legal and Social Mission" (2005) 2:2 *Canadian Class Action Review* 333.

GILLESPIE, C. "The Scope of the Class Action in Canada" (1981) 11 *Manitoba Law Journal* 215.

GIRARD, P. "The Making of the Canadian Legal Profession: A Hybrid Heritage" (2014) 21:2 *International Journal of the Legal Profession* 145.

GLENN, HP. "Class Actions in Ontario and Québec" (1984) 62:3 *Canadian Bar Review* 247.

———. "Class Actions and the Theory of Tort and Delict" (1985) 35 *University of Toronto Law Review* 287.

GOOD, M. "Access to Justice, Judicial Economy and Behaviour Modification: Exploring the Goals of Canadian Class Actions" (2010) 47 *Alberta Law Review* 185.

GOURLAY, D. "A Class Act Comes of Age: Costs and Certification as the OLRC Report Turns Twenty" (2004) *Canadian Class Action Review* 273.

GOVERNMENT OF CANADA. "Class Actions: Recent Developments in Canada" (1978) 4 *Commonwealth Law Bulletin* 128.

HAZARD JR, GC ET AL. "Historical Analysis of the Binding Effect of Class Suits" (1998) 146:6 *University of Pennsylvania Law Review* 1849.

HENSLER III, LW. "Class Counsel, Self-Interest and Other People's Money" (2004) 35 *University of Memphis Law Review* 53.

HICKMAN, F. "National Competing Class Proceedings: Carriage Motions, Anti-suit Injunctions, Judicial Co-operation, and Other Options" (2004) 1:2 *Canadian Class Action Review* 367.

HOGG, PW, & SG MCKEE. "Are National Class Actions Constitutional?" (2010) 26 *National Journal of Constitutional Law* 279.

HOMBURGER, A. "Private Suits in the Public Interest in the United States of America" (1974) 23 *Buffalo Law Review* 343.

IACOBUCCI, F. "Class Actions and IRS Settlement" (2007) *The Cambridge Lectures* (unpublished, on file with the author).

———. "What Is Access to Justice in the Context of Class Actions?" (2011) 53 *Supreme Court Law Review* (2d) 17.

IACONO, P. "Class Actions and Products Liability in Ontario: What Will Happen?" (1991–92) 13 *Canadian Insurance Law Reporter* 99.

IRVING, C, & M BOUCHARD. "National Opt Out Class Actions, A Constitutional Assessment" (2009) 26 *National Journal of Constitutional Law* 111.

JONES, C. "The Case for the National Class" (2004) 1:1 *Canadian Class Action Review* 29.

KALAJDZIC, J. "Self-Interest, Public Interest, and the Interests of the Absent Client: Legal Ethics and Class Action Praxis" (2011) 49 *Osgoode Hall Law Journal* 1.

——— ET AL. "Justice for Profit: A Comparative Analysis of Australian, Canadian and US Third Party Litigation Funding" (2012) 61:2 *American Journal of Comparative Law* 93.

KALVEN JR, H, & M ROSENFIELD. "The Contemporary Function of the Class Suit" (1941) 8 *University of Chicago Law Review* 684.

KAZANJIAN, JA. "Class Actions in Canada" (1973) 11 *Osgoode Hall Law Journal* 397.

KRUSELL, J. "'Are National Class Actions Constitutional?' A Reply to Walker, Hogg and McKee" (2012) 70 *University of Toronto Faculty of Law Review* 9.

L'HEUREUX-DUBÉ, C. "The Quebec Experience: Codification of Family Law and a Proposal for the Creation of a Family Court System" (1984) 44:6 *Louisiana Law Review* 1575.

LAFOND, P. "Le recours collectif: entre la commodité prodécurale et la justice sociale" (1999) 29 *Revue de Droit, Université de Sherbrooke* 3.

LANDERS, W, & B VANCE. "Comments: Federal and State Class Actions: Developments and Opportunities" (1975) 46 *Mississippi Law Journal* 39.

LECLERC, J. "'The Sport of Kings': Financing Class Actions in Ontario" (2012) 8:1 *Canadian Class Action Review* 123.

MACDONALD, W, & J ROWLEY. "Ontario Class Action Reform: Business and Justice System Impacts: A Comment" (1984) 9 *Canadian Business Law Journal* 351.

MARCIN, RB. "Searching for the Origin of the Class Action" (1974) 23 *Catholic University Law Review* 515.

MARCUS, D. "The History of the Modern Class Action, Part I: *Sturm und Drang*, 1953–1980" (2013) 90 *Washington University Law Review* 1.

———. "The History of the Modern Class Action, Part II: Litigation and Legitimacy, 1981–1994" (2018) 86 *Fordham Law Review* (forthcoming).

MCKEE, SG, & N HENDERSON. "Class Action Reform: The Law Commission of Ontario Review of the *Class Proceedings Act*" (2016) 83 *Defense Counsel Journal* 32.

MCLAREN, J. "The Common Law Nuisance Actions and the Environmental Battle: Well-Tempered Swords or Broken Reeds" (1972) 10 *Osgoode Hall Law Journal* 505.

MCNALLY, WE, & BE COTTON. "Guiding Principles Regarding the Constitution of a Representative Defendant and a Defendant Class in a Class Action Proceeding" (2003) 27 *Advocates' Quarterly* 110.

Miller, A. "Of Frankenstein Monsters and Shining Knights: Myth, Reality, and the 'Class Action Problem'" (1979) 92 *Harvard Law Review* 664.

Morabito, V. "Taxpayers and Class Actions" (1997) 20:2 *University of New South Wales Law Journal* 372.

———, & J Caruana. "Can Class Action Regimes Operate Satisfactorily Without a Certification Device? Empirical Insights from the Federal Court of Australia" (2013) 61 *American Journal of Comparative Law* 579.

Morgan, M. "Who Takes the Reins? A Review of Carriage Decisions over the Last Decade" (2013) 9:1 *Canadian Class Action Review* 103.

Nissen, L. "Class Actions in Canada: An Environmental Perspective" (1984) 48 *Saskatchewan Law Review* 29.

O'Grady, J. "Consumer Remedies" (1982) 60:4 *Canadian Bar Review* 549.

Oder, A. "What's Fair Is Fair? A Comparative Look at Judicial Discretion in Fairness Review of Holocaust Era Class Action Settlements in the United States and Canada" (2009) 17 *Cardozo Journal of International and Comparative Law* 545.

Papageorgiou, G. "Ontario's Class Proceedings Fund: Separating Fact from Fiction" (2015) 10:1 *Canadian Class Action Review* 83.

Pawlowski, D. "*General Motors of Canada Ltd v Naken:* Two Centuries Forgotten" (1983) 21 *Alberta Law Review* 369.

Peltzman, S. "Toward a More General Theory of Regulation" (1976) 19 *Journal of Law and Economics* 211.

Perell, P. "Class Proceedings and Lawyers' Conflicts of Interest" (2009) 35 *Advocates' Quarterly* 202.

———. "Class Action Devils and Angels" (2013) 30:3 *Thomas M Cooley Law Review* 285.

Piché, P. "The Cultural Analysis of Class Action Law" (2009) 2 *Journal of Civil Law Studies* 101.

———. "The Class Action Settlement Actors: Who Protects Whom?" (2011) 53 *Supreme Court Law Review* (2d) 57.

Prichard, J. "Class Action Reform: Some General Comments" (1984) 9 *Canadian Business Law Journal* 309.

Roach, K. "Book Reviews" (1994) 23 *Canadian Business Law Journal* 156.

Sadovnikova, A et al. "Consumer Protection in Postwar Canada: Role and Contributions of the Consumers' Association of Canada to the Public Policy Process" (2014) 48:2 *Journal of Consumer Affairs* 380.

Scott, I. "The Role of the Attorney General and the *Charter of Rights*" (1987) 29 *Criminal Law Quarterly* 187.

———. "Law, Policy, and the Role of the Attorney-General: Constancy and Change in the 1980s" (1989) 39 *University of Toronto Law Journal* 109.

——— & R Anand. "Financing Public Participation in Environmental Decision Making" (1982) 60 *Canadian Bar Review* 81.

Silberman, L. "The Vicissitudes of the American Class Action—With a Comparative Eye" (1999) 7 *Tulane Journal of International and Comparative Law* 201.

———. "The Role of Choice of Law in National Class Actions" (2008) 156 *University of Pennsylvania Law Review* 2001.

Simpson, AWB. "The Rise and Fall of the Legal Treatise: Legal Principles and the Forms of Legal Literature" (1981) 48:3 *University of Chicago Law Review* 632.

Stanbury, W. "Half a Loaf: Bill C-29, Proposed Amendments to the *Combines Investigation Act*" (1985) 10:1 *Canadian Business Law Journal* 1.

Stiggelbout, M. "The Recognition in England and Wales of United States Judgments in Class Actions" (2011) 52:2 *Harvard International Law Journal* 433.

Stigler, G. "Theory of Economic Regulation" (1971) 2:1 *Bell Journal of Economics and Management Science* 3.

Trebilcock, M. "Private Law Remedies for Misleading Advertising" (1972) 22 *University of Toronto Law Journal* 1.

Upenieks, EG, & AH Kwok. "Costs in Class Actions" (Paper delivered at the Advocates' Society, Toronto, 9 May 2017) at 7, online: www.lawrences.com/docs/default-source/publications/costs-in-class-actions.pdf?sfvrsn=5.

Valdes, F. "Procedure, Policy and Power: Class Actions and Social Justice in Historical and Comparative Perspective" (2008) 24 *Georgia State University Law Review* 627.

Walker, J. "Coordinating Multijurisdiction Class Actions Through Existing Certification Processes" (2005) 41 *Canadian Business Law Journal* 112.

———. "Are National Class Actions Constitutional?: A Reply to Hogg and McKee" (2010) 48:1 *Osgoode Hall Law Journal* 95.

Watson, GD. "Class Actions: The Canadian Experience" (2001) 11 *Duke Journal of Comparative and International Law* 269.

Wildsmith, B. "An American Enforcement Model of Civil Process in a Canadian Landscape" (1980) 6 *Dalhousie Law Journal* 71.

Williams, NJ. "Consumer Class Actions in Canada: Some Proposals for Reform" (1975) 13 *Osgoode Hall Law Journal* 1.

Williston, WB. "Revising the Ontario Rules of Practice: The Work of the Civil Procedure Revision Committee" (1977) 1 *Advocates' Quarterly* 18.

———. "The Contingent Fee in Canada" (1968) 6 *Alberta Law Review* 184.

Yeazell, S. "Group Litigation and Social Context: Toward a History of the Class Action" (1977) 77:6 *Columbia Law Review* 866.

———. "The Past and Future of Defendant and Settlement Classes in Collective Litigation" (1997) 39 *Arizona Law Review* 687.

Ziegel, J. "Review: *Report of the Ontario Law Reform Commission on Consumer Warranties and Guarantees in the Sale of Goods*" (1973) 22:2 *International and Comparative Law Quarterly* 363.

Zwibel, CF. "Settling for Less? Problems and Proposals in the Settlement of Class Actions" (2004) 1:2 *Canadian Class Action Review* 165.

Chapters

Baker, J. "Reflections on 'Doing' Legal History" in A Musson & C Stebbings, eds, *Making Legal History: Approaches and Methodologies* (New York: Cambridge University Press, 2012).

Benidickson, J. "From Empire Ontario to California North: Law and Legal Institutions in Twentieth-Century Ontario" in DJ Guth & WW Pue, eds, *Canada's Legal Inheritances* (Winnipeg: Canadian Legal History Project, Faculty of Law, University of Manitoba, 2001) 620.

Bogart, WA. "Ambiguity" in A Prujiner & J Roy, eds, *Class Actions in Ontario and Québec: Proceedings of the First Yves Pratte Conference* (Montreal: Wilson & Lafleur, 1992) 3.

Camp, JJ. "Avoiding Pitfalls and Potential Conflicts in Negotiating Class Counsel Fees and Obtaining Court Approval" in Stephen GA Pitel, ed, *Litigating Conspiracy: An Analysis of Competition Class Actions* (Toronto: Irwin Law, 2006).

Chester, S. "Class Actions to Protect the Environment: A Real Weapon or Another Lawyer's Word Game?" in J Swaigen, ed, *Environmental Rights in Canada* (Toronto: Butterworths, 1982) 78.

Cochrane, MG. "Conditions for Instituting Class Actions" in A Prujiner & J Roy, eds, *Class Actions in Ontario and Québec: Proceedings of the First Yves Pratte Conference* (Montreal: Wilson & Lafleur, 1992) 57.

Musson, A, & C Stebbings. "Introduction" in A Musson & C Stebbings, eds, *Making Legal History: Approaches and Methodologies* (New York: Cambridge University Press, 2012).

Ziegel, J. "Political Ideology and Class Action Legislation" in J Walker & G Watson, eds, *Class Actions in Canada: Cases, Notes and Materials* (Toronto: Emond Montgomery, 2013).

Monographs

Backhaus, JG et al, eds. *The Law and Economics of Class Actions in Europe: Lessons from America* (Cheltenham, UK: Edward Elgar, 2012).

Borins, S. *Recent Developments in Civil Procedure: Class Actions, Public Interest Litigation and Standing* (Toronto: Osgoode Hall Law School, York University, 1974).

Calvert, F. *A Treatise upon the Law Respecting Parties to Suits in Equity* (New York: Gale Academic, 2010).

Carson, R. *Silent Spring* (Boston: Houghton Mifflin, 1962).

Cochrane, MG. *Class Actions: A Guide to the* Class Proceedings Act, 1992 (Aurora, ON: Canada Law Book, 1993).

Finn, S. *Étude d'un recours évolutif: redéfinir la procédure sui generis du recours collectif Québécois* (2011, unpublished LLM thesis, on file at the Faculté de Droit, Université Laval).

Fisher, R et al. *Getting to Yes: Negotiating Agreement Without Giving In*, 2d ed (New York: Penguin Books USA, 1991).

Hensler, D et al. *Class Action Dilemmas: Pursuing Public Goals for Private Gain* (Santa Monica: RAND Institute for Civil Justice, 1999).

———, eds. *Class Actions in Context: How Culture, Economics and Politics Shape Collective Litigation* (Cheltenham, UK: Edward Elgar, 2016).

Knepper, P. *Writing the History of Crime* (London: Bloomsbury Academic, 2016).

McMurtry, R. *Memoirs and Reflections* (Toronto: University of Toronto Press, 2013).

Moriarity, M. *Consumers' Class Actions* (Toronto: Osgoode Hall Law School, York University, 1970).

Ogus, A. *Regulation: Legal Form and Economic Theory* (Oxford: Clarendon Press, 1994).

Posner, RA. *Theories of Economic Regulation* (New York: National Bureau of Economic Research, 1974), online: www.nber.org/papers/w0041.pdf.

Pue, WW, & B Wright. *Canadian Perspectives on Law & Society: Issues in Legal History* (Ottawa: Carleton University Press, 1988).

Ramsay, I. *Consumer Law and Policy: Text and Materials on Regulating Consumer Markets*, 3d ed (Portland, OR: Hart, 2012).

Scott, I, & N McCormick. *To Make a Difference: A Memoir* (Toronto: Stoddart, 2001).

Simpson, AWB. *Cannibalism and the Common Law* (Chicago: University of Chicago Press, 1984).

Sisson Runyan, A, & V Spike Peterson. *Global Gender Issues in the New Millennium*, 4th ed (Boulder, CO: Westview Press, 2014).

Story, J. *Commentaries on Equity Pleadings and the Incidents Thereof, According to the Practice of the Courts of Equity of England and America*, 1st ed (Boston: Hilliard Gray, 1835).

Walker, J. *Class Actions in Canada: Cases, Notes and Materials* (Toronto: Emond Montgomery, 2013).

West, J. *Public Interest Groups and the Judicial Process in Canada: The Need for a More Realistic Jurisprudence* (Ottawa: Dept of Political Science, Carleton University, 1979).

Winkler, WK, PM Perell et al. *The Law of Class Actions in Canada* (Toronto: Canada Law Book, 2014).

Yeazell, S. *From Medieval Group Litigation to the Modern Class Action* (New Haven: Yale University Press, 1987).

TABLE OF CASES

INDEX

ABOUT THE AUTHOR

Suzanne Chiodo is a lecturer in law at Oriel College, Oxford University, where she is completing her doctorate in the area of class actions. She also obtained her undergraduate degree in modern history from Oxford.

Before beginning her doctorate in October 2017, Suzanne was a class actions lawyer at Rochon Genova LLP in Toronto. She completed her LLM at Osgoode Hall Law School in December 2016, supported by funding from the Social Sciences and Humanities Research Council (SSHRC) and numerous other sources. Her book, *The Class Actions Controversy*, arises from her LLM thesis on the history of the Ontario *Class Proceedings Act*.

Suzanne has taught courses on civil procedure at Osgoode Hall Law School and has presented papers to the Osgoode Society for Canadian Legal History, the Ontario Bar Association, and the Ontario Human Rights Commission. In addition, she has published numerous papers on class actions and tort law.

Suzanne completed her articles of clerkship for the Honourable Mr Justice O'Reilly at the Federal Court. She obtained her JD with distinction at Western Law in Ontario, where she spearheaded a successful effort to establish the school's first student-run academic journal. She won numerous awards and scholarships for academic excellence, and also received the Law Society of Upper Canada prize for graduating near the top of her class.

When Suzanne is not teaching in Oxford, she lives in Toronto with her husband Joe, where she pursues her love for rock and blues music by singing and playing harmonica in a band. Her favourite day of the week is Sunday, when she attends Little Trinity Anglican Church before eating delicious food made by her Italian-Canadian family.

PUBLICATIONS OF THE OSGOODE SOCIETY FOR CANADIAN LEGAL HISTORY

2018 Philip Girard, Jim Phillips, and Blake Brown, *A History of Law in Canada : Volume 1, Beginnings to 1866*
Suzanne Chiodo, *The Class Actions Controversy: The Origins and Development of the Ontario Class Proceedings Act*

2017 Constance Backhouse, *Claire L'Heureux-Dube: A Life*
Dennis G. Molinaro, *An Exceptional Law: Section 98 and the Emergency State, 1919–1936*

2016 Lori Chambers, *A Legal History of Adoption in Ontario, 1921–2015*
Bradley Miller, *Borderline Crime: Fugitive Criminals and the Challenge of the Boarder, 1819–1914*
James Muir, *Law, Debt, and Merchant Power: The Civil Courts of Eighteenth-Century Halifax*

2015 Barry Wright, Eric Tucker, and Susan Binnie, eds., *Canadian State Trails, Volume IV: Security, Dissent and the Limits of Toleration in War and Peace, 1914–1939*
David Fraser, *"Honorary Protestants": The Jewish School Question in Montreal, 1867–1997*
C. Ian Kyer, *A Thirty Years War: The Failed Public/Private Partnership that Spurred the Creation of The Toronto Transit Commission, 1891–1921*

2014 Christopher Moore, The *Court of Appeal for Ontario: Defining the Right of Appeal 1792–2013*
Dominique Clément, *Equality Deferred: Sex Discrimination and British Columbia's Human Rights State, 1953-84*
Paul Craven, *Petty Justice: Low Law and the Sessions System in Charlotte County, New Brunswick, 1785–1867*
Thomas Telfer, *Ruin and Redemption: The Struggle for a Canadian Bankruptcy Law, 1867–1919*

2013 The Hon. R.Roy McMurtry, *Memoirs & Reflections*
Charlotte Gray, *The Massey Murder: A Maid, Her Master and the Trial that Shocked a Nation*
C. Ian Kyer, *Lawyers, Families, and Businesses: The Shaping of a Bay Street Law Firm, Faskens 1863–1963*
G. Blaine Baker and Donald Fyson, eds., *Essays in the History of Canadian Law. Volume 11: Quebec and the Canadas*

2012 R. Blake Brown, *Arming and Disarming: A History of Gun Control in Canada*
Eric Tucker, James Muir, and Bruce Ziff, eds., *Property on Trial: Canadian Cases in Context*
Shelley A.M. Gavigan, *Hunger, Horses, and Government Men: Criminal Law on the Aboriginal Plains, 1870–1905*
Barrington Walker, ed., *The African-Canadian Legal Odyssey: Historical Essays*

2011 Robert J. Sharpe, *The Lazier Murder: Prince Edward County, 1884*
Philip Girard, *Lawyers and Legal Culture in British North America: Beamish Murdoch of Halifax*
John McLaren, *Dewigged, Bothered and Bewildered: British Colonial Judges on Trial*
Lesley Erickson, *Westward Bound: Sex, Violence, the Law, and the Making of a Settler Society*

2010 Judy Fudge and Eric Tucker, eds., *Work on Trial: Canadian Labour Law Struggles*
Christopher Moore, *The British Columbia Court of Appeal: The First Hundred Years*
Frederick Vaughan, *Viscount Haldane: The Wicked Step-father of the Canadian Constitution*
Barrington Walker, *Race on Trial: Black Defendants in Ontario's Criminal Courts, 1850–1950*

2009 William Kaplan, *Canadian Maverick: The Life and Times of Ivan C. Rand*
R. Blake Brown, *A Trying Question: The Jury in Nineteenth-Century Canada*
Barry Wright and Susan Binnie, eds., *Canadian State Trials. Volume 3: Political Trials and Security Measures, 1840-1914*
Robert J. Sharpe, *The Last Day, the Last Hour: The Currie Libel Trial*

2008 Constance Backhouse, *Carnal Crimes: Sexual Assault Law in Canada, 1900–1975*
Jim Phillips, R. Roy McMurtry, and John Saywell, eds., *Essays in the History of Canadian Law. Volume 10: A Tribute to Peter N. Oliver*
Gregory Taylor, *The Law of the Land: Canada's Receptions of the Torrens System*
Hamar Foster, Benjamin Berger, and A.R. Buck, eds., *The Grand Experiment: Law and Legal Culture in British Settler Societies*

2007 Robert Sharpe and Patricia McMahon, *The Persons Case: The Origins and Legacy of the Fight for Legal Personhood*
Lori Chambers, *Misconceptions: Unmarried Motherhood and the Ontario Children of Unmarried Parents Act, 1921–1969*
Jonathan Swainger, ed., *The Alberta Supreme Court at 100: History and Authority*
Martin Friedland, *My Life in Crime and Other Academic Adventures*

2006 Donald Fyson, *Magistrates, Police and People: Everyday Criminal Justice in Quebec and Lower Canada, 1764-1837*
Dale Brawn, *The Court of Queen's Bench of Manitoba 1870–1950: A Biographical History*
R.C.B. Risk, *A History of Canadian Legal Thought: Collected Essays*, edited and introduced by G. Blaine Baker and Jim Phillips

2005 Philip Girard, *Bora Laskin: Bringing Law to Life*
Christopher English, ed., *Essays in the History of Canadian Law. Volume 9: Two Islands, Newfoundland and Prince Edward Island*
Fred Kaufman, *Searching for Justice: An Autobiography*

2004 John D. Honsberger, *Osgoode Hall: An Illustrated History*
Frederick Vaughan, *Aggressive in Pursuit: The Life of Justice Emmett Hall*
Constance Backhouse and Nancy Backhouse, *The Heiress versus the Establishment: Mrs. Campbell's Campaign for Legal Justice*

Philip Girard, Jim Phillips, and Barry Cahill, eds., *The Supreme Court of Nova Scotia, 1754–2004: From Imperial Bastion to Provincial Oracle*

2003 Robert Sharpe and Kent Roach, *Brian Dickson: A Judge's Journey*
George Finlayson, *John J. Robinette: Peerless Mentor*
Peter Oliver, *The Conventional Man: The Diaries of Ontario Chief Justice Robert A. Harrison, 1856–1878*
Jerry Bannister, *The Rule of the Admirals: Law, Custom and Naval Government in Newfoundland, 1699–1832*

2002 John T. Saywell, *The Law Makers: Judicial Power and the Shaping of Canadian Federalism*
David Murray, *Colonial Justice: Justice, Morality and Crime in the Niagara District, 1791–1849*
F. Murray Greenwood and Barry Wright, eds., *Canadian State Trials. Volume 2: Rebellion and Invasion in the Canadas, 1837–38*
Patrick Brode, *Courted and Abandoned: Seduction in Canadian Law*

2001 Ellen Anderson, *Judging Bertha Wilson: Law as Large as Life*
Judy Fudge and Eric Tucker, *Labour before the Law: Collective Action in Canada, 1900–1948*
Laurel Sefton MacDowell, *Renegade Lawyer: The Life of J.L. Cohen*

2000 Barry Cahill, *"The Thousandth Man": A Biography of James McGregor Stewart*
A.B. McKillop, *The Spinster and the Prophet: Florence Deeks, H.G. Wells, and the Mystery of the Purloined Past*
Beverley Boissery and F. Murray Greenwood, *Uncertain Justice: Canadian Women and Capital Punishment*
Bruce Ziff, *Unforeseen Legacies: Reuben Wells Leonard and the Leonard Foundation Trust*

1999 Constance Backhouse, *Colour-Coded: A Legal History of Racism in Canada, 1900–1950*
G. Blaine Baker and Jim Phillips, eds., *Essays in the History of Canadian Law. Volume 8: In Honour of R.C.B. Risk*
Richard W. Pound, *Chief Justice W.R. Jackett: By the Law of the Land*
David Vanek, *Fulfilment: Memoirs of a Criminal Court Judge*

1998 Sidney Harring, *White Man's Law: Native People in Nineteenth-Century Canadian Jurisprudence*
Peter Oliver, *"Terror to Evil-Doers": Prisons and Punishments in Nineteenth-Century Ontario*

1997 James W. St. G. Walker, *"Race," Rights and the Law in the Supreme Court of Canada: Historical Case Studies*
Lori Chambers, *Married Women and Property Law in Victorian Ontario*
Patrick Brode, *Casual Slaughters and Accidental Judgments: Canadian War Crimes and Prosecutions, 1944–1948*
Ian Bushnell, *The Federal Court of Canada: A History, 1875–1992*

1996 Carol Wilton, ed., *Essays in the History of Canadian Law. Volume 7: Inside the Law—Canadian Law Firms in Historical Perspective*
William Kaplan, *Bad Judgment: The Case of Mr. Justice Leo A. Landreville*

Murray Greenwood and Barry Wright, eds., *Canadian State Trials. Volume 1: Law, Politics and Security Measures, 1608-1837*

1995 David Williams, *Just Lawyers: Seven Portraits*
Hamar Foster and John McLaren, eds., *Essays in the History of Canadian Law. Volume 6: British Columbia and the Yukon*
W.H. Morrow, ed., *Northern Justice: The Memoirs of Mr. Justice William G. Morrow*
Beverley Boissery, *A Deep Sense of Wrong: The Treason, Trials and Transportation to New South Wales of Lower Canadian Rebels after the 1838 Rebellion*

1994 Patrick Boyer, *A Passion for Justice: The Legacy of James Chalmers McRuer*
Charles Pullen, *The Life and Times of Arthur Maloney: The Last of the Tribunes*
Jim Phillips, Tina Loo, and Susan Lewthwaite, eds., *Essays in the History of Canadian Law. Volume 5: Crime and Criminal Justice*
Brian Young, *The Politics of Codification: The Lower Canadian Civil Code of 1866*

1993 Greg Marquis, *Policing Canada's Century: A History of the Canadian Association of Chiefs of Police*
Murray Greenwood, *Legacies of Fear: Law and Politics in Quebec in the Era of the French Revolution*

1992 Brendan O'Brien, *Speedy Justice: The Tragic Last Voyage of His Majesty's Vessel* Speedy
Robert Fraser, ed., *Provincial Justice: Upper Canadian Legal Portraits from the* Dictionary of Canadian Biography

1991 Constance Backhouse, *Petticoats and Prejudice: Women and Law in Nineteenth-Century Canada*

1990 Philip Girard and Jim Phillips, eds., *Essays in the History of Canadian Law. Volume 3: Nova Scotia*
Carol Wilton, ed., *Essays in the History of Canadian Law. Volume 4: Beyond the Law—Lawyers and Business in Canada 1830–1930*

1989 Desmond Brown, *The Genesis of the Canadian Criminal Code of 1892*
Patrick Brode, *The Odyssey of John Anderson*

1988 Robert Sharpe, *The Last Day, the Last Hour: The Currie Libel Trial*
John D. Arnup, *Middleton: The Beloved Judge*

1987 C. Ian Kyer and Jerome Bickenbach, *The Fiercest Debate: Cecil A. Wright, the Benchers and Legal Education in Ontario, 1923-1957*

1986 Paul Romney, *Mr. Attorney: The Attorney General for Ontario in Court, Cabinet and Legislature, 1791–1899*
Martin Friedland, *The Case of Valentine Shortis: A True Story of Crime and Politics in Canada*

1985 James Snell and Frederick Vaughan, *The Supreme Court of Canada: History of the Institution*

1984 Patrick Brode, *Sir John Beverley Robinson: Bone and Sinew of the Compact*
David Williams, *Duff: A Life in the Law*

1983 David H. Flaherty, ed., *Essays in the History of Canadian Law. Volume 2*

1982 Marion MacRae and Anthony Adamson, *Cornerstones of Order: Courthouses and Town Halls of Ontario, 1784–1914*
1981 David H. Flaherty, ed., *Essays in the History of Canadian Law. Volume 1*

Printed and bound by CPI Group (UK) Ltd, Croydon, CR0 4YY

15/09/2026

14962400-0006